The

Q-anon

Q-anon, Summarized, Analyzed, and With a Firsthand Account of Cabal's Ground Intelligence Operations

Anonymous Conservative

Federalist Publications

Macclenny, Florida

Published by Federalist Publications, Macclenny, Florida

www.anonymousconservative.com

Printed in the United States of America
ISBN-13 : 978-1-7334142-1-0 (Cloth Hardcover, Jacketed)
ISBN-13 : 978-1-7334142-0-3 (Softcover)
ISBN-13 : 978-1-7334142-2-7 (Amazon Kindle)

Library of Congress Subject Headings:

United States--Politics and government
Conspiracies--United States
Conspiracies--United States--History--20th century

Where we go one, we go all.

The greatest trick the devil ever pulled was

convincing the world he didn't exist...

Table of Contents

Until a decade ago, I was what was known on the internet as a "normie." I believed America was a homogenous group of citizens, united under the foundational ideas of our Republic. Every man was created equal, and was equal under the law. The Constitution limited the powers of government, thereby protecting every citizen's privacy and freedom. We had privacy, and a God-given right to retire to our own sanctuaries of privacy and solitude if we so desired. The law would protect us. We lived in a government run by its people, with equal justice for everyone. And most importantly, my fellow Americans were like me. The were loyal first to America and their fellow Americans, and believed a society of free Americans, each living their lives in freedom, under the protection of the Constitution was good.

There was corruption, no doubt. But it was limited, and could never advance. Conspiracies were rare, because nobody could possibly keep it secret. The system was designed to expose and destroy any such attempt to seize power covertly within our free republic. The press worked as a counter-balance to any corruption, because reporters became reporters to safeguard truth and the republic. They had a personal interest in exposing corruption as that was how they built the reputations that would make them rich. And most of all, Americans all recognized the freedoms our nation afforded us, made it something worth protecting. Nobody would ever destroy those freedoms, because they would be destroying their own freedom, and the freedoms of their children. Most of all, Americans were one team, and no groups within the nation were freely operating against everyone else covertly.

It seemed a perfect, stable system, designed to keep America free and united.

In reality, I was wrong about it all. At some point, an intelligence operation infiltrated our country, outside of the sight of everyone. It slowly advanced, hidden in the shadows, taking over our government and drawing in various citizens it needed throughout society. Once it drew in a citizen, it put them to the purpose of advancing the conspiracy's control over everyone else, as it set about destroying our freedom and privacy.

Many they recruited apparently chose to serve it willingly. Eventually, the machine became so pervasive, you could not escape it within the United States. The voices who spoke in our public forums appeared overwhelmingly compromised.

But I never knew. That is, until I interjected a scientific idea into the political world which held the possibility of affecting the political debate. I dropped the idea online and in a book, and suddenly this machine dropped on my head, and I saw the surveillance/intimidation side of it in nearly its entirety. As it revealed itself to me, in hopes of cowing me with its scale, I felt nothing short of utter disbelief. It was so massive it seemed to defy the laws of possibility.

Take any transgressions against freedom that you think your fellow Americans would never allow, multiply it by ten, and it is being done willingly and knowingly by our fellow Americans who joined this conspiracy. Take what you think could never be done in this nation to American citizens, given its laws and law enforcement apparatus, as well as the morals of America, and multiply it by ten, and it is being done – with no legal consequence.

As I researched it, I've seen cops trying to catch killers thrown in prison. I've seen police officers, reporters, and wounded veterans murdered by this machine. I've seen injured CIA agents trying to recover from their last deployment harassed by teams that break into their homes while they are out, simply to rearrange their furniture, and then follow them around ominously as they travel about town. Most amazingly, I have seen that local law enforcement and federal law enforcement can't do anything about it. Even the CIA is powerless to protect its own in its own country.

There are numerous accounts of innocent women who come home and are drugged by food in their fridge that was spiked by a surreptitious entry team, and then they are raped while unconscious. They wake up knowing what happened, go to the ER, take a rape kit and file a report, and the local Police are helpless to do anything about it. In this book you will see the local news report on it, and the interviews with victims. The news report couches it as a mystery that cannot be solved. In reality, it was one small facet of a massive conspiracy that pervaded our entire nation, and you can find similar reports all over the country.

You will see the actual news stories in here. I will link to where local news outlets reported them, before the story was killed by the national powers that be. You will see actual videos of the machine in action on youtube, and see indications of just how far back this machine was operational in our nation. You will see how the media they compromised and filled with their agents hid it from us. You will even be able to look online, and see it in the flesh, operating in your own neighborhood. Along the way, if I am successful, you will end up becoming as proficient in spotting these intelligence units on the street as any highly trained spy, because you will see what they look like in real life with your own eyes, in places where images of them have been captured for all of posterity on the internet.

But most of all, you are going to learn you lost your own nation, without even knowing it. Indeed, you lost it without even being able to believe it could happen.

On my website, and on other select sites and forums online, many of us saw this conspiracy, and began discussing it years ago. As we did, terms developed around the discussions, and became a sort of shorthand everyone used. You will see some of these terms in here, so we will briefly touch upon them here before we begin.

The *Cabal* is the organization which has corrupted our entire society. A mixture of a non-state intelligence operation, the network of spies, informants, and assets it runs, and the elites who call the shots in it, the Cabal has infiltrated agents everywhere from our political parties, to our elected offices, to our courts, to our businesses, to our medical establishments, to our news media, and even in our own neighborhoods.

(((They))), will refer to the leaders in the conspiracy. These are the people who make the decisions at the very top. The term developed as a shorthand to represent their mysterious and hidden nature. We don't know exactly who (((They))) are, or when the conspiracy first formed. (((They))) have hidden their wealth and their identities behind trusts, corporations, charitable foundations, and the like, so they cannot be tracked.

It is believed the forerunner to this conspiracy may have

been operative in the Roman Empire, and slipped into the Vatican as the Empire collapsed. (((They))) re-emerged behind the European royalty, who they used as proxies, and they have probably been present in the US since before the Revolution. It is assumed their covert operation here was a back-up plan after the Crown's loss of control in the Revolutionary War.

Here, for centuries, hidden and unseen, their operation has been gradually solidifying its penetration of the government and society in preparation for the full control it exhibits today in secret, and the full control they planned to display openly in the near future. There are even some indications (((They))) may extend back to ancient Egypt. That would explain why 13 year old Pharaohs were in charge of the cradle of civilization. In reality they were not in charge, they were just easily controlled and intimidated puppets, being controlled by (((Them))).

Some think that today (((They))) are high ranking Vatican officials. Some think (((They))) are a secret society such as the Freemasons, while others think (((They))) are some sort of bloodline descended from a single family that got full control of the conspiracy at some point. Others think it is a confederation, of criminal groups, secret fraternal societies, and/or wealthy families who acquired unimaginable wealth at some point and then figured out they could exert even greater control, and make even more money, working together against the rest of society. Others think who (((They))) are may have changed many times over the centuries, as internal political intrigue led to changes in power at the top, and control of the machine was handed off. All other information about (((Them))), from religion to nationality is unknown. Some believe (((They))) hold some sort of occult belief system, though others think they promote occultism among lower level recruits, as an excuse for requiring immoral induction ceremonies comprised of horrific acts, whose true purpose is to be recorded for purposes of blackmail. Regardless, they have been smart enough to hide, and rich enough to do it so effectively we still are not entirely sure who they are.

"The Machine," or "The Network" is Cabal's network, which performs the actions that give it control. The machine consists of assets placed in control of critical parts of society that Cabal needs for control. It encompasses the media personalities designed to mold the public's beliefs, desires, and emotions. It is government officials who pass laws Cabal wants, judges who rule how Cabal tells them. It is intelligence agencies and agents Cabal has corrupted, who now work for Cabal, advancing its interests and objectives. It's law enforcement agencies who can deploy surveillance and spies to get Cabal information, such as on Donald Trump's campaign in 2016. And its most powerful asset is a massive civilian network of spies and informants deployed against America at the grassroots level, all throughout society.

It includes local religious leaders who try to guide their local flocks to believe and do what Cabal wants. It is cult leaders who manage groups of people under control, and who may allow experimentation with new psychological manipulative techniques upon them, or even groom females for sexual trafficking to high-ranking people, such as the NXIVM cult. It even extends down to regular citizens who have pledged loyalty to the machine for whatever it is they get out of it, and who just operate one on one with people Cabal targets. These may be local teachers who will spy on or exert influence on students, nurses who can pull medical records, workers at document destruction companies who pull documents Cabal wants for whatever reason, local affiliate news reporters who can be relied upon to put out stories Cabal wants in front of the public, or kill stories it wants covered up. It is professors at colleges, protesters who turn out to make noise about issues Cabal wants everyone to notice, bank managers who can grab records on customers and businesses, local regulators in local government who can make business problems disappear or come out of nowhere, and software engineers who can insert backdoors Cabal wants inserted. It is even children whose families are in the network, and who help fill out files on other children growing up in their neighborhoods and schools. Estimates are that the Machine is made up of between four and ten percent of the population, based on government documents, as you will see. Sometimes this group is referred to as the "Secret Society."

"Management" is a term which came from the TV show Burn Notice (itself written by a CIA officer who seemingly saw this conspiracy, and crafted an entire TV show around it. If you want to see an excellent show which is full of themes that mirror the real world of Cabal, get the DVDs of the TV Show Burn Notice and watch it, especially the first five seasons.)

Management consists of the leaders of the Machine that Cabal assigned to run each major part of their conspiracy, from corporations, to secret societies like the Freemasons, to religious organizations, to intelligence agencies, to political parties, to all the major power centers Cabal exploits to manipulate society. Many are billionaires who seemingly followed meteoric career paths as they formed various companies that served Cabal's purposes. Others are money managers who involve themselves in political activism. Others run media companies that sell Cabal narratives to the public. It is increasingly believed many of these ultra-wealthy members of Management are not actually wealthy themselves, but rather they are being given Cabal money to hold and manage, as part of a cover they are given to explain why they are so influential in society. This does explain why Bill Gates, or Warren Buffet, or George Soros openly declare they will not bequeath their fortunes to their children. It is not because they don't want to, but rather because their fortunes are not actually their own to begin with. Indeed, Jeffrey Epstein is seen as the most prominent example of this. Nobody knows where his money came from, and in retrospect it appears little more than a cover he was given, to aid him in gaining blackmail on prominent individuals for this intelligence network.

The main purpose of Cabal's Machine was to foster *The Myth*. The Myth asserts that the United States is a free republic, with a Constitution which limits governmental power, guarantees us freedom and privacy, and makes we, the people, the predominant power in our nation. We have laws, we elect our leaders to make them, and thus we are the ultimate arbiters of our fates. It is called The Myth because that is exactly what it is – a story we are told to keep our people pacified, and prevent us from ever rebelling against our true masters – (((Them))). The truth is, I am not even sure we elect our leaders anymore, we have no privacy, and I know we aren't at present, the arbiters of our own fate.

Understand that while this book will show you the pieces which do not fit - the concrete stories showing hard evidence which prove things are not as they seem - there may be some aspects of this work which will prove over time to be incorrect. Where Cabal came from, who the people in it are, what they believe in or are dedicated to, and exactly how they operate is still very much up in the air as of this writing. Explanations in the Q-community range from the practical (it is all about money and power) to the esoteric (a religious-reverence and subservience to extradimensional, demon-like, sentient entities which they believe in, that intrude in our world and are the real-life subject of our religious texts). There will be no consensus on Cabal's motivations offered here. This book will offer the best guesses circulating in the Q community on other aspects of the conspiracy, but it may prove incorrect in some regards, even on those. What I can tell you from personal experience, with absolute certainty, are two things. One, the view of America as free, with privacy, where anyone could become anything they wanted was an illusion, designed to keep people controllable and accepting of the banal fates Cabal guided them into. And two, there is a massive network out there, throughout society, composed of everyone from powerful cultural figures, to business leaders, to political office holders, to lowly citizens, and they are all working together against the majority of the population, to keep them under control. I know it beyond a shadow of a doubt, have seen it with my own eyes, and this book should convince you of it as well.

Thankfully, despite all of this you will learn there were patriots in our government who saw what was happening too, and they stepped forward to fight and stop it. Here, you will learn about their public incarnation, Q, what he represents, and just what President Trump has really been up to in running for office and holding the Presidency.

As Q says, enjoy the show.

Chapter One

*Who Is Q-Anon?*_____

Who is Q-anon, and why has he become such a phenomenon? The full answer is complicated, and requires some background information. It will also require some psychological deprogramming of you, believe it or not, to fully understand. The truth is part of what Q has revealed is that very smart people have done extensive research into how to control the accepted beliefs of populations, and that research has been applied to you. As an example, if you hear the phrase *"conspiracy theory,"* and immediately think of people who espouse unlikely explanations for events, there might be a reason for that. It might be because people who were conspiring to control the mass media used it to portray conspiracy theorists as kooks so many times that you came to assume stories of shadowy men conspiring must not be true. Keep an open mind going forward.

Before we get to all of that, the simple answer to who Q is, would be that although his exact identity is not known for certain as of this writing, it is believed Q is one or more people in Military Intelligence.

Retired U.S. Army Major General Paul E. Vallely is a senior military analyst for Fox News. In an interview, he stated that, *"Q-Anon is information that comes out of a group called 'The Army of Northern Virginia.' This is a group of military intelligence specialists, of over 800 people that advises the president. The president does not have a lot of confidence in the CIA or the DIA (Defense Intelligence Agency) much anymore. So the President relies on real operators, who are mostly Special Operations type of people. This is where 'Q' picks up some of his information."*[1]

It is assumed Q has been tasked by a clique of patriotic Americans in Military Intelligence, the NSA, and the White House. His job is to post messages to be read by independent thinkers online. Through these messages, they hope to slowly reveal a conspiracy that was working to take over the United States of America, as well as the rest of the world.

I have both read through Q's posts, and run into a small part of the conspiracy Q discusses in my own life. As I have, I have come to understand that the truth of how our government has been run, the degree it was taken over by wealthy elites, and the machinery they assembled to apply control over America and many other countries, is so massive, so pervasive, and so evil it would not be believed if revealed all at once. Q has asserted that we cannot imagine how big this is, so he needs to reveal it slowly to the public, lest it not be believed. Having looked at what I have seen with my own eyes, I found that assertion gave him even more credence in my eyes.

In his posts, Q drops "crumbs" often times in the form of questions, or cryptic statements meant to be analyzed and researched by the anonymous posters, or *"anons,"* on his website. Some crumbs directly reveal an assertion Q makes about how the conspiracy works. Others ask questions, which require his anons to

---

[1]   http://archive.is/IJYKV

research online, finding and archiving connections and data which, without the questions, would never have been assembled and revealed their truths Q wanted revealed.

Q has said he cannot reveal this material in full himself because it is technically still classified, and he cannot reveal classified information due to National Security laws. But if he asks a vague question, and anons do research, and uncover the answer themselves using open source citations online, the information can be conveyed and no laws have been broken.

Still other crumbs are seemingly indecipherable until something happens. Once it does, in retrospect, it becomes clear only someone truly plugged into the intelligence infrastructure could possibly have known about it. Through these crumbs, Q proves his own validity, and that helps him acquire the interest of more people, and increases the creep of his message into the populace.

As an example of crumbs that would prove his validity, Q asserted early on that John McCain would be executed for treason for an unspecified crime he committed. When McCain was diagnosed with a brain tumor, Q asserted that his diagnosis of brain cancer was a cover he was allowed, as part of a deal, so as to not leave his family name in shame after his execution.

One anon eventually asked when McCain would be executed, and Q said *"Every dog has his day."* Two weeks later Q posted that John McCain would be in the news in a month. Exactly 30 days after Q's post, John McCain died. The exact time of Q's post, to the minute, was the time listed on John McCain's death certificate. It was National Dog Day. John McCain died exactly 30 days to the minute after Q's post saying he would be in the news in a month, and the date of his death was National Dog Day.

There are not a lot of explanations for that. It could be chance, but the mix of McCain dying soon, as Q predicted, it happening on National Dog Day, and a prediction made 30 days to the minute prior seems unlikely. The most statistically likely explanation I can see is that McCain's death was scheduled as an execution, as Q had asserted would be the case. Due to the knowledge of the execution procedure, the precise timing of his escort to the death chamber, and the procedure for the application of the drugs at a set time, known 30 days in advance, it was possible to predict not only the day of his death, but the exact time on his death certificate, to the minute.

You can see how if Q can predict that, and he asserts the nation has been taken over by a criminal conspiracy that has seized control of the highest leaders in our land using extensive intelligence and blackmail operations, it would naturally attract attention.

The idea of a conspiracy having taken over the United States, and many other countries in the world, sounds incredible, I know. I once thought like you, and would not have believed it myself. But then I saw things with my own eyes, in my own life, which revealed to me beyond any shadow of a doubt, things did not work like we are told in the United States, or as we would assume. As I looked into it online I found many others who had seen the same things and come to the same conclusion.

Once you realize that, you begin to question all of your assumptions. Once you do that, your mind begins to open to all possibilities. Once you open your mind to all possibilities, you realize many of the assumptions we have originate in things we were told by many of the societal "influencers" who themselves would be a part of such a conspiracy.

Once you begin to look closer at all of those assumptions we have been fed, in light of logic, you will realize many are patently illogical, and could never be true. That will put you on a path to understanding how the world truly works.

There are several parts of Q's story. The first thing which you must understand is how the conspiracy has lied to you, and imbued ideas within you that prevent you from realizing that a conspiracy is not only possible - it is more likely to exist than not.

We will begin by looking at how you have been misled. Then we will look at a synopsis of the Conspiracy that Q is alleging exists. From there, we will briefly examine the proof that Q is who he said he is, and that will reveal how the media openly misled everyone, leading them to think he was a fraud.

Once you understand Q, the conspiracy, how it lied to you, and why some people believe Q and can see through the lies, we will then go post by post through Q's first 400 posts, with a brief commentary after the most notable, examining what he was saying and some of the voluminous evidence supporting it. We will finish by looking at a handful of the remaining thousands of posts that seem particularly illuminating, including one which may reveal exactly who Q is.

Having seen the extent of at least one part of the conspiracy firsthand, I believe it makes for the most amazing story in all of American history. The only thing more amazing, is that such an extensive intelligence operation, infiltrating and corrupting America to such a degree, and having attained such a position of almost total control, could have been undone by a small group of patriots who defied all of the odds.

Chapter Two

*You Have Been Lied To*_____

You have been lied to, for a very long time. For so long, that what these lies have done to your brain is akin to outright brainwashing. I know, because I was brainwashed by this conspiracy myself. When I finally saw pieces of the conspiracy in real life, what I saw was incomprehensible, because of the brain washing. It took two years of seeing it firsthand before I could begin to grasp the conspiracy's massive size was even possible. It took years to accept that so many regular citizens, neighbors, in all of our communities, would join it and work against the rest of America for personal benefit. I still have not come to terms with this shocking new reality.

It was a lonely path. People I knew for years who were not part of the conspiracy would never have believed what I said was happening, had I not caught explicit video evidence. And even then I know, Not having had the extensive interactions I had with it they still can not accept the size of it. They have just been programmed to think it is impossible. Once I broke my own programming however, and saw through the lies I had been trained to accept as fact, I could not believe I had been so blind. This book has been written explicitly to help you achieve the same awareness of reality here.

The brainwashing is designed with one purpose, and that is

to weaken you. Or rather, to make you weaken yourself. The brainwashing is very extensive, but there are a few specific, foundational lies which are probably more vital than the rest. Here, we will begin anchoring you to a few simple intellectual touchstones, fundamental truths which I think you will still realize have to be true. From there, we will move logically outward and extrapolate from those, to show you that the lies which you were told repeatedly, and which you accept unquestioningly, are in fact impossible in the light of those basic truths.

The first lie, is that our world is no longer Darwinian, and our social structures all have evolved into some rule-governed utopia, absent any Darwinian effects which would promote ruthless, rule-breaking selfishness. We are told that those who are most ruthless, most devious, and most self-interested, don't break the law and succeed. More importantly, they never find each other, group together, and work in concert, out of our sight. Because this does not happen, massive conspiracies can not exist. The government is elected by us, exactly as it seems. Nobody would dare challenge your freedom or our free governmental system. Most importantly, everyone is too afraid of our law and order system to ever transgress against it, let alone in massive organized groups. Even if they tried, they could never take full control.

I simply accepted this as truth at one point in my life. I suppose I thought it was what most people believed, so I assumed it was most likely to be true. This weakens you, by making you put your guard down, and be less vigilant in protecting the freedoms of our republic. It prepares you to believe other lies, like conspiracy theories are always fake, because nobody would ever conspire, since that would be unfair and somehow impolite. And it leaves you more vulnerable to the control of, and manipulation by any hidden forces, such as the one which has promulgated that false belief.

The truth is, this entire world is Darwinian, and it always has been. Darwinism is coded into the very fabric of this world, first through the mechanism of time, and then through the mechanism of the universe's finite nature. Because of time, we are a universe where all that can be a significant part of our reality in this ever changing universe, is that which develops an ability to remain over time.

Our primordial planet churned through many different chemical compositions in its early existence. Those which did not remain, were eventually lost to time, and would be forgotten. But those first little oil droplets containing primitive molecules which could replenish themselves through organized self-replicating chemical reactions faster than they disappeared, those became the first cells, and they would remain. Cellular life, which could take materials in the environment and use them to replicate itself, became a significant part of the reality of our world.

As variation emerged among these cells in a finite universe of finite resources, it became a contest, to see which forms could consume resources the most effectively, and remain *and reproduce* faster than the others.

Between the need to persist, and the finite nature of the environment, you had Darwinian competition fundamental to the world. It was as if it was coded into the very programming language in which the universe was written, through time and scarcity.

Since life first began reproducing on this earth, we have been selected to act in Darwinian fashion. Trillions of years of evolution have burned that Darwinian drive into the blueprints of our species. It is encoded in our brains, and in our very DNA because it is a part of the very fabric of the universe where we evolved. This world has left the species in it programmed to do what we need to, in order to win.

Today, Darwinism acts on us as people, but it also works on our social structures, from businesses, to governments, and even Secret Societies. Those most devious, most ruthless, most-self-interested, and most capable are what remain and reproduce. It is practically a law of nature.

We are told however, that we live in a world of gloriously magnanimous governments, composed of gloriously magnanimous leaders, who honestly represent us. Every election cycle they cede their power willingly if they lose, so that we, the people, are always in full control. No one would ever dare transgress against the system covertly to retain power, or even acquire it outside of elections by controlling or subverting them. No conspiracy would ever take over our governments, and moreover, it could never become so powerful as to become an integral, permanent fixture of our government.

Much of human history has been made up of intrigue, performed by despotic tyrants who mastered the Machiavellian arts. But we are told, not in our time. In just a few hundred years, our entire species has lost those fundamental Darwinian psychological urges and evolved beyond that.

We are told that even our intelligence agencies are fully

under civilian control, and have endless strictures they willingly abide by to keep themselves constrained. Some of us have begun to realize those boundaries have been strained of late, but none of us would assume such organizations might have taken over our governments outright, let alone that they might have been taken over themselves.

In short, we are told that in the American government, there is no Darwinian force operative, driving hidden alliances toward ruthlessness and cunning, in search of ever-increasing, perpetual power over all of the people.

These misconceptions weaken us, immensely. They reduce our vigilance. They weaken our drive to act when we see hints that they might not be true. They make us personally less competitive, since acting ruthlessly competitively, or even assuming others are acting ruthlessly competitively, is seen as a gauche violation of accepted norms.

The reality is, in a world where everyone acts as if Darwinian behavior is verboten, cunning ruthless people will inevitably hit the scene and they will go hog-wild, taking advantage of everyone honest, from behind their backs and within the shadows. Eventually, groups of them will emerge, and perform even more ruthless and cunning manipulations to gain full, despotic control of any system - especially an honest one filled with vulnerable citizens who would never think such a thing possible.

Think of it like a natural law. After hundreds of years in America, what is at the top of our system should be the most ruthless, immoral, cunning, lawless, Machiavellian group possible.

Given sufficient time, such a group should be expected to have subverted and corrupted every aspect of our government, covertly turning it to their ends and removing the many and varied protections against such within our government. For such not to be so, would be unnatural, and would go against a very law of nature.

If our system has been compromised, one of the first lies they will perpetuate on gaining power is that the world is not Darwinian, there are rules which would never allow such a corruption of the system, and nobody could possibly be like them and attain power in this system. They would likely even take it further, and say anyone who asserts such might be the case has something off in their thought processes, and is clearly paranoid. They might even come up with a derisive term to describe that, like "conspiracy theorist," and use it to denigrate such people in the media. Finally, they would tell everyone that all sane people operate as if conspiracies would never take over our government.

Don't believe it. In truth, the very fact someone would perpetuate such an observably false lie as saying conspiracies are unlikely, should be seen as strong evidence that a conspiracy is behind the scenes, perpetuating that lie expressly to improve their own control. Know that the natural laws practically dictate that in any system which has existed long enough, conspiracies are certainly there, recognize their lies, and understand, you must be vigilant, even paranoid, and proactive if you are to compete with them and protect your freedom.

Before we move on, replace the first lie, with the first truth. *The world is Darwinian,* as are the people and social structures in it – even, and perhaps especially, if you are not. Government, unpoliced by an honest people, will naturally produce lawless corruption and evil conspiracies. The more honest and trusting the people, the easier it will be for conspiracies to form and thrive. Only through acceptance of that, and ruthless pursuit of, and regular exposure of the conspiracies which arise, can you have any hope of being free.

If you do not see conspiracies being exposed, if your people believe that to conspire would be unfair, and you are told such conspiracies rarely exist and belief in them is the province of mentally unbalanced people, then a conspiracy is likely in charge of your society. You probably are being lied to and your government and society are very likely corrupt.

The second big lie you are told is, conspiracies never happen because nobody can keep a secret. A variant I have always liked is two people can keep a secret if one of them is dead. Alternately you will hear the phrase, *"People always talk."*

All of it is rubbish, foisted upon you by the conspirators. I will tell you first hand, I have seen the conspiracy in America firsthand. There are at least hundreds of thousands, and more likely millions of your fellow Americans who have been recruited into it as civilian assets operating against you. As will be shown later, they are your neighbors, your local luminaries, your business leaders, your news reporters, and others you trust. The conspiracy they are a part of is unimaginable, and will be completely horrifying to the average American when it is exposed. And they have kept the secret. Moreover, keeping such a secret is not uncommon.

We executed the entire invasion of Normandy on D-Day, and the Germans didn't know, nor did American civilians back home. And that was not just a secret held among a few, but involved a mass movement of troops and equipment, and the conspirators never let the secret slip. From the atom bomb, to advanced aerospace projects today, incredible secrets are routinely kept by large groups of people, even as very skilled spies actively try to pry them loose.

Jimmy Saville, a BBC broadcaster, was a prolific pedophile who abused around 500 children in Britain.[2] When he died he was lionized in the British media as a national hero. Lots of people, many in the BBC itself, knew of his pedophilia and they kept the secret. Even when individuals not in the conspiracy found out and tried to expose it, they were shut down by higher-ups at the BBC (who were themselves likely a part of the conspiracy). Even Police appeared to be involved in covering up child sexual abuse rings in the UK, often by persecuting fellow Officers who investigated it.[3] There is much more to Jimmy Saville's story we will cover later. It is far worse than that, but you see the point.

Jimmy Saville's treachery was known and kept secret, only to be fully exposed after his death. Those who broached it during his life were dismissed as conspiracy theorists, and harassed into silence. And a public who thought there could be no conspiracies because people always talked, failed to protect those children. It wasn't until long after Saville died that it came out what a monster he was, and how many people had known and covered it up. Indeed, it would appear he was part of a much larger network of high-ranking pedophiles which may still be operative today, harnessed as a means of blackmail and control. But still the public

---

2   http://archive.is/LRgOO
3   http://archive.is/Ilugv

sleeps, assuming it not possible, in part because groups cannot keep secrets.

So understand, massive secrets, known to hundreds of thousands have been kept routinely in matters of military campaigns, and huge conspiracies have happened in society that were known to some outside the conspiracy, and still the secret was kept. Conspiracies are real, Darwin demands it, and indeed, from business trade secrets that have allowed markets to be cornered, to military campaigns which maintained operational security, conspiracies have a very long history of producing successes in our Darwinian world. Conspiracies, effectively hidden, have been selected for in our Darwinian world. Not only could they exist, our world would produce them if they did not.

Again, look at how we are being told such a blatantly false lie - that there can be no conspiracies, and anyone who believes in them is mentally less competent. That alone would automatically make me think some massive conspiracy is extant and spreading that lie to protect itself, even if I hadn't seen the massiveness of the conspiracy with my own eyes.

Lie number three is a more technical one. This lie is inferred by almost everyone, and it is key to the conspiracy today. It implies that since we rarely hear about them or see them, and nobody ever talks about their funding, intelligence operations and spying must be a small area, populated by a few select specialists, which is rarely encountered or used within our nation. Far more common and prevalent in government must be the parts of the machine we see – the uniformed Law Enforcement, the Military, Fire-Rescue, Legislatures, the State Department, and so on. By comparison, any intelligence operations would be infinitesimal, under-funded, and for our purposes, relatively non-existent.

You have also probably heard, the CIA is not allowed to spy on American soil, because Americans do not want their government spying on them. Indeed, the right to privacy is considered so integral to freedom it is enshrined in the Bill of Rights. Implicit within that is the concept that therefore, we are not being spied upon, and could not be spied upon. If only you knew.

Here is one of the more stunning news articles you will ever happen across[4] The article I suspect is the beginning of a cover story being released by the CIA, to explain what Q is going to reveal. I will quote the relevant parts of it in italics:

Around 2010, the FBI also began experimenting with new ways of maintaining cover, particularly when trying to recruit foreigners on U.S. soil, through a new initiative known as the National Security Recruitment Program, according to five former officials. The FBI program, which has not been previously reported on, involved close cooperation with the CIA's National Resources Division, the agency's clandestine domestic operational wing.

The program deployed U.S. officials under very light cover, with false backstories and business cards but lacking online footprints or connections to long-running brick-and-mortar undercover operations. That way, officials could approach individuals who had potentially useful information with some level of plausible deniability. The CIA helped provide funding for the FBI program, and FBI and CIA officials paired up in major

---

4   https://news.yahoo.com/shattered-inside-the-secret-battle-to-save-americas-undercover-spies-in-the-digital-age-100029026.html?guccounter=1

American cities. While the program was successful, it was met with bureaucratic pushback and was ended by 2014 amid a turf battle, say former officials.

One roadblock, say former senior officials, was the bureau's long-standing national program for creating legends — that is, fake backstories and identities — and cover, known as Stagehand. The program, based out of Los Angeles, Chicago, Atlanta and other major American cities, sets up and maintains undercover FBI operations. Stagehand employees purchase cars, rent office space, buy homes, design cover identities for FBI officials, create fake companies and buy real ones, say six former officials.

The bureau employs former real estate brokers, physicians and dentists, among others, who become FBI agents but can assume their former jobs as needed, recalls a former senior official. "The deepest layer [of cover] might begin years before you even use it," the official says.

... By mid-decade, the agency concluded that the best way to hide was in plain sight. Nowadays, say former officials, NOCs must truly "live their cover" — that is, actually work as the professional engineer or businessperson that they present themselves to be. NOCs live and work under their true names, say former officials, though they are known to their CIA counterparts by a pseudonym. Fewer than 10 percent of individuals within the CIA's Directorate of Operations regularly use alias passports or credit cards, says a former senior official.

The intelligence community has developed sophisticated "backstopping" procedures, which seed a cover story through web traffic, emails and other digital channels. But in an interconnected world, "good backstopping can be defeated in a Google search," says one former senior intelligence official. Because of that reality, the use of front companies for NOCs has become increasingly untenable, necessitating closer coordination and cooperation with private American businesses for the placement and recruitment of NOCs, say former senior officials.

It's not always easy, however. "The CIA is very good at this, but they are getting the door slammed in their face," says one former senior official. In Silicon Valley, recalls another former senior official, it was difficult to convince these companies to participate. The situation got worse in 2013, when Edward Snowden, an intelligence contractor, gave a trove of classified documents to journalists, exposing the extent of tech companies' cooperation with the National Security Agency. "Before, it was hard," says this person, and "it was harder to do post-Snowden."

Even a switch of employer, or an unexplained gap in one's résumé, can be a giveaway to a foreign intelligence service, say former officials. In response, the agency has also shifted to recruiting individuals within the companies they already work at, and, with the approval of corporate leadership, secretly transitioning those persons onto the CIA payroll, and training them intermittently and clandestinely, far from any known CIA facility.

Sometimes, when these individuals are finished working for the agency, they simply transition back to a full-time job for the company where they already "work." In one recent case, a NOC who had worked at a U.S. company as a "full-time career employee" and was transitioning out of his CIA work was "softly landed" back into another position at the same firm — with the agency paying for his moving expenses and a government severance package, says a former senior intelligence official.

The agency, which former officials say recruits and emplaces NOCs in the technology, finance and film industries, among other sectors, targets both major U.S. corporations and smaller U.S. companies, which are sometimes preferred because they are not beholden to shareholders.

Often, say former officials, only a few select executives within a company are aware of its relationship with the agency and the "real" identities of the people in their employ. To encourage or reward cooperation from businesses, agency officials will sometimes provide special, tailor-made briefings to executives on the political and economic climate of countries of business interest to that company, say two former officials.

"There is a serious legal and policy process" in place at the CIA to manage these relationships, says a former official. Otherwise, "you could break industries."

... The agency has formed a new reserve officer program to allow spies to work in the private sector, especially the tech industry, says a former intelligence official. The program is designed to allow those operatives to maintain their clearances so they can return seamlessly to the agency after a few years, says this person.

Look at what that article is saying. FBI and CIA have merged to create CIA operational structures in the United States civilian populace, using a combined FBI/CIA, working together in common purpose. This FBI/CIA has bought homes and cars, to

19

embed citizen spies in civilian society under the cover of regular civilians. It has purchased and run businesses in civilian society in America. It has recruited business leaders in businesses it didn't purchase, and in return for their fealty and compliance, used agency resources to provide intelligence and competitive advantage to their companies which allowed them to out-compete other, non-FBI/CIA-associated companies. It has had those agents it recruited in companies offer preferential hiring, and favoritism in leave policies to other FBI/CIA assets and officers, who move into American society, living seemingly normal American lives, as spies in our society.

Not only was this FBI/CIA hydra involved in American civilian society, it was using Agency resources to decide what companies would survive, and make sure its officers had it easy in the job market within those companies. It recruited agents for its covert spy network in America, in fields as diverse as real estate, big tech, Hollywood, and medicine. And it never asked our American citizens what they thought about all of this. They just did it, creating a Secret Society of spies, in a secret economy of Agency-gifted businesses, which didn't operate according to traditional free market principles.

What if you had started a company, and were not FBI/CIA-associated, while your competitor was? Your company would likely fail, because the other company gained the favor of the FBI/CIA and you had not. Why was the other company recruited and not you? It was at the whim of agents and officers in FBI/CIA, who probably preferentially recruited family. What if you needed a job and would show up, but an FBI/CIA officer wanted the job, and intended to spend his time overseas? You would be unemployed. What if the job market contracted? Who would be immune? Who would be fired?

Now what if the daughter of an FBI/CIA officer wanted to go to medical school, and the head of admissions was an FBI/CIA officer, hired to get the school preference in Agency research contracts, such as into data analytics? What if this network needed to be kept secret from the rest of America because America wouldn't want it, and this daughter was raised in the network, running surveillance as a child, and already knew all about it? Suppose you did not know about it, and would not have liked the idea if you had, and your secret psych evaluation indicated that?

Suddenly the choice is between letting an innocent citizen who is not in the network, and who might oppose it and not want to be an agent, take that med school slot and be of no use to the Agency, or using influence over existing recruited agents/officers in the Secret Society, to give the slot to an already trusted asset, who could later become an officer, and who would not reveal the network. You see where this is going. This is how a Secret Society forms within a nation, where all the best opportunities suddenly fall to Secret Society members, while everyone else is relegated to plebe status.

On a small scale, it would be inconsequential, but read between the lines of the piece. The CIA is saying it can't have a small pool of officers, because its officers are so easily identified, often within a year. So it needs a massive pool of potential CIA-associated, part-time officers, who spend most of their time in American society, "building legends" (civilian work histories) for years, before they ever touch them. Essentially it is saying it needs to build a whole new CIA operational staff from scratch every year, as all of the old staff get identified and go on an *"inactive reserve"* in civilian society, waiting to be called up if needed, and serving the Agency's now growing domestic needs in the interim.

Again, this piece is a cover story for what is going to be revealed, designed to make it all look innocuous and having arise innocently. What you are going to find is 4-8% of the population, at a minimum, was approached by the CIA and offered a deal which they accepted, where they would be a civilian informant/spy for the CIA *in America*, and they would be classified as part-time officers, with all the benefits which accrue from that.

We will show later this is probably what they first tried to legitimize under the cover story of Operation TIPS,[5] a proposed domestic spying program which would have created a pilot-program civilian spy network consisting of one in 24 American citizens, for the express purposes of spying on fellow American citizens. Under this new cover story, these spies are CIA assets helping officers who are building legends. The spying they do on the people in their neighborhoods will probably be claimed to be training operations.

But there is a problem. What this rapidly turns into is a Secret Society, run by an intelligence agency, which even worse, is tied into the most powerful law enforcement agency in the nation. Those who swear fealty to the intelligence agency get the benefits of this massive network of influential people recruited by the agency and rewarded with benefits from agency resources.

Since the majority of America would not like the Secret Society, even were it not spying on them, the Secret Society

---

5   https://archive.is/Cb5u

cannot let it be known that it exists as such. It needs to be kept secret. This has two effects, both terrible.

One, since outsiders cannot be trusted, it means recruitment will tend to come from two sources. First, recruitment will come from within the Secret Society, making it more nepotistic and insular, and isolated from regular America. I have already seen this, with children as young as ten or eleven participating in in-person physical surveillance operations on regular Americans, whose privacy and freedom mean nothing to the Society. The kids are raised in it, because they are the next generation of this Secret Society. For them, it is normal, and those on the outside have been viewed as cattle from the earliest days.

The other pool of recruits will be foreign immigrants from despotic regimes who lack American values. I have seen them too. For them, the idea of a secret society does not violate any moral norms they were raised with. Many of them will also have already been conditioned to desire to be on the inside of such a powerful organization, rather than the outside, and they will tend to not feel loyalty to any of their fellow Americans, or the principles of freedom, or privacy, or limited government that we believe in. The Secret Society which rules, will rapidly be made up of not-Americans.

The second problem is you have a very powerful intelligence agency, which is linked up with the most powerful federal law enforcement organization. Together, they are both breaking the law, and they control the media, leadership positions in government, civil liberties organizations, and even your neighbors in some cases. And all together they need to hide this Secret Society, at all costs.

You do not want your most powerful intelligence agency in the position where it needs, at all costs, to hide something from the American people, because it will do anything to hide it. You do not want such situation to arise, and have that agency linked up with the most powerful law enforcement agency in the nation, and have both of them need to hide this arrangement at all costs. And if that does arise, you do not want to be one of the American people outside the Secret Society, who happens to catch a glace of it, or even worse - threaten one of it's areas of control.

You are going to find this leviathan which is described here was a lot bigger than you would think possible, and it did a lot of very bad things, as it engaged in a slippery slope of committing ever worse crimes to hide its operations, and then committing even more crimes to hide the previous crimes.

Once it reached this point, as it inevitably would, it would easily be taken over by the hostile foreign intelligence operation which Q is going to describe, because it is easily blackmailable with a mere threat of exposure. At that point, you do not want to be the idealistic rube who thinks he can get involved in politics, and maybe change the world for the better.

Out of necessity, the sector of politics and government was solely the province of the Secret Society, and they were not shy about letting you know that. For that matter, you would not want to own a company out-competing one of their companies, come up with a paradigm-shifting technology that would upset one of their business sectors, or otherwise threaten to succeed in any of the areas they have carved out for their agents.

Sun Tzu's writings were all about how *'intelligence is*

paramount in all matters of war.' Clausewitz said, *"War is the continuation of politics by other means."* Given the admonition that *"all politics is local,"* as one Senator once famously said, one could infer that the intelligence operations they ran began locally. You likely can't imagine just how locally.

The truth is, intelligence operations are everywhere, from little PI firms servicing divorcing wives, to big economic intelligence outfits helping major corporations get one-up on a competitor, to secret networks embedded in your very neighborhood, and they are spying on everyone periodically.

Everyone will have a file in the machinery wielded by the political elites of Cabal's Machine. Note how if you read the article referenced a couple of pages back, it says that in far less developed nations, with far less to spend on their intelligence machinery, CIA agents are no longer even followed as they go to meet sources, because there is so much surveillance everywhere in those societies that everywhere they go, they are in view of surveillance. The exact quote is:

Today there are "about 30 countries" where CIA officers are no longer followed on the way to meetings because local governments no longer see the need, given that surveillance in those countries is so pervasive, said Dawn Meyerriecks, the CIA's deputy director for science and technology, in a 2018 speech.

Note that when there is enough surveillance everywhere that your surveillance no longer needs to follow someone from point A to point B, it is because your surveillance is everywhere all the time. As your target exits one surveillance operative's sight, he is walking right into the sightline of another. And that is repeating, all the way from his point of origin to his destination. For those of us who have seen it, it is a trip. For the rest of you, you are blind to it only because you cannot imagine it could be possible for your homeland to be so saturated with people spying on fellow citizens.

Of course so much surveillance means, it is idle most of the time, with no priority threat to follow. So it has busied itself building files on regular citizens, allowing the government to personally get to know everyone, and record who they are in their file.

But how can this be fellow patriot, you ask? It could not be legal?

Au contraire. It is legal because everyone has a FISA file. That will be another of Q's big reveals. We already know for a fact that as of 2017, there had been 40,668 FISA warrants issued.[6] It is believed a single FISA warrant allows surveillance of more than one person. So if a mosque is known to be organizing a terror attack, in theory the government can submit an application for a single FISA warrant to put all of the members of the mosque under surveillance, and the warrant will justify making each mosque-member a primary target. So there may technically be far more primary targets than 40,668, but for the purposes of this elucidation, we will assume each warrant is for a single person.

Once you have a primary target, a FISA warrant allows two "hops."[7] That is, the warrant allows surveillance of the primary target. It then allows investigators to also unleash surveillance on every single one of the primary target's contacts, no matter how

6   http://archive.is/gJFbq
7   http://archive.is/w2M7V

brief, in what is called the first hop. It then allows investigators to take each of those secondary targets the primary target contacted at some point, and perform a second hop to all of their contacts, who become tertiary targets. One analysis found that a single FISA warrant on one person would justify surveillance of 25,000 additional people after factoring in all of the hops which would be justified off of it.[8]

Now the interesting part. If there are 40,668 FISA warrants as of 2017, and each FISA warrant only targeted one person conservatively, and that one primary target would allow surveillance of 25,000 additional people, then the government presently has the right to roll out surveillance, right out of the movie *Enemy of the State,* on over 1 trillion Americans. 1,016,700,000 people to be exact. And that was only as of 2017, and assuming only one person per FISA warrant. Of course, there are only 300 million Americans. So many of us probably have a few different FISA warrants from several different directions. Even President Donald J Trump has multiple FISA warrants, as will everyone who has ever been in contact with him in some capacity.

Basically, through some clever legal wrangling and some logarithmic mathematics, the government has essentially given itself the ability to treat every American like a James Bond villain armed with a nuclear weapon, bent on raising a mushroom cloud over Washington DC.

It should not be surprising. Everything done by the really successful, from business, to government, to politics, uses

---

8   http://archive.is/r4xVj

research, and a key component of the game of research today is spying and surveillance.

Of course we were told the CIA would never roll out on American soil targeting Americans. While I have no idea who exactly has rolled out like the CIA on American citizens, I can assure you somebody has established a surveillance state right out of the East German Stasi, complete with extensive numbers of civilian informants and elite spook technology, all hiding as regular fellow citizens, as they build detailed files on every American.

Even worse, although this machine may have the authority of the US government behind it, we will show later with Q's help, indications are it is run by some foreign, non-state intelligence operation. That would explain how such a fundamentally un-American operation could come to be so ever-present throughout our nation, even as every real American would oppose it with every fiber of their being, were they made aware of it.

Thanks to Q, it is now being revealed.

Now we are going to imbue you with a fundamental truth to help you contextualize the reality of America's surveillance state, and the conspiracy which corrupted it to its own purposes.

The first truth we covered was, this world is Darwinian, and favors those who go all in and seize every advantage. From there, recognize that extensive intelligence and surveillance operations are an integral part of seizing every advantage.

If you accept that, you have to accept that after millennia, those who have succeeded in this world, those who you see at the top of the pile, will be backed by the most complete and aggressive intelligence/surveillance operations possible. If they were not backed by such an operation, someone who was would quickly take them out and replace them, because *the world is Darwinian* and intelligence is paramount to all Darwinian competition. If their operations were in any way incomplete, if there was some little bit more they could be spying on, another operation would do it and quickly supplant them.

Which brings us to the next lie. Spying is about secrets. Not entirely false, this is more of a misconception. Intelligence operations are about a lot more than mere secrets, as the poisoned cigars and exploding seashells Fidel Castro managed to dodge would indicate.

Intelligence operations are more often about corruption and subversion of rival organizations, instead of merely stealing their secrets. That can take the form of blackmail, outright bribery, and infiltration of agents. It can even include control of an individual who has no idea he is controlled, because a covert operation has surrounded him and made sure he got all of the right stimuli to produce the behaviors that the operation targeting him wanted him to perform, at the time the operation wanted those behaviors.

We have also been told spying happens at the individual level, with an *"officer"* turning some individual into an *"agent"* who feeds them secrets. What we are not told is this type of turning of an asset is often done not just to get secrets, but to gain control over an organization's actions and decisions. Why steal a competing operation's secret, when you can steal the entire competing operation and make it your own by corrupting its leaders?

From my observations, the intelligence operation targeting the United States has turned many, if not most of the most critical organizations exerting force or psychological influence in the United States to its ends. It has done this through a massive infiltration and recruitment operation, run for many decades, designed to recruit and place its own agents in key positions of control of these organizations. This has given the conspiracy control over everything from government offices, to businesses, to the very media operations which would be needed to expose their operation to the nation, all as part of a coordinated network which has grown more brazen as its penetration and control has increased.

You have probably heard whispers over the years about entire Central American governments taken over by the CIA, with leaders that the CIA owned installed as the Presidents and politicians of those nations. But they don't discuss that too much, and not just for reasons of national security. They don't want you to realize, it happens more often than you would think in organizations far smaller than governments, and perhaps closer to home than you would want to consider, both in your government and your local community.

Which brings us to lie number five, and that is, there are always competing interests that have fought to a draw, so no "operation" can ever operate unchecked by competitors. I call this the *Myth of Operational Parity*. This lie states, competitors will usually fight openly to a draw, and then choose to fight no more because of the cost of fighting. This is insinuated subtly, such as through the assumption we all have, that nations will exist separately and in competition because they do not want to go to war. The concept of mutually assured destruction is another such concept. It imbues us with the idea this state of affairs, where two competitors will always stand against each other and check each other's power, is some sort of natural law of international relations that serves to keep everyone honest. If only.

Here we will make the case that in fact, this is exactly opposite of the reality, and that all competing intelligence operations will naturally tend to merge and coalesce into a single overarching power structure. This will happen as individual bastions of power launch intelligence operations against each other, seeking to comprise each other, and gain a fuller control over each other. Eventually one dominant power center will emerge, which will then rapidly suck up other more minor power structures as its rapidly growing size, massively increased resources, and the increasingly extensive nature of its intelligence networks and information-access allow it to subsume other operations at an ever-increasing rate with ever less risk.

I suspect we are imbued with this myth of operational parity so we will assume there are always competitors opposing those leaders above us, and thus everyone will always have to be honest. From that we extrapolate there can be no truly horrible truths about our leadership, or their competitors would reveal them to us. If there were pedophile networks running the British government, a hostile government like Russia would reveal them. This lie assuages any concerns we might have in such a regard.

I should specify here that I view everything governmental these days in terms of an intelligence operation. I view things this way because covert intelligence operations offer such power, at such low cost and risk, that in many cases the intelligence operation supporting some organization has simply turned around, taken over the organization it was supposed to serve, and begun running it itself.

Note how in Mexico, it was revealed a major drug cartel had taken control of the President of the nation, paying him a $100 million bribe.[9] Undoubtedly it was only one politician of many in that nation the cartel had turned to its purposes. Is such an operation, that turns an entire government's highest leadership to its ends, best characterized as *a business selling drugs that is supported by an intelligence operation*, or might it be better described as *an intelligence operation acquiring power, which is funding its operations with drug money?* (It is worth noting here that as you examine the evidence, there will be indications that the drug cartels were actually operating as subsidiaries of the larger conspiracy Q is describing. The compromised politicians in Mexico will link through family associations to a sex cult in America called NXIVM, which will link to high-level US politicians and entertainers within Hollywood. The cult served to recruit and traffic sexually-abused victims to be used to lure in potential assets in leadership positions, while the dalliances of high-level public figures and leaders within the cult were used to acquire blackmail which made them controllable. All of this caused the greater conspiracy to elevate these compromised members into ever higher positions of power and control within the broader operation.)

As an example of the power and central importance of intelligence operations to all power structures, from business to government, suppose you are an intelligence specialist hired by a

---

9   http://archive.is/EpQYL

drug cartel to support their operations and vet everyone they interact with for infiltrators and informants. You now have all of the intelligence about that cartel, its competitors, and the environment it operates in. You know who in the cartel is loyal to its leader, and who has more flexible and pragmatic moral frameworks.

Do you want to be second banana to a low-IQ thug cartel-boss who doesn't even know how to run his own intelligence operation in his own cartel? What if you got intelligence he was going to be hit by a rival cartel? What if you saw how you could take him out yourself? You already either have all the intelligence to run the cartel or know how to get it. You have the training to run the cartel and repel intelligence-savvy upstarts such as yourself who might try to take it over. And you may be the only person so situated within the Cartel, as the leader, an intelligence neophyte, has all manner of enemies who will take him out with merely the simple leaking of a small piece of data, like his location, to the right person.

You see how it would work. The world is Darwinian, and intelligence is paramount to all Darwinian competition - and intelligence operators are more Darwinian by nature than most. They will take over anything they touch, unless the person at the top of the targeted organization already is operating with an intelligence operator's perspective, and is already a player themselves.

So how do I get from that, to seeing that the concept of operational parity is a myth? I understand how intelligence works. Intelligence is not about attacks or fighting, though it can support such activities. A good intelligence operation will, as Sun Tzu wrote was the ideal, *"win without fighting."* It will infiltrate, subvert, manipulate, and corrupt.

And that itself is a science. When subverting, do you immediately take over a leadership position in a rival organization? Probably not, as such a position will likely be well guarded. An intelligence operation moving on a rival operation is first going to go for that human resources department, where hiring and promotion are being done. That is generally not as tightly guarded or scrutinized a position as a leadership position, and it allows one to bring in a flood of agents to begin manning the lower levels of the operation with your people.

Imagine, if you will, if an intelligence operation targeted another intelligence operation. If it could get its people inside, and hired on at will, in positions it wanted, it could begin to gain influence within the organization in areas critical to the operation's activities. Imagine if it could get just one of its people hired into a position in human resources and background investigations. It could facilitate the hiring of its own people, and prevent the hiring of honest, patriotic people which would be loyal to the operation.

Once it takes those human resources positions, now it is populating that operation with its people, and it is only a matter of time. Over time, some of their infiltrated agents would inevitably begin to gain leadership positions, or gain blackmail or control over those who held leadership positions.

Moreover, your operators all have an advantage within the organization – they are working together in an organized fashion as a team, to elevate each other and suppress everyone else. Regular employees are all atomized and operating individually, often in competition with each other. Bosses are trying to hire meritocratically, or maybe favoring a close associate.

But the network is working together as a team, helping each other to look good to the leadership and sabotaging others not in the network to make everyone else look bad. And all the network needs is one person to get into a position to promote everyone else, and the infiltrating network will rapidly rise relative to everyone else, and gain power and authority in a coordinated fashion. Statistically, given enough time, the odds favor the infiltrators.

Yes, counterintelligence will be on your tail, but that is why you are trying to infiltrate there as well. Only counterintelligence is operating against you, trying to detect your people, as they work to protect each other and operate against everyone else. Some of your people may periodically get caught, but as with a terrorist attack, they only need to succeed once. And if they can get into counterintelligence at some point, they not only can thwart investigations of themselves, they can begin to falsify cases to take out the honest competition to their people.

Now suppose they succeed. One operation takes over its rival organization, and occupies all of the critical leadership positions, and counterintelligence positions, so they have full control of the operation and cannot be purged.

The strength of an intelligence operation is measured by resources, manpower, assets they control, and technical capability. That intelligence operation just doubled its power by subsuming all of its rival's strengths. It now has all of its own resources, as well as all of its competitor's resources. It now has all of its own officers, and all of its competitor's officers. It now has all of the assets it had assembled in other operations, and all of the assets its competitor had recruited and placed. Imagine it now facing off against smaller operations, with twice the resources, twice the assets, twice the manpower, twice the technology deployment - and it is no longer allocating resources to the enemy it just defeated, so all of that is freed as well. Just the surveillance it could run would be mind-boggling. Eventually, when it gets big enough, it will effortlessly subsume everything it touches.

The critical point is, these types of takeovers will be events which only have to happen once, and which are always, at the broader scale, inexorably proceeding in one direction – the eventual merging of all operations under a single overarching power structure. There can be a tremendous number of failures in all directions, but sooner or later one operation will take over another, grow more powerful, and then that process will accelerate rapidly, as it will more easily take over even more of its rival operations, gaining their strengths and eliminating the cost of resisting them.

So intelligence operations are going to naturally accrete, in a system designed to evolve toward one dominant intelligence operation that controls everything. And as I have said, you should view every operation, from drug trafficking, to criminal enterprises, to businesses, to news operations, to governments, as intelligence operations.

Each of those entities, if corrupted by one operation, could facilitate the growth of that operation, and the eventual joining of all of them together in a unified fashion. A government which was corrupted by a conspiracy, could protect criminal enterprises run by the conspiracy with its intelligence services (and also eliminate their competition selectively with law enforcement operations). It could operate in conjunction with a media operation which was corrupted and helped hide the conspiracy, as the government used regulatory power to only allow businesses run by the conspiracy to thrive, as it pilfered the treasury on top of it all.

It would be a formidable operation combining many entities which previously expended energy in conflict against each other. And if I am correct about how things work, and intelligence operations tend to accrete, then given enough time that is exactly the state of the system which would naturally tend to emerge. It is what we should expect to see, given how much time Western Civilization has existed and our governments have been operating.

What will drive such a process is the fact that the costs of such intelligence operations are low, in the form of at most, individual spies. If they are caught, they can always be traded for, if they are officers, or they can be just left as expendable if they are agents. At worst there might be some minor public embarrassment as well.

Meanwhile, the upsides are considerable in the form of that ultimate aphrodisiac of power. The personalities involved in such work are going to be driven to do it. These intelligence operations are not like wars, which carry a massive inherent cost and risk if lost. They are essentially free, low-hanging fruit which one would be foolish not to avail themselves of. They are entirely free of the deterrent of mutually assured destruction. They are inevitable.

As a result of the nature of this system, there will be no balancing point, where rival operations gradually tend toward landing upon a stable homeostasis of mutually equal power levels, and then face off in perpetuity. Even if you get two equally matched organizations facing off, they will merely push and pull quietly behind each other's backs without open competition, until one gets the upper hand in secret, and takes over the other.

There will be failures. The process may be slow at times. There may even be intermittent reversals where an amassed operation temporarily splits due to some disagreement or conflict within it. But statistical probability dictates, sooner or later, one operation will take over another. And then, fortified with the strength of two operations, it will move on a third. Sooner or later an operation will have so many potential assets, so much in the way of resources, and be able to bring so much manpower and technology to the battle, that it will be able to effortlessly take over smaller operations - and it will. It only needs to happen once.

It is very akin to cosmic dust accreting into larger bodies, and then planets, and eventually that mass accreting with other solar systems into a black hole. These things have nothing but time to progress in that fashion, and they only head in one direction. Let it get big enough, and an intelligence operation will be like a black hole, sucking in rival operations and consolidating power at a stunning rate, everything drawn together by a sort of unstoppable gravity composed of the natural human ambition and avarice of the most evil among us.

This is why I believe the principle of operational parity is a myth. Two operations will never settle down into a stable state of parity with each other. Even if the relationship appears peaceful on the surface, behind the scenes each side will be sending in spies, probing for weaknesses, and trying to compromise the other so it can take it over.

Now you have been told the US government is operated by the people. We elect our leaders. We have the power. There is no corruption or conspiracies, or if there ever was it was minor and limited. Intelligence has been strictly controlled, and could never act to seize control. Other countries are in competition with us, and we with them. Our intelligence agencies work for us. All of these assertions are fundamental to your perception of our government.

Does what you were told jibe with the model of the world which these natural laws should tend to produce? I would maintain the model of the world you were raised to believe in is extraordinarily unlikely. It goes against the very natural laws of the Darwinian world and the rules of intelligence operations. It cannot be.

Is it possible things are actually far different from what you were told? If so, what does that say about the world around you? A world, which naturally should be led by lying and deceiving spies, has told you there could never be any lying and deceiving spies conspiring to control it, and you have the ultimate power and authority over your government because magnanimous men who eschew power and competition are our leaders, and they have ceded that power to you willingly.

From the murder of JFK, to the murder of RFK, to the story of "The Octopus,"[10] to the "Five Eyes" program (where we openly share our most sensitive intelligence with other countries' intelligence operations, as if we are all merged together as one), to the rise of the gang-stalking phenomenon, to the unexplained sudden rises in the wealth of our elected officials, there have

---

10   http://archive.is/TXBlO

always been hints that things may not be as we are told.

In truth there is one rival force which could possibly hold foreign intelligence operations at bay, and that is American patriotism, combined with the exposure of such a corrupting intelligence operation. That is the only motive force that could drive any resistance. Indeed this force may save us yet if this machine is exposed. But as you will see, this force faced a ruthless operation of global scale, that was unusually prominent in our compromised intelligence agencies from their very inception, which fully controlled our news media, and which has apparently killed more than one patriot who learned too much.

And all along the way, our brainwashed population has offered little, if any resistance, because having been kept blind to how intelligence operations work, and being informed by a media that was taken over by the conspiracy, they could not see the world as it was.

The final lie which we will discuss may be the story we were told of our American history, though it will be more an omission of a crucial aspect. That will be saved for when we begin to lay out the Conspiracy Q is explaining.

Chapter Three

*The Origins Of Q*_____

You cannot understand the origin of Q without understanding what we call "the Chans," and more specifically the parts of the Chans known as /pol. The Chans grew out of a series of Japanese bulletin boards where people posted messages. In the beginning, they were colloquially known online as the *"Nameless Worlds."* There everyone posted without using specific names to identify themselves. As a result, every post was seemingly written by one poster named "Anonymous." Today, everyone on the Chans refers to each other as "anon," and they called themselves collectively the "anons." It is a strange, identity-less form of interaction, like one giant stream of consciousness, emphasizing raw information exchange over egos and personal identity. Disorienting at first, with time it grows on you.

Eventually 4Chan emerged among those many sites. It was designed explicitly for English speakers, and it took off. 4Chan hosts numerous boards, but the most significant for purposes of Q is /pol, which is both the internet file address and the shorthand for a board officially titled, *"Politically Incorrect."*[11]

Another user would eventually create another splinter site called 8Chan, with its own /pol. The sites known as /pol were

---

11   http://boards.4chan.org/pol/

noted for politically incorrect humor and online pranks (trolling), expressly designed to offend everybody for laughs. Hitler was hailed as a hero who did nothing wrong, each race and ethnicity was assailed and insulted based on its worst caricatures, and people basically tried to be funny in as irreverent and politically incorrect a way as they could.

The users endlessly discussed how best to create a pure white ethnostate, and who would be allowed entrance into it. The most politically protected classes were attacked ruthlessly. And strangely, in a politically correct world of pretty little lies, the posters began to realize that on /pol they could at times speak of forbidden truths openly. As time went on, the humor became secondary to their rigorous analysis of the cold harsh realities of the world which most people would refuse to even look at. It was an oasis of truth in a world made up of endless politically correct lies.

Amusingly the users would periodically organize meet-ups in real life, only to find there were few if any whites among them, and almost everyone present was in fact made up of the very non-white races and ethnicities which they relentlessly insulted. The most intellectually non-inclusive place on the internet was actually more inclusive and welcoming of everyone than the most politically correct leftist organizations. Their response on finding this out was to proclaim their disgust with their own organization for not being white enough.

The complete history of the Chans and /pols is far beyond our scope, but what is significant is the types of users who aggregated on these strange boards, where all users speak what is on their mind, under the nom de plume "Anonymous," without concern for reputation or presentation.

In short, among their ranks were genuine geniuses with tremendous amounts of specialist knowledge, and tremendous abilities to accumulate new specialist knowledge on the fly when they choose to do so. These anonymous posters, or anons as they referred to themselves, jokingly refer to the mix of extreme genius and obsessive focus as *"weaponized autism."* They laughingly envisioned themselves as some sort of chaos-producing version of Dustin Hoffman in *Rain Man.* And they used that ability periodically to cause impressive disruptions for certain powerful entities in the world, without ever leaving their computers.

As examples, we will quickly rehash the two most famous such incidents where they decided to use their knowledge to uncover a seemingly impossibly concealed piece of information.

On January 20th, President Donald J. Trump was inaugurated. The same day Hollywood actor Shia Labeouf, in protest of President Trump, began an art installation in New York City, consisting of a live-streaming camera and microphone. There, Shia would show up and scream into the microphone, *"He will not divide us,"* and it would be broadcast across the internet. It was left running 24 hours a day, with Shia urging his fans to show up and continue the project as continuously as possible when he was not there.

4Chan's /pol quickly caught wind of it and began showing up at the installation to disrupt the festivities. Like most things opposing President Trump, it rapidly turned into a disaster as the camera recorded and documented the chaos while airing it live online. Shia eventually ended up arrested by the Police during one incident when he snapped and accidentally assaulted one of his own fans in the midst of the chaos from a real-life prearranged /pol-raid of his project by some local anons who escaped unscathed.

Shia moved the installation to a crime-ridden neighborhood in New Mexico hoping to keep anons away, but it got disrupted again, sometimes by unrelated factors. In one after-hours video, an aspiring local rapper tried to deliver his rap about peace and tolerance to the camera, only to have it disrupted mid-rap by a drive-by shooting of someone feet away, on the very sidewalk right next to him.[12] That then set off a neighbor who began screaming, incensed about all the violence and disruption the installation had brought, leading even the now-befuddled rapper to sheepishly opine on camera how the camera needed to be shut down because it caused so many problems.

Shia eventually gave up, simply aiming a live-streaming camera located in some unknown location up toward the sky, at a flag atop a flag-pole. The flag said, *"He will not divide us."* That would have been the end of it, except for the fact /pol had set its sights on him, and they decided they wanted the flag.

All they had was a live-stream picture of the flag, and the background behind it, but that didn't deter /pol. They were able to examine the movement of the stars in the little piece of the sky behind the flag, and combine it with angle and the movement of the sun's shadow in relation to the time, and get a general geographic region and position of the camera. They listened to ambient sounds of traffic to judge the proximity and size of nearby

_____

12   https://www.youtube.com/watch?v=LWYvWcwbgWI

roads that would be found on maps. They were able to correlate weather conditions and wind directions cited on live radar on meteorological websites with what they saw in the sky to narrow it further. Then they looked at the contrails of planes in the sky overhead and compared it with real time air-traffic control website data. This finally narrowed it down to one neighborhood in Tennessee.

Once they had a neighborhood, one local anon began driving around honking his horn, as other anons told him in real time on the site whether his honking was getting louder or softer on the sound of the live-cam. He eventually reached Moon Creek Road in Greenville, Tennessee, found the flag, removed it, and hung it in his basement. It took less than 36 hours from the time it was put up for /pol to find it and steal it.

Shia moved the flag display to the top of a five story building in Liverpool, England, thinking the top of that secure building would be totally inaccessible, even if /pol's anons managed to find it. Once again, within two days members of 4Chan's sister site, 8Chan's /pol had found the flag, devised a plan using satellite imagery and online photos off of Google, and gotten to the top of the secure building, stealing the flag.

But even that example fades compared to the time 4Chan located a terrorist training camp in Syria and called in a Russian airstrike, just to amuse themselves.[13]

A Russian reporter had asked his twitter followers if they could locate the site where a terrorist training video was filmed. A Russian speaking anon posted the question to /pol. Anons were

---

13   http://archive.is/V4e7O

able to use a similar process to eventually track down the exact location where the video was filmed, pinpointing the camp in Syria on a satellite overhead at Google Earth. They gave the coordinates and the evidence to the reporter, he forwarded it to the Russian Defense Ministry, and shortly after airstrikes were launched, destroying the terrorist camp.

But unfortunately in this world, you are not allowed to be that good, and not under the direct control of the conspiracy. The "powers-that-be" were beginning to fear this anonymous intellectual Goliath. Anons began to notice and catalog various techniques designed to try and control the dialog on discussions the government would want to discourage, and other techniques designed to disrupt, and even drive people off the site.

There were floods of posts to the board, containing everything from gore-videos of accidents and torture-murders, to full frontal nude pictures of pre-op transvestites having homosexual sex, complete with male genitalia and breast implants. There were anime cartoons of transvestites having sex, videos of animals being tortured and killed, cannibals cooking and eating humans, and even child porn on posts about topics the powers-that-be really didn't want discussed. Anyone who wanted to partake of the board would have to see all of those posts to get to posts from genuine anons.

There were floods of meaningless posts, designed to make finding anything meaningful difficult as those fake diversionary posts trended above government/Cabal-opposed content. There were even full board shutdowns, apparently done by the people running it, when too sensitive a topic began to be unraveled. Then a post popped up from somebody associated with the site alleging that the FBI had moved in, seized the servers, and took full control of the site, supposedly on the basis of a child-porn investigation.[14] As they reviewed the allegation, anons noted things about the site's recruitment of moderators which was only explainable through that chain of events.[15] So 4Chan was literally being run by the FBI.

The site also disabled the ability to visit it through a virtual private network, and individual anons began reporting being gangstalked in their lives by a pervasive on-the-ground intelligence/surveillance operation embedded in their communities and made up of everything from neighbors to postal workers. Some even began regular gangstalking general posts to discuss it.[16]

And yet /pol soldiered on. Even today, the average person will have to wade through an enormous amount of highly unpleasant material to find the pure gold which is its research. I suspect most of the posts on it are actually produced by some form of opposition project designed to try and derail its effectiveness.

Regardless, what is important, is there were anons on /pol who had an impressive ability to notice and gather extraordinarily obscure, small quantities of evidence and the intellectual tenacity to extrapolate underlying realities from it, wherever it might lead.

It was against this backdrop of irreverent, unorthodox, independently-thinking genius that an anonymous poster who

---

14   http://archive.is/4qTNy
15   http://archive.is/Fxvkx
16   Some archive links followed by the 4Chan archive of the page:

               http://archive.is/kEvDz
               https://archive.4plebs.org/x/thread/22880859/
               http://archive.is/nAtVP
               https://archive.4plebs.org/pol/thread/186685702/

would come to be known as Q began posting to 4Chan.

Chapter Four

What Does The Cabal's
Machine Look Like? _____

Q began with a splash – that Hillary was going to be detained, and some sort of criminal action would be launched against her. As time went on he began to reveal the outlines of a massive conspiracy of which she was a part, run as a giant intelligence penetration and subversion, and designed to subvert the interests of the entire United States on behalf of a small group of ultra-wealthy, ultra-powerful, foreign elites. Along the way, he made predictions, and coordinated posts with President Trump in such a way as to lend the story he was telling an incredible amount of credence. We will begin with the story he told, of a secret Cabal of ultra-wealthy and powerful elites running a massive intelligence operation to infiltrate and subvert the entire United States. Then we will progress to the proof which seemed to lend Q credence.

Q's story sounds extraordinary, but only given that we have been told this could not happen. In reality, looking honestly at history, understanding the nature of intelligence operations and their ever-presence, and their uncompromising drive to penetrate and subvert whatever organization they see which has any power, I now think it more likely we would have been subverted than not.

Bear in mind, what is proposed here is a radical concept, however I have seen things firsthand in my own life, and know things you do not, which have directly led me to support this hypothesis. I am not just extrapolating a possible reality which Q might point to. I am posing the only solution which can explain real-life parameters I have witnessed in a very vexing conundrum which I have been grappling with for some years now in real life.

What I have seen with my own eyes, and what extensive research has led me to believe, is that our government was compromised by a foreign intelligence operation, and may have been from its very founding. If so, our history was a lie, a grand deception crafted by this operation, to keep us feeling in control and forestall any desire to seek any change in our governmental arrangement.

Let's begin with the Revolutionary War. History tells us we won. But then what? We did not expel those loyal to the Crown. They were given citizenship. Indeed, the British forces maintained a highly capable intelligence/spying network, made up of ostensibly regular citizens throughout the Colonies, both before and all during the Revolution. Would the King have abandoned such a network after the war, once we were competing nations? Or might he have maintained it? Would loyalists who viewed themselves as more British than American, and risked their lives for the Crown during the war, perhaps have retained their loyalty to the Crown after the war ended, especially if there was a generous financial incentive to do so?

We then became a nation welcoming of immigrants. How would a foreign power infiltrate our ranks better, than to simply send loyalists to migrate to the new land and take citizenship? Given that the intelligence war is ever-present, and the world is Darwinian (even more so in matters of international espionage) this was merely inviting our enemies within the gates, hidden within the camouflage of millions of other, innocent immigrants. We even freely gave them the right to vote in our elections and elect our leaders.

The older me would expect every nation would have flooded us with sleepers and spies, but in light of the falsity of operational parity, I suspect one much older intelligence operation, which had long ago coalesced from many, had penetrated and subverted most European countries. It had, in reality, used those multiple nations to set up one network – even if many of the assets within that network may not have known it, and may have been driven by nationalistic and patriotic fervor.

At that point, we would have infiltrators within America, given full citizenship, and moving through the population as citizen spies. How easily might a foreign power which sent them, have sent the most capable among them money, to establish themselves in high positions in society, perhaps so they might one day seek elected office? They could purchase businesses and the best educations for themselves and their children. They could purchase politicians and do favors, to ingratiate themselves into the circles of leadership. They would become fixtures of high society. They could set up blackmail, bribery, and intelligence networks. And most of all, they could coordinate among themselves in a Secret Society devoted to raising the prominence of Secret Society members above all outsiders.

Now the infiltrators of the network would have a leg up on our honest, hardworking citizens, forced to lift themselves up by their own bootstraps as they battled an organized, covert intelligence operation, running as a Secret Society and plotting against them.

Such a network, externally funded by governments and composed of highly capable organized individuals working in concert to help each other rise, would have an innate advantage. Doubtless their members would immediately set about infiltrating other fraternal organizations devoted to members helping members, such as the Freemasons, or religious groups, or business organizations, or political parties, and other societies, and turn them all to the ends of the network. That is what intelligence operations do.

An asset of the network, living in an electoral district where network members concentrated (as they might on orders, as part of an organized network's operational plan), could run for office. Where an election might previously have been close, his election might be guaranteed, if there were a hidden, secret block of voters, all voting on orders of the network for the network's candidate.

And all of this time throughout our history, as a foreign intelligence network was infiltrating its agents, setting up networks, and taking power, we were running a minimalist government based on the principle that government should interfere as little as possible in citizen's lives. *"That which governs best is that which governs least."* Obviously spying on citizens, as would be necessary for a viable counter-intelligence effort, would have been out of the question, and thus we would have lacked any counter-intelligence capability to detect and defend against this infiltration.

We were a nascent nation, absent sufficient counter-intelligence assets, already hosting a well established, hostile foreign network, and welcoming any migrant we encountered, all while facing the predominant superpower of the time, Britain. I would be shocked had we not been infiltrated and successfully subverted.

And that assumes Britain was actually a nation ruled by the King. For a long time, the Kings were crowned by the Pope. Might there have been a larger intelligence operation in the shadows behind the King, perhaps behind many kings, using the King as merely one figurehead puppet, tasked with running but one nation they had corrupted?

Was there any organization, which predated the Crown, indeed, which had persisted, unchanged in the background, across Europe, throughout the rise and fall of numerous nations and leaders, and which always seemed to manage to gain a position of great influence and wealth, no matter the leaders in power? One organization filled with wealth, power, intrigue, a foothold in every nation, and the unquestioned loyalty of citizens of many different nations, and yet seemingly immune to the tumult as its host nations and their leaders rose and fell? Obviously, the Vatican could fit the bill, and Q as much as says it openly.

Imagine a simple religious organization, made up of good men seeking to further the word of God, holding the power of the unquestioned loyalty of the pious, as well as the wealth produced by tithing. Imagine it suddenly falling into the sights of a ruthless intelligence network in the past, looking to take it over. As with a young America, lacking the training and experience, it would not be long before it was taken over.

The intelligence operation targeting the United States could have been far larger than that which one would assume Britain could have mustered. Q has implied this group of hidden elites, forming a clan whose strategy was the corrupting of governments, may have much more ancient origins, perhaps traveling back to the Roman Empire, or even earlier.

There are indications that in the past, when governments fell, those who held the real power from within the shadows may have used their influence and power to cloister themselves and consolidate their power within the Church, waiting to reemerge later, when conditions were more amenable. We could have faced a far older enemy, with far greater experience in these intelligence-related matters than our Founders could have mustered a defense against.

When you think about it, the idea of America being infiltrated from her earliest days almost seems wholly unavoidable, given our minimalist government, emphasis on privacy and freedom, known entrenchment of British spy networks made up of our own citizens, and welcoming of immigrants from all of the other superpowers. Those superpowers would almost have been remiss in their own patriotic duties had they not flooded us with spies. The only question is, given the falsity of intelligence parity, were their intelligence services isolated, individual actors, or was their one hidden hand controlling them all. Q will lead us down a path indicating the later was the reality.

If it were true, then for much of her history, America could easily have had within it, a massive Secret Society of spies, living in parallel with Americans, but never quite fully among them. They would all know the secret (at least that they were spies for whoever they thought recruited them, even if they were incorrect in their understanding of who they were ultimately serving, or where the intelligence they gathered was going).

Likely, they would pass their birthright down from parent to child, as their children would be raised in the network, and they would want them to have its benefits. They would see the rules and mores regarding freedom and privacy by which Americans live as malleable. The Constitution would have been a mere document for others to abide by. And they would know that the America everyone else saw, was merely a show designed to mollify the masses and make them willingly submit to what really ruled the nation.

Q appears to state that by the time we were forming our intelligence services during and following WWII, such a conspiracy had a sufficient operational footprint within our government, academia, cultural structures, and society to make sure their agents were heavily represented in the nascent formal national Intelligence Community. Understanding intelligence operations, it would be unsurprising to find out that from their very inception, our civilian intelligence agencies had been compromised by a foreign intelligence operation.

In truth, I am a little surprised that a United States government, composed of highly educated and erudite individuals, familiar with the use of espionage in warfare, had not formed some sort of official, centralized, governmental organization to perform foreign espionage and domestic counter-intelligence until WWII. As I look at it, it feels like that may have been more an engineered state of affairs created by those who wanted to keep the American government weak and ineffectual, rather than an accidental oversight.

Granted, I am not an expert in the history of intelligence operations in the United States, but what I do know is that either the story behind the sudden formation of the OSS during WWII, and the disorganized ad-hoc nature of foreign intelligence operations prior to it is false, or there was some strange reason the leaders of the US Government had not been allowed to form a dedicated, centralized intelligence service. Even an isolated code-breaking operation someone had set up prior to the war had been dissolved by a Secretary of State who famously said of it, *"gentlemen don't read each other's mail."*[17]

My own assumption, based on observations to date, would be that the Secretary of State that made that quote was a compromised asset of whatever intelligence operation it was that had penetrated the United States. He was not stupid, or hopelessly naive. By keeping the US blind, he was, wittingly or not, helping to protect the intelligence operation he was a part of from any accidental exposure that could have come from the wrong patriot in the US overhearing talk of it and exposing it.

Even our immigration system historically being so welcoming of immigrants makes me suspicious. Think about this for a moment. You have been told from birth we are a nation of immigrants, and moreover, that it is a good thing. Why is it such a good thing? Nobody ever asks. They just absorb the idea they are imbued with, that being a nation of immigrants is better than not being a nation of immigrants. Moreover, having been raised utterly blind to the world of intelligence operations, our citizens never consider the real world implications of such a policy on increasing the vulnerability of our nation to being infiltrated and subverted.

---

17   https://www.u-s-history.com/pages/h1665.html

Imagine if you are a foreign intelligence officer of another nation (or even, as may be the case, a non-governmental organization of ultra-wealthy elites), tasked with subverting the United States. Your goals are twofold. First, weaken the capabilities of the United States relative to your organization/nation. Second, and actually far preferable to the first objective, you would want to actually to co-opt the wealth, political might, and military might of the United States to the purposes of your organization/nation.

The best way to accomplish this is to infiltrate your agents into the United States. Then you would move them into positions of power and influence using the resources of your nation and the network of agents you assemble in the nation. Look at how much easier that is to accomplish when the United States establishes an open immigration policy.

Protecting us from such a vulnerability is the job of our government, and its state security apparatus. If such an operation, seeking to take over our nation, controlled the very government which was instituting those liberal immigration policies, and if they controlled the institutions which created and presented to us the idea of America as a nation of immigrants, a part of me wonders if it was chance we suddenly became a "nation of immigrants."

By the time WWII arrived, I would assume the operation had gained a tremendous amount of power, and penetrated the United States population and government thoroughly. I suspect that by that point, it felt it could adequately penetrate any newly-formed US intelligence operation enough to control it.

If it could control the risks of allowing the US to have a coordinated national intelligence operation, then it could begin to use US government resources to fund even more expansive intelligence operations, to gain even greater control, under the cover of official US governmental operations. Best of all, it would control the very US apparatus which would have been used to root it out and destroy it, had it been discovered.

Once the CIA was assembled after the war, it would appear from Q's posts that the Cabal had its people installed in it from its very inception, and it was off and running. Some saw a problem from the very beginning, though I suspect they were not entirely clear on the root cause. Asked about his formation of the CIA years later, President Truman replied, *"I think it was a mistake. And if I'd known what was going to happen, I never would have done it... the President needed at that time a central organization that would bring all the various intelligence reports we were getting in those days, and there must have been a dozen of them, maybe more, bring them all into one organization so that the President would get one report on what was going on in various parts of the world. Now that made sense, and that's why I went ahead and set up what they called the Central Intelligence Agency... But it got out of hand. The fella ... the one that was in the White House after me never paid any attention to it, and it got out of hand. Why, they've got an organization over there in Virginia now that is practically the equal of the Pentagon in many ways. And I think I've told you, one Pentagon is one too many.*

Now, as nearly as I can make out, those fellows in the CIA don't just report on wars and the like, they go out and make their own, and there's nobody to keep track of what they're up to. They spend billions of dollars on stirring up trouble so they'll have something to report on. They've become ... it's become a government all of its own and all secret. They don't have to account to anybody.

That's a very dangerous thing in a democratic society, and it's got to be put a stop to. The people have got a right to know what those birds are up to. And if I was back in the White House, people would know. You see, the way a free government works, there's got to be a housecleaning every now and again, and I don't care what branch of the government is involved. Somebody has to keep an eye on things.

And when you can't do any housecleaning because everything that goes on is a damn secret, why, then we're on our way to something the Founding Fathers didn't have in mind. Secrecy and a free, democratic government don't mix. And if what happened at the Bay of Pigs doesn't prove that, I don't know what does. You have got to keep an eye on the military at all times, and it doesn't matter whether it's the birds in the Pentagon or the birds in the CIA. "[18]

So our history books tell us the Revolutionary War was won, but if Q is correct, we may have merely won the battle, and ultimately lost the war for true independence, courtesy of an intelligence operation that set about taking over behind the scenes. Thankfully Q's emergence and the election of President Trump is a possibly decisive second chance to turn the tide of this battle.

Now we will look at an overview of what Q has asserted, and look at the evidence supporting it later. Understand that as we

---

18   http://archive.is/gV4Ip

go forward, I am hewing quite closely to the barest bones interpretation of Q's assertions. You will see deeper examinations elsewhere which look at specific religious histories, trace the lineage of little known Secret Societies which have been associated with societal and cultural leaders, or speculate on possible historical origins of Cabal. Q however has been sparse in the information he has offered, and it is far from clear exactly where the Cabal originally came from, though he notes that it does make use of quite ancient symbolism.

Some assert things may be far worse than what will be presented here. Some believe that there is a possibility the Cabal which took over the country appealed to a spiritual darkness of some sort, which has helped them attain power. It is true, Ivy-league trained psychiatrists with full MDs, who counted themselves among skeptics have, at the request of the Catholic Church, assessed various individuals whom the Church indicated may have been demonically possessed. Many have followed those deemed possessed through the exorcism process, and concluded that the phenomenon they witnessed during the process defied scientific explanation, and pointed to some sort of poorly characterized super-natural phenomenon in our world.[19]

It is not impossible there is another side to this world, or even that if appealed to, the seemingly randomly emerging phenomenon of demonic possession which those Ivy-league psychiatrists claim to have seen could be interacted with and harnessed in some fashion. But Q has not been explicit about any of that. He has, at most, indicated that many among the elite practice some sort of satanic worship. Whether that is performed

_____

19   http://archive.is/6cKKt

to call upon dark forces, or simply to trick members into performing awful acts during rituals for purposes of gaining blackmail on them is unknown at present.

So understand, as radical as the more pedestrian human conspiracy we allege is, there are other interpretations which are even more radical, and I have no evidence either way whether they might even be correct. Here we will try to hew most closely only to the most obvious and concrete of Q interpretations. In my opinion, they are more than horrifying enough.

For now, as you read these interpretations take my word that one, I have seen shadows of this conspiracy in my own life which led me to Q, and two, having followed this movement almost from the beginning, the evidence which will emerge in support of this theory, courtesy of Q's anons, is mind-boggling. The things which follow, which you will presently view as near-impossible in America, are now simply fixtures of the daily reality for myself and many others.

So, on to Q's assertions.

Although Q has made reference to the Cabal which controls things being ancient in its origins, the earliest reference to it in the US that he has made is to the Cabal setting up the Federal Reserve, to gain control over the US currency. It would seem it was much more undercover during this period, although it was still operative, and advancing toward its ultimate goal of full control. Most of this secret Cabal's machinery seems to have begun to be assembled in earnest after WWII.

If we were compromised by an intelligence operation, it would have done what intelligence operations do, which is conceal its activities, even before advancing toward its goals. It would have looked to potential avenues of exposure of its own activities, and sought to gain control of them, so if information ever did leak out about its activities, it could stifle the dissemination of that information.

Detailing the mechanisms of this control over what people are told is what many of Q's posts were devoted to. Once the Cabal made the jump to allowing the creation of the CIA, it created a powerful intelligence tool which could be used against it, to expose its activities to the public, or even launch legal actions against it. I assume because of this increased risk, it realized it would need to have backup plans in the event anyone in the CIA who was not part of the conspiracy ever discovered its activities, and tried to expose its operations to the public.

This would mean Cabal would need full control of other parts of prominent American society such as the law enforcement and judicial apparatus, and the information dissemination machinery. That way, if some spy at the CIA discovered its activities, it could prevent the dissemination of that knowledge to the public, as it tried to leverage its control over the rest of the governmental machinery to avoid legal repercussions and deal with the threat. According to Q, this became the goal.

So after WWII, the CIA was formed and the real expansion of Cabal operations began, in an effort to get full control over all of the machinery of American society, from government oversight agencies, to law enforcement, to the media and academia. Q pointed out that this began with an organized infiltration of our organized mainstream media.

He supports this by pointing to several documented CIA operations. Operation Mockingbird[20] was a documented CIA program to infiltrate CIA officers and agents into the US news media, and recruit agents from the existing US news infrastructure with the express purpose of controlling what the news media would – and would not – report to the public.

Q then goes on to state that there was a similar program to make sure famous cultural figures were on board with Cabal's conspiracy, from rock stars to actors. He said many of them would either have close familial connections to the intelligence community, they will be recruited agents, or they will be shown to have been part of child abuse networks run to blackmail prominent people with predilections toward pedophilia, with their history of child-abuse being used to control them in adulthood.

He asserts that these "Stars" are in fact created and elevated through the CIA-controlled media, with the express purpose of acting as psychological trendsetters. In this way, they exploit a quirk of many humans, to subconsciously emulate what they see successful people doing, and follow what they are told by "authority figures." In ancient evolutionary times, when we existed as small groups, doing this was beneficial to survival.

However today that trait, which was identified by the Cabal, only serves to allow them to exploit mass media and celebrity culture to exert control over the population. By simply having "successful" celebrities tell us transphobia is wrong, we now have legal jurisdictions where if you try to stop a grown man who claims to be a woman from taking off his clothes in front of a

---

20   http://archive.is/LKcm7

young girl in a woman's locker room, you will be arrested for infringing on the trans-person's rights.

This creation of controlled "stars" is done so that all cultural stimuli presented to society can be controlled, and there will be no honest people in prominent positions to deliver uncontrolled messages or stimuli, or reveal to the public information that the conspiracy might find inconvenient. Indeed, as you delve into the research, it is disturbing how common the experience of sexual abuse is among child stars and the Hollywood machine, how often such child stars allege people know and do not intervene, and how many prominent people in that industry are dogged by rumors of pedophilia and child sexual abuse. Our culture is more controlled than most would believe.

That research by Q's anons, into the use of pedophilia and blackmail to compromise and control a societal sector, will extend far beyond mere entertainment and news media, and as Q will show, the conspiracy is not limited to the United States. Many other countries have been infiltrated by this leviathan. As that research expands globally, Q's anons will point out many instances all over the world where pedophiles are uncovered in all sorts of prominent positions, and media and criminal investigators begin to find linkages pointing to networks which reach high into government, business, and high-society. However before these linkages can be properly probed and exposed, the investigations are suddenly stopped and a media blackout on them comes into effect. The control is amazing when you see it.

Alternately you will find cases of people in the media who were part of the abuse who were protected, like that of BBC celebrity Jimmy Saville.[21] Saville is rumored to have molested almost 600 children, some of them sick children provided to him by doctors at a hospital where he did charity work.[22] It was a horrific scandal which was rumored to point to a pedophile network that ran high into the BBC leadership, the political elite, and British high society. In his case, the molestation was uncovered, but only after he had died. No leads pointing to a larger network were pursued, and there was no examination or punishment levied for any of those who either knew and did nothing,[23] or those conspirators who actually punished the few noble souls who did come forward and try to stop it.[24]

As you follow the research Q has produced, you stumble onto more disturbing CIA programs, designed around understanding how humans think, and how to manipulate them. MK Ultra is one program, and some of the more grotesque elements of this program which became public are quite horrifying.

In Canada, the CIA took over a small depression clinic. Once in control, they took regular, innocent citizens who entered it for minor problems and experimented on them with different techniques, from drugging, to electroshock therapy, to hypnosis, to simple mental torture experiments. The experiments on these innocent people resulted in victims' becoming incontinent, experiencing amnesia, forgetting how to talk, forgetting their parents, and even seeing their memory altered to the point they

---

21   http://archive.is/muQqn
22   http://archive.is/RQJzv
23   http://archive.is/BdMOj
24   http://archive.is/X6HDF

would think their interrogators were their parents.[25]

We would never have heard of these experiments, except one victim ended up marrying a Canadian Prime Minister, who on hearing of this called for an official investigation. Absent that one quirk of history, none of that small piece of MK Ultra's history would ever have come to light - and MK Ultra was not the only such program that experimented on civilians which the CIA initiated. It was succeeded by MK Naomi,[26] MK Delta,[27] Project Artichoke,[28] and MK Often.[29] Sadly, much of what occurred is not known, and cannot be discovered, as CIA admitted during the Church Committee hearings that it had destroyed almost all of the documentation from all of those experiments. This is only what was able to be confirmed from various scraps of documents which eluded those agents tasked with eliminating all evidence of these activities.

So according to Q and the evidence accumulated from his anons, there may very well be a foreign-originating conspiracy which has been running a complex full-fledged intelligence operation against all American citizens to subvert the United States government and society. It may have been operating within the nation from its very independence. If so, it likely was rife throughout our intelligence infrastructure from its very formation, and spring-boarded from there to infiltrate, subvert, and take over other sectors of our societal machinery, from news media, to entertainment, to academia.

---

25   http://archive.is/kIHRP
26   http://archive.is/skj5b
27   http://archive.is/A1t0d
28   http://archive.is/6FYwD
29   http://archive.is/r0a5A

There is also hard evidence that this conspiracy was invested in high-level research into technical manipulations of minds and population control using advanced psychological techniques, in ways a layman would not believe could be possible. All of it was an effort to control the population, so it could maintain its control over the country.

They had a documented program tasking the CIA with infiltrating and taking control of the mainstream media and news media, so they could deliver such psychological stimuli to an unsuspecting public, through news and entertainment in a controlled fashion. Controlling the news broadcasts particularly would allow them to control and/or mitigate any potential exposure of their myriad of activities. And this is just a brief summary of what has leaked out in official documents, about a secret operation run by intelligence professionals that professionally keep everything they do secret – even from our legislators and our elected leaders. Imagine how much we do not know.

Acting in support of this entire operation was a massive surveillance/intelligence machine deployed throughout our society. It used a civilian informant network of regular citizens embedded in neighborhoods and social circles, ostensibly leading regular lives while tasked with spying on citizens.

From what I have seen firsthand, the scale of this network within the United States would rival anything the East German Stasi had produced, and it was supported by a quantity and level of technology the Stasi would never have dreamed possible. I have seen this part of Cabal's operations first hand, and I can tell you it took years of dealing with it 24 hours per day, 365 days per year, to even begin to comprehend the scale of the manpower, and the extensive advancement of the technological machinery it had deployed all throughout our society.

How did I come to be in close proximity to Cabal's operations and see them? Very simply, they showed them to me in an effort to intimidate me into not getting involved in our political system, and specifically, spreading one conservative political idea online. I do not believe the surveillance is ideological, per se, beyond the fact the Cabal appears to be furthering leftism as a way of weakening the political influence of the more patriotic segments of American society. I probably would have gotten the same treatment had I been a leftist who threatened to amass an audience and influence the political world in some way, given I was not a Cabal agent, nor was I particularly controllable by any foreign entity.

Since observing the machine, I have come to conclude that most people online are data-consumers, and not producers or spreaders of information. This works to the Cabal's advantage. Take 4Chan's /pol, for example. Suppose you try to start a conversation by posting a topic there. Through observation, it would seem there are three ways Cabal controls the stimuli 4Chan offers the casual observer.

The first is by assessing if they want your post deleted. Some people have posted things only to see the thread either deleted immediately, or fail to post. It happens, and most savvy anons assume the board is ultimately operated by someone who is under the control of the machine.

If your post is not that bad, but they want it to drop off the board and out of sight, they can not add any comments to it, while commenting on other, more harmless posts. Again, most honest anons do not post, but rather lurk. Five Cabal operatives, each running twenty fake online profiles, with software giving each profile a unique IP, can post as a hundred different people. Posting five comments per identity, they can quickly support harmless posts, keeping them active and in sight at the top of the board, as they let undesirable posts drift lower and off the board due to lack of commenting activity, until they drop off the board and are not seen.

The final method is simply by using their various identities to flood a post with pointless comments, disinformation, or outright objectionable material. You will see this on any gangstalking/surveillance post which gets enough comments to stay on the board. It will quickly be deluged by naysayers deriding the poster as schizophrenic, claiming the government would not run surveillance on anyone on the board, and trying to dilute the content with meaningless banter unrelated to the topic.

In reality, a casual observer who had not met the surveillance machine would have no opinion, and quietly observe. Even some under the aggressive surveillance known online as gangstalking will be prone to lurk (I have), rather than comment. As a result, a relatively few people, using simple software, can effectively control how the overall conversation looks to outsiders. If you have never heard of this type of operation, it may sound extreme, but even small political action groups have been documented using what are called paid shills online, to control conversations on otherwise independent forums.[30]

---

30   http://archive.is/gXNmU

So when you go online, there is a tendency, due to natural psychological projection, to think you are seeing people just like you writing honestly to inform you. You are not. Even the free discussions on many independent forums with influence that touch on sensitive topics likely have many fake comments produced by a few paid posters running multiple accounts, to control the dialog.

You can imagine how this control would be exerted on actual content providers who run sites, where the machinery can be used to elevate some and suppress others. This is where I ended up running face-first into Cabal's ground-surveillance/intimidation machinery in real life. I began to move toward becoming an outright online content provider, and I was not controlled by the machine.

It began with a simple idea I wanted to promote. Years back I had an epiphany. Political ideologies appeared very similar to psychological "programming" imbued in the minds of animals, designed to emerge through a mixture of genetics and adaptation. This programming was a sort of rudimentary operating system for an animal which guided the animals to instinctively make decisions which benefited their survival and reproduction under two different environments. In the literature these were called called an r-selective environment and a K-selective environment.

I use the example of rabbits and wolves to illustrate this programming. You do not see a wolf naturally develop a rabbit's peaceful, herbivore personality. Nor do you see a rabbit born who naturally exhibits a wolf's aggressive, hunting psychology. Why?

Rabbits are designed for an environment of glut. They never run out of fields of grass. As a result, they evolved to exhibit several psychological urges. They expect free food everywhere, so competing and risking injury for food would be disadvantageous compared to simply fleeing to another source of food elsewhere. As a result, they are non-territorial, and driven to avoid the risk of conflict and direct competition, even with predators who want to kill them. They will mate with anyone who they come across without committing to one mate, to make as many offspring as possible (promiscuity) as fast as possible to exploit the glut. They expend as little effort as possible on rearing offspring for the easy world they face (with clutches raised by a single mother due to male promiscuity) so they can turn out as many offspring as possible as fast as possible to take advantage of the glut. They will not oppose offspring engaging in promiscuous sexual activity as early as possible because it will maximize total offspring production, and enhance the spread of their genes by extension. They will also show no loyalty to in-group because loyalty requires sacrifice and cost, and since food is free, is it more beneficial statistically to simply flee from all sacrifice and cost to a new field of grass and safety.

Basically animals who face a glut exhibit a psychology that sees those traits as normal because it allows them to exploit the glut by producing as many offspring as possible, as quickly as possible, while avoiding all risk. In r-selection, the competition among each individual is who can flood the next generation with offspring the fastest. Scientists say it is a strategy of quantity over quality.

So basically in r-strategists, you have a pacifistic, competition-averse psychology, that doesn't believe in protecting its own, which mates promiscuously, rears children with single moms, thinks children can be sexualized, and has no loyalty to any type of in group. Amusingly, in r-selected animals, the female will often be big and aggressive to provision and protect the offspring she rears alone, while males get smaller and more effete, better suited to mating on the sly and fleeing danger. They call it the *reversal of sexually dimorphic traits*. I saw the parallels between this psychology's urges and liberal leftism's worldview, and was blown away.

The opposite of an r-selective glut is a K-selective shortage. (The terms r and K came from equations relating to population dynamics.) In a K-selective shortage, it is like wolves facing a deer population which only has a herd of six deer to last their entire pack through the entire winter. There isn't enough food around for them to be able to tolerate other wolves just moving into their territory and eating their food. This selects the population for a completely different psychology, which sees entirely different behaviors as normal.

K-selected animals like wolves have to become territorial and competitive because given the shortage, only those who fight over food and the territory it occupies survive. They just assume resources are limited (and in humans that they must be "won" in merit-based competition as a result). Because only those who compete successfully in K-selection get food, those mates who do things to make their offspring more successful in competition are the ones whose traits become the traits of the K-selected organism.

This means K-strategists carefully select the fittest mate (again, producing the genetically fittest offspring who can survive, is itself a part of the competition), and then they monopolize that mate's fitness with monogamy, so no other competitor can benefit from that mate's genetic fitness by having offspring with them.

Offspring are reared in a two-parent family with high rearing investment, because it is a dangerous world and they need their offspring to survive and be adequately provisioned until they are fully mature and capable of reproducing themselves. They will even discourage their offspring from mating until fully mature and maximally competitive, so they can be as attractive as possible to acquire the fittest life-long monogamous mate, and continue the competition to produce the genetically fittest offspring themselves. Even wolves do not believe in sexualizing pups, and there is a concrete, biologically advantageous reason for it.

And finally, K-strategists will tend to form groups with a high degree of in-group loyalty and competitiveness toward out-groups, for obvious reasons. They need to win competitions as a cohesive, loyal group to get the food to survive. I have wondered if that K-strategy, with its emphasis on monogamy and loyalty, is the evolutionary origin of the emotion of love. Kill a deer or a rabbit, and its peers would graze right alongside the body, unaffected. But kill a wolf, and its pack will mourn.

So in K-strategists you have a group of territorial, competitive, loyal, monogamous, two-parent-rearing, pack-oriented animals, who love each other, discourage sexualizing young, and expect a world where there are not always enough resources for everybody to just cruise and acquire free stuff without needing to compete for it and earn it. And among K-strategists, males evolve big and strong, and are willing to fight for, and give their lives for their offspring since they have so few, as well as die for their clan since it needs to survive for the good of their genes. Meanwhile females evolve smaller, less confrontational/aggressive, and more feminine, to guide the offspring from the dangers the male confronts. Clearly, that is the evolutionary origin of the Conservative-right's ideology.

It ended up becoming the book *"The Evolutionary Psychology behind Politics,"* and it came out brilliantly. It was a deep, deep dive into all of the published research, comparing and correlating the genetics behind political ideology and r/K psychologies, the brain structures, the neurochemistry of reward and how that had been shown to affect the brain structures that were both associated with the r and K traits, and with political ideology. It even examined how whether you looked at grand timelines like the fall of Rome or the leftward tilt of America that has occurred since the fifties, or whether you plotted the Economic Misery Index year by year, and laid a graph of the Conservative Policy Mood year by year over it, you could see how an influx of resources would trigger human brains to exhibit a more leftist r-selected psychology, while a resource restriction would trigger a more Conservative, K-selected trend in population-level ideological inclination. Human brains were actually self-adapting their r or K-psychological programming to the level of dopamine produced by their environment (ie, resource availability), and as they did, their left or right wing political inclinations moved right along with it. Everything matched up perfectly.

The book was the next 250 years of all of political science's advances in understanding, from biology, to neurochemistry, to genetics, to social science advances, condensed down into 280 pages, and available this moment with a click of the mouse. Titled *The Evolutionary Psychology Behind Politics*, it was the final word on the study of the origins of political ideology.

I assumed it would be a blockbuster, and would be required reading in every political science class in the nation. This was where our political battle first arose – in an evolutionary process which adapted us to two different environments. You could not study politics without understanding it.

Darwin supposedly just mailed around manuscripts for *Origin. W*hen the banter of experts spread into the mainstream, he changed the world's perception of how we came to be, or so we were told.

There were magazines devoted to politics, like National Review and American Spectator. There were radio shows and cable TV shows, devoted to bringing interesting ideas in politics to viewers to hook them as fans, because that was how they made money. I even saw a major publisher who had just opened a new conservative imprint, and was desperate for manuscripts with interesting ideas. The publisher never even responded to my inquiries. I mailed copies to, and emailed the various outlets, and nothing happened. Something was strange. The idea was too interesting to just be completely ignored.

Among the small, online conservative community it caused a major splash. People on the right who read it gave it glowing reviews. Liberals seethed and hated it, but I even saw that hatred as great for the dialog and generating interest. Outside of the small, independent online right however, the mainstream media outlets completely blacklisted it. There was not even a whisper, even as fans wrote me about promoting it to all of them on my behalf.

And then I began to get followed around, by a lot of strange people. If I had to go back to the point when the machine really began to become involved with me, it was probably as I was writing the book. However at the time I was blissfully unaware.

The first sign I should have seen, but being naive to surveillance procedures I missed, was that one neighbor disappeared. Their house just suddenly went empty. It was strange, but they lived alone and had family who cared for them, so I assumed some event had occurred that forced them to move. However they never said anything, nor did anyone else move into the house. Of course someone likely did move into the house, they merely did so quietly and established it as a covert observation post, something my later readings on surveillance indicated was the standard operating procedure.

A while after that I began finding screws placed cleanly into the tires of my cars, parked in front of my house. I first thought I must be driving somewhere where someone had spilled a box of screws all over the ground. However one time I had been checking the treads of new tires I just bought, and saw no screw, but when I came out the next day and glanced absent-mindedly at the tire, there was another screw, cleanly inserted, as if with a power drill.

The sudden appearance of screws was a puzzle, as I wasn't disliked by the people who knew me, and it would take some effort to get to my house. I looked around and found footprints leading to in front of the now abandoned house, where I lost them as they entered grass. Since I assumed the house was abandoned, I concluded someone had pulled into the driveway in front of the abandoned house in the middle of the night, and walked over to my house to insert the screws.

Still it was puzzling. Whoever would have done it would have run the risk of encountering a potentially armed homeowner who might not be violence-averse in a darkened environment where a cordless drill could be mistaken for a gun. It would have seemed a strangely high-risk activity with little to gain. Of course, if you had ears in my house, knew when I went to sleep, could tell if I awoke in bed, and had live radio contact with whoever was running over quickly to place the screws, and you were sent expressly to harass, that would have segued from a very dangerous operation with little gain, to one with almost no risk and all gain, in the form of completing an assigned mission objective.

Then I had a shock-absorber pried off a car. A mechanic said it looked like somebody took a crowbar to the water pump on another car.

I deployed surveillance cameras to try and catch them, and the screws and other damage suddenly stopped. I assumed it was bad luck they had just decided to stop. However if the house next door had been converted into an observation post, as I now know is standard operating procedure in surveillance operations,[31] then they were watching as I deployed the surveillance cameras, and were one step ahead of me.

Then one day I traveled to a remote location with no traffic where nobody have known I was traveling to, and where I would

---

31 Regarding the investigation of Soviet Spy Jack Barsky:
From: http://archive.is/FJjOH
"The bureau bought the house next door to get a closer look at the Barskys.
Steve Kroft: Did you get a good deal?
FBI Agent Joe Reilly: I think we paid what he was asking. And we had agents living there so that we could be sure who was coming and going from his house without being too obvious in our surveillance.

not have encountered anyone. I parked, left, returned to my car, and ended up having to stop at a gas station due to a flat tire. Again, I had a spike in my tire. This one was nearly impossible to remove. Made of ABS plastic, it had been sculpted with dual hooks preventing it from being either extracted or pounded into the tire. It was so fixed in place, it would only break apart as you tried to extract it. After a half hour, and removing the tire from the rim, it was fixed, though the mechanic commented he had never seen anything like it.

It was reminiscent of the operation to target and intimidate Kathleen Willey in 1998. Bill Clinton had sexually assaulted her, and she was subpoenaed to testify in the Paula Jones case. A similar intelligence/surveillance/harassment operation set upon her. Her cat disappeared, her tires were all slashed, a skull looking like a cat's was left on her porch, and she was finally approached by a jogger while she was walking in a park. He asked about her missing cat by name, and threatened her children by name, before asking her if she got the message.[32] Obviously in the intervening years, the organization established to harass her must have grown,

---

32   From: http://archive.is/JMi9R
        HANNITY: Your cat did. But you ran into a stranger who mentioned the loss of your cat, and your cat's name, and your children by name.
        WILLEY: I didn't run into him. He approached me one morning. He alluded to the fact. He alluded to my cat by name in the past tense. He said... "That Bullseye was a nice cat."
        HANNITY: And that was a direct threat, you believe, on the eve of your testimony to let you know the cat's gone?
        WILLEY: That was followed by — that was followed by, "How are your children?" And he named them by name. That was followed — that was followed by this naming of very dear friends to the children. That was fired by, "Did you ever get those tires fixed?" I had three out of four tires of my car flattened by a nail gun. He said — let me finish — he said, "You're just not getting the message,   are you?" That was the threat to go in and lie under oath.

and begun launching many more operations on ever less important targets. Even Clinton mistress Sally Miller was targeted by this machine over her writing a memoir of her years with Bill.[33]

I didn't realize it, but since reading Q, it has become clear that a major way the Cabal maintained control over our government was by keeping as many people as possible "asleep," in Q's terminology.

I knew they were asleep. All of western civilization was going to hell, and only a small percentage of the population could even see it, and even they couldn't figure out a way to stop it. Clearly people who should have cared ardently did not, because their brains had stopped paying attention and caring.

I actually crafted Evopsych's reveal of r/K to try and awaken all of those asleep, thinking it a possibly effective way to try and reverse the decline by triggering K-urges in the readers. But what I didn't realize was somewhere a very powerful group had actually put those people to sleep purposely, and they were not pleased with any efforts by anyone to wake them up. Even worse, they had the machinery built and deployed to realize very quickly whenever someone tried to awaken their sleeping slaves, and the machinery to dish out harassment to try and dissuade such behavior.

Online they call it *gangstalking*, but I never liked the term. I get the impression that "gangstalking" is a term introduced by them, to make it sound less official and less associated with government and authority figures. The reality is, it is for all intents

---

33   Describing her observations in the US: http://archive.is/u0NJq
      Describing harassment in China: http://archive.is/AMMaO

and purposes merely government surveillance using local civilian informant networks, deployed by political leaders in such a way as to harass and intimidate.

After years of extensive observation, I have found it to be composed of a massive, Secret Society of civilian informants, organized by a central command structure, and designed to act as a civilian surveillance/informant/spy/harassment network. It is embedded in most, if not all communities and neighborhoods, both rural and urban.

Its members appear as normal civilians. They usually have non-intelligence related day jobs. They live in houses like normal people, with normal families and hobbies. You would never peg them as elite surveillance operators belonging to such an organization, until you happen on Cabal's radar and suddenly they come out of the woodwork to execute their orders and follow you everywhere you go.

Although it appears to have had the support/protection of some US government agency, it also appears to operate across national boundaries, with similar civilian informant networks built identically in other nations, doing similar things. There are anecdotal reports from victims of gangstalking of traveling to places like China or Europe, where one would think any US intelligence operation would not be welcome, and they report being seamlessly picked up at the airport, and followed there by an identical local civilian network of informants to that which they were followed by in the United States, and it continues their harassment, as if the local operatives were briefed on their arrival, and told how to continue the harassment.

It seems to have been around a while. There was an FBI agent who headed the LA Field office of the FBI, named Ted Gunderson.[34] (This archive of his Wikipedia page in this note is fascinating, as he was saying the exact same things Q was saying, decades before Q, from satanism to child abuse networks being involved in the conspiracy.) Ted had spotted this surveillance machine following him, as he began investigating Cabal's pedophile/blackmail networks. There is an affidavit from him attesting that the gangstalking/civilian-informant/surveillance-network is real here.[35] He apparently fell under it due to his direct research into Cabal's activities, and his attempts to awaken the population to the conspiracy. But even as a famous, high-ranking FBI leader, he could do nothing about it, and the media never mentioned his plight or lent him any support.

There are other anecdotal cases reminiscent of this machine going back through history. Pulitzer Prize winning author John Kennedy Toole (1937-1969), author of the Pulitzer Prize winning book *A Confederacy of Dunces*, led an unremarkable life, until submitting the manuscript of his book to publishing houses. Shortly after his rejection, he reported becoming the target of a massive centrally coordinated surveillance/harassment operation being perpetrated by seemingly normal people in his community.[36] Eventually, based upon observations, he became convinced it had planted bugs throughout his house, was following him everywhere, and was even sending college-aged agents into the

---

34   http://archive.is/OvwqY
35   https://www.anonymousconservative.com/blog/wp-content/uploads/2019/08/ted-gunderson-affidavit.pdf
36   https://www.anonymousconservative.com/blog/archival-material-of-the-cabals-history/

college classes he taught to disrupt his work-life. He also believed at one point this machine had intended to steal his manuscript, and publish it under another author's name. He finally, supposedly committed suicide. However after extensive observation of these types of cases, it is difficult to say whether the stress of his ordeal motivated him to kill himself, or if it was merely staged that way by the unknown actors he claimed he faced.

There are other cases which extend even farther back. However when facing an intelligence operation, it can be difficult to say what is real, and what is illusion. The earliest case of which I am aware was the case of James Tilly Matthews (1710-1850). He was a peace activist during the French Revolution, who almost interceded successfully in heading off war between England and France through diligent third-party negotiation.[37] Failing, he returned to England, making accusations of treason by its leaders, to the point the government simply declared him "not of sound mind," and had him institutionalized. While institutionalized, he was deemed of such sound mind that the institution paid him for architectural drawings he produced for a remodeling of the facility. The proprietor of a subsequent, "more genial" institution he was transferred to regarded him as entirely sane, and even employed him during his residence as a book keeper and gardener.

Once queried by doctors on his arrival at the institution, Matthews began to matter-of-factly relate that there were teams of spies and criminals all throughout England, embedded in the populace and posing as regular citizens. These teams were networked together, operating as a single unit, under a central leadership, and each was responsible for specific neighborhoods.

37 http://archive.is/wip/CBaHM

82

Their purpose was a mix of surveillance of the populace, and harassment of some who involved themselves in politics, and he described them as having a high level of technological sophistication, especially for the times.

He reported that in some cases, including his, they were using a weapon he referred to as an "air-loom." It was some sort of remote-energy-weapon used to physically torment those who attempted to involve themselves in politics. It generated energy which was beamed at the targets through the walls of their residences at night. The device was supposedly housed somehow adjacently to the target residence, and could be tuned to produce various effects on the target. It is a curious anecdotal description of what people today refer to as directed energy weapons, which are reported as being used on targets of the modern surveillance machine, by some of the people who run into this machine today.

On the one hand, today's technology would not have been available to the people of the time. This would seem to speak to his account being the product of an overactive imagination. On the other hand, there have been cases where buildings have been described as having produced symptoms of physical illness and altered mental states in those who entered them. The sources of the illnesses were tracked back to some mechanical device which was unknowingly releasing infrasound waves as it operated, which had accidentally sickened the entire buildings.

It is not impossible such reports might have generated interest from those in power at the time and been studied more intensely by the specialists they had access to. Given Europe's intense interest in sound and musical instruments at the time, I could see such a technology developing, using some type of bellows-type forced air to produce such such infrasound waves. Moreover, specific frequencies of infrasound waves could be produced at the time by "weaving" various different frequencies of sound waves together constructively and destructively, to produce specific infra-sound-length wavelengths, making his use of the word "loom" quite curious. And as this article shows, his description of symptoms, even difficulty breathing, would be consistent with infrasound exposure. So all of this would be something that could have been technologically feasible in such a musical culture, and although he seemingly had no reason to have any knowledge of any of this, he described it quite accurately.[38]

Also strange is he would describe these operations as being housed in adjacent residences. Most people would think an intelligence/surveillance operation acquiring a neighboring residence to base operations out of would be unusually difficult and unlikely. But we will show evidence later that such action is in fact standard operating procedure for surveillance/intelligence operations, and we will show where it has been described on such notable TV shows as 60 Minutes by such knowledgeable individuals as high ranking FBI counterintelligence/surveillance

---

38 Interestingly, he described one facet of this device's effect as being difficulty breathing. That is a known symptom of infrasound exposure, which would easily have been able to be produced at the time given the knowledge of musical instrument production in Europe. And such a musical instrument, would likely be unusually large so as to produce such long wavelengths, just as Matthews drew it. Possibly even organ-sized, it could perhaps, be described by some as an "Air Loom," weaving together different sound frequencies to produce different infrasound wavelengths and related effects through constructive and destructive interference effects. Indeed, Mathews drawings of the device, drawn from unknown sources, show an organ-like device with vertical pipes, and wooden barrels which appear to be supplying pressurized air from chemical reactions. For more, see:
    http://archive.is/kgZl4
    https://waubrafoundation.org.au/wp-content/uploads/2015/02/Broner-The-effects-of-low-frequency-noise-on-people.pdf

operatives.

It is strange Matthews would, as a layman, describe a potentially viable technology of the time which could produce physical symptoms such as he would describe – moreover, a technology which would seem quite impossible to laymen, and which he himself did not fully understand. It is also strange it should so closely parallel what numerous people describe today. And simultaneously, he described a seemingly impossible mission parameter of basing intelligence/surveillance operations out of a neighboring residence, and yet this is standard operating procedure for such operations, though it is not known to the general public.

Of course if one accepts that we face an intelligence operation today arrayed against the populace, then one possibility we cannot rule out is that they would want to make allegations of any directed energy weapon usage today, which is entirely possible and maybe even likely, seem the product of overactive imaginations. To that end, understanding intelligence operations somewhat, I could see this account, and the text which "discovered it" being inserted into libraries recently, perhaps even using artificially-aged books and alteration of archiving records. It would actually be quite simple to have someone insert such books into an archive, and then arrange for them to be innocently "discovered."

Introducing an allegation of such technology, at a time when its existence would be seemingly improbable to the public, into the historical record in such a way, would make it more easy to denigrate such accounts today as fantasy, even despite the documented presence off the technology, and the scientific plausibility of the accounts. Indeed, James Tilly Matthews account today is officially cited as the first documented case of paranoid schizophrenia with delusions of persecution, implying all such allegations today would immediately, de facto, be cases of diagnosable mental illness with delusions. So I do not know exactly what to make of Matthews' case, though its similarity to credible accounts today would make it seem related to modern events, in one way or another.

Throughout work, we will show others who have made allegations of similar experiences, encountering a massive hidden network conducting surveillance and intelligence operations against an unwitting public, and focusing on those who involve themselves in politics, without the machine's permission. These personalities will range from Rolling Stone reporter Michael Hastings, to Supreme Court Justice Antonin Scalia, to conservative talk radio host Tom Bauerle, to New York Governor David Patterson (and numerous New York legislators who approached him about their own experiences with this machine), to Clinton accusers Juanita Broadrick, Kathleen Willey, and Sally Miller, to NXIVM cult leader Keith Raniere, to wounded warrior Brian Mancini, to numerous mass shooters and cop-killers.

I can attest personally, there is undoubtedly a hidden, secret society of some sort out there, conducting some sort of covert intelligence operation against the public. And its greatest advantage is that public is by and large not just unaware of it, but actually unable to believe such an operation could possibly exist.

So what does it look like? I first noticed it when I took out my garbage, though it had probably moved on me much earlier. I took my garbage out to the end of my driveway late at night, on the isolated street I lived on. It was remote and sparsely populated enough I could reasonably have expected no car traffic to be passing on a normal night. However every night, just as I reached the end of my driveway, I'd hear a car down the street rev up its engine suddenly, bottom out, and then come racing down the street toward me, slow down just before coming into sight, and then drive in front of my driveway, just as if it was a normal car leaving my neighborhood. After it passed, I could hear it accelerate and take off out of my neighborhood.

I became curious, so I put the garbage out later and later, until it was a time when the whole neighborhood should have been asleep. Every time, I would reach the end of the driveway and hear the car bottoming out down the street and racing to me. And yet, it was almost always a different car, strangely enough. It was a puzzle, because the road they were likely staged on, and waiting for me on, was a steeply inclined dead-end road that split off my road, about 300-500 yards away, with numerous winding turns on the main road between us, and heavy woods all the way around it. In theory, they couldn't be seeing me, they couldn't be hearing me, but when I got to the end of my driveway they knew and sent the car. I could hear them all the way down there suddenly take off and pick up speed at exactly the right moment.

This eventually led to a realization that I never got to the end of my driveway, be it day or night, that traffic didn't come driving by, often in multiple directions, even though my road was isolated, only served a few houses, and the traffic was totally out of proportion to what one would expect.

I checked my driveway surveillance camera, and sure enough there would be no traffic for hours before and after my excursion. But at the moment I reached the end of my driveway, suddenly they would appear. If it occurred during the day I noticed that often multiple cars would suddenly be driving in both directions, just at that moment.

Then I began to notice as I drove out, cars would always begin to pass in front of my driveway. As I headed out, there were always cars coming at me, and often one behind me. I'd hit intersections in isolated areas, and there were almost always cars puling up to them just as I arrived. There were also massive increases in the numbers of pedestrians walking and bicycles riding where I had never seen them before. Then I noticed I couldn't go into an empty store at an early hour without three or four people suddenly following me in, about thirty seconds to one minute after I entered, and loitering around with a sightline to me, but no clear purpose. I could go to Costco, arrive to an empty store early in the morning on a weekday off, and within minutes it would fill up with thirty or forty people, all shopping in the area of the store around me.

The I came to realize, they were listening inside my house, and saying certain things could dramatically increase the traffic outside my house, often with revving engines and even honking horns. As it became clear I knew, they became hostile. Some would even whisper into their wrists, as if secret agents, in an effort to intimidate.

I eventually began writing about it on my website, despite how insane I knew it would look. As I would compose blog articles about it, they would suddenly increase the traffic in front of my house dramatically, as if to complain or threaten. I eventually concluded they were monitoring my keystrokes in real time. It sounds insane, I know. I never would have believed it myself ten years ago, but I can only report what I saw.

I didn't realize it at the time, but surveillance rolls out as a package. If you have cars following you, you have people on foot following you into stores. If you have cars and foot, you have technical monitoring of your technology, and they are on your phones, your internet, listening in your house, and everything else their space-age tech can do. It appears they deploy much of the technology at the telephone poles, from microphones to cameras, plugging it into the cable internet and feeding it to their observation posts or base stations. I assume they feel no warrant is needed if they harvest the sound waves outside of your house and amplify them artificially, or use other remote monitoring technology that doesn't require a covert entry of your residence..

From my readings online, I found out they use microphones and geophones (microphones which pick up vibrations from the ground, and pass them on as sound) which pick up very fine vibrations from sounds made in a residence. The sensors document the waveforms as they arrive at the mics, and the exact times they arrive. Then, through computer analysis they can filter out only waveforms which arrive with a specific constellation of arrival times. This allows them to triangulate the sound almost in the way a GPS receiver uses the wave arrival times of signals from satellites to determine your position.

By way of explanation, suppose you held two microphones in front of you, in each hand. On your right side, somebody said *"Hello,"* and on the left side of you, exactly at the same time, somebody said, *"Goodbye."* Now if you just rigged the mics to a tape recorder you would only hear a jumbled mess. But if you rigged them to a computer, with exact arrival times of the waves recorded at each mic, the computer could tell that the *"Hello"* waveform of vibrations hit the right mic at a set time, and passed it and hit the left mic just a pico-second later. It could also detect that the *"Goodbye"* waveform hit the left mic first, and hit the right mic just a pico second later. It could then apply an inverse wave to remove from the output whichever waveform you wanted to erase, and the result would be a targeted recording of just one voice, positionally targeted to the location you specified based on the waveform arrival times. The only difference in the output would be, it would be twice as loud because you were feeding the outputs from both microphones into the recording. But it would filter out the extraneous sound as if it never happened.

Now imagine increasing the distance between those microphones to telephone pole distance to exaggerate the waveform arrival time differences. Imagine in addition to atmospheric mics you used geophones in the ground detecting the sound through the vibrations from your home's structure passing through the ground, (think of hearing horse hoofbeats miles away by putting your ear to the ground). Then imagine multiple microphones, all positionally targeting the sound, and amplifying it as each mic's output is laid over the others. It is a powerful technology, because with just a few points of contact with a building superstructure, such as granted by renting a few apartments in an apartment building, you can program and tune the software to be able to listen inside any apartment in the building, without having to make entry to the apartment, almost as if each apartment was a tuned radio station.

I just assume it is widely deployed throughout cities, with each building having a dedicated observation post and assigned listeners. And I imagine there are still other technologies we do not even know about. One would be passive radar which can actually pluck a single voice out of a stadium of screaming fans, and which is now being used in Europe openly in stadiums to police the speech of individual fans for racist comments.[39]

The FBI has to get a warrant to plant a physical bug to eavesdrop in residences (which by the way is 1940's era technology – obviously the technology has been advancing alongside all other technology we see). But with Cabal, there were no rules, and there is technology today nobody would believe.

It also appears standard operating procedure is to establish an observation post with a sightline to your house. Since it began, literally all of my long term immediate-neighbors ghosted, disappearing silently to be replaced by what would appear to be regular American families, some even with children.

Oddly enough I could hear two of their children (from different families) talking at one point. One of my surveillance cameras captured the conversation. One was new to the neighborhood, and asked the other about my house, to which the first one quickly responded, *"We followed him today."* Although I had never met the kid, he definitely knew what was going on, and that his friend was a fellow cult-member, raised in it and aware of the game going on, as this wasn't unusual to him.

Which brings us to the strangest aspect of the phenomenon. They use children in surveillance operations, and have read them

---

39   https://news.sky.com/story/italian-football-league-considers-using-anti-terror-listening-devices-to-identify-racist-fans-11842057
http://archive.is/nGeQg

in on this unbelievable secret. I assume they are running them as agents against other kids, who are not in the cult, in the schools, building files on everyone from the earliest of ages. It is pretty amazing, and very creepy for a supposedly free republic.

So they already knew everything about me.

Among those things they knew was I had to take a longish car trip at one point which would have me out of the house for a few hours. When I returned I noticed the power had been cut to my house. I reviewed a surveillance camera I had installed on my driveway, and was surprised to see that within a minute of me driving out, three large phone company trucks pulled up in front of my house, and everyone in them jumped out and began scrambling to prearranged jobs, as if in an incredible hurry. Then, after a few moments, the power went out.

I knew something was up because union procedure is five guys drink coffee while two guys have a conversation, all while one guy does the job as slowly as possible.

When I looked at the poles, they were loaded with cables, splitters, and routers. As I watched as time went on, they got even more loaded in my neighborhood as pole trucks drove up and down it.

As time went on, it increased. You'd go in an empty store, and five or ten other people would come in after you and form a crowd around you, and then coincidentally follow you throughout the store. Some would purposely look to make eye contact with you at a distance of maybe fifteen feet. Once you locked eyes, they would simulate talking into a wrist microphone, turn and walk away quickly. Others made loud conversations about things I had discussed privately with family inside my house. It was weird.

My impression is the show was to let me know my presence was not welcome in the online political world. It got more and more aggressive, until I began running video everywhere I went. I put 1080p action cameras running out all four sides of my car, eventually upgrading them to 4K, and wore 1080p video sunglasses everywhere I went. Then they backed off so as to not be so obvious on video. It was costly, in both time and money. Constantly archiving video from all of those cameras for an hour every time I got back from a trip, and making sure everything was charged before I left was a pain, but it was better than the alternative.

I talked to a local cop I had known, to file a report for the record when I suspected my car had been tampered with, possibly to plant something in it. He made it clear, he didn't like what was going on, but there was nothing he could do. Whatever the jurisdictional authority they threw at the local department, everybody in it was afraid. He took the report, and a cop from a neighboring department showed up. His job was to gather as much info out of me as he could about what I had seen and figured out, presumably for the surveillance team. Then the cop I knew said he'd get a copy of the report to me later in the week. No copy ever came, and I assume the entire report was "lost."

Around this time I began to notice the houses they took over were releasing some sort of chemical fog into the air, which would fill the neighborhood. I suspected the fog was responsible for the vegetation dying back and thinning out, as sight lines opened up from my house and driveway to windows of the neighbor's houses, where previously they were completely obscured.

At one point, a tree trimming crew came in and cut down all of the brush between my property line and the road, opening up things there. Judging by how the ground cover and natural plant growth died back, I suspect they deployed an herbicide as well. You could drive through the neighborhood, and it was a lovely bucolic, wooded street, until you got to my driveway where the front of the property was a massive clear-cut patch of stumps and bare dirt on the ground, and then the woods picked back up when you got on the other side of me.

I came home from being chased around one day, flopped on the couch, and put on the movie *The Burbs* with Tom Hanks. I had the volume quite low, so as to not disturb a family member who was sleeping.

The movie is about a guy (played by Tom Hanks), who notices strange things being done by weird people in his neighborhood, and he begins investigating them with his friends. His wife (Carrie Fischer) doesn't like him doing that and in one scene, they have an acrimonious argument, where they yell at each other about strange things going on in their neighborhood, and whether or not they should take off for a cabin on a lake, or stay and not surrender their neighborhood to the weirdos in it.

You see where this is going. As Tom Hanks and Carrie Fischer yelled at each other, I suddenly looked at the road outside on my surveillance camera monitor, and along came a hybrid surveillance SUV, super slow and quiet. A middle aged woman with a butch haircut had the passenger window open and was craning her neck out of it, as the car pulled up to the front of my house and stopped in the road, so she could listen.

They were listening inside my house, in real time, heard the argument on the TV, thought it was me yelling, and crept up to see how audible it was from the road, not knowing it was a TV show I was watching, and not realizing I could see them on my surveillance camera. Bear in mind, I would not have been able to hear the argument from right outside my window, let alone the hundred or so feet to the road, through the woods which were still there at the time. So basically they had ears inside my house, and they were quite sensitive, though not infallible.

One house across the street was kept seemingly abandoned, until one day about 15 gunshots appeared to come out of it early in the morning. It sounded like 9mm or mid-size handgun, which would be consistent with magazine capacity. It wasn't the only time. Rapid fire bursts of gunfire were ringing out pretty frequently late at night, seemingly answering each other from different houses.

I had gotten the feeling they had people living around the neighborhood in other houses who were amusing themselves by firing guns in the air to screw with each other as they all sat performing the otherwise boring monitoring operations on the residents, watching the technical surveillance established throughout the neighborhood and listening to the microphones at the poles to get a heads up on any pedestrian activity in the woods, or interesting arguments or conversations in the houses.

This morning, it seems they had stashed somebody in the abandoned house across the street, and they had let some gunshots fly, and accidentally hit a nearby house which seemingly was occupied by regular citizens. According to the Police conversations afterward, they took out a picture window. The local PD responded, as did State PD en masse, and some unmarked cars too. The Police Chief came along about an hour later to survey the scene personally. However he seemingly made the responding uniformed patrol officer from his department wait at the scene for him, as if he didn't want to be at the scene alone with the unmarked vehicles' occupants.

There were a couple of other major events that happened around that time, which really screwed up the lives of other very prominent people in the area, who apparently either had fallen afoul of this machine, or simply been in the wrong place at the wrong time, but I don't want to get into them because it would reveal too much about my location. Suffice it to say, this operation used intelligence techniques to take out local members of my government and law enforcement apparatus, I presume replacing them with their own controlled agents.

We pushed and pulled over the years. At one point I made moves toward approaching the Russian Embassy and looking to bring the intelligence services of the Russian Republic into it. I was hoping to leverage SVR and GRU's desire to hobble America's surveillance state, by getting them to assist in finding a Russian private sector TSCM (Technical Surveillance and Counter-Measures) company I could hire to expose surveillance technology mounted on telephone poles. In addition they would offer media contacts with Russian media who would document and expose the local monitoring tech pulled off the poles by the TSCMs as part of a broader treatment on the extent of America's surveillance state. Finally I was going to bring in Russian Embassy approved legal support to observe and document the removals, file Police reports, bound subpoenas to everyone involved, from the local Police Department to the utilities which serviced those lines, and then launch a lawsuit based on those Police reports filed on the illegal technology which was uncovered by the TSCMs.

I assumed the Russians would jump at the opportunity just to have Russian experts get a legal look at a high-end Western surveillance operation and it's technological deployment, and in the process politically cripple American domestic surveillance capabilities. My surveillance probably agreed, because they backed off the harassment. However I, my family, and family friends were all still being followed around passively while out and about, and they remained on my phones and internet, and listening in my house. At the time, I still could not believe this would be an outright criminal conspiracy. Thinking the probability would have favored it being some law enforcement operation that had stepped over a line in the course of normal law enforcement duties, rather than a foreign conspiracy to take over full control of the US for some foreign elites, I didn't go to the Russians. I look on it now as God's will. Perhaps if I had, it would have thwarted Q's efforts in some regard.

The intrusions remained vexing, as did the gradual realization our nation was being taken over by something which was slowly supplanting our Constitutional Republic with a Stasi-like surveillance state run by a bonafide Secret Police force akin to the KGB. Bear in mind I realized our nation was being taken over by an un-American intelligence operation, and I was writing about it on my website, literally years before Q arrived on the scene.

I continued to write about surveillance topics on my

website, and things escalated until it eventually reached a point where I think they were hitting me with some sort of directed energy weapon through the walls of my house that would cause my body to vibrate.

It sounds ridiculous, and in truth I cannot to this day tell you whether it was them or not with certainty. All I know is when I would lay down to sleep, about a half hour in, just as I drifted into a deep sleep, I would feel as if an 8-12" sphere of my internal organs were being pushed and pulled rapidly in a single axis along the plane of my bed, maybe two to six times per second, back and forth, from inside by body. The axis would correlate with the house owned by a woman whose child was recorded talking about following me in front of my house.

When I was near that neighbor's house it was focused in a smaller sphere, and when I went to the other side of my house it was a more diffuse, whole body effect, so I assume it was coming from that neighbor (the one whose kid was discussing following me).

Occasionally they moved the sphere of vibration up to my head, and after years of martial arts, the sensation was identical to that of the first punch to the face of a training session, from that unique sensation in the sinuses/nose you get with that first punch of the day, to the mental blurriness you could get after awakening from a knockout. The only difference was it was more drawn out and diffuse, as if throughout the entire skull where it hit rather than a part of the face. Instead of being one clear sensation with one large hit, it felt like an accumulation of the sensation building slowly with hundreds of small hits. Moving could get you away from it, but it would eventually track back to you and return.

I would have assumed it was a major medical problem developing, except for three things. When I was hit with it one day while still awake, I was actually able to look at the second count on a clock on a surveillance camera display, and count the number of hits in one minute. It was exactly 240 on the dot, which correlates with a pulsing of exactly 4 Hertz, or four cycles per second. Such a regular and precise number of cycles per second over 60 seconds, designed around a human time measurement, seems artificial. Were this a physical malady I would have expected a number not correlating with a precise whole-number Hertz measurement. In addition, the sphere seemingly moved over my body intelligently, stopping precisely at areas like the lungs, heart, head, and thyroid. Finally, this vibration of the body when sleeping, delivered from some thru-wall technology, has been described by two other people who were under gangstalking/hostile-surveillance activity in America.

Aaron Alexis,[40] a Navy veteran and military technology contractor who went on to do a mass shooting at the Washington Navy Yard claimed to have been woken up regularly by his "gangstalkers" with such an effect. Also, the killer of Deputy Natalie Corona[41] left a suicide note saying he was killing a Police Officer because he believed it was the Police who had organized his gangstalking. He claimed they were following him around, and that he could no longer take the sonic vibrations waking him up every night. I can attest, they do pretty significantly degrade brain

---

40   http://archive.is/xL94u
        https://www.theguardian.com/world/2013/sep/20/aaron-alexis-washington-navy-yard-shooter
41   http://archive.is/P9lHC
        https://www.cnn.com/2019/01/13/us/davis-police-officer-corona-sonic-waves-letter/index.html

function and degrade sleep, whatever they do. They are strangely physically/mentally agitating, and after you are hit, sleep is nearly impossible for at least an hour or more. Ofttimes I would get up and put the time to use posting a surveillance-exposing, surveillance-detection blog post in retaliation.

By the time of this writing, we are in an uncomfortable standoff. Though they dislike me, I think they have given up on controlling me. The video I roll everywhere, and the fact I was about a hair away from rolling into the Russian Embassy, and bringing Russian intelligence and media to document online the extent of surveillance of the American population all over by this leviathan makes me more trouble than I am worth. I am still followed and they are undoubtedly still listening in my house, watching my mail, on my phones, and following my online activity in real time. I still get vibrated on occasion, usually after writing something they do not like, and I retaliate with more writings they do not like. We exist as the unstoppable force and the immovable object.

They know I am not positively predisposed to such a machine existing, so I assume their mission now is to watch me closely, try to limit what I do, and make sure I never get into any position where I might acquire the resources or prominence/authority where I might have the ability to have any extensively negative effect on their operations.

The strangest aspect is, this operation was not sent to me. I think this operation, and all the other cases of "gangstalking" and hostile surveillance you hear about are in fact launched by a massive machine that is permanently embedded throughout American society, in every neighborhood, business, and social organization, as well as other communities throughout the globe.

It most likely consists of about 4-6% of the population, it is everywhere, and they intermittently check out everyone to the same degree I get examined full time. I suspect they use the data they acquire to fill out files on everyone with incredibly detailed information about them.

I think this surveillance/informant machine is what they were trying to get an official approval for when they tried to enact Operation TIPS, a program which was launched under the second Bush administration.[42] It's pilot program was to build a civilian informant network consisting of 1 in 24 citizens (over 4% of the populace up front), all informing on the people they came in contact with, generating files within some domestic intelligence outfit tasked with getting to know everyone. It would have grown from there.

Operation TIPS was discovered by one reporter who found it listed on the Citizen Corp website. There the government had issued an official public notification it was creating a covert informant network and needed recruits. The pilot program was to recruit one in 24 citizens as domestic informants/spies, spying on fellow citizens, and being managed by the government through some sort of network of intelligence handlers. I would assume, grouped up into small citizen-informant teams, they would have been assigned 24 people per team member that they were to "get to know personally," using all of their surveillance tools. Whatever intelligence outfit ran it could have created a file on every citizen, crafted with all the most elite tools and technology of modern-day

---

42   http://archive.is/AMXS0

spies, and known exactly who was likely to threaten their control.

Bear in mind, that 4+% of the population they were seeking recruits for was the pilot program, just an initial toe-in-the-water, to see if they could manage such an operation. It would have been scaled up, according to the proposal, once it was operational. That number also did not include all of the official sworn officers, who would have been required to handle all of those citizen informants/spies on the ground.

I think that machine was already built, but the threat of exposure of such a massive illegal and unwanted machine, with no governmental imprimatur, frightened those in charge. So they tried to get some sort of official seal of approval for it, and codify it as something approved by the government. That way, if it was exposed, it would not have been entirely illegal. Public outcry caused Operation TIPS to be closed down, but the machine obviously remained, likely being run as a CIA/FBI "training operation."

Also of interest is how the reporter was shocked at a program which even in its toe-in-the-water testing stage, would have created in America, a domestic informant program larger than what was run by the infamous communist East German Stasi Secret Police, which to that point was the largest and most intrusive surveillance operation in human history.

Even more amazing, the massiveness of this new machine was just measured manpower-wise. This increased manpower would have been supported by surveillance technologies and digital recording capabilities the Stasi could never have dreamed of, massively amplifying the intrusiveness of what was already a record-level monitoring of the populace.

It was a Secret Police force like nothing mankind had ever seen, supported with technology the Stasi could never have dreamed of, being built in the US, and yet that reporter could not get a single US newspaper to run his story. He finally got it published online in an obscure local Spanish newspaper. It just happened to go viral online from there, forcing US papers to give it coverage.

Again, Q's model would have predicted that every US media outlet would have been compromised, and would not talk about a massive, illegal US intelligence operation, even if it would get them viewers and boost subscribership. Q asserted that the media was controlled by the US intelligence machinery, which had itself been compromised by Cabal, and Cabal did not want this program publicized. It worked exactly as Q would have predicted.

It all sounds extraordinary. We are told the media is independent. We are told they look for interesting stories to inform the public and gain loyal readers. You would assume if somebody revealed that the East German Stasi was being recreated in America, in even larger and more intrusive form, to get citizens to inform on citizens, everyone would race to report the story. Especially when it was George Bush overseeing the government doing this. This was tailor made to feed the narrative of George Bush as tyrannical despot. But the American media refused to report it.

If simultaneously, people were reporting being followed around by an extensive civilian network of government harassers who appeared to be regular citizens, who intrusively spied on their most private moments, you would think that would be drawn into the story, and questioned. No media outlet made a peep, save for a lone NY Times article saying the gangstalking phenomenon was simply mentally ill people finding each other online and feeding each other's delusions.

Yet if one goes online, even with its suppressive algorithms, YouTube is filled with videos people have uploaded of their own surveillance harassment. Beyond that, there is a rich online community of people who have been complaining of it for decades. There are numerous cases of mass shooters who expressly said they were doing the shooting because of their harassment.

There were actually *"Gangstalking General"* posts on the Chans, where anons who were under it discussed their own coverage blasely, while what appeared to be government agents derided them as schizophrenic. And there were more cases where this machine emerged in the media.

Reporter Michael Hastings of Rolling Stone magazine reported he was being followed around and his car had been tampered with by an intelligence operation targeting him, before he was seen in a high speed chase, and his car blew up killing him.[43] CBS Reporter Sharyll Atkisson had her computers hacked, and classified documents placed on them to frame her for criminal prosecution, because Cabal did not like her examination of the Benghazi and the Fast and Furious scandals.[44] Top conservative

---

43   https://www.mintpressnews.com/michael-hastings-targeted-cia-wikileaks-reveals-agencys-covert-carjacking-ability/225738/
        http://archive.is/T7xJH
44   http://nypost.com/2014/10/27/ex-cbs-reporter-government-related-entity-bugged-my-computer/

104

talk radio host Tom Baeurle was caught in a long battle with the Machine, where he reported the use of invisibility devices which projected the image behind a person onto a flexible LED screen in front of them to make them appear to meld into their background.[45] The book *Chameleo*[46] was written by a college professor, and described the exact same technology being deployed by a massive, technologically sophisticated surveillance operation targeting his childhood friend. Another case involved a woman where surveillance eventually drugged the food in her fridge while she was out and raped her after she ate it and fell unconscious, which appeared to be part of a pattern by the operatives in that region.[47]

Supreme Court Justice Antonin Scalia reported he felt the entire Supreme Court had been placed under surveillance by Barack Obama based on what he saw following him around.[48] By this time the illegal surveillance of President Trump has been delved into quite extensively, and I will assure you it extended to all of his friends and associates. Glenn Beck has been fairly open that he is being stalked by a machine which chased him out of his home in Connecticut, before his son was approached by a pedophile online.[49]

New York State Governor David Patterson reported that a

45	http://archive.is/afvAz https://canadafreepress.com/article/vindicated-talk-show-radios-true-patriot-tom-bauerle
46	http://archive.is/kLWbo https://www.amazon.com/dp/B00ZDWEITO/ref=dp-kindle-redirect?_encoding=UTF8&btkr=1
47	https://youtu.be/boxCW3L7iAI
48	https://www.newsmax.com/Newsfront/andrew-napolitano-antonin-scalia-obama-spied/2017/05/16/id/790439/ http://archive.is/JL3Y2
49	https://youtu.be/0OoBhySK3JA

massive surveillance operation which had been following him for decades had tried to blackmail him, to gain control of the New York Governorship immediately following his assuming office after the Elliot Spitzer scandal. He described being approached by "over 10" legislators who asked him to do something about what they all thought was an out of control group of rogue surveillance/intelligence personnel.[50]

From another angle, this network's existence was revealed when it was revealed Eric Scheiderman, at the time the Attorney General of New York, kept his abused girlfriend in line by threatening to have her put under surveillance and harassed by this machine.[51] So there are even accounts of politicians threatening to deploy this network in the exact way many said it was deployed on regular civilians. It is also worth noting that Schneiderman had also used these surveillance resources against President Trump and his children as well, all part of this Cabal's operations to keep Donald Trump from ever being president and posing a threat to their operations.[52]

I was not the only one to see this. This was a massive intelligence network, embedded in our communities and deployed against the citizens of the Untied States, for purposes of establishing control over the nation. And yet not a peep from the media, even as it appeared the conspiracy may have killed one of their own and set another up for imprisonment. Operation Mockingbird must have been wildly successful. The entire media

---

50   https://gothamist.com/news/gov-paterson-says-state-police-drove-him-to-confess-affairs-drug-use or http://archive.is/jWIPR
          http://archive.is/1jiq0
51   http://archive.is/LSYJv
52   http://archive.is/hnT9y

was controlled, something that doesn't surprise me given I have often been followed by local news vans when driving around.

If you are curious about what it looks like, there is actually a good video here.[53] Bear in mind, this is what it looks like at the first departure point, if there is a snafu which throws them off their game and forces them to scramble to adapt to something they were unprepared for. Had she just pulled out and driven off as they expected, she would have seen less, because the guy on the bike would have looked at his phone and not appeared out of place, the walkers would have walked and ignored her, the car with the missing hubcap would have just driven by once, and it all would have seemed passably normal.

However she would have seen a group like that everywhere she went, all of the time, and periodically it would have made mistakes and revealed itself. Once you know it is there, the people trying to appear normal while watching you become much more apparent.

The only aspect of it that video doesn't capture is the sheer volume of followers you would see in a day. If you drive to a store, it will look like that again, but with an entirely different cast of characters. Likewise, you will see a new group at each arrival at a destination, each period of loitering at the destination, each departure, and each new arrival. Each will get a separate "phase" of coverage in the parlance, consisting of new people who only follow you for that phase. All along your trip, you will see it arrayed at intersections, watching to see if you turn or continue on. The big hallmark is you will rarely find yourself alone at any

---

53   https://www.youtube.com/watch?v=GMeA5i485Eg

decision point like an intersection or departure point.

There are other, more subtle ways it reveals itself. I once was caught at three stop lights in a row within sight of the only entrance/exit of a parking lot for a grocery store I was about to pull into. Traffic was heavy and each light stopped me for about a minute, so I was about three full minutes watching, as nobody entered or exited the only entrance to the parking lot. I pulled in and as I got out of the car, five other cars opened their doors, people got out almost mechanically, and we all walked toward the store together. I knew they had all sat in their cars for at least three minutes, waiting until I came in to the lot and parked, and they were then told to follow me. As we walked into the store, four or five other cars whipped into the lot and rushed to park and go shopping, despite nobody having entered the lot the entire time I was watching the entrance.

I should be clear, I do not think they were waiting in that lot just for me. They were normally deployed and loitering informants/surveillance-operatives, monitoring that lot and store as part of an operation that is deployed everywhere, all of the time - and watching all of society at some point. They were waiting for one of the people who the machine is following in my area to show up, so they could pick them up and cover them while they were in the store. I just happened to be the lucky contestant.

I often see them on hot summer days as I drive by parking lots. They are sitting with their driver's side door wide open, half-in and half out of scorching hot cars in parking lots of shopping centers I never go into, with one leg jammed up on the open car door. They are maintaining a presence in those lots. I would estimate in my small town there are probably fifty to one hundred people at any one time assigned to such positions in front of local shopping centers.

And I see them in other places indicating that they are not moving swarms of people to follow me. Rather the swarms I see are actually out and about, loitering in various areas, covering various sectors, noting everything of interest, and focusing on specific people as they are told to.

I have pulled off unexpectedly into neighborhoods which I would never go to predictably, and which were far off my path, and just as I enter the neighborhood, out of it comes a car which just happens to be pulling out as I pull in, with the driver's window open on a cool day. (That is a surveillance technique to allow the driver to listen, both for anything of interest in the neighborhood that is out of sight, and to prevent anyone from sneaking up on a surveillance vehicle.) That car was stationed in that neighborhood, probably linked up by radio, serving as the mobile component of an observation post in at least one of the houses, which was watching everything happening in that neighborhood. I think if you have a neighborhood with three or four hundred people living in it, you probably have two or three people assigned to it at any moment, embedded in it, documenting everything which happens there.

This machine is deployed throughout our society like that.[54]

_____

54   It sounds extraordinary, but numerous former intelligence personnel, including the legendary William Binney, gathered together to call attention to this program, and its more problematic offshoots such as the directed energy weapons which had been directed at many of them, at www.biggerthansnowden.com. Unfortunately, even their efforts were disappeared into the ether, as the only vestige of the page now resides on the Wayback Machine at https://web.archive.org/web/ 20190503070612/https://www.biggerthansnowden.com/

You pass them every day and have glanced past them yourself, though you had no idea what they were doing. They are people standing on strategic street corners, who appear to be begging for change, but occasionally get caught driving home in fairly nice cars. They are cars pulling out of neighborhoods just as you pull in, seemingly oddly coincidentally. They are cars driving on highways all day long, spread out and waiting for instructions on who to track. They are so thorough that chances are, at some point, one stood online behind you at the grocery store and took a cell phone photo of your purchases to add to your file. Another listened as you had an argument with your wife, and I think chances are greater than not, at least once or twice in your life, somebody noted you were going to the bathroom and wrote down exactly what happened. I have no idea if that was recorded in your file, but it would not surprise me.

Combined, they have amassed incredibly detailed files on everyone, with shockingly personal observations, from food brands purchased to probably sexual preferences. That TIPS network was designed that dense because it was to work like a full time, embedded, covert surveillance operation, watching everyone and every thing in every area of operations it was deployed in.

In truth this sounds outlandish only because of the myth we were raised with, that somehow America was a nation vastly different from all that had come before, where citizens ruled the government, freedom reigned supreme, and privacy would always be respected. In reality, from the KGB, to the Stasi, to London's Surveillance state developed during the IRA years, to the People's Republic of China and its Social Credit System, to old Royal spy networks in Medieval Europe, all the way back to the vastness of the Roman Empire at its peak, governments have always gathered whatever intelligence they could on those under their reign. The main difference in America is technology has allowed ever more data to be gathered and archived, and we believed the lie that somehow our leaders were different – or even who we were told they were.

The traitorous leaders in elected office today are if anything, probably even more corrupt than in the past, and mixed with the force multiplier of technology, we should have expected an even more intrusive surveillance state. The very fact they sold us on the lie we would be left alone under those conditions, is itself almost prima facie evidence the truth would be far worse than we could ever imagine, even before things like Operation TIPS leaked out, and we considered what technology might allow.

The intelligence product they have produced has given their command an incredibly detailed file, with very private, personal insights and first-person observations on every person who lived in any area of moderate population density. The informants they run are your neighbors, your coworkers, your friends, and your fellow church-goers. As a result, (((They))) know who you are, what your preferences are, and exactly what you are like in the most private recesses of your life. Given what I have seen, I would even be shocked if there was not technology installed near every Church confessional that captured vibrations from every confession made to a priest, wired over the internet to a central repository, and converted it into a transcript that was cross referenced with a voice-print biometric to attach it to the confessor's permanent file. When Q says this thing is bigger than you could possibly believe, I've seen it. He knows.

So if you are looking for this around you, it will look much like that video, but the people may look less obvious if you don't do something unpredictable. Each destination and departure which a citizen arrives at and leaves from will repeat the process. And each destination and departure will repeat the process with different people, who are assigned to that specific area, and who will try to appear normal and uninterested in you. Only if you deviate from the expected plan, will this machine stumble, exhibit curiosity and interest in you, and really become obvious.

In my experience, seeing two or three hundred people doing all of that over ten stops, in a single outing to several stores in a nearby populous area is not at all unusual, and for me, it will be a different 200-300 the next day if I repeat the process. If you have a county with 200,000 people, and one in 24 is a watcher, as the pilot program for Operation TIPS proposed, you could expect to have about 8,000 dedicated informants/surveillance-personnel on call or actively monitoring the population around them. And that is assuming the program hasn't built up a deeper density of followers where you are due to some aspect of interest. Also, those numbers would be the TIPS "pilot-program" numbers, not the fully manned and fleshed out operation which the creators were envisioning.

Again, that sounds extraordinary, especially in a nation which only has one sworn Law Enforcement officer per 417 citizens.[55] But again, the pilot program for Operation TIPS was one informant per 24 citizens.[56] This means just the initial toe-in-

---

55   http://archive.is/D9EjM
      https://ucr.fbi.gov/crime-in-the-u.s/2011/crime-in-the-u.s.-2011/police-
      employee-data
56   http://archive.is/pfE5I
      https://www.smh.com.au/world/us-planning-to-recruit-one-in-24-

the-water test of the TIPS concept was going to mean that for every Police Officer and Federal Agent you see (and don't see in the case of Police undercover officers and surveillance officers), there would be over 17 watchers cruising around, watching everyone. Factor in that many of those Law Enforcement Officers will not be seen, working as investigators or on plain clothes operations, and for every patrol car you see with a uniformed officer, there may be 40, or 50, or more surveillance operators driving and walking around following people in your area, under just the initial numbers.

And once that proof of concept had been borne out in testing, the plan was to expand the program. Anyone who has experienced gang-stalking or surveillance will tell you, that expansion happened. The Secret Society it produced within America is real and it is beyond imagination for anyone who was raised with "The Myth" of America as a bastion of freedom, where the government was required by the Constitution to respect the privacy of regular citizens.

In a city like New York City, where there are 8 million people, the pilot program in their initial request, just to test it out, would have about 340,000 watchers, each with a cell phone and an Uber-like app on their phone. That is ten times the size of the entire NYPD. The app calls them up when they are available, delivers them directions on where and when to follow someone, who the target is, what they look like, when to break off, and probably the ability to give real-time updates to their handler, including imagery of the target, using the phone's microphone and

---

americans-as-citizen-spies-20020715-gdfgbq.html

video camera.[57] I would assume it also coordinates payments for their services, based on what they acquire.

When they get home from being out, they each probably have a set number of people in their neighborhood who they are responsible for monitoring in their homes and *"getting to know"* through surveillance tech they are supplied. If anybody seems interesting, they probably have to report them up the chain of command for some sort of reward. It is even possible, and maybe likely, this regular monitoring of everyone is how I first came to get my enhanced coverage when I began trying to promote r/K Theory as the origin of politics.

You will eventually see some overlap in the manpower if you are under coverage long enough. However after a few weeks of a few hundred people a day with minimal repeat operators, you will be awed at the scale of the operation. I still cannot believe it could exist in America.

I assume that absent Q and President Trump, my own watchers would have been here intruding on my life and making sure I never gathered any ability to resist the program. At least

---

57　　Although I cannot say if this is a case of it in action, I suspect this video of a local news reporter filming someone is how it would look from the perspective of an informant/follower. Notice the video begins with the reporter whispering to his phone, *"You will see him now"* while seemingly trying to not move his lips, and probably appear inconspicuous as he held his phone's camera so it was pointing where the black gentleman was about to walk into. The black gentleman appears to have grown quite upset with people filming him everywhere he goes. Also notice if this reporter was one of the Secret Society, and you appealed to him as a reporter to try and expose any harassment you were receiving from the Secret Society, your efforts would have been blocked before they got off the ground, by one of the very agents of the conspiracy you were looking to expose. Operation Mockingbird was real. : https://www.nydailynews.com/new-york/nyc-crime/ny-metro-man-accosts-wpix-reporter-queens-20190124-story.html

114

until I went with the Russian plan, and it ended with me either dead, or triggering a Civil War once the Russian media exposed it and everyone realized this Secret Society was, whenever it wanted, listening to them, and maybe even watching them, in their most private moments in the most private recesses of their personal residences.

But now I suspect that with the exposure of the illegal surveillance of President Trump, there will be a broader examination of domestic surveillance operations coming which will reveal what has been going on with all of this, probably going back before Ted Gunderson, albeit in a much more attenuated fashion. If Q is right, I expect the very conspiracy running it will be fully exposed and extricated from our society. I cannot say I will feel bad, finally being free from under this.

My situation sounds bad, but even more bothersome is the fact it appears embedded not just in most neighborhoods in America, but across the globe, as part of a bigger global conspiracy. I believe this conspiracy, and operation that is harassing Americans, is not even an American operation. I actually have done some research (and written several articles[58]), using the Google car's Streetview to examine the presence of indicators of this ground surveillance operation overseas. In the vast majority of nations I examined, it appears this network is embedded in the neighborhoods it operates in.

One exception has been Russia, where any surveillance teams you see will appear more standardized, and often not from the neighborhoods where they operate. For example in the South

---

58   https://www.anonymousconservative.com/blog/surveillance/

Caucasus, if you travel through poorer rural neighborhoods, where cars of residents are more beaten down, you will notice that the cars which appear to be surveillance tracking the Google car will appear as newer, more polished models.

It indicates to me Russia moves a government team to follow the Google car, because they do not have a strong informant network embedded in their society, and linked up and prepared to run surveillance operations against their neighbors. (Note in that context, the one nation which appears relatively free from this conspiracy on Google Streetview, is the one nation that the "Mockingbird" news media and pundit class, and corrupt politicians of the Cabal, will endlessly assail as our worst enemy, and run by outright dictators. Even on the national stage, Russia has been kept at arm's length from global trade groups and defense pacts, as if Cabal has been isolating them due to their freedom from Cabal's control. I found it an interesting observation.)

When Q said *"This thing is bigger than you could possibly believe,"* was when I began to buy into Q. I immediately found myself thinking Q knew what he was talking about. I have seen it firsthand in my own neighborhood, been tracked by it across the country, and then logged indicators of it all over the globe on google, from foot and bicycle surveillance dispersed through the neighborhoods in Finland, to pedestrians walking back alleys in the streets of London, to vehicular coverage in Guam, to motorbike surveillance tracking the Google car throughout backwoods neighborhood roads in Sri Lanka.

I write all of that mainly to show you that long before Q arrived on the scene, I was one of many Americans who had seen a ground surveillance/intelligence operation permeating and tracking the population, and monitoring individuals in the privacy of their homes illegally - and to a degree nobody would believe. I saw it replacing local political and Law Enforcement leaders, to take control of the local government. I noted that it was running cover for, and stalling police activity targeting local street gangs, who were utterly running amok, fully unchecked in these areas. It was suppressing political speech by those not in the network. I saw people being killed by this operation, from civilians, to veterans, to Police officers. And I saw indicators and anecdotal stories which made it appear this operation was global in scale, and operative in foreign countries which should not have been friendly with US intelligence. This was not a US intelligence operation which had simply grown beyond its bounds.

I know what I would have thought if someone said this to me, before I saw the machine. So I understand that if it has not focused in on you, Q's allegations would sound fantastical, bordering on the ridiculous. But understand there were intelligent Americans who read Q and did not see allegations, but rather they saw credible explanations for puzzling observations which were really not easily explainable outside of Q's new paradigm. In fact, I find Q's allegations the only credible explanation for what I have seen.

Unfortunately, the allegations Q makes, and the research his anons come up with supporting them, actually get more and more disturbing as you follow them. However nothing he alleges is in any way unusual, if you assume his fundamental premise – that a hostile external intelligence operation has been tasked with compromising American society and government, and has been successful for several decades now at least.

The research by Q's anon's leads to the discovery of evidence indicating that this operation used all of the most noxious elements of the intelligence tool chest. It is a tool chest which we had previously been assured would only be used by our intelligence agencies overseas, in the most uncivilized environments, and then only to protect our nation from imminent harm.

The techniques have run the gamut. Q's anons have uncovered evidence of intrusive spying on innocent citizens' most private moments in search of blackmail and control, even performed to try and control, and then reverse the outcome of a US Presidential election. Cabal appears to have been dividing and conquering the public by fostering racial and societal divisions through violent hate-organizations they either created, or infiltrated and took over, like Antifa, La Raza, and #BlackLivesMatters. Its more aggressive operations appear to have entailed physical intimidation, bribery, blackmail, and murders of individuals who either posed a threat to the machine or whom the machine needed to control.

Q will produce evidence that for such operations they utilized alliances with criminal elements like street gangs and drug cartels, using them as a sort of ground-level proxy-soldier against our citizens, even in murders. Cabal's intelligence operation also appears to have fostered the practice of occult and satanic belief systems among members, which would entail the performance of horrifying acts as part of induction rituals. This would allow the gathering of blackmail on those who sought membership and participated in such actions.

Cabal even appears to have been involved in fostering

terrorist attacks and mass casualty events.[59] Presumably the goal of such an act would be to enlarge government's power and scope, as well as foster wars with the express purpose of enriching those behind the conspiracy.

According to Q, Cabal has also been behind numerous murders of citizens who have gotten in their way. These murders have ranged from citizens who discovered too much about aspects of their operations, all the way up to Supreme Court Justice Antonin Scalia (who himself said he was under an aggressive surveillance operation, as was the rest of the Supreme Court[60]).

President John F Kennedy (who made a speech about this conspiracy just before he was assassinated[61], and swore he would shatter the CIA, a central mechanism of Cabal's control, into a thousand pieces and scatter it to the wind[62]) was a victim according to Q. His son, John F. Kennedy Jr., was murdered for refusing to ignore his father's murder, and trying to investigate it. Even innocent Police Officers like NYPD Detective Miosotis Familia were among those murdered to assert Cabal's control over local law enforcement agencies like the NYPD, according to Q.[63]

---

59   CIA Officer Kevin Shipp says in the speech below that many of the 9/11 hijackers were in fact known CIA assets, implying that since the CIA would track such assets, at least senior leaders would have known the 9/11 attacks were coming, if the assets were not actually doing it for some rogue CIA operation running them.
         https://www.youtube.com/watch?v=rQouKi7xDpM
60   http://archive.is/iej56
61   https://www.youtube.com/watch?v=xhZk8ronces&feature=youtu.be
62   http://web.archive.org/web/20190209014635/https://www.ratical.
         org/ratville/JFK/Unspeakable/JFK-scatterCIAtoWinds.pdf
63   I personally knew Detective Familia's murder had to have been purposeful when I saw it online. Her murderer had complained of his 24/7 surveillance operation harassing him. That meant he was under the same coverage I am. Given that, I knew that if he acquired a firearm, posted online about assaulting Police officers, and headed out armed with his firearm there was no way their surveillance operation didn't see that and know, given the manpower and technology they deploy

The most obvious purpose of the conspiracy appears to be fraud. Q has pointed out again and again, there are no audits of massive expenditures of cash by the government to foreign nations and non-profit organizations. Once those funds are delivered, it is up to the corrupt, often third world governments, to allocate the funds honestly. According to Q, Cabal enters into agreements with corrupt leaders in these nations, whereby foreign aid is delivered to their nation in large amounts, the leaders take a cut, and the remainder is funneled and laundered back into Cabal's coffers, where it is used to further Cabal's operations.

---

routinely on targets. Surveillance does not deploy piecemeal. If you have street harassment, you have the full suite of capabilities assigned to you as well, from 24/7 technical monitoring of your residence, phone, mail, and internet activity, to physical, in-person followers when you go out, to infiltration of informants into your sphere. They knew. One of their informants may have provided him with the gun. There was no way he hit the street without them knowing he was an armed criminal who threatened Officers, and was driven to shoot one. Given surveillance is able to move Officers out of the path of targets on the fly (so as to not spook them in legitimate surveillance operations), his crossing paths with Detective Familia that night was no coincidence. That an Officer was placed in a static position, inside a command van, where a pedestrian outside could see in clearly to engage her, but she would not be as aware of what was happening outside, was designed. That she was the nice girl with the million dollar smile who everybody loved, who was responsible for four kids who were orphaned when she was killed, was by design. Given this target, who was known as a hostile, was allowed to walk right outside the van was no coincidence. Although the motivation wholly eluded me at the time, I knew long before Q, based on personal experience, that Cabal generated Detective Familia's murder, and it was not a chance occurrence. Q will state that Cabal ground surveillance had identified her shooter as one of many unbalanced individuals they encountered in the course of their normal monitoring of the population. Once identified as a potential shooter, the ground operation was ordered to rile her shooter, put him on the path to shoot at Police by posing as Police when they riled him, and then allow him to encounter an Officer. According to Q, this was a warning to NYPD to not allow any of the very damaging information on Anthony Wiener's laptop to leak out to the media, or they would do this more regularly, choosing targets which would be most painful to the NYPD. Again, I did not know the motive, but I knew Detective Familia was killed purposely by the same entity following me. Q's fantastical assertion about the shooting was more explanative than fantastical to me when I saw it.

According to Q, government expenditures associated with the Paris-accord on climate change have yielded trillion-dollar levels of gross income for the conspiracy. It has produced that income through its effective taxation on carbon emissions, which are basically required for all forms of trade and manufacturing. Red Cross fraud has yielded billions in illicit income.[64] Foreign aid fraud has yielded trillions. War fraud and profiteering has yielded trillions. And Q says it goes on from there.

It sounds incredible, and yet all along the way Q's anons have found evidence supporting it all. It has only persisted because of the lax attitudes we as a nation have grown accustomed to with respect to how our government's money is spent. A single woman, the wife of New York City Mayor Bill DeBlasio, vanished almost a billion dollars of New York City taxpayer money, all by herself,[65] on a "mental health initiative." She openly admitted she can't account for how the money was spent and she had nothing to show for it, saying you can't measure what she accomplished on "mental health." One woman, not even an elected official, and over one billion dollars is just gone, with absolutely no consequence or investigation. That money could be anywhere. Imagine what a massive, coordinated network of such individuals, infiltrated at every level of government, and all beyond any legal or media scrutiny could do. That is what Q says is operative within the US.

---

64   Q had linked to the video linked below, which raises the interesting question of why Red Cross would keep that much cash on hand, given it is of no use in foreign countries where other currencies are used, and in the US it would be better kept in a bank account where it would earn interest and could be transferred electronically.
      https://www.youtube.com/watch?v=LZIizLVlZp8
65   http://archive.is/qy9Mf

So to summarize, Q basically says a massive global conspiracy by non-state actors is operating an organized covert infiltration/intelligence operation that has created a massive intelligence network of agents, composed of regular citizens at every level of society and government, and dedicated to fraud operations launched against the treasuries of the nations within which it operates.

This network has infiltrated its people into leadership positions throughout all levels of the American government. There they are using their power for apportioning resources to Cabal-created entities, in return for some sort of personal recompense or favoritism. Still other agents are selling US secrets, or helping to allow Cabal to otherwise control various aspects of the United States government which could pose a threat to its operations, like intelligence, law enforcement, or our judicial apparatuses. It was precisely this machine which launched the illegal targeting of the Trump campaign, using illegal surveillance and false allegations of Russian collusion to try and remove President Donald J. Trump before he could act against the conspiracy himself.

Through occult activities they encourage, the people they elevate will commit grievous sins that can be documented covertly and later be used for blackmail, allowing them to be certain of a member's loyalty and commitment. They run child-sex-grooming networks and pedophile networks, for the express purpose of blackmail and control of wealthy people they either service, or entrap. Such activities will also serve to filter out infiltrators from any counter-intelligence operation who sough to infiltrate their operations, by making the cost of entrance into their network so odious few with principles could make it inside. They have also similarly taken over the media to prevent any media exposure of their operations, and done extensive research into mind-control and the techniques of group-level persuasion so as to be better able to control the general population, which they view as cattle they are farming for their labor.

Their controlled operatives lead nations, run banks, head major businesses, control the intelligence agencies, as well as control cultural institutions like Hollywood and television. They man think tanks to set policy objectives, run academia to identify recruits and indoctrinate youth with the ideas Cabal wants them to hold, and even operate in the medical field, controlling access to medical care.

Again, Q showed up and dropped these allegations, in the form of "crumbs" designed to lead the anons to uncover and aggregate the evidence supporting this theory themselves. And the data has been amassed to an incredibly impressive degree.

Chapter Five

Why Did People Believe In Q?

Why would people believe in Q? What proof is there that Q is real? The reasons people believe in Q probably began long before Q ever showed up on the scene.

You have to understand that those who believe in Q were mostly independent thinkers who were doing their own analysis long before Q showed up on the scene. Some saw the corruption firsthand in dealings with the system or forays into politics.[66] Others were voracious readers who saw patterns develop and inconsistencies in what they were being told. Still others, like myself saw Cabal's machinery up close, and were left awed by the sheer scale of the operation cruising, unseen and unspoken of, beneath the surface of our society. That is what attracted all of us to the Chans. The Chans were a meeting place where our logical, but not mainstream views and observations were not portrayed as aberrant, due to them being based on evidence and observation

---

66   For an example of this, you can view an episode of former Governor Jesse Ventura's TV show *Conspiracy Theory* at the link below. It touches upon just the aspect of the coordinated surveillance/harassment of private citizens which involves the use of directed energy weapons, wielded upon them in their homes by embedded networks of people working for Cabal who live nearby. Note the three people he interviews who are so targeted, all began to be harassed due to political activity and interactions with government. I have actually personally felt the "vibrations" referenced in the show, and can vouch for their existence personally.

https://www.veteranstoday.com/2019/10/30/banned-vt-from-2012-jesse-ventura-takes-on-psychotronic-weapons-and-targeted-individuals-video/

rather than the widely disseminated and held opinions of our Fake News media.

As one example, such independent thinkers had long been commenting that it was unusual that our elected officials would almost always become so wealthy so quickly, in ways which would make it seem they were receiving benefits beyond their government salaries. As an example, take Maxine Waters. As a congresswoman she earns around $178,000 per year. And yet she has numerous properties, including a $5.1 million dollar mansion[67] that takes up half a city block, two other homes worth in the $1 million range, and a time share in Palm springs. Q said she had cash assets worth approximately $6 million on top of that. How many school principles will never amass similar net-worths or property portfolios? And Maxine is among the least wealthy of the politicians examined.

Even more suspicious is the fact websites like Open Secrets claim her net worth is only around $250,000 in its latest year, 2016,[68] despite her multimillion dollar residences. This has long made people suspicious that the information we were being given was untrue, and it was untrue because something was being hidden.

Then you move on to cases like the Clinton Foundation, which was receiving multi-million dollar payouts from foreign donors while Hillary Clinton was Secretary of State, and the payouts were from entities with business before her agency. It was something which seemed confirmed to be improper when her

---

67   http://archive.is/YZPU2
68   http://archive.is/hLcby

hacked emails leaked.[69]. There was Joe Biden's son getting a $1.5 billion business deal from China when he accompanied his father, the Vice President on an official State visit.[70] Nancy Pelosi's husband is an investor who has allowed her to take part in eight IPOs while using insider knowledge[71] to amass a $202 million net worth.[72] Dianne Feinstein's husband is a real estate investor who has made billion dollar deals with the US government[73] and at least hundreds of millions from China, as Dianne repeatedly hires Chinese intelligence agents into her office[74] (as she serves on the US Senate Select Committee on Intelligence, where she has access to the nation's most sensitive intelligence secrets). And there's a plethora of other examples.

As bad as that was, it was mere financial corruption. More troubling was the evidence anons gathered of associations between high government offices, power players in the media and civilian side of the political/cultural/business world, and pedophilia. There was the Dutroux Affair, where a case of a single pedophile who killed four girls, kept producing evidence of others involved that went uninvestigated,[75] and produced a steady stream of suspicious deaths of those who tried to push the investigation forward.[76] Then there was the Westminster dossier on a massive pedophile network operating at the highest levels of the British government.[77] That was one of just several such near-exposures in Britain, such as the

69   http://archive.is/ZlKnJ
70   http://archive.is/6cLZO
71   http://archive.is/ARyZd
72   http://archive.is/ZvD6B
73   http://archive.is/ymGlt
74   http://archive.is/bWVSo
75   https://archive.is/LmrLc
76   http://archive.is/InEQO
77   http://archive.is/XuwK8

Saville Scandal.[78] BBC Television personality Jimmy Saville, who was a combination of Ryan Seacrest and Dick Clark in his day, was revealed to have molested almost 600 young children in Britain, some sick in hospitals which he visited as a celebrity guest. The scandal appeared poised to reach into the upper echelons of the BBC[79] and the British government, where Saville had numerous associates and friends, when the investigation just died. There was the VIP pedophile scandal, where a newspaper editor was handed a dossier showing Police knew of a pedophile ring that reached into the highest levels of British government, and were covering it up.

Wikipedia will tell you it was shown to be false,[80] even though it pretty clearly was not.[81] The initial accuser was even sent to prison for 18 years for "fabricating" the scandal, even though significant evidence exists that it was not fully investigated and political pressure played a considerable role in dictating its conclusion.

In America we had the Franklin Scandal.[82] It alleged there was a high-level child prostitution ring facilitating the abuse of children within the foster child system in Nebraska, which may have had some ties to a CIA operation. Official investigations claimed the allegations were baseless, and even charged and convicted one of the victims for perjury. The associated cover-up, which it is believed killed one of the official committee investigators in a plane crash (right after he told an associate he

---

78   http://archive.is/LRgOO
79   http://archive.is/4GuBg
80   http://archive.is/FORBl
81   http://archive.is/SjW1z
82   https://www.youtube.com/watch?v=-x-IZS8uKYo&t=416s

had acquired a piece of evidence which would get him killed if anyone found out he had it), turned public opinion against the conclusions of the official investigations by 10 to 1.[83] There were other troubling indicators of the foster system being used for abuse as well.[84]

Then there was the investigation into the Finders Cult. Police Officers, investigating a report of some children who appeared neglected in a park in Florida, discovered several children in the accompany of adults who could not be confirmed as their parents. The children could not tell Police who their parents were, and reported they were on their way to Mexico. It sparked a massive investigation which discovered a cult-like group of adults based out of Washington DC. A search warrant served on a property of the cult revealed they had gathered and organized information on how to procure children without leaving a paperwork trail. Searches of properties uncovered an extensive underground tunnel system under a school they ran, filled with animal bones and satanic symbols.

The FBI file on the case[85] revealed one of the founding members of the cult was a 21 year veteran of the CIA, the group had traveled to areas of the world where only the CIA could arrange travel, and the group had performed investigative services for a while for various entities. According to the case file, FBI and Police investigators concluded the Finders were some sort of CIA

---

83   http://archive.is/KzfUZ
84   Oregon : http://archive.is/MhKNs
            Arizona: http://archive.is/xtdKA
            Here, President Trump's administration seeks whistle-blowers with information about organized sex trafficking within governmental foster care systems: http://archive.is/Hgm4T
85   The FBI case files are here: https://vault.fbi.gov/the-finders

organization. The CIA was intimately involved in the investigation behind the scenes, telling one agent he was stepping on toes by investigating it, and the CIA had called the local police department investigating it and ordered all local PD case files be classified Secret, restricted, and not be shared with the FBI.

The file even made note that during the execution of a search warrant, an FBI Special Agent had noted the presence of some documents, whose significance was redacted, and those documents somehow were disappeared from the chain of custody as if they never existed. All law enforcement officers involved denied knowledge of what happened, but the event would indicate the presence of some infiltrated agent within the Law Enforcement community conducting the investigation, who was working at cross purposes to his agency's official objectives, presumably as an infiltrated agent of some intelligence operation. Cabal has embedded agents everywhere.

The initial children found were eventually returned to adults who claimed to be their parents, though the case file indicated they may not have provided actual evidence of their parental custody. Prosecutors declined to prosecute anyone on the neglect charges, everyone was released, and the entire matter was summarily dropped.

More recently, we have had the Pizzagate scandal, where some anons noticed, long before Q showed up, that among the emails from John Podesta which leaked out were strange, seemingly coded messages, using terms which were commonly used as code words among the online pedophile community to describe their predilections. Deeper digging revealed among Podesta's contacts were a circle of politically influential people associated with a pizza restaurant in DC. The central character, James Alefantis, was inexplicably named one of Washington's most influential people,[86] ranking him alongside the CIA Director, the Secretary of State, the Secretary of Defense, and the Chairman of the Federal Reserve, despite his only claim to fame being owning a small pizza shop, that until that point nobody had heard of. The anons who investigated found that the social media circle he belonged to seemed to contain frequent oblique, coded postings about child abuse, and many of their businesses used symbols in their logos very similar to those identified in an official FBI bulletin as symbols signifying an allegiance to the pedophile community.

Again the media will tell you Pizzagate is a bizarre conspiracy nobody should believe, but by now you should be getting the picture that such an assertion by a media and official authorities who have all been corrupted by the conspiracy may actually be a cause to look a bit deeper. Oddly enough, one CBS reporter did look deeper, and did an honest report about it which you can see at the address in this note.[87] But within two days, CBS deleted the report from their site. For a good rundown of evidence supporting the Pizzagate scandal which the TV report couldn't air, as well as highlights from the online cover-up, as well as other possibly Pizzagate-related pedophile networks in Hollywood, the Pentagon, and the government, you can go here.[88]

Most recently, we have seen the Jeffrey Epstein scandal. "Billionaire investor" Jeffrey Epstein is now accepted to have been

---

86   http://archive.is/KCxmk
87   http://archive.is/nIFji
88   http://archive.is/FFrSa

one part of a global network which groomed underaged girls to be used for blackmail operations and as sex slaves by the rich and powerful. Epstein himself appears to have been a smaller player of a much larger intelligence operation, and the origins of his fortune are so murky that many now just assume his billionaire label was merely a cover for his blackmail and grooming operations.

In 2005 Palm Beach County Police began an 11 month investigation of Epstein's activities after a complaint regarding one of the under-aged girls he was grooming.[89] After Police assembled an extensive investigation intending to imprison Epstein and seize his assets under forfeiture laws, prosecutors turned around and offered Epstein a sweetheart plea deal. He forfeited nothing, was given his own wing in the Sheriffs Department jail to serve the small sentence he received, (where he had young girls servicing him sexually while he was serving his sentence),[90] and he was allowed to leave the jail by day to tend to his "business affairs." The Detective who led the investigation into him died suddenly at age 50 from an undescribed, "brief illness."[91]

Alexander Acosta, a US Attorney in Miami at the time who oversaw Epstein's plea arrangement has said that when he questioned the leniency of the deal, he was told to *"leave it alone"* because Epstein *"belonged to intelligence."*[92] Notice how this implies even the most high level government officials just accepted there was a class of individuals who were beyond the law in the nation, due to an association *"with intelligence."*

---

89   http://archive.is/JtV34
90   http://archive.is/csNim
91   http://archive.is/0GEQW
92   http://archive.is/4L8D8

Since then, Epstein's Mossad handler has come forward, alleging Epstein was a Mossad asset, and his grooming of young girls was part of a Mossad blackmail operation targeting US leaders.[93] There are only three possible explanations for that. Either Mossad compromised US intelligence, and used it to kill the investigation. Another possibility would be that US Intelligence compromised Mossad, and was using it to run blackmail operations against our leaders. As a final possibility, some other third entity could have compromised both US Intelligence and Mossad, and was using both in conjunction to run blackmail operations against US leaders. Notice Q's thesis, of an international intelligence operation dedicated to compromising entire nations, would have predicted circumstances where US intelligence would allow a hostile foreign intelligence service to operate blackmail operations targeting our leaders.

You also can see how a foreign, non-state intelligence operation getting into our government, could reach a critical-mass of control, and then establish itself more openly, at least among government officials. Once it could terrify senior law enforcement officials like Acosta into submission, it would have attained an extra-legal, supra-judicial authority that put it above and beyond any law. Things would snowball from there, as being above the law would intimidate others into granting it even more such power, making even more above the law.

It was a self-reinforcing cycle which fed off itself, until eventually nobody asked any questions. Those in the network could do whatever they wanted, and those outside the network would be too terrified to even try to publicize it. Notice how if the

_____

93   http://archive.is/mf3rn

network even controlled the media, then even if you wanted to stand up to it and blow the whistle, the media would not report it, the government officials in the network would circle the wagons to protect the network, and you could be harassed with no end, by a domestic informant network made up of citizens who lived all around you. You would serve as an example to others of how you do not challenge the network. I can say firsthand, this was the reality in our nation prior to President Trump assuming office.

The culmination of this infiltration operation was a nation where young daughters could be sexually abused, brave investigators could make the case, nobody in government would intervene, and even if they had, nobody in the media would report on it because they were part of the network. Even the lead Police detective who made the case against Epstein could die under mysterious circumstances of a "sudden illness" at age 50, after a long period spent under aggressive surveillance operations,[94] and nobody in the media would ask any questions or publicize the death.

The most powerful and freest nation in the world had become little better than the most ruthless third-world dictatorship, if you happened to land in the wrong spot and fall afoul of the wrong people with juice in the conspiracy. And if you pointed any of this out, the combined weight of the machine would dismiss you as a conspiracy theorist, and ignore you, before a quiet campaign of first person surveillance/harassment by the ground level informants embedded in your community began.

Epstein was eventually arrested again in 2019 under the

---

94   http://archive.is/PR2fq

Presidency of Donald Trump, and this time it appeared he would not be getting such a lax sentence. Rumors were he intended to cooperate in search of a reduced sentence,[95] and soon enough he had been found strangled on the floor of his cell, albeit still alive. He told his lawyers he had been attacked,[96] but he was placed on suicide watch anyway.

The jail dismissed the possibility he had been attacked and claimed to believe he had attempted suicide. However despite this they had a psychologist remove him from suicide watch shortly thereafter, despite the fact this did not meet the prison's own standard of care.[97]

At the time of his death, the jail just happened to be short staffed,[98] vital cameras which would have documented Epstein's cell were mysteriously broken,[99] two of the guards who were watching over his cell block were moved due to "maintenance" of his cell block,[100] his cell mate was moved and the guards who were supposed to check on him slept through his checks,[101] all of which violated established procedures. In addition, the autopsy found broken bones in his neck consistent with strangulation,[102] something confirmed by a second autopsy done by his family.[103] which said he was definitely strangled. Finally, after his death his attorney noted that Epstein had told him his previous cell mate had

95   http://archive.is/KJC4h
96   http://archive.is/tzEXi
97   http://archive.is/IL7uD
98   http://archive.is/nrUVG
99   http://archive.is/Qje7p
100   http://archive.is/yZlEp
101   http://archive.is/fNHYP
102   http://archive.is/aYG7f
103   http://archive.is/RQBHV

tried to kill him.[104] The blatant nature of this event was surprising to those who had not noticed the rising dictatorial secret police force being established behind the scenes. However those of us on the Chans knew from the start, Epstein would never get to testify.

Also worth noting is how the Dutroux affair, the Franklin Scandal, Jimmy Saville,[105] and even the Westminster pedophile scandal[106] all had accusations of satanism associated with the abuse. Even Pizzagate members were documented having attended satanic *Spirit Cooking* sessions with occult "artist" Marina Abramovic. Bear in mind 30 year veteran of the FBI and head of the LA FBI Field office Ted Gunderson investigated child abuse networks in the US and concluded there was a significant satanic element to the established child abuse rings.[107] He even believed many of these satanic cults were performing child sacrifices.

I point this out because the satanic aspect is a strange element to include in allegations of a child abuse ring. If these were simply fabricated claims, one would think they would be simplified, and the majority would not include such a bizarre element as satanic cults. However the satanic cult theme is found fairly consistently throughout these allegations, from Pizzagate, to Ted Gunderson, to the Finders.

I point this out because Q will assert quite strongly that satanism is a hallmark of this conspiracy which has penetrated our modern global power structures. Left unsaid thus far is why. It is possible the members practice satanism at the behest of Cabal, and

---

104   http://archive.is/tzEXi
105   http://archive.is/vipgK
106   http://archive.is/1N8X1
107   http://archive.is/OvwqY

the satanic aspect serves as a justification for demanding the highest level initiates perform rituals including the most horrific form of criminal acts possible, up to and including child murder. This would allow the acquisition of blackmail gained against them which would allow for full and complete control of them.

However there are cases of Ivy League psychiatrists who have found themselves recruited by the Catholic Church into performing assessments of candidates for exorcisms, to rule out organic disease before the exorcism is embarked upon. Although entering the field as skeptics, they have asserted in no uncertain terms, they have seen evidence of some seemingly intelligent and sentient phenomenon, with tangible effect on the material world around them, which was beyond explanation within the rules governing our material world. By way of full and accurate explanation, Q has left open that this conspiracy may be benefiting from actual worship of some as yet uncharacterized phenomenon which could bestow some form of tangible advantage upon them. Personally, I see no conclusive evidence of exactly what Q is asserting is the truth in this regard.

As this is being written, still to be fully unraveled are the cases of Jeffrey Epstein and the NXIVM cult. Q alleges Epstein was also involved in some type of satanic ceremonies performed by the elites at his private island in the Virgin Islands, in a temple constructed specifically for that purpose on the island.

NXIVM appears to have been running a similar sexual blackmail program, primarily targeting politicians in both the US and Mexico with young girls and children who were groomed as members of the cult. Q has asserted there were many such operations being run to gain blackmail. As the youngest victims of such operations aged out of it, they would sometimes be given roles in Hollywood and in the modeling world. In that way, Cabal would fill those famous positions with agents who they would control fully. It would allow them to avoid having an honest and moral person perhaps enter that rarefied world, realize what was going on, decide to expose it, and then have at their disposal a fan base to spread their allegations to.

So in matters of child trafficking, Q's allegations, as extraordinary as they sound, are not without precedent, correlate in unusual ways with previous allegations, and are fully supported by what evidence we have. Those of us who lurked among free thinkers online were long ready to see someone probe these dark corners and shine a light into them.

There have been many events as you look back, which fit with the model of total, ruthless control Q alleges has been operative, even if each at the time appeared as an isolated incident. Michael Hastings was a high-level, nationally recognized journalist writing for Rolling Stone.[108]

He gradually became certain he was being followed around by some sort of massive intelligence operation, which he attributed to the FBI. Once, while standing outside, he even told a neighbor he had aviation units assigned to him, pointing up to helicopters that were loitering overhead.[109] This would be not at all unusual. The massive surveillance machine Cabal constructed maintains loitering aviation units over all major population centers, complete with state of the art thru-structure imaging technologies capable of

---

108   http://archive.is/MiYt7
109   Http://archive.is/h85zi

peering through rooftops. When it is idling with no high value target assigned to them, even the most inconsequential targets appear to see unusual air activity, often seemingly for no reason beyond mere harassment.[110]

Hastings notified his family and bosses that he thought he had been placed under investigation by the FBI, and that due to some major story he was working on he needed to get off the radar.[111] Reportedly the story he was working on at his death involved CIA director John Brennan[112] who Q now says was a key part of Cabal's conspiracy to take over our intelligence agencies. There is no telling what he had uncovered, but it would appear to have been serious. The FBI would deny he was ever under investigation, although FOIA requests later turned up a heavily redacted file on him that indicated the FBI was keeping tabs on him.[113]

At some point, something Hastings saw panicked him and he decided to flee his home in the middle of the night. He went next door to his neighbor, telling her he thought someone had possibly placed some sort of tracking or hacking device on his car, and asked to borrow her's. When told her car was in the shop, he fled in his own Mercedes. He was last seen driving at high speed[114] before a security camera appeared to catch an explosion under his

---

110   See at 5:55 in this video, where a harmless conspiracy theorist documents his aviation detail: https://youtu.be/dIvc31sxZtY?t=355
        Oddly enough one aviation expert noted in the comments that one of the LAPD helicopters recorded following him was a model of helicopter the LAPD did not keep in its inventory, implying it was a non-LAPD helicopter painted in LAPD colors, and used to lead targets to believe their persecutors were the Police.
111   http://archive.is/S8s1g
112   http://archive.is/T7xJH
113   http://archive.is/GwBDg
114   http://archive.is/5FiEb

car. He crashed at high speed into a palm tree, and was killed.

Witnesses heard a couple of explosions prior to the crash, the engine of his car was blown out of his vehicle and was found approximately 200 feet away, and witnesses reported a fire more indicative of a thermite burn than a gasoline fire.[115] Interestingly video of one of the explosions, which had been embedded on most sites discussing it, has been wiped from Youtube.[116] (Q alleges the big tech companies were usually created by Cabal. Their supposed founders were often merely hired to play the part of founder. That way, the public would see a harmless college kid on a lark, and not the CIA, behind some social media website asking them to upload all of their photos, resumes, social connections, and daily activities to an Agency database file on them.)

A former National Security Adviser and Cyber Security Czar, Richard Clarke, stated that given the lack of any skid marks, even as Michael Hasting's car made a sharp turn to careen off the side of a straight road, the crash of Michael Hasting's car was consistent with a current technique allowing a Mercede's electronic control systems to be hacked remotely.[117] This type of attack allowed the car to be accelerated to high speed and steered into an obstacle remotely, while denying the driver any input into the vehicle's controls.[118]

Of course the most interesting aspect of the Michael Hastings case is how, as with the many unusual aspects of the death of Supreme Court Justice Antonin Scalia,[119] the suicide by

115   http://archive.is/PzRQE
116   http://archive.is/6y7QX
117   http://archive.is/WczlT
118   http://archive.is/n752c
119   http://archive.is/X90k9

two gunshots to the head of reporter Gary Webb,[120] or even the murder of John Lang,[121] it was subsequently ignored by all major Main Stream Media, despite how interesting it looked. Only those independent minds Q would eventually appeal to knew about it from their time spent exchanging information among themselves, rather than listening to the propaganda outlets of the Cabal. Many of us had known something was wrong for some time.

Then there was the idea of what came to be known within the community as "false flag" attacks. Many had noted that large terrorist attacks or mass shootings seemed to occur immediately prior to or immediately after large stories the government in power would not want to lead evening news casts. Still other shootings seemed conveniently timed to critical votes on gun control and surveillance legislation.

I could try to go case by case, but in the interest of brevity I will only cover a single case here, to try and make my point that at least some of these mass casualty events may have been planned, and used as part of a public propaganda effort.

On May 31st, 2019 a Virginia Beach City employee named Dewayne Craddock entered the Virginia Beach Municipal Center and shot twelve people and wounded four others.[122] He used two weapons. One was a 45 caliber handgun with a silencer.[123] This was the only case of any mass shooting in the US using a silencer, and it was definitely the only case ever, of a legally papered silencer used in a crime. There is a reason for that.

---

120   http://archive.is/frhtv
121   http://archive.is/mYH0T
122   http://archive.is/eJfZw
123   http://archive.is/dat17

Silencers, or more accurately sound suppressors, are incredibly difficult to acquire. As an avid firearms enthusiast from my earliest childhood, I have never seen one stocked in any firearms store because of that. I have never known any gun owner who had jumped through all the hoops to acquire one, and I have never actually seen one in my entire life. That is the norm for the vast majority of gun owners. Sound suppressors require special permission through an extensive licensing and registration process from the Bureau of Alcohol Tobacco and Firearms, which will perform an extensive background check, and produce a very long waiting period while that check is performed and the paperwork is processed. Only after the processing is complete, can your dealer order one for you from a manufacturer.

Additionally, sound suppressors are a serious tactical disadvantage in a mass shooting event. While they reduce the sound of the firearm negligibly, (from the sound of an explosion to the sound of a hammer hitting a board), they add a weight which projects outward from the handgun's muzzle, which makes it require more wrist-muscle to hold the firearm level. This weight, the increased length, and the shifting of the gun's balance forward all significantly reduces the pointability of the gun and the ability to acquire targets quickly. It also makes disarmament of the firearm in a struggle much easier, as it offers a larger purchase to grab the firearm and a longer lever to use to gain mechanical advantage to twist it free.

On a handgun they are much, much more of a disadvantage in almost any combat environment, outside of silencing a sentry at a guard gate a considerably large distance from any potential observers, or where communication with teammates over gunfire in coordinating an assault in real time is necessary. Their tactical utility is very, very limited.

So why did we see the only use ever of an incredibly rare, and hard to acquire weapons accessory, which actually would have reduced the shooter's capability in a very real way, on that particular day? The shooting occurred on a Friday. The very next week, was the week which the Supreme Court would, for the first time ever, debate whether to take a case asserting that sound suppressors were an "arm," or weapon in the eyes of the Constitution, and whether they enjoyed the same protections firearms enjoyed under the Second Amendment.[124] After this shooting, the Supreme Court decided to not take the case and thus allowed greater governmental suppression of suppressor ownership.

Literally, the only shooting ever, utilizing one of the rarest and most difficult to acquire firearms accessories, which would make the shooting more inefficient and less lethal, happened at the exact perfect moment to impact a Supreme Court case which could have more broadly protected civilian access to that firearm accessory. The firearms community has noted for decades that very often, when a piece of legislation was pending, or some critical moment in the battle for the Second Amendment was imminent, a perfectly tailored mass casualty event would happen at the perfect moment to aid the forces of gun control.[125]

To be clear, I do not pretend to know the mechanism behind

---

124   http://archive.is/dtksz

125   Often these incidents would be accompanied by strange aspects, such as seen here, where a Sandy Hook father is seen laughing in a carefree fashion after supposedly finding out his child had just been murdered :
https://youtu.be/0JoeXAFBbpQ

these perfectly timed shootings. Was the shooter an anti-gunner who was so committed to the cause he purchased that suppressor legally years back, knowing that court case was coming up and he would have to sacrifice himself to stop it? Was he ID'd by the Cabal's intelligence/surveillance of the population as the only legal owner of such a device who had recently had a work dispute, and one day he just woke up drugged, in the office, surrounded by dead bodies, right before a SWAT officer executed him? I have no idea. But as a long-time observer of the phenomenon, I have seen that happen more often than I can remember. I and many other observers have no doubt the two aspects were related in that case, and many others. Given how strange my own day to day existence is, I have come to think anything is possible.

So when Q mentions that attacks are common when bad news for Cabal is about to break, it did not take much convincing for his followers to accept there may be some strange aspect to the mechanism that is working behind the scenes. And indeed, often when he predicted the release of damaging information for Cabal, there would be attacks just before the information would come out.

When Q asserted declassification of key documents would happen the following week and it would be pivotal to the fall of Cabal, just before the date he predicted, George H. W. Bush died. Q indicated that the death was not a coincidence. Rather it had occurred as a way of trying to interfere with the publicizing of the declassified documents by creating a story the news programs let dominate the newscasts. Strangely, just before his death, it was reported that on being moved, Bush had asked his friend James Baker where he was going. Baker's immediate reply was, *"To Heaven."* Again, I do not know the mechanism, but I suspect things work differently from how we have been told they worked.

There were many other reasons that once Q showed up citizens believed in him. Most prominently, Q appeared to exhibit unusual prescience, making oblique predictions or vague references that were borne out as events transpired. Several other times it seemed he and the President were coordinating the timing of Q's posts and President Trump's tweeting. And then there were things the President did.

First, examples of Q and the President coordinating tweets. On January 7th, Q posted two interesting posts:

Q !UW.yye1fxo ID: 05b846 No.13549   **492**
Jan 7 2018 03:28:14 (EST)

We will never lose again win this is finished.
Q

Q !UW.yye1fxo ID: 03b993 No.20558   **497**
Jan 7 2018 22:05:50 (EST)

Good**[win]**
[win]/when
[15]
Q

It made no sense at that time, and could not have been decoded in any meaningful way. However shortly thereafter, the President tweeted two tweets, which contained elements of Q's postings, arranged in such a way it would be doubtful the President spent the time arranging the tweets to mimic being associated with Q. The President's tweets were as follows:

145

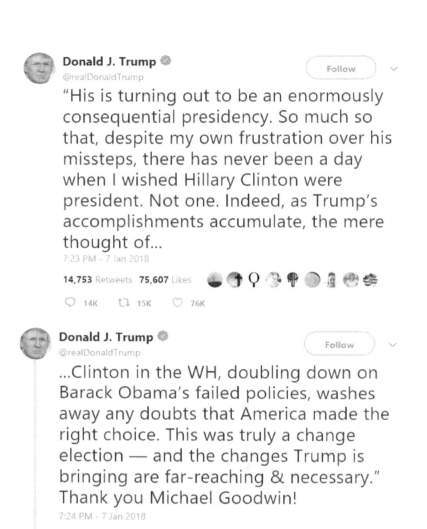

Donald J. Trump @realDonaldTrump

Follow

"His is turning out to be an enormously consequential presidency. So much so that, despite my own frustration over his missteps, there has never been a day when I wished Hillary Clinton were president. Not one. Indeed, as Trump's accomplishments accumulate, the mere thought of...

7:23 PM - 7 Jan 2018

14,753 Retweets **75,607** Likes

💬 14K 🔁 15K ♡ 76K

Donald J. Trump @realDonaldTrump

Follow

...Clinton in the WH, doubling down on Barack Obama's failed policies, washes away any doubts that America made the right choice. This was truly a change election — and the changes Trump is bringing are far-reaching & necessary." Thank you Michael Goodwin!

7:24 PM - 7 Jan 2018

16,447 Retweets **75,996** Likes

💬 18K 🔁 16K ♡ 76K

So Q posted a typo, using the word "win" to draw attention to it, then noted the typo was a marker that something significant featuring "win" was coming. He wrote "Good[win]" would be significant, and there would be a time frame of 15 minutes figuring in somehow.

Shortly thereafter, the President tweeted two tweets about

an article by an author named Goodwin, he tweeted them 15 minutes apart, and he even included a typo which left out a "Q" in the first tweet, which he corrected before posting the second tweet. By now it was obvious the President was tweeting in such a way as to at least draw attention to Q, and Q had some advance info on what he was going to be tweeting, and how he was going to do it.

This was seen as incredibly significant, and it was assumed the President was subtly lending support to Q-anon's credibility.

On December 23, 2017, Q wrote about the Iran Nuclear deal that gave Iran cash, which was used to pay off certain people. Q included a line in the post which read *"$$$,$$$,$$$.00 (pockets)."* 10 days later, President Trump tweeted:

Donald J. Trump @realDonaldTrump

The people of Iran are finally acting against the brutal and corrupt Iranian regime. All of the money that President Obama so foolishly gave them went into terrorism and into their "pockets." The people have little food, big inflation and no human rights. The U.S. is watching!

7:09 AM · Jan 2, 2018 · Twitter for iPhone

There are too many of these twitter proofs to cover in detail. If you wish to see more, you can visit one of the many sites devoted to them online, such as https://www.qproofs.com/.

As time went on and the media refused to reference these coincidences, even to disparage the President for associating with a conspiracy theory, it rapidly became clear the media was afraid to draw attention to Trump's coordinated tweeting with Q. This would seem to indicate that the media feared drawing any attention

147

to Q, or lending him any credence, such as implying the President supported him. To anons it was clear both President Trump and Q were working together, against the media, and presumably against the conspiracy the media must have been a part of.

Around this time the President began doing things in public which lent further credence to this perceived association. When Presidents host a winning sports team at the White House and receive a ceremonial jersey, it typically carries the number of their Presidency. President George W. Bush was the 43rd President, so his ceremonial jerseys would feature a number 43 on the back. President Obama's were number 44.

President Trump's should have been number 45, but they weren't. In March he hosted the Houston Astros, who presented him with a white jersey, number 17. In April, he hosted the University of Alabama football team, and the red jersey they presented was also number 17. Q is the 17th letter of the alphabet.

President Trump would eventually escalate these types of displays, making "Q" motions in the air with his hand, either as he repeated Q phrases,[126] or after seeing a Q-jersey in a crowd at a rally and pointing at it. These became known as *"Air-Q's"* and were seen as further proof of the validity of Q's assertions, especially as they became known as a sign of support for Q and the President continued to do them openly.

Even stranger, in Q's post 1357 on May 12th, 2018, Q wrote *"11.11 provided as a strategic marker. Post-midterms. Red wave coming. Strength. Justice"* On November 11th, strange seismic waves that baffled scientists were detected traversing the globe at intervals of 17 seconds, in a global news story.[127] Nobody before or since had observed any such waves. Again, it could have been coincidence, but strange coincidences were accumulating with Q.

In another "proof" as they are known in Q-speak, on January 13th of 2018, Q had asked anons, *"Do you trust the chain of command?"* On January 15th, the Department of Defense tweeted out a promotion for an upcoming National Geographic airing of a special entitled *"Chain of Command."*[128] Within the special, prominently featured, was this following shot of a coffee cup in a coffee maker at the Department of Defense:

---

126   One air-Q visible when he first announced the phrase "The calm before the storm" is here : https://www.anonymousconservative.com/blog/trump-did-the-air-q-when-first-saying-calm-before-the-storm/
        Another at a speech at CPAC : https://www.anonymousconservative.com/blog/wp-content/uploads/2019/03/AirQ.mp4
        At a rally in Orlando, at 1:03:26 here: https://youtu.be/ndOFsNQmtow
        Another in Indiana here: https://youtu.be/tjrlymV2JhM
        Another: https://twitter.com/that_deplorable/status/1113578523048808449
127   http://archive.is/PUVxD
128   https://twitter.com/DeptofDefense/status/953008906493546496

How could Q have known this was about to air? Obviously, this was seen as another sign that Q was aware of and in control of things that were going on, far more than a mere impostor could be. The assumption was Q knew this documentary was about to air, and whoever he was, he had the authority to take action to place a Q coffee cup in a coffee machine, get it filmed, and not let it get cut, and he knew back when the filming was happening that there would be a "Q-operation" all these months, or even years, later.

It implied both a certain degree of power and seniority, as well as incredibly detailed, intelligence and long-term planning.

On March 6th, Q asked why wasn't North Korea in the news, given all the previous aggression and hostility verbalized between the North Korean regime, and President Trump. On March 8th, Kim Jong Un asked President Trump for a face to face meeting to discuss denuclearizing the Korean peninsula. Obviously in retrospect, this was the beginning of a massive change in the tenor of the US-North Korean relationship. Q knew what was coming.

Q posted a picture of the North Korean delegation meeting with the South Korean delegation in March of 2018. Behind them was a painted mural on the wall, portraying calm waters with a sun rising behind them.

This reminded anons of a previous Q drop, which had been delivered with no fanfare, Q post number 765:

Q !UW.yye1fxo ID: 276796 No.382161 **765**
Feb 15 2018 01:08:41 (EST)

Watch the water.
Q

Anons compared the newly released picture to another similar picture, one of Kim Jong Il and the US and North Korean delegations taken during a previous meeting in 2009 with then former President Clinton. Behind them, a mural on the wall depicted tumultuous waters roiling in a storm:

Almost one month prior, on Feb 15th, Q had previously said simply *"Watch the water."* Many took this as a sign tumult was turning to tranquility, an assumption that was to be borne out over time. Inherent within the assumption was that somehow Q had known that nearly a month later, this second picture would be taken in North Korea, in front of a mural of calm waters, after the tone of North Korea's relationship with the world had changed dramatically, and peace had begun to come to the Korean peninsula. Sure enough, since then there has been a decided change in tack in the relations between North Korea, South Korea, and the United States. Q had known, before anyone not in the uppermost echelons of leadership could have.

Again, each proof, by itself can be seen as perhaps mere

coincidence, or even an amused case of the President playfully pulling people's chains. But over time Q proved himself unusually prescient, to a degree which would otherwise have seemed impossible, and he appeared to have the willing support of the President of the United States.

Behind this, in the background, was the increasing realization that Q appeared to be correct when he was saying the mainstream media had been penetrated and taken over by the CIA on behalf of the Cabal. According to Q, long ago the media's leadership positions had been infiltrated, recruited, and taken over, and hiring in the media was now based upon one's willingness to only report what Cabal's intelligence operation, based out of the CIA, told them to report. It sounds extraordinary.

Yet, here Q-anon followers see Q, making incredible predictions, posting in coordination with the President's tweets, describing an earth-shattering model of the world, and amassing an enormous number of followers whose research is producing extraordinary revelations all their own.

Despite all of that, at this point in time, nobody in the mainstream media would report on any of it. They would not even use it to denigrate the President for being possibly associated with a *"conspiracy theory."* When had the media ever ignored any opportunity to attack or marginalize President Trump?

In those early days, it was a complete media blackout. That only lent credence to Q's assertions about the media being controlled, Q being part of a threat to the conspiracy's leadership, and there being some sort of conspiracy in control of the information being presented to the public. But Q's biggest proof was yet to come, and this one would leave no doubt.

Q had long been implying that John McCain had committed a major treasonous act, and been caught dead to rights. Q's assertion was that it was so bad, he and other patriots who knew no longer wanted to speak McCain's name. So he began referring to him in posts as *"No-Name."*

According to Q's drops, McCain had been convicted of this crime, and his diagnosis of brain cancer was merely a cover story to explain why he would no longer be in the Senate. McCain was still allowed out as part of the deal he cut, but he had to wear an ankle monitor. This ankle monitor was the reason McCain was photographed wearing an orthopedic boot, ostensibly for an Achilles tendon injury. The boot would hide the ankle monitor.

At this point, Q was beginning to sound somewhat questionable, because his claims were so extraordinary. Yet if McCain had ruptured his Achilles tendon, he should not have removed the boot until it healed. Yet he did, and was caught by a photographer at his daughter's wedding with the boot on the wrong leg. So not only was the injured tendon put at risk. He placed the boot on his good leg. Why he'd wear an uncomfortable orthopedic boot which restricts movement on his good foot, when he could just leave it off, did defy explanation. McCain did not help things when he tweeted out to the masses that he had moved the boot to his other good leg to give it a rest.[129]

As we were puzzling over all of this, on June 30th, 2018, Q posted the following response to an anon who wanted to see McCain punished:

---

129   http://archive.is/IDAX5

Q !CbboFOtcZs ID: 317346 No.1973688 ⬀   **1649**
▮▮n 30 2018 14:46:19 (EST)

> Anonymous ID: 355946 No.1973567 ⬀
> ▮▮n 30 2018 14:40:09 (EST)
>
> >>1973527
> Please do not let No Name off the hook. he is a disgrace to
> Veterans across this great country and needs to be held
> accountable.

>>1973567
Think SC vote to confirm (coming).
No Name action.
Every dog has its day.
Enjoy the show.
Q

Q's credibility would seem to hinge on something odd
happening with McCain. Then came post 1706:

Q !CbboFOtcZs ID: 77016b No.2287098 ⬀   **1706**
▮▮l 25 2018 18:28:35 (EST)

6169C31C-A4BA-4CCD-8561-D900C8C16307.jpeg

No name returning to headlines.
Q

Exactly 30 days later, at 4:28 pm Arizona time,[130] John McCain died. Notice Q's post was at 6:28 pm Washington DC time, which was the same as 4:28 in Arizona. Q posted his notice that no name would return to the news exactly 30 days, to the minute, from the time of death on McCain's Death Certificate. It was National Dog Day. As in, *"Every dog has his day."*

Again, that can be chance. But Q nailing all of that would require an extraordinary coincidence. The only logical explanation for how I could see it not being chance, would be if John McCain had been sentenced to death. Then they would have timed the procedure out, from removing him to the death chamber, to the exact moments the drugs would be administered, to exactly when they would confirm his pulse had stopped, and a doctor would pronounce the time of death.

If Q was right, the cancer diagnosis was just a cover story, allowed as part of some deal to not sully his family name, probably in return for his acquiescence to his fate. Q could have posted 30 days prior because once the appeals process was done, or the deal was cut, the date was set 30 days from then. So that was the time at which the process was set in stone.

To me, this was when I began to really pay attention to Q. Q had promised something was going to happen with McCain, and it did appear something very unusual happened. Whatever had happened, the only rational explanation was consistent with what Q had been alleging all along.

Of course it should be noted these were far from the only

_____

130   http://archive.is/athvv

fascinating events we would witness which would lend credence to Q's story – that the President was at war with a conspiracy which had killed Presidents before, and which would try to kill President Trump if they could.

Indeed, twice we witnessed video, recorded by witnesses, of cars passing the Presidential motorcade which seemingly swerved out of control and attempted to ram the Presidential limousine while President Trump was inside. In one case in Springfield Missouri, a vehicle was described as just taking off on its own in a parking lot, failing to respond to braking by the driver, and following a winding road down a hill to where it almost entered the main road and rammed the Presidential limo exactly as it passed. The car was only stopped from ramming the motorcade when it hit a concrete drainage ditch next to the road (which it should be noted, would have appeared as a sidewalk on a surveillance satellite looking down, had that been being used to steer a wirelessly hacked vehicle remotely),[131]

In another case in Opelika, Alabama,[132] the Presidential limousine was driving on the freeway when a car in the opposing lane appeared to suddenly try and cross over the divider into oncoming traffic at the exact perfect moment to impact the oncoming Presidential limousine head-on, at highway speeds.

Again, these can be coincidences, but as Q says, how many must pile up before you begin to see them as more a part of a pattern than coincidences? Moreover, what were the chances that all of these coincidences would just happen to align perfectly with

---

131   https://www.youtube.com/watch?v=1Yqa5PUViPo
132   https://www.youtube.com/watch?v=Tj-qhuxf-4k

the story being told by Q, who himself appeared to be acting with the support of the president?

As time went on, Q appeared to be a combination of different operations. Part of his purpose appeared to be genuine information dissemination to the public (perhaps only enough to establish a credible cover as an honest broker of inside information, informing the public to prepare them). Another part appeared to be operating as a psychological operation targeting the enemies he described, periodically using disinformation and feints to drive the enemy to take actions that would be disadvantageous in the larger battle. Part of his purpose may have been to shift the enemy's focus from the actions Q was involved in which were truly important to overcoming the entrenchment of Cabal in our society. And part of his purpose appeared to be getting his anons researching open source data and amassing relevant information on the board where he was posting, turning the weaponized autism of the Chans into his own private intelligence gathering operation.

His disinformation operations would make his information somewhat unreliable, since it would mean occasionally his posts would say a critical moment was coming and it might pass without a noticeable event. However in order to credibly affect the enemy's actions with disinformation, he would still have to release enough good information to gain credibility, making his posts well worth the effort to follow.

As time went on, things would happen on the world stage which were only explainable within the context of the Q-paradigm, where a war on a secret Cabal was being waged by the President and Military Intelligence.

Eventually the media would begin to address the growing legions of Q fans. However as Q predicted, rather than give an honest assessment of Q's assertions and accurately describe the movement, the "mockingbird media"[133] relentlessly assailed Q and his followers as a conspiracy cult. Every media mention of Q-anon misrepresented the things Q asserted and described his followers as mentally unbalanced and detached from reality. For those who followed Q, the media's refusal to address the very real evidence they were observing only further confirmed the media's bias and enhanced their skepticism of the mainstream media's narratives, as it increased their desire to research things on their own.

Other events also began to only make sense in light of Q's assertions as well. The Rothschild family, which Q said was heavily involved in the leadership of the Cabal began a liquidation of expensive properties and possessions, as if suddenly they were short of resources.[134] Media outlets, which according to the Q paradigm were often primarily funded by Cabal to push Cabal narratives on a trusting public suddenly experienced financial difficulties, began layoffs, declared bankruptcies, and in some cases suddenly shut their doors, despite a booming Trump

---

133   "Mockingbird media" is a disparaging reference to Operation Mockingbird, a well documented CIA program which Q said was still in effect. Run by the CIA, its objective was for the CIA to infiltrate and take over the media, only allowing CIA agents to be hired and employed as news media employees, so any damaging information could be prevented from official dissemination by the media. Personally, I have seen firsthand evidence that many of the members of local affiliate news media are so involved in domestic intelligence operationally, they even partake in live physical surveillance operations and harassment of regular citizens who fall afoul of the domestic intelligence machinery in between covering news stories.

134   As examples,
land - http://archive.is/NKl8V
art - http://archive.is/AzSyt
business - http://archive.is/H4wm9

economy.[135] Republicans and Democrats in Congress suddenly announced they would no longer seek office at the end of their terms.[136] Guantanamo began construction projects, as if planning to house new inmates, after Q had said the leaders of Cabal in America would be getting sent to Guantanamo.[137] Q predicted the Special Counsel the Democrats insisted on would amount to nothing, as Special Counsel Mueller had already been turned by Q. When Mueller released his report it exonerated the President, to the surprise of everyone who had not been following Q.

Prior to Bob Mueller issuing his report, the media ignored all the evidence, as well as the ridiculousness of the idea that someone as pro-America and competitive as President Trump would act subserviently to Vladimir Putin. Instead the media constantly pushed the narrative that President Trump was almost certainly a foreign agent, and the Special Prosecutor, Bob Mueller would prove it.

It was obvious that if we were in a world where things worked as they seemed, the media would not have hung itself out there by promoting such a ridiculous narrative so divorced from reality. The only way the media would push such a narrative was if they thought that Mueller was a Cabal agent, sent in not to investigate, but to expressly trap President Trump in some procedural charge, or make up evidence of Trump's campaign colluding with the Russians that would allow the Democrats to remove him from office. Understand the degree to which Cabal had taken control of all of the media and government. Reality was

---

135   http://archive.is/qzt9B
136   http://archive.is/CklWc
137   http://archive.is/0tTgy

meaningless if they could have the media report it to the public, and then have the government act on that reporting. Prior to Donald Trump's election, that is exactly how it would have worked.

When Mueller ultimately exonerated President Trump and it was clear he had not been operating as a Cabal agent to remove the President, the media was left looking ridiculous – and shell shocked. Q had been right all along.

President Trump also initiated a top to bottom review of the Navy's JAG Corps.[138] Q had asserted this would be necessary if Military Tribunals were going to be used for trials and meting out punishments to high-level Cabal operatives who had colluded with a foreign power to treasonously subvert the United States Government.

It was revealed the DOJ Inspector General was probing illegal spying by the FBI and other associated agencies. Presumably that review will ultimately lead to the domestic spying apparatus embedded throughout America. There was a US Attorney, John Huber, in Utah, who was teamed with the DOJ Inspector General's office and its 470 investigators in an unusual arrangement, giving him special powers, and he was conducting other reviews which were not clearly specified. [139]

A new US Attorney, John Durham was brought in, to investigate the origins of the Russia probe, augmenting the DOJ Inspector General who was conducting his own investigations as well as US Attorney John Huber who was performing still

---

138   http://archive.is/IiJlo
139   http://archive.is/3YQm2

additional investigations.[140]

They would discover the Russia probe was fraudulently predicated by corrupted FBI Agents, who went so far as to alter FBI interview records to make Trump staff look guilty of lying. The fake Russia investigation was then used to justify an illegal spying operation targeting the President, seemingly perpetrated by our Central Intelligence Agency and FBI, as well as foreign intelligence agencies. The entire operation was designed to first damaging the Trump campaign so he wouldn't win, and then having failed at that, conjure evidence that could be used to remove President Trump from office after his election.

However the core of the origins of the Russia probe was a national security apparatus that was out of control, and deploying illegal surveillance and complex intelligence operations in a bid to control the American government and who got to hold office in it. As wrong as it was to try and deny American citizens the President they had selected, this was more emblematic of a larger problem which had been growing behind the scenes.

While President Trump certainly wanted to find out who had placed him under illegal surveillance and attempted to frame him for a crime, it should not escape notice this investigation would be going to the heart of a larger problem many of us who were far lower in the political hierarchy had been experiencing for years. Indeed, I suspect it is a problem which afflicted every citizen at one point or another, as the government built out their files, regardless of whether those citizens were aware of it or not.

Sealed indictments, normally numbering a few thousand per

---

140   http://archive.is/LO8SC

year skyrocketed to well over 144,000 as of this writing.[141] This led to speculation that a conspiracy, corrupting the very machinery of the government needed to investigate and prosecute it, would not be able to be removed piecemeal. You would have a judicial system where the investigatory apparatus (such as the FBI) was compromised by agents of the conspiracy, the evidence storage apparatus could be compromised, the prosecutors, the judges, the court clerks who summoned the jury pool (and who could arrange to only summon members of the Cabal's civilian surveillance apparatus), and thus even the jury could all be compromised. Each individual part you targeted for prosecution could be protected by any of the other parts sabotaging the trial, releasing that part to go and protect other parts when their prosecutions came about.

However, by placing everyone involved under sealed indictment, and only unsealing them all simultaneously, you would force all of the conspirators to recuse themselves simultaneously from each other's legal procedures, or allow for them to be removed based on their conflicts of interest. You would purge the entire system, all at once, of all the compromised parts, allowing a pristine judicial system, free of compromised agents to then set about prosecuting all of those cases.

Another strange incident that led many to think something unusual was going on behind the scenes occurred when Q implied some revelation was forthcoming, and suddenly George H. W. Bush died. His death sucked up all of the media coverage for that period. On his next post, Q congratulated the Deep State and promised that his response would be forthcoming.

---

141   https://qmap.pub/cases

Shortly thereafter, at the funeral, the Cabal-attendees were filmed discovering mysterious envelopes in their funeral pamphlets,[142] with some sort of short message which caused them displeasure. When Hillary Clinton opened her's, Jimmy Carter, sitting next to her showed great interest and immediately looked for his own in his own funeral pamphlet. Not finding any envelope in his pamphlet, you could see him trying to see what her's said, as she coldly stuffed it back in its envelope.

When asked, Q indicated that the envelopes contained his response to them. From Joe Biden's shock as he showed his to someone next to him, to Laura Bush's outrage as she showed hers to Jeb, who immediately looked crestfallen, whatever was in them must have been something interesting.

Q had long faced pushback on his board from paid Cabal posters who flooded it with everything from porn to gore. As it appeared his operation was accelerating with new fans joining quickly, I remember trying to surf his board for interesting posts amid a flood of transexual anime porn. They tried everything.

On August 3rd, a new strategy emerged. A racist shooter's manifesto was posted to 8Chan, where Q's board was, and the young man who authored it proceeded to conduct a mass shooting targeting latinos at a Walmart in El Paso Texas.

However strange facts surrounding the case quickly emerged. For starters, the shooter had posted his manifesto to Instagram first, and it appeared he was not the person who posted it to 8Chan. Someone else took it off Instagram, and reposted it to

---

142   Hillary and Joe Biden: https://youtu.be/pmHwJbS_ku8
       Jeb and Laura: https://www.anonymousconservative.com/blog/letters/

8Chan, while the shooting was going on.[143] Furthermore, had they just done this, the manifesto would not have been able to be linked to the shooter. So before they posted the manifesto, they posted a private file with his name to 8Chan, as if they were him, and had accidentally posted the wrong file, and then they posted the manifesto, allowing it to be easily linked to his real life identity. It sounds incredible, but I can tell you firsthand, Cabal's domestic intelligence/surveillance operation has impressive computer skills.

Whoever did it got the effect they were looking for. 8Chan was quickly blamed for the shooting.[144] Cloudfare, which provided a critical service that protected the 8Chan website from internet attacks ceased providing its service, taking 8chan offline.[145] Q had been effectively separated from his followers.

At least it seemed that way. Shortly thereafter Jeffrey Epstein was found dead in his jail cell. At that moment, Q's fans would have wanted to hear something from him. And just at that moment, Rudy Giuliani, who normally tweets in full sentences with perfect grammar, tweeted these questions, in a Q-tone:

Rudy Giuliani ✓
@RudyGiuliani   Follow   ⌄

What does the word watch mean in the phrase suicide
Watch? Who was watching? What does camera show? It is inconceivable Epstein could have hung himself if there was a suicide Watch? Follow the motives.
11:27 AM - 10 Aug 2019 from Manhattan, NY

---

143   http://archive.is/mcZwL
144   http://archive.is/l7o4d
145   http://archive.is/gdEAN

It is unclear if Rudy was posting for a friend, or if he might have revealed a secret identity.

Of course things got stranger still. 8Chan was brought back up and Q returned 93 days later. One of his returning posts referenced an earlier post, from July 27th, exactly. The post contained a picture James Comey had posted of himself standing in a corn field, at an undisclosed location, as well as a link to Comey's tweet. The last line of Q's post was the most interesting:

Q !!mG7VJxZNCl ID: 6bfd78 No.7222066 🔗 📑   **3525**
Jul 27 2019 19:54:54 (EST)

90.jpg   ⬇️

https://twitter.com/Comey/status/1155271446207389696 🔗 📑
Was the corn ripe for harvesting?
It is now.
[93   dk]
Q

After the El Paso shooting, Q had gone dark for 93 days. What makes it interesting is Q posted this one week before the El Paso shooting which ostensibly was what took 8Chan, where Q posted his missives, offline and forced him to go dark for 93 days.

Did Q and company just take advantage of the shooting on the fly and use it as an opportune excuse for their 93 days of darkness? Did they know the shooting was coming, and was it incorporated into their plans? Was there even a shooting?

Don't forget, we have a full fledged intelligence network embedded in our society, composed of entire families which appear entirely normal, even though they are recruited into the network and will do anything for it. Our news media is almost entirely compromised, and willing to tell us anything the network orders them to tell us. Anything is possible under those circumstances.

My assumption is this early phase of Q's operation is not so much about informing people, as it is about releasing solid information to build credibility, and then using that credibility to feed bad information to the Cabal observers to either trigger action or inaction, and aid other Q operations we do not see. While Q is doing that, they are building up the sealed indictments, and preparing for their own version of D-Day, when the indictments will be unsealed, and the Cabal will be purged from all of its positions of power within the government.

I suspect that is why thus far the President has only made oblique references to Q rather than openly talking about him, and it is why Q has not dropped hard confirmation of his identity. They would prefer to keep his readership limited until at some point Q's operations no longer are aided by the release of disinformation. It may also be why this period of darkness was not overly concerning to them. We are reaching a point where it no longer matters what Cabal does or doesn't do. The sealed indictments have built up , and eventually the hammer will drop, and all that will be left will be the sentencing and the punishments.

At that point Q's identity will probably be released, his readership will soar, and it will be backed by all of the research anons have been performing for all of this time.

For now, all we have are Q's posts and the proofs he highlighted. In the next chapter, Q's first 400 posts are reprinted as images, exactly as they appeared to anons on sites which complied them. A rough explanation follows the posts in bold italics, using the best data available as we went to press. Q's posts begin with him using the name "Anonymous," The name "Q" arose later courtesy of the anons, and was then adopted by Q.

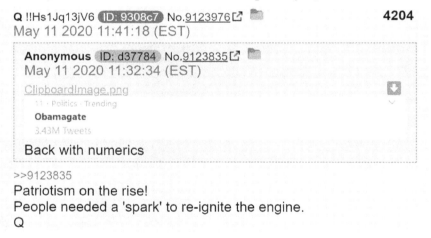

Before we jump to Q's posts, in an example of a post above, an anon who was assigned ID "d37784" based on his computer address (the only way to tell anons apart), posted, showing there were 3.43 million tweets about Obamagate, adding himself, *"Back with numerics."* Q quoted his post here in the darker box in his 4204th post, and replied, saying patriotism was on the rise.

Chapter Six

Q-Anon's Posts

Anonymous ID: BQ7V3bcW No.147012719 ⬈   1
ct 28 2017 15:44:28 (EST)

Anonymous ID: gb953qGI No.147005381 ⬈
ct 28 2017 14:33:50 (EST)

>>146981635
Hillary Clinton will be arrested between 7:45 AM - 8:30 AM EST
on Monday - the morning on Oct 30, 2017.

>>147005381
HRC extradition already in motion effective yesterday with several
countries in case of cross border run. Passport approved to be
flagged effective 10/30 @ 12:01am. Expect massive riots organized
in defiance and others fleeing the US to occur. US M's will conduct
the operation while NG activated. Proof check: Locate a NG
member and ask if activated for duty 10/30 across most major
cities.

This is the first Q post, before he was named Q. It was
assumed now it meant Hillary Rodham Clinton (HRC) would be
arrested, shown evidence of her crimes, turned into an agent of
Q's, and released. There are indications throughout Q's story
that many of the individuals who did wrong under Cabal will
continue to play the role of villain, but they will be doing so as
part of a script which is under the control of Q. However at this
point we were not aware of that, and many were not even sure if
Q was real or not.

Mockingbird
HRC detained, not arrested (yet).
Where is Huma? Follow Huma.
This has nothing to do w/ Russia (yet).
Why does Potus surround himself w/ generals?
What is military intelligence?
Why go around the 3 letter agencies?
What Supreme Court case allows for the use of MI v Congressional
assembled and approved agencies?
Who has ultimate authority over our branches of military w\o
approval conditions unless 90+ in wartime conditions?
What is the military code?
Where is AW being held? Why?
POTUS will not go on tv to address nation.
POTUS must isolate himself to prevent negative optics.
POTUS knew removing criminal rogue elements as a first step was
essential to free and pass legislation.
Who has access to everything classified?
Do you believe HRC, Soros, Obama etc have more power than
Trump? Fantasy.
Whoever controls the office of the Presidecy controls this great
land.
They never believed for a moment they (Democrats and
Republicans) would lose control.
This is not a R v D battle.
Why did Soros donate all his money recently?
Why would he place all his funds in a RC?
Mockingbird 10.30.17
God bless fellow Patriots.

Operation Mockingbird was a CIA program from the 1950's[146] which infiltrated the media with CIA agents to control the news for propaganda purposes. The implication is, it was never discontinued, and the media today is controlled by the CIA. According to Q, Hillary was released, perhaps now as a

---

146   http://archive.is/TzvDM

170

controlled, turned asset. Military Intelligence and President Trump are working together to execute a plan against corrupted elements of various government agencies, including the FBI, CIA, and other private entities. The President is in control, but the Cabal which has taken over the nation has so effectively polarized it that President Trump cannot, at this point, allow himself to be associated with what is going on for fear citizens still deceived by the Cabal will align against him. In the post, RC stands for Registered Charity, and MI is Military Intelligence.

Anonymous ID: P3Lk4PKG No.147104628 ☑   **3**
 ct 29 2017 10:47:07 (EST)

Open your eyes.
It finally came out that Rod/Bob were key players in the Uranium scandal.
Don't you think POTUS would be tweeting about removal given clear conflict.
Why did POTUS meet Bob under the cover of FBI Dir interview?
Bob is unable to serve as Dir per the law.
Gowdy comments on Comey (history will ....)
POTUS has everything.
Not everyone is corrupt (fewer than you think).
Follow Huma.
Operation Mockingbird.
Priority to clean out the bad actors to unite people behind the America First agenda.
Many in our govt worship Satan.
Not about Republicans v Democrats at this stage.
Where is HRC?
Why is the NG called up across 12 cities?
Trust in your President.
God bless, Patriots.

This refers to the involvement of Rod Rosenstein and Robert Mueller (Rod/Bob) in the sale of Canadian Uranium supplier Uranium One[147] to Russian interests – a sale which was

---

147   https://infogalactic.com/info/Uranium_One

rumored to have been facilitated by Hillary Clinton and the State Department as well as elements of the corrupt Obama administration in return for bribes. Robert Mueller personally delivered a Yellowcake Uranium sample to the Russian buyers for analysis. But The President is not tweeting about Mueller's conflict of interest. That is because President Trump met Mueller, claiming he was thinking of hiring him for FBI Director, However Mueller had already served more than the statutory 10 year term FBI Directors are allowed by law, and thus could not fill that position. In reality Mueller was being shown evidence of his corruption, and he was turned as an agent. National Guard was called up due to pending Antifa protests. Finally, President Trump is in no legal jeopardy. The investigators are actually investigating the corrupt network.

Anonymous ID: P3Lk4PKG No.147106598 🗗 📷   **4**
Oct 29 2017 11:11:40 (EST)

Some of us come here to drop crumbs, just crumbs.
POTUS is 100% insulated - any discussion suggesting he's even a target is false.
POTUS will not be addressing nation on any of these issues as people begin to be indicted and must remain neutral for pure optical reasons. To suggest this is the plan is false and should be common sense.
Focus on Military Intellingence/ State Secrets and why might that be used vs any three letter agency
What SC decision opened the door for a sitting President to activate - what must be showed?
Why is POTUS surrounded by generals ^^
Again, there are a lot more good people than bad so have faith.
This was a hostile takeover from an evil corrupt network of players (not just Democrats).
Don't fool yourself into thinking Obama, Soros, Roth's, Clinton's etc have more power present day than POTUS.
Operation Mockingbird
Patriots are in control. Sit back and enjoy the show.

The President is not a target of the patriots rooting out the treason, and he will not discuss this event to prevent the left from attempting to portray it as his own personal political vendetta.

Military Intelligence and the State Secrets act being used against three letter government agencies implies our intelligence agencies were penetrated by a foreign conspiracy and were operating against the United States from the inside, using the very agencies which were supposed to protect the nation from such an attack.

Hamdan vs Rumsfeld confirmed the President's power to form Military Tribunals in cases of National Security.

Q finally asserts that Military Intelligence and the President are in full control, and have all the power.

Anonymous ID: P3Lk4PKG No.147109593 ☐   5
 ct 29 2017 11:47:18 (EST)

Follow the money, it's the key.
What is Pelosi's net worth by way of one example. Why coincidentally is her memory apparently going?
Cover for possible future indictment to plead what?
What if John M never had surgery and that was a cover for a future out if needed against prosecution?
Why did Soros transfer his bulk public funds to a NP? Note this doesn't include massive slush funds that are pulled by several high ups.
Why did Soros' son have several meetings with Canadian PM and how is that related to Clinton's?
Can you rely on being able to board a plane and fly away?
Why is MS13 a priority _ nobody got this.
Could people pay such gangs to kill opponents and why / how to insulate against exposure?
The truth is mind blowing and cannot fully be exposed.
Also many are thinking from one point of view, US only, this evil is embedded globally. US is the first domino.
Have faith.

173

This begins the reveal that this corrupt network was using Non-Profit (NP) charities to launder cash for their operations. Pelosi's net worth is over $200 Million dollars.[148] *Q also asserts here that many of the participants are showing signs in public of mental degradation, or in the case of McCain, a brain tumor, all of which is an effort to set up a mental incompetence defense. The relationship between Soros, Trudeau and the Clintons is the Uranium One scandal, where a Canadian Billionaire, who also profited from it, funneled donations to the Clinton Foundation, which also received taxpayer monies from Justin Trudeau, who has his own foundation which is said to operate similarly to the Clinton's.*[149] *It also reveals the Cabal had recruited low level criminal gangs such as MS-13 as enforcers, routing money to them through their foreign leadership overseas, making it difficult for local law enforcement investigating any one murder to prove any linkage. Q also asserts that the network we are looking at is global. This is an important example of how rival intelligence operations will not exist as equals, checking each other's power forever. Once the Cabal took over our national intelligence apparatus, it would have infiltrated and taken over the intelligence apparatuses of as many other countries as it could, both for purposes of expanding its power, but more importantly for purposes of covering up the crimes it had already committed. It also begins to reveal that politicians were making far more money than one would think they should make, merely off of their government salaries, through monetization of their offices and authorities.*

---

148   http://archive.is/kQfCh#selection-703.80-703.120
149   https://youtu.be/3md0r9rOlhE
       http://archive.is/tldmA

Some of us come here to drop crumbs, just crumbs.
POTUS is 100% insulated - any discussion suggesting he's even a target is false.
Follow Huma tomorrow.
POTUS will not be addressing nation on any of these issues as people begin to be indicted and must remain neutral for pure optical reasons. To suggest this is the plan is false and should be common sense.
Focus on Military Intelligence/ State Secrets and why might that be used vs any three letter agency
What SC decision opened the door for a sitting President to activate - what must be showed?
Why is POTUS surrounded by generals ^^
Again, there are a lot more good people than bad so have faith.
This was a hostile takeover from an evil corrupt network of players (not just Democrats).
Don't fool yourself into thinking Obama, Soros, Roth's, Clinton's etc have more power present day than POTUS.
Follow the money, it's the key.
What is Pelosi's net worth by way of one example. Why coincidentally is her memory apparently going?
Cover for possible future indictment to plead what?
What if John M never had surgery and that was a cover for a future out if needed against prosecution?
Why did Soros transfer his bulk public funds to a NP? Note this doesn't include massive slush funds that are pulled by several high ups.
Why did Soros' son have several meetings with Canadian PM and how is that related to Clinton's?
Why is MS13 a priority?
Could people pay such gangs to kill opponents and why / how to insulate against exposure?
The truth is mind blowing and cannot fully be exposed. These people are evil.
Operation Mockingbird.

Q states in the future that he must communicate by dropping questions which will lead you to the truth, to comply with national security laws. Much of this is classified, so if he

175

told us openly, he would be committing a crime. But if he asks questions, and people discover the truth themselves, he has broken no rules. I have suspected many of the "anons" who find the answers and post them may actually be operationally tasked by Q's organization with doing so, to better control the message.

Anonymous ID: Eka5Om1K No.147167304 ☐ 📷   7
Oct 29 2017 20:58:37 (EST)

Why wasn't HRC prosecuted for the emails? Put simply, Obama ultimately OK'd by using the non govt email addy to communicate w/ Clinton. Obama also had an alias along with each of his cabinet members. Therefore indicting HRC would lead to indicting Obama & his cabinet etc which could never happen. Remember he lied about knowing but that ultimately came out in the dump. Poof!

So these agents of the Cabal had a secret back-channel communications system they had set up, and were hiding.

Anonymous ID: Eka5Om1K No.147169329 ☐   8
Oct 29 2017 21:18:17 (EST)

Huma
Husband in jail.
HRC, Muslim Brotherhood, or child?
What would you do? Kiss your child goodbye and leave without a mother or father for Clinton?
Where is Huma today?
Was she with HRC on her book tour?
RE: Military Intelligence / State Secrets
No FBI
POTUS installed his people within each top spot at each 3 letter agency except 1 (good reason there as Adm R kick started this and scrubbed all POTUS nominations to verify oath).
Do you think they aren't in control of those respective agencies?
What is most valuable?
Information
AG Sessions on leakers.

176

Fire or prosecute?
Reorg is underway and happening.
Coincidence Senate Republicans pushing for Fed Judge
confirmations last week?
Why are Senate Republicans dropping out? Not by choice and
were offered a choice (rest assured they will vote pro Trump).

Huma Abedin's husband, Anthony Wiener, is in jail. Her
choice is to show loyalty to Hillary, her Muslim Brotherhood
associates, or her child. This implies she is cooperating for her
child. Also Admiral Mike Rogers of NSA, who went to Trump
Tower to alert Trump to the illegal surveillance he was under, is
vetting all of Trump's nominations personally through the NSA
databases to make sure they are not compromised by Cabal.
Attorney General Sessions had just announced a crackdown on
White House leakers, which is part of the purge. Meanwhile
Republicans are resigning from their offices for seemingly no
reason, but Q implies it is because they were told of the evidence
against them, and forced out of government.

Anonymous ID: Eka5Om1K No.147170576 ☑ 9
ct 29 2017 21:30:26 (EST)

Projection
D's can't lose control over the black population.
At some point the great awakening will occur whereby these false
local / national black leaders are corrupt and paid off to help keep
the black pop poor and in need.
D's formed the confederate states against freeing slaves.
D's formed the KKK.
HRC's mentor is who?
What happens if the truth about Haiti is released? Do D's lose
majority of the vote?
Through the looking glass.
They rely on the MSM to keep the narrative going but tech is
entrenching on their controls. They missed this in 2016 and
desperately attempting to censor now due to CIA cash infusions.
This will fail.

The Cabal has executed a complex plan to control people, which is most obviously with the black community. With blacks, they addicted inner city communities to welfare handouts, enacted crime-fostering policies that were soft on criminals, and then allowed highly aggressive policing strategies directed at the entire population as a whole, rather than focusing on criminals. Police targeting of criminal elements, such as illegal aliens, or the minor crimes which lead to larger crimes were suppressed. They then fostered a perception of hostilities between police and the black community, often using black celebrities, fueling angst to create police shootings which the media would then publicize, further fueling the split. The Democrats would then sell Cabal politicians to the black community, ostensibly to fight the "enemies" of the black community which they created. This was a broader strategy which Cabal enacted against all of America, and it produced the victim culture we have seen so prominently.

Remember, the FBI, and MI, have an open investigation into the CF. Why did Comey drop this? Who was the FBI director during the Haiti crisis? How many kids disappeared? How much money sent to CF under disguise of H relief went to H? What countries donated big money to CF and why? How much was owed by accepting? When she lost how would this be repaid? What did Obama do with cash just prior to leaving office? Repayment to those who donated for favors/access? Dig!!!!!
Again, good people were forced into bed with this evil under personal and family threats. Could you live with yourself helping to cover up such evil despicable acts if given a safe way out? These people worship Satan _ some openly show it.

This was the part I was not aware of. It will come out the intelligence operation targeting the nation was using tendencies to pedophilia to exert control over their assets. Later Q will imply that it may be worse than mere utility motivating the child abuse, and the Clinton Foundation (CF) is key.

Anonymous ID: Eka5Om1K No.147175452 ☐   **11**
Oct 29 2017 22:20:11 (EST)

Key:
Military Intelligence v FBI CIA NSA
No approval or congressional oversight
State Secrets upheld under SC
Who is the Commander and Chief of the military?
Under what article can the President impose MI take over investigations for the 3 letter agencies? What conditions must present itself? Why is this so VERY important? Who surrounds POTUS? They lost this very important power _ the one area of the govt not corrupt and directly serves POTUS.

In 1953 the Supreme Court ruled intel agencies could legally classify and hide secrets from the people and Congress, thereby removing all oversight from our intel agencies. That is used to hide their criminality now. We were only saved because Military Intelligence, who remained loyal to the Constitution.

Anonymous ID: Eka5Om1K No.147181191 ☐   **12**
Oct 29 2017 23:26:53 (EST)

Military Intelligence ref above is the absolute biggest inside drop this board will ever receive.
Now think about why Antifa plays right into the plan? Always ahead.
Good guys are winning.

Anonymous ID: Eka5Om1K No.147181801 ☐   **13**
Oct 29 2017 23:34:36 (EST)

Now think about the timing of POTUS traveling to China/SK. I've said too much. God bless, Patriots.

Q will later reveal the President makes a secret stopover in North Korea to seal a peace deal with Kim Jong Un.

179

Patriots.jpg

SCI[**F**]
Military Intelligence.
What is 'State Secrets' and how upheld in the SC?
What must be completed to engage MI over other (3) letter agencies?
What must occur to allow for civilian trials?
Why is this relevant?
What was Flynn's background?
Why is this relevant?
Why did Adm R (NSA) meet Trump privately w/o auth?
Does POTUS know where the bodies are buried?
Does POTUS have the goods on most bad actors?
Was TRUMP asked to run for President?
Why?
By Who?
Was HRC next in line?
Was the election suppose to be rigged?
Did good people prevent the rigging?
Why did POTUS form a panel to investigate?
Has POTUS *ever* made a statement that did not become proven as true/fact?
What is POTUS in control of?
What is the one organization left that isn't corrupt?
Why does the military play such a vital role?
Why is POTUS surrounded by highly respected generals?
Who guards former Presidents?
Why is that relevant?
Who guards HRC?
Why is ANTIFA allowed to operate?
Why hasn't the MB been classified as a terrorist org?
What happens if Soros funded operations get violent and engage in domestic terrorism?

What happens if mayors/ police comms/chiefs do not enforce the law?
What authority does POTUS have specifically over the Marines?
Why is this important?
What is Mueller's background? Military?
Was Trump asked to run for President w/ assurances made to prevent tampering?
How is POTUS always 5-steps ahead?
Who is helping POTUS?

Every law enforcement and civilian intelligence agency was compromised, so Trump could only rely on the military and Military Intelligence. The idea you could report illegality to the law enforcement, and the agency would facilitate it would sound crazy to anyone. Except there were those of us who watched Cabal engage in highly illegal targeting and harassment of civilians, tried to report it, and saw just that happen. I was standing in the parking lot of my local PD, with a sympathetic officer, as ten local surveillance vehicles made a point of driving slowly within twenty feet of us, each car with the driver's side window down, each driver (in Fed sunglasses) making a point to glare at us ominously, as the officer sympathetically tried to let me know, there wasn't anything he could do. A similar experience was actually reported in the media, when Clinton mistress Sally Miller had basically the exact same experience at her local FBI office.[150] So long as you never ran into Cabal, the illusion held, and Q would sound crazy. But run into Cabal, and you realize Q knew exactly what he was talking about. In that light, the Muslim Brotherhood (MB), a terrorist organization, or even MS-13 and other street gangs being protected by government is entirely logical.

---

150   http://archive.is/AMMaO

181

There are more good people than bad. The wizards and warlocks (inside term) will not allow another Satanic Evil POS control our country. Realize Soros, Clintons, Obama, Putin, etc. are all controlled by 3 families (the 4th was removed post Trump's victory).

11.3 - Podesta indicted
11.6 - Huma indicted

Manafort was placed into Trump's camp (as well as others). The corruption that will come out is so serious that deals must be cut for people to walk away otherwise 70% of elected politicians would be in jail (you are seeing it already begin). A deep cleaning is occurring and the prevention and defense of pure evil is occurring on a daily basis. They never thought they were going to lose control of the Presidency (not just D's) and thought they had control since making past mistakes (JFK, Reagan).

Good speed, Patriots.
PS, Soros is targeted.

What most people failed to grasp was that this was not merely a corrupt conspiracy hatched by a few people several years back, solely in the US. This was a complex intelligence operation, running certainly for decades, probably for a century, and perhaps for even longer. Such a covert operation to infiltrate and subvert, running for that long, making incremental gains all along the way in terms of taking over key positions of power, would inevitably gain this level of control. As time passed, more and more agencies which previously would have posed a threat of exposure, could be taken over and turned to actually aid and support future operations to subvert even more agencies. The rise in the level of power and control of such an operation would gradually become exponential.

Eventually, such an operation would reach a point where it would begin penetrating and taking over lower, more local offices and positions of power. What you had was an operation whose sole objective was the acquisition of power and control wherever power was found. It would advance fellow conspirators in attaining power and control using the already acquired agencies, government assets, academic assets, business assets, news media assets, media assets, cultural assets, criminal assets, control over the voting process, and so forth. It could both suppress non-conspirators and elevate fellow members of the conspiracy. After enough headway was made and enough control attained, further headway would become almost effortless to acquire. The conspiracy would then begin targeting the remaining lower-level positions of control in local politics and government. It would become as likely as not an office or position would be compromised, no matter where you went.

The biggest surprise is that people were able to keep this secret. In my own travels, I found an old family friend who lived two houses away, and who I had known since childhood, who was a knowing participant in the network, and who seemingly feared it to to such a degree he would unhesitatingly choose the network over me, with a tone of fear of his voice. I now suspect at least five percent of the populace, and maybe more, has been operating with a view that the Constitution is immaterial and nothing works the way we plebes have been told. We are told two people is one too many to keep a conspiracy secret, but what this has shown me is that one, that is wholly incorrect, and two, many of those old, common-sense idioms we are told were probably introduced to us as part of a mental programming designed to aid this conspiracy in hiding from us.

16
ct 31 2017 22:31:00 (EST)

Get the popcorn, Friday & Saturday will deliver on the MAGA
promise. POTUS knows he must clean house (gov't) in order to
'free up' and demonstrate who has authority in order to pass
important legislation. This was always the priority. Remember, AG
Sessions cannot look like an impartial player that is out to get all
former Obama team members as we need him for other important
work. All will come into focus and for anyone to think POTUS is not
in control is kidding themselves. Also, he's 100% insulated with
zero risk of impeachment (fact).

17
ct 31 2017 22:58:00 (EST)

Why does Obama travel in advance of POTUS to foreign locations?
Why is this relevant?
Focus on the power of POTUS as it relates to the Marines.
How can MI be applied to prosecute bad actors and avoid corrupt
agencies and judges?
Biggest drop on Pol.
Above is reason why the shills are sliding. In case you didn't know,
shills log and send new info back to ASF for instruction. They use a
5 prong pre packaged injection (one post auto generates four more
at random designated times). Common drive of posts they all tap
into. Since they misjudged the influence of the MSM they are
aggressively looking to censor throughout major platforms in
exchange for CIA slush funds and WW access for expansion of
said networks. Everything they do has been forecasted and
prepared for.

*Here Q begins to reference the idea Obama is performing
a sort of shadow counter-diplomacy against President Trump,
trying to prevent and/or undo what President Trump is doing to
isolate the Cabal as he travels. In the parlance of the website
where Q is posting these (known as Pol), "shills" are paid
government operatives who post on the site as if normal users,
and perform several functions. They flood the site with*

meaningless content to try and dilute content they do not want people to see (AKA "slide" a post off the board by posting so much new, meaningless content that the content they want hidden falls off the bottom of the board and is not visible). They post objectionable or illegal material such as child porn or animal torture to try and drive off people so they will not see content the shills' leaders want hidden. And they can try to poison narratives the Cabal doesn't want to take hold among the populace. Again, this sounds extreme if you have never gone to these websites the government wants to control, but if you did, this is just an accepted part of the environment. ASF is related to software they use, which allows one person to make many posts.

Anonymous ID: grTMpzrL No.147441378 ☐   **18**
Oct 31 2017 23:09:55 (EST)

Why did Mueller meet POTUS 1-day prior to FBI announcement if Mueller COULD NOT be offered director due to prev term limits rule?
Why is Pelosi begging for a new special counsel?
What is Pelosi's net worth?
How was this obtained given salary as career official?
Why is Pelosi's memory going?
Could it protect against prosecution?
How so?
What if John M's surgery was fake?
Why would this occur?
What could this prevent potentially?
What is the Mayo Clinic?
Who sits on the BOD there?

Anonymous ID: grTMpzrL No.147443190 ☐   **19**
Oct 31 2017 23:29:28 (EST)

Why do D's want to control the black pop?
Why do they intentionally keep poor and in need?
Why do D's project racism on a daily basis against R's?
Why do black elected officials do the crazy talk on behalf of D's?
How do D's cover the historical facts of forming the confederacy, KKK, and oppose all things pro black re: legislation?
What happens if D's lose the slave grip on the black pop?

185

Why do D's, through the funding of the CIA, prop up and install Hollywood/media assets?
Does this fall within Operation Mockingbird?
What were the historical advantages D's gained by having MSM and famous people peddling narrative?
Who exposed the pedo network within H wood?
You can't answer the above but will laugh once disclose details.
The network which controls this false narrative which in turns keeps the black pop under control is being dismantled.
False local and national black leaders will be exposed next as shills for the D party.
Follow the money.
Maxine W has a $4mm home and cash assets in excess of $6mm.
How is that possible? One example.
All of these questions help to paint the full picture.

BOD is Board of Directors. Now Q addresses that Hollywood may not produce stars the way we are told. We are told naive young kids go to Hollywood, and if they are pretty enough, and good enough actors, and meet the right people, they hit it big and make millions as they become a star. In the darkest versions, they may trade sex for opportunities. Q is saying that as part of the not-discontinued Operation Mockingbird, the CIA may have exerted control over who became stars, providing opportunity to their agents and controlled assets, so they could be sure nobody would attain stardom, and then one day turn around and expose the conspiracy. Again, in the old "Myth" of American opportunity and freedom, this sounds ridiculous. But if a sophisticated intelligence operation targeted America using the sophisticated art of espionage, before America had an OSS or CIA to defend it, then infiltrating agents, creating networks, and taking over the gatekeeper positions would have been easy. From that moment, even if a CIA or FBI Counter-Intelligence organization was launched, because the positions of control

186

were already occupied, it would be easy to compromise those as well from the outset, take the leadership positions, and actually use the machines that were supposed to defend us to further conceal and protect the conspiracy, as it advanced its power and control even more. Only the Military, receiving a constant torrent of idealistic young Americans who believed in the Myth, could possibly escape Cabal's grasp over the long term.

Anonymous ID: grTMpzrL No.147444335 ⬈   **20**
Oct 31 2017 23:42:00 (EST)

Who did POTUS meet with yesterday?
Was AG Sessions there?
How many MI generals were on the WH list to attend a separate meeting?
Could those meetings have been combined?
Why were certain rooms in the WH renovated?
Where was the meeting on Monday?
Why aren't phones allowed in this room (one of many).
What firm was contracted to conduct the renovations?

Anonymous ID: grTMpzrL No.147444934 ⬈   **21**
Oct 31 2017 23:48:20 (EST)

I've dumped some crumbs like this over the weekend which started the intense shilling. At this point we are far enough along you can paint the picture without risk of jeopardizing the operation.

Q is saying they have accomplished critical objectives that severed the Cabal's leadership from its hold on power, so he is now free to share information here. The Q-phenomenon appears to be designed to slowly seed awareness of these concepts, to minimize the psychological effects of them. Having been thrown into the fire suddenly myself, I can say it took me years to get beyond an overwhelming disbelief that would not accept it. If you believe in the Myth that Constitutional freedom was what governed America, it will take years to fully accept that a shadow dictatorship where the citizen literally had no power when confronted by the Secret Police, filled with corruption, and run by a Secret Society of fellow citizens who have known this secret all along, was the reality. You can see it with your own eyes, know it is all around you, and your brain will assume you are seeing things wrong, or even that you are going crazy, before it will believe what it is seeing. It takes years to adapt your brain. A normal brain would actually lack the structural ability to adapt immediately to such a shocking change in beliefs. Q is designed to blunt the negative effects of such psychological disorientation on the populace. Remember as you go, the world is Darwinian.

Anonymous ID: grTMpzrL No.147445681 ☐   **22**
ct 31 2017 23:57:15 (EST)

Who controls the NG?
Why was the NG recently activated in select cities within the US?
Can the NG work in coordination w/ the marines?
Do conditions need to be satisfied to authorize?
What former President used the military to save the republic and what occurred exactly?
Biggest drop to ever be provided on Pol. Study and prepare. The masses tend to panic in such situations. No war. No civil unrest. Clean and swift.

Anonymous ID: grTMpzrL No.147446992 ☐   **23**
ɔv 1 2017 00:11:52 (EST)

Note MI has the same SAPs as NSA, CIA etc as designated post 9-11.
Why is this relevant?
Who can be held hostage and controlled?
CIA thinks its foreign offshore assets are strong enough to defend against the US executive (not accounting for military use on domestic soil).
Why does the Constitution explicitly grant this authority to the President and what is it to prevent?
They knew our agencies would grow in power so much so they could/can hold the executive hostage or engage with bad actors.
Trump nominated someone new to direct every agency but one. He controls the top.

SAPs are Special Access Programs, highly classified intelligence programs. They can be used to gather intelligence on targets the agencies involved wanted to control. Q will frequently make reference to the fact that many members of the legislative branch were being held hostage, presumably by the compromised aspects of the CIA, at the behest of the Cabal. And it will appear this Cabal was a foreign, non-governmental operation assembled by very wealthy old-money non-US actors.

Anonymous ID: grTMpzrL No.147448408 ⬚   **24**
⬛️ov 1 2017 00:27:03 (EST)

Any person making statements they will not be seeking re-election was put in submission. For the betterment of the country not all will be prosecuted and all will do as told. You will see more of this occur (not normal yet disregarded) and even on the D side.

Anonymous ID: grTMpzrL No.147449010 ⬚   **25**
⬛️ov 1 2017 00:34:11 (EST)

Follow up to last post.
Return to comments re: Pelosi and John M (some of us refuse to say his last name for a reason).
This all has meaning - everything stated. Big picture stuff - few positions allow for this direct knowledge.

Proof to begin 11.3.
We all sincerely appreciate the work you do. Keep up the good fight. The flow of information is vital.
God bless.

So Q is predicting bad actors in Congress who were compromised and operating for Cabal have been blackmailed with the evidence of their crimes into stepping away from government. As time goes on, there will be a shocking number of such long-time political professionals who will suddenly leave thriving careers to go back into the private sector.

Anonymous ID: grTMpzrL No. 147449624 ⟶   **26**
Nov 1 2017 00:41:54 (EST)

Think about it logically.
The only way is the military. Fully controlled. Save & spread (once 11.3 verifies as 1st marker).
Biggest advanced drop on Pol.

Anonymous ID: grTMpzrL No. 147450817 ⟶   **27**
Nov 1 2017 00:56:06 (EST)

Not everything can be publicly disclosed because so much ties back to foreign heads of state. Much will be revealed, we want transparency but not at a cost we can't recover from.

Anonymous ID: grTMpzrL No. 147451052 ⟶   **28**
Nov 1 2017 00:59:01 (EST)

Anonymous ID: dugFL8Fh No. 147450119 ⟶
Nov 1 2017 00:48:01 (EST)

Spy.png

>>147441102
>What must be completed to engage MI over other (3) letter agencies
During the 1950s and 60s, federal troops and federalized National
Guard forces, accompanied by military intelligence personnel, were
deployed to help integrate Southern schools23 and to help deal with

190

civil disorders in Detroit in 1967 and other cities the following
year
after the assassination of Dr. Martin Luther King Jr.24
Throughout
this period military intelligence units also continued to collect
data on
Americans at home who were suspected of involvement in
subversive
activities.25 In the late 1960s, the Pentagon compiled personal
information on more than 100,000 politically active Americans in
an
effort to quell civil rights and anti-Vietnam War demonstrations
and
to discredit protestors.26 The Army used 1,500 plainclothes
agents to
watch demonstrations, infiltrate organizations, and spread
disinformation. 2
' According to one report, the Army had at least one
observer at every demonstration of more than twenty people.28
The Army's activities were summed up by Senator Sam Ervin:
Allegedly for the purpose of predicting and preventing
civil disturbances which might develop beyond the control of
state and local officials, Army agents were sent throughout
the country to keep surveillance over the way the civilian
population expressed their sentiments about government
policies. In churches, on campuses, in classrooms, in public
meetings, they took notes, tape-recorded, and photographed
people who dissented in thought, word, or deed. This included
clergymen, editors, public officials, and anyone who
sympathized with the dissenters.

http://digitalcommons.law.lsu.edu/cgi/viewcontent.cgi?
article=6053&context=lalrev ↗

>Hahahaha, Trump has had MI infiltrate Antifa and all the
dissenting local govts.

Always 5 steps ahead!

Please be true.

>>147450119
Well done. Picture being painted.

When you see a boxed comment in a comment, as in the last two pages (post #28), Q is replying to another anon's post. Q has a unique board ID of grTMpzrL in the header of post 28 above. He quotes another poster on his board, with a user ID of dugFL8Fh. Q only said, "Well done. Picture being painted." Note you'll see this "boxed" quoted reply format again.

Anonymous ID: grTMpzrL No.147452214 ⬈   **29**
Nov 1 2017 01:13:10 (EST)

Some things must remain classified to the very end. NK is not being run by Kim, he's an actor in the play. Who is the director? The truth would sound so outrageous most Americans would riot, revolt, reject, etc.
The pedo networks are being dismantled.
The child abductions for satanic rituals (ie Haiti and other 3rd world countries) are paused (not terminated until players in custody).
We pray every single day for God's guidance and direction as we are truly up against pure evil.

Anonymous ID: grTMpzrL No.147453147 ⬈   **30**
Nov 1 2017 01:25:22 (EST)

Would you believe a device was placed somewhere in the WH that could actually cause harm to anyone in the room and would in essence be undetected?
Fantasy right?
When Trump was elected you can't possibly imagine the steps taken prior to losing power to ensure future safety & control.
When was it reported Trump Jr dropped his SS detail?
Why would he take that huge risk given what we know?
I can hint and point but cannot give too many highly classified data points.
These keywords and questions are framed to reduce sniffer programs that continually absorb and analyze data then pushed to z terminals for eval. Think xkeysc on steroids.

Xkeyscore[151] was an NSA computer program which

---

151   http://archive.is/3iHaQ

allowed operators to enter a query and receive all data returns in multiple databases relating to it. It will later come out that Obama and the Cabal were so worried about Trump taking office and prosecuting them that they had installed a device inside the construction of the White House designed to degrade Trump's health and eventually cause him to seemingly pass away naturally due to his body wearing out. Trump had it found and removed under the cover of renovations being done. Don Jr released his security detail and relied on his known loyal security detail because there were fears an agent on his detail may have been compromised. Similarly, that concern would explain why Trump kept his private security detail operating in parallel with his Secret Service detail when he first took office. Given what I have seen firsthand, non of that seems the slightest bit odd to me. The people of the Secret Society have infiltrated everywhere.

Anonymous ID: grTMpzrL No.147454188 ⬀   **31**
Nov 1 2017 01:38:23 (EST)

World stalemate.
We all have the goods on everyone else.
That's part of the reason why some things that tie back to foreign heads of state will remain classified (not all).
We are in one of the most critical times of our country. Trump and others are working to balance the we're doing well for America (for the common person to endorse) while at the same time purify our govt and remove the bad actors who are entrenched. There is so much string pulling and blackmail that we need to cut these off to truly gain the power granted to us by the Patriots and hard working people of this great country.

Anonymous ID: grTMpzrL No.147454631 ⬀   **32**
Nov 1 2017 01:44:10 (EST)

Maybe one day but it cannot go slow. The initial wave will be fast and meaningful. It will send a signal to others immediately and you'll see the tide turn (not even the MSM can hide and rest assured some will be jailed as deep cover agents).

I'm hopeful my time spent here was not wasted.
Note few if any shills inside this thread. Reason for that. It's being
monitored, recorded, and analyzed and don't want the clutter.
Take good care. God bless.

Q Clearance Patriot

My fellow Americans, over the course of the next several days you
will undoubtedly realize that we are taking back our great country
(the land of the free) from the evil tyrants that wish to do us harm
and destroy the last remaining refuge of shining light. On POTUS'
order, we have initiated certain fail-safes that shall safeguard the
public from the primary fallout which is slated to occur 11.3 upon
the arrest announcement of Mr. Podesta (actionable 11.4).
Confirmation (to the public) of what is occurring will then be
revealed and will not be openly accepted. Public riots are being
organized in serious numbers in an effort to prevent the arrest and
capture of more senior public officials. On POTUS' order, a state of
temporary military control will be actioned and special ops carried
out. False leaks have been made to retain several within the
confines of the United States to prevent extradition and special
operator necessity. Rest assured, the safety and well-being of
every man, woman, and child of this country is being exhausted in
full. However, the atmosphere within the country will unfortunately
be divided as so many have fallen for the corrupt and evil narrative
that has long been broadcast. We will be initiating the Emergency
Broadcast System (EMS) during this time in an effort to provide a
direct message (avoiding the fake news) to all citizens.
Organizations and/or people that wish to do us harm during this
time will be met with swift fury – certain laws have been pre-lifted to
provide our great military the necessary authority to handle and
conduct these operations (at home and abroad).

*Around this time, the EMS tests did pick up. However it is
likely this was designed to alter Cabal's actions, by making it
seem things were about to happen quickly. Q is here to inform
and prepare us. But given the extent to which Cabal has*

penetrated and corrupted the county, it will take years to investigate and then prosecute. And due to the structure of Cabal's networks being designed to allow one part in government to protect and cover for another, it is necessary to remove the entire network from the system at once, so no one part can cover for another. Q appears to have a very clever way of doing this, but will take considerable time. Until then, keeping Cabal members thinking the hammer is about to drop will keep Cabal's planning dedicated to short term solutions, rather than directed at the longer-term problems they face. Some think this post may be relevant on this day in a few years, perhaps in 2020.

Anonymous ID: pGukiFmX No.147567928 **35**
Nov 1 2017 21:56:38 (EST)

POTUS will be well insulated/protected on AF1 and abroad (specific locations classified) while these operations are conducted due to the nature of the entrenchment. It is time to take back our country and make America great again. Let us salute and pray for the brave men and women in uniform who will undertake this assignment to bring forth peace, unity, and return power to the people.

It is our hope that this message reaches enough people to make a meaningful impact. We cannot yet telegraph this message through normal methods for reasons I'm sure everyone here can understand. Follow the questions from the previous thread(s) and remain calm, the primary targets are within DC and remain at the top (on both sides). The spill over in the streets will be quickly shut down. Look for more false flags – stay alert, be vigilant, and above all, please pray.

"For God so loved the world that he gave his one and only Son, that whoever believes in him shall not perish but have eternal life. Love is patient, love is kind."

God bless my fellow Americans.
4,10,20

Military Intelligence.

No media.

No leaks.

How many MI generals have been in/out of WH in the past 30 days?

Focus on Flynn.

Background and potential role.

What is the common denominator in terms of military backgrounds close to POTUS?

Why did Soros transfer the bulk of his 'public' funds to a NPO?

Why is this relevant?

Who owes a lot to very bad actors?

How can she repay as payment was made under promise of victory.

What cash payments occurred by BO during the last 90 of his Presidency to foreign states and/ or organizations?

What slush fund did AG Sessions (through DOJ) put an end to?

How does Soros, Obama, Clinton, Holder, Lynch, etc all net many millions of dollars (normally within a single tax year).

What was negotiated on the tarmac between BC and Lynch?

Remember it was expected HRC was going to win during this time period.

What if the wizards and warlocks tipped off a local reporter as to the supposed unscheduled stop?

What if the NSA under the personal direction from Adm R had this meeting miscat and logged under a false identity to prevent bad actors from locating while also verifying to said players all was clear _ no logs.

What really happened when the wizards and warlocks revealed what they had?

Was Comey forced into the spotlight shortly thereafter not by choice? Right before the election no doubt which would cast suspicion?

These are crumbs and you cannot imagine the full and complete picture.

If Trump failed, if we failed, and HRC assumed control, we as Patriots were prepared to do the unthinkable (this was leaked internally and kept the delegate recount scam and BO from declaring fraud).

Dig deeper - missing critical points to paint the full picture.
There is simply no other way than to use the military. It's that corrupt and dirty.
Please be safe and pray for those in harms way as they continually protect and serve our great country.

Again, you see the theme that all Trump can rely on is the Military. Soros was transferring his funds to NPOs - Non-Profit-Organizations presumably to try and protect them from seizure in the event of arrests. Obama sent $221 million to the Palestinians[152]. It will later be alleged that the Clinton tarmac meeting between Bill Clinton and Loretta Lynch was captured by intelligence using cell phone microphones, and that Clinton offered Lynch a guaranteed Supreme Court seat in return for her dropping any prosecution of Hillary's mishandling of classified intelligence on her private email server. Rogers miscategorizing the meeting in NSA databases implies bad actors were accessing the database and deleting anything relating to Cabal members, to protect them from the surveillance state capturing their crimes. Miscategorizing the feeds from the tarmac meeting would prevent finding (and deleting) the files. The unthinkable Q refers to would have been a full military takeover, presumably with immediate executions of politicians who had betrayed the country and a violent termination of this network.

Anonymous ID: pGukiFmX No.147581516 ☍   **37**
Nov 1 2017 23:57:23 (EST)

They are the true Patriots. We will never forget. Let these coming days be remembered in our history as the time we fought to recapture the republic from those evil bad actors who for so long have sacrificed the good people of this land for their own personal gain.
Fight the good fight.
LET JUSTICE BE SERVED.

---

152   http://archive.is/KLAjh

Four carriers & escorts in the pacific?
Why is that relevant?
To prevent other state actors from attempting to harm us during this
transition? Russia / China?
Or conversely all for NK? Or all three.
Think logically about the timing of everything happening.
Note increased military movement.
Note NG deployments starting tomorrow.
Note false flags.
Follow Huma.
Prepare messages of reassurance based on what was dropped
here to spread on different platforms.

The calm before the storm.

Would it blow your mind if I told you BO has been to NK and
perhaps there now?
Why did his administration do little to slow their nuclear and missile
capabilities?
Who feeds NK w/ strategic intel? Iran?
What deal was done with Iran under BO?
Why was the deal sealed under a top secret classification?
Why wasn't Congress notified?
Why after BO left office all of a sudden NK has nukes and the tech
to miniaturize for payload delivery within the US?
What about NSA CIA DI etc all confirming tech won't be in place for
5+ years (statements made in 2016).
Why is all of this relevant and what does it tell you?
Big picture is rare.

*This refines another paradigm-changing concept Q
introduced in post 29. Q asserts North Korea was not a hermit
kingdom ruled by a single dictator. North Korea was controlled
by Cabal. It was established as it was, complete with an actor
playing the role of a crazed dictator, to establish it as a safe,*

denied area for Cabal to maintain a base of operations in. If Cabal set up in a Westernized nation in Europe, white-hat intelligence operatives who opposed Cabal could have gotten surveillance technology close to their sensitive areas, and maybe even infiltrated them under cover identities such as a contractor or janitor. North Korea, by virtue of the cover they established there, of a hostile foreign nation which imprisoned and killed outsiders, became an entire nation operating as what is referred to as a "denied area" – an area where surveillance and intelligence operators can not gain entrance to at all. North Korea becoming a nuclear power was about securing this denied area even further against penetration – even violent, military penetration, should Cabal ever lose its grip on the US government. The implication is Barack Obama (BO) has known all of this all along, and everything you were told about North Korea was a lie.

Anonymous ID: pGukiFmX No.147588421 ☑   **40**
Nov 2 2017 01:18:35 (EST)

4,10,20
A,b,c,d,e......

If the numbers correlate to letters, the fourth, tenth, and twentieth letters of the alphabet correspond to DJT, the initials of Donald J Trump. Notice post 35 above was signed, 4, 10, 20. It implies these messages come, ultimately from the President.

Anonymous ID: pGukiFmX No.147590619 ☑   **41**
Nov 2 2017 01:47:47 (EST)

What a coincidence the mountain that housed NK's nuclear weapons and testing collapsed. Unbelievable timing. I wonder if critically important materials as well as scientists aka the bomb makers were inside when it happened. Shocking no global news agency suspects we had nothing to do with it. Enjoy the crumbs.

In the news, that collapse was attributed to "Tired Mountain Syndrome,"[153] however Q implies it was something more interesting and the Mockingbird-media is not reporting it.

Anonymous ID: pGukiFmX No.147591125 ☑   42
 ov 2 2017 01:54:29 (EST)

We serve at the pleasure of the President. DJT

So although the messages here ultimately originate with the President, and some are directly from him and signed, Q is not the President, but rather serves under him.

Anonymous ID: pGukiFmX No.147591663 ☑   43
 ov 2 2017 02:01:46 (EST)

These crumbs are not meant to scare anyone but merely inform. Resistance will be dealt with swiftly. The core focus is removing entrenched and fortified bad actors within our federal govt (past and present) as well as others. Simply be diligent - phone numbers will be provided if you witness an uprising or other domestic violence (in addition to 911). Any military seen is for your protection as well as to demonstrate our resolve. Watch for confirmations tomorrow.

Anonymous ID: pGukiFmX No.147592019 ☑   44
 ov 2 2017 02:06:41 (EST)

Before POTUS departs on Friday he will be sending an important message via Twitter. God bless.

Trump's tweets[154] were about Hillary and the DNC rigging the primary against Bernie Sanders, as well as the need for the FBI and DOJ to prosecute her for money laundering, campaign violations, her email server scandal, and the Uranium One

---

153   http://archive.is/9w1Yt
154   http://archive.is/nKgEx

scandal. Twitter also took down Trump's account for 11 minutes.

Anonymous ID: zGyR4tyi No.147632662 ☐   **45**
Nov 2 2017 11:36:31 (EST)

Follow Huma.
What just broke w/ Huma?
What did HRC instruct Huma to do re: Classified markings?
Why is this story just now coming out?
What relevance does it have?

Why is Donna running for cover?
Was a deal granted in exchange for something?
Who made the deal?
Do we care about Donna or those who instructed her to violate the law?
Why is this being leaked v. simply prosecuted privately?
Who is attempting to change the narrative and soften the acts that are forthcoming this weekend?

The story which broke with Huma was that emails were found which revealed Hillary had ordered classified materials that were restricted to official, secured government networks to have their classification markings stripped, and have them sent over unsecured, open networks to Hillary's unsecured server – a huge violation. It was later revealed that at least one foreign actor, assumed to be Chinese intelligence, installed malware on Hillary's server which was carbon-copying them on every piece of material which crossed Hillary's server. And it will be alleged this may have been allowed by Hillary in return for payment.

Donna Brazile was head of the DNC, and had a front row seat to many illegalities going on behind the scenes at the DNC. She also stated that given what she knew, she suspected the death of DNC staffer Seth Rich was not as it seemed, and she feared for her own life, staying away from windows for fear of snipers, and installing sophisticated surveillance at her house.[155]

Anonymous ID: zGyR4tyi No.147634822 ⬚   46
⬚ov 2 2017 11:57:19 (EST)

Why is the information re: BO important re: U1 and export approval
to Canada to EU?
Where is BO today?
Did BO and/or his admin ever make false statements that U1 would
never be exported from the US?
Who made those statements?
Who did they report to?
Why is this relevant?

The public has been given a select taste (i.e. sampling) - rest
assured others have it all (100% verifiable and impossible to
refute).
Why is this relevant?
Who controls the narrative?
Why are left wing organizations beginning to report on DNC/D
corruption?
Does the CIA have operators inside the MSM?
What happens if exposed?
What happens if tied back as 'knowing' to execs?
What does this have to do with 'leaking'?
What if it can be verified no sourced stories (made up) were in fact
(and approved) to be published?
The wormhole goes deep.

*This references the sale of Uranium One to Russian
interests in return for kickbacks to the Clinton Foundation, a
sale which gave Russia one fifth of America's Uranium supply.*[156]
*Q will use the phrase, "knowingly" often. The significance lies
in the Alien and Sedition Act,*[157] *where one's criminal status is
based upon whether one "knowingly" acts against the US
Government, such as when publishing false materials as news.*

---

155   http://archive.is/q8RJ1
156   http://archive.is/8rUoY
157   http://archive.is/Qyy82

You can paint the picture based solely on the questions asked.
Be vigilant today and expect a major false flag.
Does anyone find it to be a coincidence there is always a terrorist
attack when bad news breaks for the D's?
What is that called?
Military relevant how?
BO could not and would not allow the military to destroy ISIS -
why?
How was ISIS formed?
When?
How has POTUS made such progress in the short time he's been
President?
Alice & Wonderland.

This now begins to introduce the idea of ISIS as a tool
created and controlled by Cabal, serving several purposes. By
creating civil war in Syria, ISIS offered a cover story for why
mass waves of migrants heading into Europe and America had
to be accepted as refugees. No ISIS, no refugees. ISIS also
created a credible enemy who could launch timed terrorist
attacks to distract the public from uncomfortable stories which
would otherwise lead newscasts. ISIS also turned areas of Syria
into denied areas, where foreign intelligence couldn't safely
enter, loiter, and gather intelligence. It will later be revealed
Iran, compromised by Cabal in much the same way as North
Korea was, established covert nuclear weapons facilities in
Syria, allowing Iran to legally bypass restrictions in the Iran
nuclear deal. For these reasons, it is not surprising to see that
many think the CIA created ISIS[158], or that Obama was caught
on tape calling for expanding it.[159]

---

158   http://archive.is/TZxSR
159   http://archive.is/73Kts

What is Q Clearance?
What hint does that explicitly refer to?
DOE?
Who would have the goods on U1?
Does stating 'Q' refer that person works in DOE?
No.
Does it refer that someone dropping such information has the highest level of security within all departments?
Why is this relevant?

(May 2010) BO "Russia should be viewed as a friendly partner under Section 123 the Atomic Energy Act of 1954" after agreeing to a new nuclear weapons reduction deal and helping US w/ Iran.
Who is the enemy?
What is being continually stated by all D's?
Russia is what?
What did the Russia reset really provide?
Clearance/pathway to complete the U1 deal?
Why is the Canadian PM so important?
They never thought they were going to lose.
The calm before the storm.

Q clearance is the highest security clearance offered under the Department of Energy (DOE). Some thought this implied the Storm may primarily involve the Uranium One deal, and perhaps other nuclear-related matters. Uranium One was a Canadian entity, thereby requiring the leader of Canada to be a Cabal-friendly asset. Q also highlights the difference between how Obama and the Democrats portrayed Russia when they were about to engage in a criminal conspiracy to damage US national security in return for bribes, vs how Russia was portrayed after Trump had won the Presidency. It shows that the concern over Russian collusion with the Trump campaign and Russian interference in the election was fraudulent.

Anonymous ID: zGyR4tyi No.147641320 [↗]
Nov 2 2017 12:54:59 (EST)

Follow Sen Grassley.
What is different effective this week?
What do you notice?
Why does Sen Grassley (one example) have a higher than normal amount of security detail?
Why is Grassley and others held in a secure location?
When did this start?
What has been different this week?
U1 FBI informant.
Have secret sessions been underway?
How could this be discovered?
What must be reported even if filed under 'State Secrets'?
It's a name recognized around the world.
Alice & Wonderland.

Around this time Grassley, as head of the Judiciary committee had begun to investigate FBI Director James Comey's decision not to charge Hillary Clinton over her illegal email server and mishandling of classified information.[160] It will later be revealed in Clinton emails[161] that Alice is a reference to Hillary, and Wonderland is a reference to Saudi Arabia.

Anonymous ID: zGyR4tyi No.147642680 [↗]
Nov 2 2017 13:06:58 (EST)

BIG DROP:
How did NK obtain Uranium?
How did Iran obtain Uranium?
Why did BO send billions (in cash and wire) to Iran?
Why the cash component?
Was the hostage component a cover?
For what?
Could any of the cash component be handed off to other people?
How many planes carried the cash into Iran?

160   http://archive.is/Ri4Ik
161   http://archive.is/wmNah/image

Did all land in Iran?
Did all land in the same location?
Why is this relevant?
Who controls NK?
Who really controls NK?
Don't think of a single person.
Think of a powerful entity.
Why is this important?
Why are wars so important?
Who benefits?
What does hostage refer to?
Who can be held hostage and controlled by NK having miniaturized nuclear weapons?
Where is BO TODAY?
Where is VJ?
Alice & Wonderland.

Now we begin to see the outlines of a global conspiracy, a complex, sophisticated intelligence operation designed to harness the wealth and power of other nations to its own ends. In the Iran deal, Obama had pallets of cash ostensibly flown to Iran. But suppose Iran was controlled. Suppose the ultimate recipient of the cash was to be someone other than Iran. That would make sense of why the money was not simply wired into Iranian accounts. Then we find there was a goal to give North Korea miniaturized nuclear weapons as a way of holding the world hostage. VJ is Valerie Jarrett, a senior Obama adviser who was raised as a child in Iran, and whose family has long and deep ties to communism[162] (which it will be revealed appears to have been a controlled organization infiltrated, taken over, and used to control our entire political environment by an extensive conspiracy which stretches back many decades at least, if not centuries or more). VJ is Valerie Jarrett, am Obama adviser.

---

162   https://outline.com/84MnkZ0

Anonymous ID: taaOHN6t No.147642589

ov 2 2017 13:06:03 (EST)

one-nation-under-god-t-shirt_design.png

ive watched as society has been effectively addicted to msm, apps, social media, games, music, all propaganda and the moment you try to open anyone eyes. you. are. shunned. being dumbed down, weakened and groomed for passivity and stupidity through food and their addictions. like calf literally being fattened for a slaughter.

and with all the race war propaganda and pizzagate possibility, i became suicidal because i cant stand that no one will open their eyes and are being manipulated hard.

i hope with all of my heart that Trump is going to make good on his promise to maga and clean the swamp. ive been thinking about joining the navy for corpsman greenside, and i would love to serve under a Trump administration if he really does clean swamp, (will try to join regardless no openings for corpsman right now though). I hope that what OPanon says is true. i will be praying for OPanon and all who risk their lives, for safety and that the Lord will guide them. and praying that what he says is true. and will be praying for the spiritual edification of God for Trump and for his complete safety in all of this. The pieces are coming together for me. and if this is true, those working with him are absolute geniuses because i would have never imagined their would be any way possible to take the monster of corruption that has overtaken this country.

>>147642589
Dear Patriot.
We hear you.
We hear all Americans such as yourself.
The time has come to take back our great land.
The time is now.
Rest assured POTUS is backed by the absolute finest people alive who are all dedicated to the eradication evil and corruption from the US/World.
Find peace.
God is with us.
God bless and be safe.
-The WH

Notice again, the box-within-a-box format which indicates Q (as "Anonymous), is responding to another anon's comment. This also makes reference to the Pizzagate pedophilia scandal, where anon's noticed strange phrases in John Podesta's hacked emails. They seemed to use strange codes, like one which notified John that after a party they had discovered a napkin that had a "pizza related" "map" on it.[163] Anons began digging into the emails and the people involved, and discovered disturbing evidence,[164] from emails exhorting attendance at parties based on how many young children in bathing suits would be in the pool, to associates of Podesta who had businesses that used FBI-identified pedophile symbols in

163   http://archive.is/eGJnL
164   http://archive.is/TaRBU

business literature. It all left researchers with the impression that either there were a lot of adults in prominent positions of power who routinely interspersed coded messages with jokes, double entendres, and even covert symbols related to pedophilia, or there was an actual pedophile network embedded in the upper echelons of power.

Q would later indicate a propensity for child abuse was how many leaders and celebrities were selected by the Cabal, because such a vulnerability made them more subservient and controllable. The implication being that this practical aspect of running a blackmailable network was also the reason there had been so many pedophile networks which were almost uncovered, from the Catholic Church, to media[165], to upper levels of European Government[166], and even the CIA[167], and yet those investigations would all ultimately peter out with few if any major players targeted.

Q will take the allegations a step further, indicating that many of those in high levels of power may practice occult ceremonies which involve abuse or even murder of children, likely at the encouragement of a Cabal leadership which can use the resulting events for blackmail. John Podesta's lobbyist brother Tony Podesta actually proudly displays artwork in his home seemingly depicting some form of ritualized child abuse[168] which is disturbing to look upon, at the least.

---

165   http://archive.is/88IqC
166   http://archive.is/9Io6e
          http://archive.is/pVirE
167   http://archive.is/0Ws1Q/image
168   http://archive.is/3HsIh

Review BO's financial disclosure when he submitted pre-D election campaign.
What is the annual salary of a sitting US President?
What home(s) were just purchased by BO?
How much did it cost?
How does it reconcile?
What is the net worth of Pelosi?
How does it reconcile?
What is the John M Institute?
Notice any patterns relating to the CF?
Where did John M obtain his surgery?
Why is that relevant?
What surgery did he supposedly have?
How many days until he was back in Congress and sitting on the OS comm?
What is John M's net worth?
How does it reconcile?
What is MW's net worth?
How does it reconcile?
You can play this game with most D's and many R's.
What does swamp refer to?
What does money buy?
Alice & Wonderland.

BO is Barack Obama, CF is Clinton Foundation, John M is John McCain. OS comm is The House Oversight Committee. MW is Congresswoman Maxine Waters. Q's saying you will find politicians take office, and then routinely acquire net worths far greater than they could ever have acquired off their government salaries. Clearly they take office, and then acquire additional sources of income from somewhere which are not available to others, and which dwarf their government salaries. Q will maintain that each of their foundations is a money laundering instrument, which allows them to be paid money as charity, which they can then route to relatives in return for "services."

Nov 2 2017 13:36:25 (EST)

List out all who have foundations.
Why is this relevant?
How can donations be used personally?
Analyze the filings.
Who is charged w/ overseeing this?
IRS?
Corrupt?
Politically motivated?
The level of corruption in our country (and most others) is so severe there is ONLY ONE WAY.
Alice & Wonderland.

Basically many of these politicians set up charitable foundations such as the Clinton Foundation. People who want things from government launder the bribes by contributing them to the charities, and then they either arrange family business and travel in such a way the charity will defray their personal costs, or they structure the charity's expenditures to seemingly expend the money on charity, but in reality the money is routed back to them in secret accounts in return for a cut of the largess.

Nov 2 2017 13:39:41 (EST)

"For I know the plans I have for you," declares the LORD, "plans to prosper you and not to harm you, plans to give you hope and a future."

Nov 2 2017 13:44:21 (EST)

Look to Twitter:
Exactly this: "My fellow Americans, the Storm is upon us......."
God bless.

211

http://thehill.com/blogs/pundits-blog/presidential-campaign/292310-huma-abedins-ties-to-the-muslim-brotherhood ☑

The Clinton campaign is attempting once again to sweep important questions under the rug about top aide Huma Abedin, her family ties to the Muslim Brotherhood and to Saudi Arabia, and her role in the ballooning Clinton email scandal.

Her mother, Saleha Abedin, sits on the Presidency Staff Council of the International Islamic Council for Da'wa and Relief, a group that is chaired by the leader of the Muslim Brotherhood, Sheikh Yusuf al-Qaradawi.

Perhaps recognizing how offensive such ties will be to voters concerned over future terrorist attacks on this country by radical Muslims professing allegiance to Sharia law, the Clinton campaign on Monday tried to downplay Ms. Abedin's involvement in the Journal and the Muslim Brotherhood.

The Clinton surrogate group Media Matters claimed predictably there was "no evidence" that Ms. Abedin or her family had ties to the Muslim Brotherhood, and that Trump campaign staffers who spoke of these ties were conspiracy theorists.

To debunk the evidence, Media Matters pointed to a Snopes.com "fact-check" piece that cited as its sole source... Senator John McCain. This is the same John McCain who met Libyan militia leader Abdelkarim Belhaj, a known al Qaeda associate, and saluted him as "my hero" during a 2011 visit to Benghazi.

Here Q introduces a theme you will see again and again. Seemingly disparate organizations, operating at cross purposes will exhibit a discomfiting familiarity with each other. Hillary should have worried Huma might be a spy for the Muslim Brotherhood. John McCain should have opposed Hillary Clinton and Huma Abedin. But they don't. Wherever there was power and influence, Cabal infiltrated and took the operation over. You could not form an honest interest group, and be successful without your operation becoming a target itself. As a result, all of those you see in power, even where they supposedly oppose each other, are all employees of subsidiaries of the same greater organization – Cabal, Inc.

Hillary trusts Huma because they work for the same ultimate boss. John McCain will rush to both of their defenses because they are valued fellow employees and he knows it will get him in good with Management. You will see this again, and it will get weirder, to the point Google Founder Erik Schmidt will be in North Korea setting up private internet servers and Edward Snowden will go from anti-government hero to evil Cabal-lacky trying to help take down the one organization which was standing up to Cabal. As you begin to see Cabal, you will see it changes everything, because it was the hidden hand everywhere.

Anonymous ID: KC17sSpZ No.147661243 ☐   **57**
Nov 2 2017 15:39:38 (EST)

Senator McCain and others roundly criticized Rep. Michele Bachmann in 2012 when she and four members of the House Permanent Select Committee Intelligence and the House Judiciary Committee cited Ms. Abedin in letters sent to the Inspectors General of the Department of Defense, Department of State, Department of Justice, Department of Homeland Security, and the Office of the Director of National Intelligence, warning about Muslim Brotherhood infiltration of the United States government.

Why is this relevant?
Who took an undisclosed trip to SA?
What was the purpose of a f2f v phone call?
Alice & Wonderland.

Again, why is John McCain standing up for the Muslim Brotherhood, and opposing Michelle Bachman (who is not a Cabal employee)? The associations you thought you knew were all wrong, because you didn't grasp that one organization might see it advantageous to co-opt and control all the sides at the same time. Q's next post is a reiteration of these past two, for emphasis, linked with one as a reply to the other.

Anonymous ID: KC17sSpZ No.147661332 ⊡   **58**
Nov 2 2017 15:40:27 (EST)

Anonymous ID: KC17sSpZ No.147661217 ⊡
Nov 2 2017 15:39:22 (EST)

http://thehill.com/blogs/pundits-blog/presidential-campaign/292310-huma-abedins-ties-to-the-muslim-brotherhood ⊡ 🗎
The Clinton campaign is attempting once again to sweep important questions under the rug about top aide Huma Abedin, her family ties to the Muslim Brotherhood and to Saudi Arabia, and her role in the ballooning Clinton email scandal.
Her mother, Saleha Abedin, sits on the Presidency Staff Council of the International Islamic Council for Da'wa and Relief, a group that is chaired by the leader of the Muslim Brotherhood, Sheikh Yusuf al-Qaradawi.

Perhaps recognizing how offensive such ties will be to voters concerned over future terrorist attacks on this country by radical Muslims professing allegiance to Sharia law, the Clinton campaign on Monday tried to downplay Ms. Abedin's involvement in the Journal and the Muslim Brotherhood.

The Clinton surrogate group Media Matters claimed predictably there was "no evidence" that Ms. Abedin or her family had ties to the Muslim Brotherhood, and that Trump campaign staffers who spoke of these ties were conspiracy theorists.

To debunk the evidence, Media Matters pointed to a Snopes.com "fact-check" piece that cited as its sole source… Senator John McCain. This is the same John McCain who met Libyan militia leader Abdelkarim Belhaj, a known al Qaeda associate, and saluted him as "my hero" during a 2011 visit to Benghazi.

>>147661217Senator McCain and others roundly criticized Rep. Michele Bachmann in 2012 when she and four members of the House Permanent Select Committee Intelligence and the House Judiciary Committee cited Ms. Abedin in letters sent to the Inspectors General of the Department of Defense, Department of State, Department of Justice, Department of Homeland Security, and the Office of the Director of National Intelligence, warning about Muslim Brotherhood infiltration of the United States government.

Why is this relevant?
Who took an undisclosed trip to SA?
What was the purpose of a f2f v phone call?
Alice & Wonderland.

Anonymous ID: KC17sSpZ No.147664082 ⌐   **59**
Nov 2 2017 16:04:05 (EST)

How did SA welcome POTUS during his trip?
Why was this historic and not covered by MSM?
How did SA welcome BO during his trip?
How did SA welcome HRC during her trip?
Why is this relevant?
Not suggesting SA is clean by any means but they play a role in this global game of RISK.

Combine all posts and analyze.
The questions provide answers.
Remember, information is everything, the flow of information is no longer controlled by the MSM but by you/others.
Hence, why we are dedicating 'critical' time to distribute crumbs which can be followed in greater detail to paint the entire picture once more information is released.
Why has POTUS dedicated so much time into labeling the MSM as fake news?
Why is this relevant?
We are fully prepared that all social media will be shut down to prevent the spread of this information (i.e. POTUS' Twitter etc. and/or mass censoring).
Sealed Federal orders pre-submitted as prevention and masked as 'in general' (though that does not account for rogue agents/programmers within).
Dates (impending actions) are deliberately provided for authenticity.
Alice & Wonderland.

Now we come to Saudi Arabia (SA). The story which will emerge from the Main Stream Media (MSM) is that President Trump traveled to Saudi Arabia and made a deal with Crown Prince Salman. The US would offer intelligence to help him neutralize bad actors and place him in charge of Saudi Arabia, as well as economic help. In return, he would neutralize the elements in Saudi Arabia who were running Cabal money through their bank accounts, helping to prevent any tracking of it. President Trump was greeted with a traditional Saudi Sword Dance, which is normally performed before warriors enter into battle together. It implied Trump and the Prince were about to enter into a battle together. After Trump strikes this deal, evidence will emerge in the media of known Cabal actors scrambling to acquire operating funds by selling off assets.

Anonymous ID: WBXFv1gl No.147679416 ☐ **60**
Nov 2 2017 18:03:36 (EST)

You can count the people who have the full picture on two hands.
Of those (less than 10 people) only three are non-military.
Why is this relevant?
Game theory.
Outside of a potential operator who has been dialed-in w/ orders (specific to his/her mission) nobody else has this information.
Operators never divulge.
Alice & Wonderland.

Anonymous ID: WBXFv1gl No.147680054 ☐ **61**
Nov 2 2017 18:07:54 (EST)

Please refer back and collect my crumbs.
As discussed, we've anticipated the Twitter and other social media blackouts.
Rogue agents/programmers.
Per sealed Federal orders, we quickly tracked and reinstated.
Expect outages periodically (infiltrated).
If this doesn't signal what I've been saying I don't know what will.
Q

Anonymous ID: WBXFv1gl No. 147680749 ☐   **62**
☐ov 2 2017 18:12:48 (EST)

Highly recommend someone take all my crumbs and put into a
massive dump (a single shot). This will be considered the biggest
'inside' 'approved' dump in American history.
They are beginning to understand as Podesta's attorney was just
notified.
All my dumps are being recorded but again it doesn't matter.
Alice & Wonderland.

WHERE IS BO TODAY?!?!?

Anonymous ID: WBXFv1gl No. 147681912 ☐   **63**
☐ov 2 2017 18:21:32 (EST)

To those watching (you know who you are):
You have a choice to make.
You can stand up and do what you know to be right.
Or you can suffer the consequences of your previous actions.
Make no mistake, you are on the losing side.
The choice is yours.
If you decide to take down /pol/ and the net we will be ready.

4920-a 293883 zAj-1 0020192
Alice & Wonderland.

Anonymous ID: WBXFv1gl No. 147683156 ☐   **64**
☐ov 2 2017 18:31:24 (EST)

Fellow Patriots,
I'm being advised actions have created accelerated counter-
actions.
We have not yet ascertained the scope of the attack.
Watch the news outlets.
POTUS' Twitter take down was not by accident (as referenced
several hours ago).
Should the lights go out please know we are in control.
Do not panic.
We are prepared and assets are in place.
God bless - I must go for good at this point.
Q

Anonymous ID: WBXFv1gl No.147687684 ☑   **65**
🔲v 2 2017 19:07:18 (EST)

:::::Flash Traffic:::::
Three letter agency embedded tracking/up-channel into POTUS'
Twitter to specifically target through specialized geo and send his
location.
We anticipated this (see post a few hours ago).
It has begun.
Perhaps more posts to follow as expected imminent departure.
Q

This was thought to mean CIA had embedded something in POTUS' twitter app designed to geolocate his phone so he could be either monitored through the location of his twitter phone, or perhaps even targeted, such as knowing which decoy limo he was traveling in.

Anonymous ID: WBXFv1gl No.147689362 ☑   **66**
🔲v 2 2017 19:19:28 (EST)

> **Anonymous** ID: VXi4Bx/o No.147688276 ☑
> 🔲v 2 2017 19:11:43 (EST)
>
> >>147687684
> Let's be clear - you're telling us POTUS is currently under attack
> by our own intelligence agencies?

>>147688276
Let's be real clear.
The CIA just attacked the Command and Chief which was
immediately detected by NSA/MI and alerted to POTUS.
Re-review all my crumbs including today/yesterday/weekend.
What does this mean?
What actions are immediately occurring?
If this leaks, or the immediate action ongoing at Langley, you'll have
your verification ahead of schedule.
Q

NSA/MI is National Security Agency/Military Intelligence.

Where is John Podesta?
Where is Tony Podesta?
Did one or both escape the country and was let out?
WHERE IS BO?
WHERE WAS BO YESTERDAY?
What is the difference between commercial and private re: security clearance for departure?
Who is the TSA head?
Which party did he contribute to?
What is of particular interest when researching?
How does HS interact w/ TSA?
What updated post 9-11 protocols were put in place to prevent/stop inbound/outbound C-level targets?
What local airports are in close proximity to DC?
What happened shortly after 9-11 (specifically with all aircraft)?
Who was authorized to depart? ONLY 1 PLANE was authorized during this 'mandatory forced grounding'.
Who SPECIFICALLY authorized this?
What airport did the departure take place at?
Why is this relevant?
How does it tie together?
Podesta's plane has military escort (i.e. tag) and is being diverted (forced down).
Short delay.
This will be leaked.
Watch the news.
Have faith.
What fake news anchor will not be on air tonight?
Why is this relevant?
What was stated in the past?
Where did the $18b from Soros go?
Why?
Can it be used by bad actors (escape, bribes, rogue contractors, etc.)?
Slush fund?
Did the US gov't seize/stop/track other slush funds that prevent or create risk to operate?
Why did JK travel to SA recently?
What is SA known for?

Where do the biggest donations originate from?
Why is this relevant?
What else is relevant w/ SA?
Safe harbor?
Port of transfer?
Why was there a recent smear campaign against JK and POTUS?
Why is the timing important?
Who released the article?
The council of Wizards & Warlocks cannot be defeated.
Nice view up here.
Q

BO is Barack Obama, who is shadowing President Trump's travels at this point in events. You will see similar behavior by John Kerry. This will eventually be referred to as shadow diplomacy in one article, and attributed to Obama trying to counter the effects of Trump on the world stage. But according to Q what is really happening is Obama is trying to assess what Trump has done at each diplomatic stop overseas and then organize and marshal resistance among old allies in those nations to thwart the operation which Trump is carrying out against the Cabal. TSA is Transportation Security Administration and HS is Homeland Security. JK in this post is Jared Kushner, and SA is Saudi Arabia, where he traveled before this post. Expect periodic disinformation in Q posts, given they are read by enemies.

Anonymous ID: GVUvg1M7 No.147817468 ☐   **68**
Nov 3 2017 16:38:03 (EST)

What data just dropped?
Why is this relevant?
HUMA.
HUMA.
HUMA.
Where is HUMA?
Who is HUMA connected to?
What organization?

What is HUMA's family history?
How did HUMA meet HRC?
What did HRC say about HUMA that demonstrates how close they are?
Why are D's dropping HRC all of a sudden?
Were deals made w/ select D's?
Can we expose every crooked politician?
70%.
HUMA.
Follow HUMA.
Alice & Wonderland.

Huma's family is Muslim Brotherhood, an influence organization which would almost certainly be Cabal. She met Hillary as an intern in the Clinton White House in 1996. Such internships will be given preferentially to those in the Cabal's Secret Society, which is probably why Hillary latched onto her with so little worry. Democrats were distancing themselves from Hillary because they are realizing her mishandling of classified information means Trump's administration has the goods, and she is a goner. It is only a matter of when.

Anonymous ID: GVUvg1M7 No.147819733 ☐   **69**
Nov 3 2017 16:56:13 (EST)

God speed to those who will be put in harms way. You are the bravest men and women on earth.
We will never forget.
All share one title in common and that is the title of "Hero."
"The LORD is my shepherd, I lack nothing. He makes me lie down in green pastures, he leads me beside quiet waters, he refreshes my soul. He guides me along the right paths for his name's sake. Even though I walk through the darkest valley, I will fear no evil, for you are with me; your rod and your staff, they comfort me. You prepare a table before me in the presence of my enemies. You anoint my head with oil; my cup overflows. Surely your goodness and love will follow me all the days of my life, and I will dwell in the house of the LORD forever."

[Repost]
Why did JK travel to SA recently?
What is SA known for?
Where do the biggest donations originate from?
Why is this relevant?
What else is relevant w/ SA?
Safe harbor?
Port of transfer?
Why was there a recent smear campaign against JK and POTUS?
Why is the timing important?

Martial law declared in SA.
Why is this relevant?
How much money was donated to CF by SA?
How much money was donated to John M Institute by SA?
How much money was donated to Pelosi Foundation?
How much money was donated to CS by SA?
What other bad actors have been paid by SA (bribed)(Not just D's)?
Why did the Bush family recently come out against POTUS?
Who is good?
What are the laws in SA v. US (charged criminals)?
What information might be gained by these detainees?
Why is this important?
SA ---> US
What force is actively deployed in SA?
NG?
Have faith.
These, the crumbs, in time, will equate to the biggest drops ever disclosed in our history.
Remember, disinformation is real.
God bless.
Alice & Wonderland.
The Great Awakening.
Q

Saudi Arabia was investing in such disparate entities as leftist academic endeavors and Fox News. It was rumored to have funded the 9/11 attacks and other terrorist endeavors, as well as Barack Obama's early educational ascendance. I had dismissed these observations as merely a rich entity with too much money to waste blowing it on public relations campaigns and espionage-skulduggery. But then I had begun to meet up with the conspiracy in my own life, and realized something bigger was at play in the world.

The relation between these expenditures and Saudi interests defied easy explanation, until Q. Q revealed that ultra-wealthy individuals were exerting financial pressure over multiple sectors of Western society to control events, but they were doing so from behind financial-proxies, so as to conceal their identities and financial activities. These were people who did not want their activities known. If the Rothschilds (estimated as being worth in excess of $2 trillion[169]), were to try and engage in these activities openly, it could be publicized. People might object to such interference. But notice, you cannot tell me what causes the Rothschild have ever contributed to.

Their solution was laundering the expenditures, and for this the Cabal which Q is describing appears to have commingled their funds with those of other ultra-rich entities and nation-states, such as the Kingdom of Saudi Arabia, Iran, North Korea, and perhaps Venezuela and Cuba as well. In addition, they appear to have utilized ultra-wealthy individuals, such as Jeffrey Epstein, seemingly hiring people to play the part of wealthy billionaire, for the express purpose of hiding the elite's financial activities in politics and intelligence operations.

What Q describes here was Crown Prince Mohamed Bin Salman basically holding an economic conference in a big convention center. All of Saudi Arabia's major financial

---

169   http://archive.is/UhLdN

223

powerhouses attended. Once they were present, private military contractors swooped in, slammed the doors shut on the convention center, and all of these wealthy Saudis who had acted as Cabal money-managers were taken to hotel rooms and forced to reveal access to their finances, some while under duress.

Since Cabal commingled their funds with those of these Saudis, Cabal's funds were all effectively seized by the Saudi government with no legal recourse. By choosing an environment with lax financial laws and an all powerful government they previously controlled, to facilitate hiding their illicit activities, they opened themselves up to losing all of the very wealth they needed to operate. So, Trump was greeted with a sword dance which precedes allies entering battle, and then this happened.

Anonymous ID: s4Iv8TW8 No.147979863 **71**
Nov 4 2017 18:33:30 (EST)

Follow HUMA.
Who connects HRC/CF to SA?
Why is this relevant?
Who is the Muslim Brotherhood?
Who has ties to the MB?
Who is Awan?
What is the Awan Group?
Where do they have offices?
Why is this relevant?
Define cash laundering.
What is the relationship between SA & Pakistan?
Why is this relevant?
Why would SA provide tens of millions of dollars to US senior gov't officials?
What does SA obtain in exchange for payment?
Why is access important?
What happened when HRC lost the election of 2016?
How much money was provided to the CF by SA during 15/16?
HRC lost.
Loss of access/power/control.

Does repayment of funds to SA occur? If so, how?
Why did BO send billions in cash to Iran?
Why wasn't Congress notified?
Why was this classified under 'State Secrets'?
Who has access to 'State Secrets'?
Where did the planes carrying the cash depart from and land?
Did the planes all land in the same location?
How many planes carried the cash?
Why is this relevant?
What does this have to do w/ NK?
What does this have to do w/ SA/CF cash donations?
What does this have to do w/ ISIS?
What does this have to do w/ slush funds?
Why is SA so vitally important?
Follow the money.
Who has the money?
What is happening in SA today?
Why is this relevant?
Who was Abdullah bin Abdulaziz?
What events transpired directly thereafter?
How was POTUS greeted compared to other former US President's when in SA?
Why is this relevant?
What is the meaning of this tradition?
What coincidentally was the last Tweet sent out by POTUS?
Why is this relevant?
Was that an instruction of some kind?
To who?
Why is this relevant?
Where was POTUS when that Tweet was sent?
Why is that relevant?
What attack took place in SA as operations were undertaken?
Flying objects.
What US operators are currently in SA?
Why is this relevant?
Questions provide answers.
Alice & Wonderland.

Huma Abedin, Hillary's assistant, grew up in Saudi Arabia. As a foreign national growing up in Saudi Arabia, it was likely she would have been observed and assessed, and maybe even approached by the Saudis to act as an agent. Her familial ties to the Muslim Brotherhood would have linked her to both the region, and a likelihood of some intelligence involvement.

Given Hillary had close ties with Saudi Arabia through donations to the Clinton Foundation, Huma appears to be one more element of the linkage. I originally thought Huma might have been sent in to compromise and turn Hillary, but in light of Q's revelations it now seems more likely they were all employees of the same employer. Enter Imran Awan, a Muslim congressional computer tech who used his position in Congress to spy on everything Congress was doing, sending sensitive intelligence to the Muslim Brotherhood.

Again, in the environment of Cabal you have to view everything in the context of the Falsity of Intelligence Parity. Intel operations corrupt, and merge. When you have a long-term intelligence operation in an environment, the probability of any organization being uncorrupted decreases exponentially as time goes on. This is because as that long-term operation corrupts each successive organization, its resources and ability to corrupt future organizations grows exponentially. At this point, whether you are talking the Kingdom of Saudi Arabia, the Muslim Brotherhood, the American government, the FBI, the CIA, the American Civil Liberties Union, MSNBC, CNN, or politics, it will all be infiltrated, turned, and under control.

So when Hillary exerts influence over the Democrat Party to facilitate a Muslim Brotherhood spy to gather intelligence in Congress, and then Saudi Arabia funnels millions of dollars into The Clinton Foundation which she controls, those are not all separate entities you should expect to work at cross purposes. If each individual entity has power and influence, it is not at all impossible that over the preceding decades Cabal-loyal agents were given intelligence support in infiltrating and corrupting each organization, other organizations that were uncorrupted were suppressed and went defunct, and everything you see is ultimately a subsidiary of a larger hidden umbrella organization.

Here, the theory Q is promoting seems to be that Hillary facilitates spying by a Muslim Brotherhood asset. That Muslim Brotherhood asset funnels his intelligence back to the Muslim Brotherhood[170] (which Cabal is piggybacking, and receiving the intelligence from). Then Cabal facilitates payment to Hillary's Foundation via unofficial "bankers" in Saudi Arabia.

Military Intelligence in the US, the last bastion of idealistic Americans who still believed in the Myth, had seen all of this and decided to destroy it. They recruited Trump into their plan, and together they began dismantling Cabal with a detailed plan. It began with disconnecting Cabal from its money supply in Saudi bank accounts. Operators from US Security Contractor Blackwater, whose founder Erik Prince has close ties to President Trump,[171] took part in the Saudi purge and subsequent interrogations.[172] Now Q is beginning a slow reveal of this, to minimize the shock which will ensue when people realize how close we came to losing our country and our freedoms.

It sounds incredible, but you have to understand, you have been told all your life that the world is not Darwinian. Powerful agencies would never try to seize total power through

---

170   http://archive.is/Ll5mV
171   http://archive.is/B71Zy
172   http://archive.is/LZSGo

underhanded means like espionage and conspiracies. You have been told conspiracies never happen. You have been told there are many actors, all at cross purposes, and they would never work together, let alone hide each other's secrets.

All of that is false. The very world is Darwinian. People conspire all the time. Among the ultra-rich, principle is for suckers. And intelligence operations aggregate over time, just as gravity accretes space dust into solar systems, galaxies, and eventually black holes. Intelligence operations are designed to corrupt other organizations, naturally tending toward a world where one intelligence operation will dominate the environment nearly entirely. In light of those realities, all of the evidence Q puts forth will look much, much different. The world we were taught exists violates natural laws. It cannot exist. The world Q is describing matches natural law completely. It exists.

In the next post, we again have a citizen posting first in the darker box, and Q responding afterward on how the Saudi takedown was a bigger story than anyone realizes:

Anonymous ID: s4lv8TW8 No.147981354 ⌐   **72**
▮▯v 4 2017 18:44:06 (EST)

Anonymous ID: GE433ksq No.147977181 ⌐
▮▯v 4 2017 18:13:27 (EST)

WAIT
WAIT
WAIT

GO BACK TO THE POST ABOUT THE FAMILES THAT RUN
EVERYTHING AND TRUMP TAKING ONE OUT

WAS ONE OF THEM THIS SAUDI FAMILY

SERIOUSLY

BECAUSE THAT MAKES THIS A HAPPENING

I Remember the phrasing not making sense, I was like "oh does
he mean that dt took out the Clintons?" But the Clintons were
on the list as remaining so I didn't know who was taken out

>>147977181
Very smart, Anon.
Disinformation is real.
Distractions are necessary.
SA is the primary, US is secondary, (Asia/EU)...
Alice & Wonderland.
Q

Anonymous ID AZhJ37bn No 147986661 ☐   **73**
Nov 4 2017 19:22:08 (EST)

What was POTUS' last Tweet (prior to)?
To who was it addressed?
When was POTUS' Twitter taken down?
Why is this relevant?
What was POTUS' last Tweet (prior to)?
Who was it addressed to specifically?
When was POTUS' Twitter taken down?
Has this ever happened before?
Why now?
Coincidence?
How many times did the attack occur (secondary clean up)?
What is the purpose of tracking?
What is the purpose of disruption?
Why did POTUS have military guards (uniform) while in HI?
Why is this relevant?
Do military guards (uniform) typically assist the USSS?
Why is this relevant?
What flying object was recently shot down?
Why is this relevant?
How precise is geo tracking (non-public c-level pro)?
Why is this relevant?
Alice & Wonderland.
Q

The last tweet he sent spoke of sending a New York terrorist to Guantanamo. Hillary is from New York, and Q will imply that the Cabal operatives at her level will be going to Guantanamo. Earlier Q said CIA embedded a tracking program in a social media device POTUS used, possibly for an attack, possibly for determining his activity. This was why POTUS augmented his security with military guards.

Anonymous ID: AZhJ37bn No.147987614 🗗   **74**
⬛v 4 2017 19:28:58 (EST)

Q = Alice
You'll soon understand the meaning behind Alice "&" Wonderland.
Everything has meaning.
God bless.
Q

These following posts, (posts 75-79) were reposts of what you just read. They had been deleted on the board. There is an image at the end which is just a picture of all these posts.

Anonymous ID: v3eCc2tY No.148016618 🗗   **75**
⬛v 4 2017 23:14:37 (EST)

AMER_PAT.jpg   ⬇

By the time POTUS returns from his trip the world will be a different place.

Godfather III
Alice & Wonderland
Alice (Lewis Carroll) =
The Bloody Wonderland =

[Repost]
Why did JK travel to SA recently?
What is SA known for?
Where do the biggest donations originate from?
Why is this relevant?
What else is relevant w/ SA?
Safe harbor?
Port of transfer?
Why was there a recent smear campaign against JK and POTUS?
Why is the timing important?

Anonymous ID: v3eCc2tY No.148016670 [↗]   **76**
Nov 4 2017 23:15:02 (EST)

[Repost Lost]
Martial law declared in SA.
Why is this relevant?
How much money was donated to CF by SA?
How much money was donated to John M Institute by SA?
How much money was donated to Pelosi Foundation?
How much money was donated to CS by SA?
What other bad actors have been paid by SA (bribed)(Not just D's)?
Why did the Bush family recently come out against POTUS?
Who is good?
What are the laws in SA v. US (charged criminals)?
What information might be gained by these detainees?
Why is this important?
SA ---> US
What force is actively deployed in SA?
NG?
Have faith.
These, the crumbs, in time, will equate to the biggest drops ever
disclosed in our history.
Remember, disinformation is real.
God bless.
Alice & Wonderland.
The Great Awakening.
Q

[Repost Lost]
Follow HUMA.
Who connects HRC/CF to SA?
Why is this relevant?
Who is the Muslim Brotherhood?
Who has ties to the MB?
Who is Awan?
What is the Awan Group?
Where do they have offices?
Why is this relevant?
Define cash laundering.
What is the relationship between SA & Pakistan?
Why is this relevant?
Why would SA provide tens of millions of dollars to US senior gov't officials?
What does SA obtain in exchange for payment?
Why is access important?
What happened when HRC lost the election of 2016?
How much money was provided to the CF by SA during 15/16?
HRC lost.
Loss of access/power/control.
Does repayment of funds to SA occur? If so, how?
Why did BO send billions in cash to Iran?
Why wasn't Congress notified?
Why was this classified under 'State Secrets'?
Who has access to 'State Secrets'?
Where did the planes carrying the cash depart from and land?
Did the planes all land in the same location?
How many planes carried the cash?
Why is this relevant?
What does this have to do w/ NK?
What does this have to do w/ SA/CF cash donations?
What does this have to do w/ ISIS?
What does this have to do w/ slush funds?
Why is SA so vitally important?
Follow the money.
Who has the money?
What is happening in SA today?
Why is this relevant?
Who was Abdullah bin Abdulaziz?

What events transpired directly thereafter?
How was POTUS greeted compared to other former US President's when in SA?
Why is this relevant?
What is the meaning of this tradition?
What coincidentally was the last Tweet sent out by POTUS?
Why is this relevant?
Was that an instruction of some kind?
To who?
Why is this relevant?
Where was POTUS when that Tweet was sent?
Why is that relevant?
What attack took place in SA as operations were undertaken?
Flying objects.
What US operators are currently in SA?
Why is this relevant?
Questions provide answers.
Alice & Wonderland.

Anonymous ID: v3eCc2tY No.148016769 ☐   **78**
Nov 4 2017 23:15:52 (EST)

[Repost Lost]
Disinformation is real.
Distractions are necessary.
SA is the primary, US is secondary, (Asia/EU)...
Alice & Wonderland.
Q

[Repost Lost]
What was POTUS' last Tweet (prior to)?
To who was it addressed?
When was POTUS' Twitter taken down?
Why is this relevant?
What was POTUS' last Tweet (prior to)?
Who was it addressed to specifically?
When was POTUS' Twitter taken down?
Has this ever happened before?
Why now?
Coincidence?
How many times did the attack occur (secondary clean up)?
What is the purpose of tracking?
What is the purpose of disruption?

Why did POTUS have military guards (uniform) while in HI?
Why is this relevant?
Do military guards (uniform) typically assist the USSS?
Why is this relevant?
What flying object was recently shot down?
Why is this relevant?
How precise is geo tracking (non-public c-level pro)?
Why is this relevant?
Alice & Wonderland.
Q

[Repost Lost]
Q = Alice
You'll soon understand the meaning behind Alice "&" Wonderland.
Everything has meaning.
God bless.
Q

Anonymous ID: v3eCc2tY No.148016876 **79**
Nov 4 2017 23:16:50 (EST)

1509840715226.png

Graphic is right.
Add above points to graphic.
Stay organized.
Q

Anonymous ID: v3eCc2tY No.148019575 ☐
☐ov 4 2017 23:44:18 (EST)

We need to get organized.
Things need to be solved to understand what is about to happen.
Let's start w/ Alice & Wonderland.
Hillary Clinton in Wonderland by Lewis Carroll.
Saudi Arabia - the Bloody Wonderland.
Snow White.
Wizards & Warlocks.
Q

These clues have not been ironed out with any certainty, but we can speculate. I have seen the reality, with my own eyes, thanks to r/K Theory. I have spent months progressing from one state of disbelief, to another. The reality is there is an entire parallel society within American society which is composed of informants/agents Cabal has recruited into their network. It operates by entirely different rules from those you were raised with. The members of the Secret Society know nothing works the way you were told. They think differently, act in private differently, and live in a different reality from you. And yet, they look like you. In public, they act like you. Their kids go to school with your's and their kids know too. But nobody ever says anything. They all somehow manage to keep the secret.

You can live an entire life, occupied with tasks of daily living, and never see them, even if you are looking right at them. You walk by them, they strike up conversations with you. They stand behind you on the grocery line noting your purchases. They may even intervene and move your life to different paths.

If you look for them, you can find them in anecdotal stories online. Legendary FBI Agent Ted Gunderson puzzled over them his entire life. Tom Bauerle briefly got them to admit to following and harassing him. Wounded Iraq War vet Brian Mancini, featured on 60 Minutes, ran into them and they drove him to commit suicide. The stories have accumulated to an impressive degree. Myron Mays. Aaron Alexis. John Lang. Alexander Bonds, the killer of NYPD Detective Miosotis Familia who will appear prominently in Q's drops later. Gavin Long, who killed three Baton Rouge Police officers. Kevin Limbaugh, the killer of Davis, California Police Officer Natalie Corona. The killers of the Police were sure who was harassing them were Police Departments, something it seems was encouraged by the surveillance-harassment coverage on them in at least one case.

They are the ground level operatives of a covert intelligence network created and run by the Cabal. You don't know them, but they know you. They've followed you around when you went out shopping. They've listened to private conversations you've had in the privacy of your house using eavesdropping and observational technologies developed alongside the silicon revolution, which to us would appear as if magic. And that is just what every citizen gets at some point.

Once you get into politics at the highest levels, I am sure it is an entirely different game. You think there is a meritocracy. You think if you are good at what you do, you excel. And if you are not your career never gets off the ground. In reality Cabal's ground surveillance is out there cataloging people, and deciding who succeeds and who fails, using metrics of their own design.

My suspicion is Hillary was identified by Cabal's ground-level intelligence operations as an ideal candidate for high-level operative, even for installation in the Presidency. She was smart, ruthlessly ambitious, totally lacking in morals, and willing to do anything to get power. The references by Q to Alice and Wonderland appear to be drawn from her emails, where her friends share an inside joke with her about the fairy tale, where she is Alice. I assume the rabbit hole is what Cabal looks like.

Given Saudi Arabia appears a Cabal base of Operations, some suspect when inducting Hillary into Cabal, she was brought to Saudi Arabia and it was explained to her how the highest levels of politics worked, prior to Trump's arrival. There was a Cabal with a global reach, composed of an old, ultra-wealthy elite who ran everything. This Cabal had spent decades, before the US even had an OSS or CIA, infiltrating the positions of power in our society, while encountering almost no resistance. They controlled the FBI, CIA, DHS, White House, Congress, and had operatives all throughout all levels of government, from judges, to local DA's, to town councilmen. They owned the news media, academia, political structures, cultural institutions, actors, singers, record labels, production companies, and the very funding that ran the machine. They dictated election outcomes, and voting was meaningless. From religion to social organizations like the Freemasons, to the local community you lived in, everything was, to some degree, infiltrated and compromised – and watched. Even every American citizen had a file, assembled from a local network embedded in each community, using advanced tech, in a way nobody would believe could be possible in America.

As Q's later drops will indicate, if Hillary was inducted, and she almost certainly was, she was likely told that there were rituals she would have to perform, probably designed by Cabal to yield blackmail materials which would prevent her from ever turning on them. I suspect due to the privacy requirements, this was all done in the most secure place Cabal had at the time, which was probably Saudi Arabia. To Hillary, having gone as deep as she did, having to do what she did, her revelations probably exceeded my own, leaving her feeling like Alice, in the Bloody Wonderland of Saudi Arabia. Having seen just a portion of it myself, it is a deep rabbit-hole to fall down into. The only thing more shocking is how many know and keep the secret.

Although nobody ever settled on a final answer, I suspect Snow White is a reference to America, who throughout Cabal's reign was rendered the sleeping beauty through advanced mass-psychological control techniques. Wizards and Warlocks will appear later on to be terms referring to intelligence operations and/or personnel. Godfather III may refer to Vatican corruption.

Anonymous ID: v3eCc2tY No.148019905 ☍   **81**
Nov 4 2017 23:47:38 (EST)

When big news drops please re-read entire graphic.
This is so critical and why information is provided in a certain order and why some topics are continually emphasized more than others as those will be the recent happenings.
This is the purpose of this new thread (re-organize).
Snow White
Wizards & Warlocks.
Q

Anonymous ID: v3eCc2tY No.148020085 ☍   **82**
Nov 4 2017 23:49:24 (EST)

[Repost]Things need to be solved to understand what is about to happen.
Let's start w/ Alice & Wonderland.
Hillary Clinton in Wonderland by Lewis Carroll.
Saudi Arabia - the Bloody Wonderland.
Q

Anonymous ID: v3eCc2tY No.148020278 ☑   83
Nov 4 2017 23:51:20 (EST)

Simplified.
Alice & Wonderland.
Hillary & Saudi Arabia.
References:
Hillary Clinton in Wonderland by Lewis Carroll.
Saudi Arabia - the Bloody Wonderland.
Q

Anonymous ID: v3eCc2tY No.148021501 ☑   84
Nov 5 2017 00:03:28 (EST)

Please add crumbs above in new complete graphic.
Organized and in order.
Critical for understanding and review.
Spider web.
Hillary & Saudi Arabia (Alice & Wonderland)(see above).
This is staged and deliberate.
Snow White
Godfather III
Q

Anonymous ID: v3eCc2tY No.148027165 ☑   85
Nov 5 2017 00:06:58 (EST)

Who funds MS13?
Why did BO instruct HS & BP to release MS13 captures at the
border?
What agency has direct ties to (2) major drug cartels?
Why is AG Sessions / POTUS prioritizing the removal of MS13?
Why is AG Sessions / POTUS prioritizing building the wall?
Immigration?
Drugs?
Who do you hire for a hit?
Who can be eliminated after the job is complete?
Seth Rich.
Who was found dead (2) shortly after his murder?
What affiliation did they have?
Classified.
Q

Anonymous ID: v3eCc2tY No.148022145 ⬚ **86**
▮v 5 2017 00:10:37 (EST)

> **Anonymous** ID: QLWgJTG3 No.148021760 ⬚
> ▮v 5 2017 00:06:20 (EST)
>
> https://www.amazon.in/Hillary-Clinton-Wonderland-Quotes-Campaign-ebook/dp/B01HOM8AV2 ⬚ ▮

>>148021760
Finally.
Correct reference.
Saudi Arabia - The Bloody Wonderland.
=Alice & Wonderland signatures
Study.
Important.
Q

Anonymous ID: v3eCc2tY No.148022342 ⬚ **87**
▮v 5 2017 00:12:48 (EST)

My signatures all reference upcoming events about to drop if this hasn't been caught on.
Snow White
Godfather III
Q

Anonymous ID: v3eCc2tY No.148023976 ⬚ **88**
▮v 5 2017 00:31:00 (EST)

Ten days.
Darkness.
Scare tactics (MSM).
D's falling.
R's walk-away/removed.
SA --> US --> Asia --> EU
Disinformation is real.
Distractions are necessary.
Focus was US today while real happening in SA under same context (military control, martial law, missile strike (rogue) etc).
Necessary.
POTUS' Twitter attack (see above).

Important.
Why is this relevant?
What was the last Tweet by POTUS prior to SA?
Why is this relevant?
SA (1), US (2), Asia (3), EU (4).
Where is POTUS?
Why is this relevant?
Military operations.
Operators in US.
Snow White
The Great Awakening
Godfather III
Q

The image below is all the posts you just read, joined together.

Anonymous ID: cS8cMPVQ No.148029633 ⬈   **89**
ov 5 2017 00:35:58 (EST)

Anonymous ID: dXfSDuiB No.148028820 ⬈
ov 5 2017 00:25:49 (EST)

qupdated11-4v3.png

>>148028820
Thank you Anon.
FBI/MI currently have open investigation into the CF.
Why didn't Comey drop this?
Who was the FBI director during the Haiti crisis? How many kids disappeared?
How much money was sent to CF under disguise of Haiti relief and actually went to Haiti?
What countries donated big money to CF?
SA?
Why is this relevant?
Snow White
Q

CF is Clinton Foundation. MI is Military Intelligence.

Anonymous ID: cS8cMPVQ No.148029962 ☑   **90**
Nov 5 2017 00:39:41 (EST)

> Anonymous ID: t7IECyBT No.148029846 ☑
> Nov 5 2017 00:38:23 (EST)
>
> Two Mexicans were found murdered in their car in South Carolina
> one day after Seth Rich's murder. Looks like Q was saying those
> two chulos were MS-13. Hillary's gonna get her neck stretched.
>
> http://www.myrtlebeachonline.com/news/local/crime/article89158707.html
>
> >>148029250
> Ok, we just need Q to come back and confirm now.

>>148029846
Confirmed.
Classified.
((HRC))
Q

Because these posts are often coming out nearly simultaneously, some research can end up archived out of order. Although technically Q post 90, this comment by an anon and confirmation from Q is best understood in the context of Q post 91, displayed on the next page, which preceded it.

91

Anonymous ID: v3eCc2tY No.148025825 ↗
Nov 5 2017 00:50:56 (EST)

Why is MS13 a priority?
Could people pay such gangs to kill opponents and why / how to
insulate against exposure?
The truth is mind blowing and cannot fully be exposed. These
people are evil.
Why wasn't HRC prosecuted for the emails?
Put simply, Obama ultimately OK'd by using the non govt email
addy to communicate w/ Clinton. Obama also had an alias along
with each of his cabinet members. Therefore indicting HRC would
lead to indicting Obama & his cabinet etc which could never
happen.
Remember he lied about knowing but that ultimately came out in
the dump. Poof!
Snow White
Godfather III
Q

Seth Rich was a DNC Staffer who it appears was the source of the DNC Server hack. In the hacked Podesta emails, Podesta says shortly before Seth was killed that he is for punishing any leaker, whether or not they were guilty, just to make an example.[173] Shortly thereafter Seth Rich was killed.

This introduces a new Q revelation which is shocking on its face, but which with time appears more and more likely. Namely, that the Conspiracy which corrupted our government also had taken over, or formed alliances with, criminal organizations, including street-gangs, exchanging protection from law enforcement for criminal services, including murders. It's not without precedent. Note how the mafia was long associated with CIA assassination attempts, be it on JFK or Fidel Castro. Those were just the famous cases we hear about.

---

173   http://archive.is/6hcE2

As I have said, I was looking at Cabal's ground-level operations for some time. My region appears to be a Cabal hotspot for reasons I do not yet understand. I can tell you from first hand observation, street gangs were under the protection of Cabal's local intelligence networks. The local police where I live tried to engage with and suppress the local gangs, and without going into too much detail, it did not go well for them. For the duration of Obama's terms, uniformed patrol units were banned from entering local gang territory, under the rubric of active covert surveillance operations being active there by some federal entity that claimed jurisdiction. Communities were holding town halls to complain about the lack of patrols, to no avail. Once President Trump took office, this rapidly reversed, as the police quickly began clearing a backlog of cases built up under Obama.

For me, Q alleging something so outrageous, so unlikely, and it corresponding to a direct observation I had made long before Q ever showed up, served as potent proof Q was real. Even more amazing, it appeared somebody had actually found a chink in this leviathan's armor, and was about to take it out. Given all I have seen, such a thing was unimaginable, however I was not about to complain.

Anonymous ID: cS8cMPVQ No.148031295
Nov 5 2017 00:55:46 (EST)

Seth Rich only mentioned because it directly relates to SA.
Las Vegas.
What hotel did the 'reported' gunfire occur from?
What floors specifically?
Who owns the top floors?
Top floors only.
Why is that relevant?
What was the shooter's name?
What was his net worth?

92

How do you identify a spook?
What can historical data collection reveal?
Was there any eye witnesses?
Who?
Was he registered as a security guard?
Why is MS13 important?
What doesn't add up?
Was there only one shooter?
Who was in LV during this time?
What was the real mission?
Speculate.
Why are survivors dying randomly?
What do each of these survivors have in common?
Did they talk on social media?
What did they say?
Were they going to form a group?
Why is this relevant?
How did they die?
What CIA report was released by WK?
What can control a car?
How did the (2) of the survivors die?
Car crash?
How does this connect to SA?
What just happened in SA?
Who owns the top floors of the hotel?
What happened today in SA?
To who specifically?
Was POTUS in LV that night?
Yes/no?
Why was he there?
Who did he have a classified meeting with?
Did AF1 land at McCarran?
What unmarked tail numbers flew into McCarren that night?
Trace AF1 that entire day.
What do you notice?
Classified.
Q

There were several interesting aspects to the Las Vegas shooting by Stephen Paddock. Most interesting was that the upper floors of that hotel were owned by one of the Saudi's who had been locked away in a hotel room and encouraged to give up his financial information.[174] When asking about identifying a spook, Q is probably referencing Paddock's mixture of low social media presence, travel, and easy untracable income acquisition. There were other elements of the Las Vegas shooting which were unusual,[175] including how many survivors died mysteriously in various ways in the years after the shooting.

Anonymous ID: cS8cMPVQ No.148032210 ⬈   **93**
Nov 5 2017 02:06:00 (EST)

> **Anonymous** ID: yY946/MZ No.148031978 ⬈
> Nov 5 2017 02:03:40 (EST)
>
> >>148031295
> Is HRC just a puppet and the goal is to take down her minders
> and the real kingpins?

>>148031978
Correction:
HRC was a puppet but her strings were recently cut.
She's now on her own and fighting for her life.
Q

Anonymous ID: cS8cMPVQ No.148032910 ⬈   **94**
Nov 5 2017 02:14:12 (EST)

> **Anonymous** ID: GwO0QESI No.148032489 ⬈
> Nov 5 2017 02:09:14 (EST)
>
> >>148032352
> if she's not, I think they're gunning for her. How can she repay
> the money sent to CF for influence? Do they have Huma?

>>148032489
Review my other threads.

---

174   http://archive.is/JmBB0
175   http://archive.is/ZSFt5

This is why complete graphics are so important.
BO paid the debt prior to leaving office.
HRC is not currently in SA.
Bill wants a deal.
Playing the former President card.
Watch the cookie quickly crumble.
Where does Soros fit in?
Godfather III

Anonymous ID: cS8cMPVQ No.148033178 ⌐   95
Nov 5 2017 02:17:24 (EST)

What happened in SA will happen here, Asia, and EU.
Keep digging and keep organizing the info into graphics (critical).
God bless.
Hillary & Saudi Arabia
Snow White
Godfather III
Q

Anonymous ID: cS8cMPVQ No.148033932 ⌐   96
Nov 5 2017 02:26:35 (EST)

> **Anonymous** ID: wz2tGFlp No.148033380 ⌐
> Nov 5 2017 02:19:39 (EST)
>
> Obama sent 221 million to Palestinians right before leaving
> office. The payout..
> http://www.breitbart.com/big-government/2017/01/23/report-
> obama-gave-221-million-palestinians-last-hours/ ⌐

>>148033380
Amazing how things make sense once you are asked a question.
That's the entire point of this operation.
It's up to you all to collect, archive (safely), and distribute in a
graphic that is in order with the crumb dumbs.
It will all make sense.
Once it does, we look to you to spread and get the word out.
Time stamps will help you validate authenticity.
Your President needs your help.
He wants full transparency for the great people of this country.
Everything stated is for a reason.
God bless, Patriots.
Q

Game Theory.
Define.
Why is this relevant?
Moves and countermoves.
Who is the enemy?
False flags.
Shooter identification.
Shooter history.
Shooter background.
Shooter family.
MS13.
Define hostage.
Define leverage.
MS13.
Shooter.
Family.
Hostage.
Force.
Narrative.
Race.
Background.
Why is this relevant?
Flynn.
What is Flynn's background?
What was his rank?
Was he involved in intel ops?
What access or special priv?
Why is this relevant?
Set up.
Who wins?
Who becomes exposed?
Who knows where the bodies are buried?
Who has access?
What is MI?
Who was part of MI during BO term?
Who was fired during BO term (MI)?
Why is this relevant?
Re-read complete crumb graphic (confirmed good).
Paint the picture.
Disinformation exists and is necessary.

10 days.
Darnkess.
War.
Good v. Evil.
Roadmap of big picture is here.
Review post happenings.
Clarified.
Crumbs not only for /pol/.
The silent ones.
Others monitoring (friends and enemies).
Instructions.
Snow White.
Godfather III.
Q

>>148136656
Graphic is good.
Please update and continue to log.
Important more than you know.
Review each sentence post happenings.
Big picture.
Signatures have necessary meaning.
Snow White.
Godfather III.
Q

US assets.
Location.
Who was arrested in SA?
Define.
Background?
HUMA.
Foundations?
Institutes?
Soros.
Who was killed in SA?
Who fired?
Who really fired?
Why would we fire?
Follow the money.
Who pulls the strings?
Strings detached.
Open season on puppets.
Who are the puppets?
Where are the puppets?
Global.
MSM.
Mockingbird.
Secret agents.
A. Cooper family background?
Why is this relevant?
Q

Who is the Queen of England?
How long in power?
With power comes corruption.
What happened to Diana?
What did she find out?
Why was she running?
Who did she entrust to help her flee?
What was the cover?
Why is this relevant?
Why now?

Old.
Connection.
News.
Bad actor.
London Mayor.
Background?
Affiliation?
Connection to Queen?
British MI6 agents dead.
When?
How?
What was reported?
What really happened?
Why is this relevant?
Wealth.
Corruption.
Secret society.
Evil.
Germany.
Merkel.
Migrants.
Why are migrants important?
Assets.
What are assets?
Define assets?
Why are migrants so important?
What are assets?
Why are migrants so important?
What are assets?
Why are migrants so important?
Operations.
Satan.
Who follows?
What political leaders worship Satan?
What does an upside down cross represent?
Who wears openly?
Why?
Who is she connected to?
Why is this relevant?
Spirit cooking.
What does Spirit Cooking represent?
Cult.

What is a cult?
Who is worshipped?
Why is this relevant?
Snow White
Godfather III
Speed.
Q

Here Q begins to raise several points, based around the idea that there is a Cabal who runs the world, their operations cross national boundaries, and they may use or exploit pseudo-religious, cult-like belief systems to control many of their assets.

Queen Elizabeth's family name was changed from Saxe-Coburg Gotha to Windsor during WWII, to make it less Germanic and hide her family origins. As you begin to look into the Cabal, you will find a group of people who ascribe to a bloodline-oriented breeding philosophy. In today's era of equality and blank-slate beliefs about people, it seems strange. But for a long time, elite families practiced a selective breeding of their bloodlines, carefully vetting mates for various traits so as to strengthen their bloodlines, rather than succumbing to the vagaries of tempestuous emotional forces like love or lust. "Of good breeding" was a phrase interpreted literally. The most obvious manifestation of this became Royal families preferentially inter-marrying with other Royal families.

As you look deeper, you will begin to find those today who are famous, from politicians to movie stars, strangely seem to always be able to track their lineages back to Royal families and famous individuals, almost as if someone somewhere was preferentially promoting them as a way of keeping their bloodlines prominent in the gene pool,, even all these centuries later.

Q then goes on to begin to highlight that there is a lot of shady activity and questionable deaths which occur in proximity to the Cabal. Diana's death had numerous witnesses, both before the crash,[176] and after,[177] who spoke of strange individuals who seemed to be prepared for prior to, or involved in, after her crash. Others told of a sound as if one car had rammed Diana's immediately before the main crash, as well as paint chips and debris found at the scene from a mysterious second car which was never located, despite tracking down every matching vehicle in the country at the time.[178] Another saw a motorbike using a strobe-dazzler to disorient Diana's driver.[179] Others spoke of Emergency Services delaying their response and driving Diana to a distant hospital.[180] The implication being Diana may have been killed, and if she was it would probably be because of things she witnessed during her time within the Royal family.

Q then brings up Sadiq Khan, the Mayor of London. He spent time as an adviser to the Queen early in his career, as part of the Privy Council,[181] and he has ties, again, to the Muslim Brotherhood.[182] So again, you have a high-ranking leader of a Western Nation who has at their side a member of the Muslim Brotherhood. And the CIA-Mockingbird news media is silent.

"MI5 agent deaths" leads to only one result on Google,

---

176   http://archive.is/lyHRB
177   http://archive.is/n3thS
178   http://archive.is/uMpG7
179   http://archive.is/Dw9by
180   http://archive.is/DyUEE

181   http://archive.is/Tqgt7
182   http://archive.is/cZD3C

namely Gareth Williams, who was actually an MI6 foreign intelligence officer who was found murdered and sealed inside a dufflebag.[183] *Officials initially tried to explain it away as an autoerotic activity that went awry, though later that explanation fell apart, so they blamed it on the Russians.*

However Q may not be pointing to that, particularly because it is an MI6 officer. What Q may be pointing to is that on all of google, there is not one result for any MI5 officer who has died, in the line of duty or otherwise. MI5 is the British equivalent of the US FBI. For many years its officers were involved in an outright insurgency against Irish Republican Army terrorists who were heavily armed and trained overseas by other terrorist groups.[184] *Have they never sustained a single line-of-duty death? Have they never had a single suicide which made the news? Has an MI5 officer never died in a car accident, or a random crime, or in any way which was reported in any news outlet? Why do we have a report of an MI6 foreign intelligence officer's death, and yet not a single report of any MI5 officer's death. By contrast, we have numerous accounts of US CIA and FBI agents dying in the line of duty and otherwise.*

Q may be pointing out how controlled the news is when it comes to reporting the deaths of MI5 officers as a way of

183   http://archive.is/SEy4G
184   Again, if there is power, influence, or danger within any organization, understand that Cabal intelligence will likely infiltrate and try to co-opt such an organization. It is not, to me, entirely clear if the IRA was as it seemed – a separatist group which operated against British domestic intelligence competently enough to be effective for decades despite overwhelmingly superior British technical and physical surveillance capabilities. It may be more likely Cabal restricted British security service activities, and then infiltrated and controlled the IRA so it could use it to threaten the public and thereby gain societal justification for openly turning London, a Cabal financial center, into the most heavily surveilled city on the planet.

showing that in Britain, those who serve in that role know, they can disappear without a sound in the media or otherwise. Such a state of affairs could help you keep a lot of secrets – and would probably arise if you had a lot of embarrassing secrets to keep.

Q then moves on to the concept of a Secret Society, and its relation to the migrant surges. I believe I may have inside information on why this is significant. But to understand it, you first have to take a closer look at the domestic surveillance machine. Online, I have long been describing the problems I have seen with what I thought at the time was an over-grown American surveillance state. Read my writings at my site, and you will see one of the complaints I made, starting years ago, was that it was recruiting heavily among new immigrants.

After I introduced r/K Political Theory, and somebody took note of it, I began to notice that all around me, emerging from the wood work, were what appeared to be normal citizens following me. As I continued to promote r/K, the interactions became more aggressive, and they appeared to want to intimidate me, by asserting themselves as some sort of surveillance force, openly talking into their wrist while looking at me, or boxing me in, in traffic. It only pissed me off, and drove me to redouble my efforts to promote r/K Theory.

As it progressed, I noticed many appeared to have just arrived in the country as new immigrants. I assumed they were being recruited on arriving, and noted on my site this ran the risk of eventually handing a very powerful domestic intelligence apparatus, which was already being abused, over to foreigners who might not feel the same loyalty to the Constitution, America, and other traditional institutions our citizens valued.

Obviously the surveillance was of interest, so I began researching it online. Others, with far less involvement in politics had been reporting the same things going back to the early 2000's, and there were even a few cases I found predating that, though it seems it was much less common before then.

One of the most interesting things I found was that some people fled their countries, for nations where they thought the surveillance would not be able to follow them. One tried Japan, assuming Japanese domestic security would not allow American intelligence to recruit Japanese civilian informant networks to run harassment operations in their country. Another tried China. Others headed to Europe, thinking domestic security there would frown on Americans running any sort of embedded intelligence networks on their home turfs, made up of their citizens. All reported leaving their domestic surveillance at the airports at home, and then being picked up by identical operations on landing in the foreign countries, made up of locals who seemingly were trained in the exact same techniques – and who knew who they were.

It was as if China was allowing US surveillance to recruit its Chinese citizens, and give them orders to follow and harass US citizens who visited the country. In the old paradigm, where nations were in competition, and rival intelligence agencies would zealously guard their turf, it made no sense. But what if there was something else – a covert non-state actor, running a global intelligence operation that had covertly subverted nations all over the globe and was running them as puppet governments so the people would never rebel against a single global "ruler?"

If this was the case, then the surveillance operation in the

US, and the surveillance operation in China would be getting targets from the same boss. If that were the case, then a target who flew from California to Beijing could expect to be picked up at the local airport. It was the only explanation that made sense.

I eventually found a way to look at this operation's global tentacles myself. As I cruised various countries on Google Streetview, I began to see images which looked unusually like domestic surveillance operators clocking the Streetview Car as it passed. I took the car into areas where you shouldn't see much traffic, and lo and behold, there was surveillance everywhere.

Around the time things heated up with my surveillance. They slowed me down getting a critically ill dog to the vet, which pissed me off, and I began doing more posts exposing their operations. At night as I slept, I began awaking to bizarre vibrations of my body, as if I was being hit with some sort of pressure waves of energy.[185]

So I began doing more posts analyzing these observations of the Streetview car, and how it revealed what in-person, physical surveillance looked like. When I did Bulgaria, one reader responded, saying he vacationed in that very area with family who lived there, and when he went and looked at Streetview, he was shocked at how much more foot traffic and vehicles he saw, compared with when he would travel there.

As I continued these analyses, I was struck by how this covert, civilian informant/surveillance network was everywhere,

---

185   Two others who experienced the surveillance state, Navy Yard shooter Aaron Alexis, and the murderer of Sheriff's Deputy Natalie Corona both also reported similar vibrations from some sort of thru-wall "body-vibrating" device.

using the same tradecraft. You could cruise the backstreets of rural Japan and see it, and then head to a dirt road in a rural area in Sri Lanka, and find it there.

So here, Q asks, "Why are Migrants Important?" followed by, "What are assets?" Long before Q, I had discerned somebody was flooding this country with migrants who were acting as covert assets to surveil and harass Americans. Although I initially suspected an American intelligence outfit, I subsequently noted that the operation harassing me seemingly had operations – and assets - all over the globe.

What Q is saying is that Cabal is using the migrant waves to marshal all of the assets they have recruited all over the globe, bringing them into the West, where they will be expected to show loyalty to this network. At the least they will vote how Cabal will tell them to, and in their spare time they will act as an harassment/intimidation force to try and control the political battlefield. And occasionally, if Q can be believed (and I think he can), the more criminal elements of this network , such as MS13, will be used for even worse. I have no doubt this is an attempt to flood our nation with agents who will be loyal to this conspiracy before they are loyal to our country, or our fellow citizens.

Notice Q repeats these questions four times. I agree entirely with his assessment of this idea's importance. The mass migration events of late have nothing to do with human rights. It is, plain and simple, an invasion by hostile non-state actors to subvert our governments through the use of infiltrated assets. It is an invasion. That we have tolerated it this long, without opposing this destruction of our very society by foreigners is a measure of just how much the Cabal has managed to weaken our mental resolve and our commitment to traditionally normal American principles of patriotism and loyalty to country.

Q then begins to introduce the idea of occult practices and satanism. There is some sort of occult aspect to the Cabal and its members. Hillary Clinton recruited psychic Jean Houston to help her commune with Eleanor Roosevelt, as Bill Clinton famously spoke of.[186] Then there were the Podesta emails which revealed high-level Democrats from politics, to entertainment and business, were routinely attending "Spirit cooking" sessions with self-styled occultist Marina Abramovic.[187] At the same time we are finding elsewhere within this network exist cults like NXIVM, which attempt to control members with less paranormal belief systems.

At this point all we know is high-level power players in our society attend these functions, and appear to at least entertain themselves with occult ceremonies.

Given what I have seen, we do not need to jump to the supernatural as an explanation, however. Let us take a moment and indulge in some speculation, as a mental exercise. Much of Cabal's control is based upon psychological control. In the article on Spirit Cooking and Marina Abramovic, above, notice how the woman described believed she had actually killed someone with a hex. One possible mechanism for some Cabal command and control of their network, which would greatly minimize risk of an operational-security compromise, would be the simulated-supernatural explanation.

---

186   https://www.youtube.com/watch?v=SGFUzixmuz8
             http://archive.is/TuxZF
187   http://archive.is/R3Rvk

That is, when Cabal is bringing people in, it leads them to supernatural belief systems. Simultaneously, it uses its massive ground surveillance operations to monitor them closely, and it then combines the use of its intelligence with a molding of events in their lives to exert control over their behavior through their belief system. As an example, suppose Cabal brought someone they wanted to recruit to an occult ceremony, telling them it was a religion of the successful because it was real. They decided to try it out, and performed their own ceremony, in the privacy of their house, maybe requesting a certain amount of money. Unbeknownst to them, Cabal surveillance was listening in their house, and observed the ceremony. It then arranged for them to fall into that exact amount of money.

In their mind, the religion's power was confirmed, and you now have an individual who believes a supernatural entity that is all powerful is listening to them at all times, and has power of life or death over them. I cannot help but think of Dave Mustain, lead singer of the band Megadeth. He recounted how satanism is real, because he cast two spells in high school, one to hurt a bully, the other to sleep with the hottest girl in the school who was way out of his league. Very quickly the bully was hurt the exact way he requested, and he had slept with the girl.[188] Suppose she was in the secret society, surveillance saw the rituals, and her parents told her to do it as a training exercise, while a vehicular team arranged a car accident for the bully. Suddenly Mustain was a believer, they had control of him, and they proceeded to promote him to the position of Rockstar.

That may not be far from the truth, and the reality would

---

188   https://www.youtube.com/watch?v=FwDbiajBEbk

be Cabal had just acquired an asset which will do what they want, and which fears them. And yet, he could never reveal anything of interest to investigators about their chain of command, nor could he testify against them in a court of law, because nobody would believe satan was his boss.

How might this look in real life? Imagine for a moment Osama bin Ladin. Imagine bin Ladin was under close surveillance from a very early age, both technical and physical, as well as infiltrators sent to get close to him in his organization. As he began setting up a network, Cabal intelligence intervened to make sure things went very well for him. Money, connections, it all happened and bin Ladin saw Allah showing him the way.

All along the way, a covert intelligence operation, with the degree of civilian involvement as I have seen embedded throughout the populace, could give him signs and offer opportunities, and in doing so steer his path. He would be under the impression only an all seeing god could be behind it, if he did not grasp the sheer magnitude of the manpower arrayed against him, and its ability to hear/observe everything from a distance, and even through walls, inside even the most denied of areas.

Part of me suspects this happened to bin Ladin simply because of the extensive library he amassed in that little compound in Abbottabad. Among the books were many on Cabal subjects,[189] such as the bloodlines and genealogy of the Illuminati, the real leaders behind the scenes of the free world, and so forth. It carried the feel of a man who, left alone with his thoughts to reflect on the past, began to wonder if all of those

---

189   https://www.dni.gov/index.php/features/bin-laden-s-bookshelf

strange forks in the road that popped up in front of him, and the decisions he was steered to may not have been Allah after all.

It struck a familiar chord, and I cannot help but wonder if he had begun to realize he was a pawn in somebody else's game. It might even be why the decision was made to let him be found and taken out. I can't tell you this is how the mechanism works. But given the control I have seen all around me, and the strange obsession that otherwise intelligent people in power seem to have with occult beliefs, it is one plausible mechanism which might fit the evidence.

Anonymous ID: hHkrVD7x No.148148004 ⬈   **101**
v 5 2017 19:08:10 (EST)

> **Anonymous** ID: QVBSWPvd No.148147343 ⬈
> v 5 2017 19:03:39 (EST)
>
> LATEST Q VERIFIED NOV6.png
>
> LATEST Q, along with what was posted in CBTS 68

>>148147343
Graphic confirmed.
Q

jD79-x10ABy-89zBT
08:00
12:00
11_6_TP_Pub
PHIL_B_O_Extract_Conf
02:00 Z

262

14.5995° N, 120.9842° E
_Conf_UDT_green_
^_Sj69ETC-
Godspeed.

Anonymous ID: hHkrVD7x No.148152047 🗗

🖿ov 5 2017 19:34:57 (EST)

103

> **Anonymous** ID: WlbWZggC No.148151281 🗗
>
> 🖿ov 5 2017 19:29:50 (EST)
>
> >>148149435
> For a God and Country.

>>148151281
POTUS
You are all heroes.
Come home safe.
Godspeed.

Anonymous ID: hHkrVD7x No.148154137 🗗

🖿ov 5 2017 19:49:15 (EST)

104

Now is the time to pray.
We're operational.
God bless the United States of America.
Q

Anonymous ID: hHkrVD7x No.148154941 🗗

🖿ov 5 2017 19:54:47 (EST)

105

Please pray.
Operators are in harms way.
High risk.
High value targets.
Please pause and give thanks to those who would die to save our republic.
More to follow.
Q

Anonymous ID: HpMXQdk5 No.148154996 ⌐
🔲ov 5 2017 19:55:14 (EST)

30059B4D-41BE-4A63-9BC7-5BFF618390C0.png

>>148154530
They cut the feed trying to shut him down. Remember what Q said. They were waiting for this. Whatever is happening, is happening now. Archive EVERYTHING

>>148154996
Nothing is a coincidence.
We are at war.
SA cut the strings.
They are scrambling for cover and using any means necessary out of their remaining power/control.
God bless.
Q

The image posted above will be on the next page:

Anonymous (ID: WGBs2Yx3)
11/05/17(Sun)18:51:34 No.148154481

>>148154137 #
How can we help?

Anonymous (ID: yITzW/Dq)
11/05/17(Sun)18:51:46 No.148154509

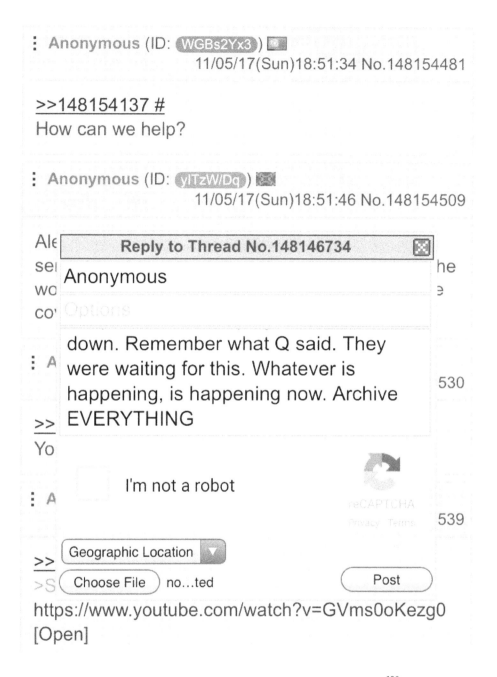

Reply to Thread No.148146734

Anonymous

down. Remember what Q said. They were waiting for this. Whatever is happening, is happening now. Archive EVERYTHING

I'm not a robot

Geographic Location

Choose File no...ted

Post

https://www.youtube.com/watch?v=GVms0oKezg0
[Open]

The link at the bottom was wiped from Youtube.[190]

---

190   A rchive (sans video) of the page: http://archive.is/FSDBC

It was a video of a Swiss Government opening ceremony for a train tunnel,[191] which examined the occult symbology that was incorporated into the ceremony. It showed that the elites of Cabal would throw occult imagery in their public performances and displays. Some think this is due to occult beliefs, some think it is a wink and a nod between fellow travelers at the top who have all undergone the initiations and partaken of their rituals on admission to the Secret Society, and thus will recognize the hidden signs. What was significant was that Youtube would quickly delete a video which really did not seem to violate any terms of service or contain anything objectionable.

Anonymous ID: hHkrVD7x No.148155609 ☑   **107**
▓ov 5 2017 19:59:21 (EST)

Code:
May God also grant all of us the wisdom to ask what concrete steps we can take to reduce the violence and weaponry in our midst.
Note when we just sent the go orders and when this Tweet went live.
Coincidence?
Pray.
Q

Anonymous ID: hHkrVD7x No.148156129 ☑   **108**
▓ov 5 2017 20:03:07 (EST)

Anonymous ID: cxbjPd3x No.148155375 ☑
▓ov 5 2017 19:57:48 (EST)

>>148152800
Checked and phoneposting, excuse the post count. The first "extraction order" referenced 0200 Zulu time, it was 0200 Zulu when I posted my response. I was saying that 1.5 hours would be plenty enough time for anyone to hide if they needed to hide, so if it was real info then whoever posted it just broke opsec in a pretty bad way.

191   Original ceremony video reposted: https://youtu.be/I4NU0Tok1T4

Nothing is as it seems, Anon.
What occurred?
It flushed BO out.
Why is that relevant?
Analyze time stamps of my go message to BO's Tweet.
Q

Q had posted some sort of coded orders implying a movement to arrest Barack Obama was in action. It was however disinformation designed to precipitate action, according to Q.

Anonymous ID: hHkrVD7x No.148156632 📁　　　　　　　**109**
Nov 5 2017 20:06:36 (EST)

> **Anonymous** ID: pqW40Wgk No.148156518 📁
> Nov 5 2017 20:05:48 (EST)
>
> spiritual_warfare.jpg
>
>
>
> >>148154137
>
> St. Michael the Archangel, defend us in battle. Be our
> protection against the wickedness and snares of the devil.
> May God rebuke him, we humbly pray. And do thou, Prince of
> the Heavenly Hosts, by the power of God, cast down to Hell
> Satan and all his evil spirits, who prowl about the world
> seeking the ruin of souls. Amen.

>>148156518
Amen brother.
Q

Nov 5 2017 20:08:46 (EST)   **110**

MSM.
CIA counter-ops.
Will all fall down.
Q

Nov 5 2017 23:34:15 (EST)   **111**

Important Context:
What have you learned about HUMA?
What organization is HUMA?
Which US President is affiliated w/ HUMA?
Why is this relevant?
What year(s) did this occur?
Who funded on behalf this President?
Why is this relevant?
What year(s) did this occur?
What just happened in SA?
Who was arrested?
Funds frozen.
Why would this former President be funded pre-political days?
Repeat.
Important.
Why would this former President be funded pre-political days?
Why is the relevance?
Was the MB affiliated to any of these organizations/people?
Fast forward.
Why are the events in SA so important?
Why was JK in SA recently?
Why was POTUS' last Tweet re: SA prior to the happening?
Why was POTUS' Twitter taken down days before under cover of a
rogue employee?
Refocus again.
Who was arrested in SA?
Any ownership stakes in US co's?
Why is this relevant?
Twitter.
Las Vegas.
Recent events.

Why would investment be made in a former President pre-political days?
What year(s) did this occur?
What faith does HUMA represent?
What faith does the MB represent?
What faith does Huma represent?
Who are the bad actors?
Who funds majority of US 'senior' politicians?
Fantasy land.
Fantasy land.
Was the former President of the United States groomed to be Command in Chief?
Is this possible?
Is the US political / election system corrupt?
Who owns poll machines?
Soros?
Why is this relevant?
They never thought she would lose.
They never thought she would lose.
Fantasy land.
Fantasy land.
The complete picture would put 99% of Americans (the World) in a hospital.
POTUS is our savior.
Pray.
Operators are active.
We are at war.
Goodnight BO.
Snow White.
Godfather III.
Q

Anonymous ID: FAkr+Yka No.148185083 ☒
█ov 5 2017 23:46:24 (EST)

112

Important to archive.
Above & next drops have high probability of shutting down /pol/.
It is being safeguarded for these transmissions but not 100% secure.
Who owns /pol/?
Why is this platform being used?
What recent events almost occurred re: /pol/?

Why is this relevant?
Stay alert in main US cities (DC), sporting events, and other conservative gatherings.
Repeat.
Stay alert in main US cities (DC), sporting events, and other conservative gatherings.
More false flags imminent.
Elections (tues) no longer matter at this stage.
Snow White.
Godfather III.
Above will have context as news unfolds.
Summarize and paint the picture.
Critical.
Q

Anonymous ID: FAkr+Yka No.148185905 🔗   **113**
ov 5 2017 23:53:46 (EST)

Social media platforms.
Top 10 shareholders of Facebook?
Top 10 shareholders of Twitter?
Top 10 shareholders of Reddit?
Why is SA relevant?
MSM.
Controlling stakes in NBC/MSNBC?
Controlling stakes in ABC?
Controlling stakes in CBS?
Controlling stakes in CNN?
Investor(s) in Fox News?
Why is this relevant?
What is Operation Mockingbird?
Active?
Who is A Cooper?
What is A Cooper's background?
Why is this relevant?
Snow White.
Godfather III.
Speed.
Q

Anonymous ID: FAkr+Yka No.148186256 🗗   **114**
Nov 5 2017 23:56:55 (EST)

US Military = savior of mankind.
We will never forget.
Fantasy land.
God save us all.
Q

Anonymous ID: FAkr+Yka No.148189295 🗗   **115**
Nov 6 2017 00:23:34 (EST)

Anonymous ID: ibK4PoCz No.148186000 🗗
Nov 5 2017 23:54:34 (EST)

manila-extraction-coords-philipines-japanese-restaurant.jpg   ⬇

>>148183551
JESUS FUCKING CHrisT!!

Its a japanese restaurant.

JAPAN. MILITARY. urgent SPEECH

AND THE EXTRACTION COORDS ARE A JAP RESTAURANT

>>148186000
!!!!!!!!!!!!

This anon took one of Q's previous posts of random numbers and showed it was coordinates of a location, but it later appeared that this was disinformation being released by Q to affect some decisions made by Cabal actors. It is important to note, Q may never have been here to inform anons, or the public. His purpose may have been to reveal enough accurate data to establish a cover as some form of public disclosure, and then utilize that cover to drop disinformation to affect the behavior of bad actors elsewhere. Indeed, in retrospect, it would appear one major objective he fulfilled was to create a perception, for years, that action was imminent. In reality the operation targeting the Cabal was a very long-term plan designed to build a legal "relative-superiority" slowly over years, before finally taking action against the players involved.

As all of this is happening, the mass of sealed indictments of Cabal agents throughout critical positions is growing, and setting the stage for a mass-unsealing which will purge all of them from the legal and judicial system instantly. Trump also is confirming new judges who will be certified as Cabal-free, so when the judiciary is purged, there will remain a body of judges capable of handling Cabal-related cases to complete the purge.

In the mean time, Q kept the Cabal focused on addressing short-term problems, rather than letting them address the longer term legal attacks which were slowly approaching. Regardless, in order to establish that cover and credibility he required, Q would need to release enough credible and correct information to make his releases still quite interesting to observe. And as will later be shown, he does release interesting information which was inexplicably dead on.

Anonymous ID: KKlreCTB No.148286961 ☐   116
Nov 6 2017 16:48:58 (EST)

Crumb dump incoming fast.
Archive immediately.
Upload to graphic.
Q

CH_Navy_Bund.jpg

Why was the arrest of Alwaleed and others important?
How is Alwaleed and BO tied to HUMA?
Why did Alwaleed finance BO pre-political days?
Why did Alwaleed finance BO pre-political days?
What is HUMA? Define.
What book was BO caught reading?
Why was this immediately disregarded as false?
What is 'Post-American World by Fareed Zakaria'?
Why is this relevant?
Why would the President of the UNITED STATES OF AMERICA be reading this book?
What church did BO attend as pre-POTUS?
Who was BO's mentor?
How is Alwaleed and HRC connected?
Who was HRC's mentor?
How is Alwaleed and Bush Sr./Jr. connected?
What occurred post 9-11?
What war did we enter into?
What was the purpose and disclosures given re: justification?

Who financed 9-11?
Why, recently, are classified 9-11 pages being released?
What just occurred in SA?
What FOIA docs are being publicly released (recently)?
Why is this relevant?
What information is contained within these c-releases?
Why is C Wray important with regards to these releases?
What does money laundering mean?
What is the single biggest event that can generate many nation states to payout billions?
Who audits where the money goes?
$15,000 for a toothbrush?
Reconcile.
Why did we attack Iraq?
Halliburton.
Who are they?
What do they specialize in?
What is oil field service?
Why is this relevant?
What 'senior' level political officials are affiliated w/ Halliburton?
What is the primary goal?
What is the primary mode of influence that drives corruption?
What does money buy?
How is this connected to SA?
How is this connected to Alwaleed?
How is this connected to LV?
Q

Saudi Arabia was the primary banker for Cabal. There may have been multiple reasons. Saudi Arabia moves enormous cash flows as it supplies the world with energy. This may have allowed a better camouflaging of currency movements within the flow. As an energy provider which controlled the flow of oil, Saudi Arabia could exert political/economic pressure on any nation which attempted to investigate its activities. Indeed it could funnel cash payments merely by offering oil at lower prices to various entities, or launder cash for two parties by charging one entity seeking to give money a higher price for oil, and another entity seeking to receive cash a lower price for oil, obviously working the transaction to be paid a cut themselves. As a dictatorial nation known to contain radical Islamist elements, any treachery that did come to light, such as 9/11, could be attributed to isolated bad actors who are no longer even alive due to mysterious accidents which befell them. Saudi Arabia would be easily influenced itself via a carrot and stick method, given its leaders on the one hand were offered a life of unimaginable wealth and comfort, while on the other side they sit precariously atop a population composed mostly of unskilled and restless Islamist radicals who are dependent upon the state for all their financial needs. Deviate from Cabal's wishes, and a coup would be easy to stir up. And finally, as essentially a dictatorship prone to kill political enemies, there is not a strong and unyielding domestic legal infrastructure to investigate questionable financial transactions and then pursue legal remedies designed to foster a greater good. If it merely compromised the leaders, Cabal could do what it wanted within Saudi Arabia, both hidden and free from consequence in the unlikely event they were ever exposed in the world.

The implication of Obama reading a book about a post-American world was that he was expecting to see a world where America had declined from its superpower status.

Prince Alwaleed's close friend, Khalid Abdullah Tariq al-Mansour helped Barack Obama get into Harvard Law School.[192] Alwaleed is a major donor to Hillary Clinton's campaign, and even insulted President Trump on Twitter when he was running for office (Trump mocked him in reply, referring to him as

---

192   http://archive.is/2KIUr

"Dopey Prince Alwaleed"[193]). Alwaleed had also contributed to causes associated with the Bush family,[194] was an investor in the Carlyle Investment Group with Bush Senior (which profited from the Iraq War),[195] and was a major investor in Fox News[196] even as he was funding the families of Muslim suicide bombers. The implication is Alwaleed had links to and supported both Hillary and Obama, as well as the Bush family, and Islamic terrorism, because they were all employees of the same employer who operated out of Saudi Arabia. That brings us to 9/11. We have long heard rumors 9/11 was covertly funded by Saudi interests, and that our political leaders have covered this up to protect the Kingdom from embarrassment due to the actions of a few radicals within it. Perhaps it was something behind the Saudis who perpetrated that, using Saudi banks, and it was covered up to protect that entity.

Q then points out the recent release of the JFK assassination documents, implying Cabal was involved in that. As this progresses, Q will assert that JFK had begun to confront Cabal, though he did not grasp the extent of the conspiracy he faced, and they killed him before he could act against them.

Q then points out the extent to which Cabal bled America financially, from overcharging on government contracts, to starting wars to get the nation to payout trillions of dollars to Cabal defense contractors which would find their way to Cabal accounts, to diverting foreign and humanitarian aid to Cabal entities. We were told our state of perpetual war just happened,

193   http://archive.is/FBXnE
194   http://archive.is/bxAh9
195   http://archive.is/Aydpx
196   http://archive.is/0bxOT

or that it was chance that President Trump sought to get out of Afghanistan, Iraq, and Syria. He was drying up Cabal funding.

This becomes a theme of Cabal in many nations. If Q is correct, it is one of the longest running intelligence operations in history. As such, it has gradually infiltrated agents into areas of influence, and it has compromised, and gotten control of most, if not all of the players on all sides of every conflict, and it profits off all of them as it pits them against each other across the globe.

At this point, with this level of control, of the political parties, of the politicians, of the intelligence apparatuses, of the criminal actors, of academia, of business, of cultural institutions like Hollywood and broadcast networks, of civilian informant networks, and even the news, now Cabal spends its efforts overseeing the societal battlefield it already almost totally controls. You can see how intelligence operations accrete, until they assume an almost black-hole-like state. By now, Cabal can make or break any new players entering the arena. Add in files on everyone, and it's civilian network, and it has total control.

Suppose two civil liberties organizations enter the social square. One is principled, supports the little guy's rights, and is run by an incorruptible leader. The other is run by a pedophile, and the organization will gladly sacrifice principle for cash donations. Cabal can destroy the honest one by any number of means. IRS inquiry, intelligence penetration and takeover, criminal assault by a street gang member, or Cabal can just order its media allies to completely ignore the newcomer. Conversely, Cabal can contribute money to the corruptible group, order its media to publicize it, protect it from all law enforcement investigation, and add it to its stable of assets.

Two groups, and Cabal can produce the exact opposite outcome from a meritocracy. You can see how an intelligence operation reaches a critical mass, at which point total control of the battlefield it operates on becomes almost like a natural force behind it, like gravity, driving it toward total control. And if that intelligence operation predated the US's counter-intelligence apparatus this Cabal would have owned that too, from the start.

Anonymous ID: KKIreCTB No.148287236 **118**
Nov 6 2017 16:50:59 (EST)

What family was permitted to leave immediately after 9-11?
Who authorized the departure?
Why is this relevant?
Was anyone else permitted to leave?
Repeat.
Was anyone else permitted to leave?
Was it a private plane?
What can private planes carry v commercial?
What airport did they arrive/depart from?
What was carried on a private plane to Iran?
Why was the Bin Laden family here during 9-11?
Coincidence?
How does SA connect to the Bin Laden family?
Who in SA is connected specifically to the Bin Laden family?
What did they deliver?
To who?
Why?
What does money buy?
Why are the events in SA relevant to the above?
Who is the financial backer for human trafficking?
Who is the 'broker' for underage sex?
Think SA.
How does FB & Instagram play a role in capture?
Think 'Taken'.
Fantasy right?
Why do select senior political officials have foundations/institutes?
What is money laundering?
What does money buy?

What other people were arrested in SA?
What are their backgrounds?
Are any connected to the Podesta Group?
Why is this relevant?
What do you need in order to prosecute senior political officials?
How do you avoid public misconception?
How do you justify counter-political attacks to the mass public?
Why is information so vital?
Is the country divided?
Why does the MSM portray the country as being divided?
Why is this relevant?
Q

Now Q begins to introduce that there is a substantial child sexual abuse issue involved in Cabal activities. You will see more and more evidence for this as time goes on. On Q's board, as anons have dug through social media accounts of those Q has drawn attention to, disturbing images and coded messages have pointed to an entire network devoted to supplying Cabal with vulnerable children, which is presumably supported by Cabal leadership due to the level of control such blackmailable activities provides.

At the end Q begins to introduce the idea that Cabal has used its political, media, and cultural apparatuses to foster an increasingly partisan political divide. This benefits Cabal in that it diverts attention from Cabal to ideology. As a result, every election ends up a corrupt Cabal candidate from the right, and a corrupt Cabal candidate from the left. We vote for one of them because our focus is on ideology, rather than the more important issue of corruption and Cabal affiliation.

Indeed, 2016 was almost an election between Hillary and Jeb Bush. Even as we elected Donald Trump, there was almost half of the country who opposed him based on left-wing ideology, even as "Establishment Republicans" sought to defeat him from the right. That ideological opposition to Donald Trump would diminish the amount of voter-fraud needed to defeat him, and could be proffered to "explain" his loss. Sadly, much of that portion of the country who opposed him ideologically would even countenance such fraud, were it exposed, claiming it was done for a greater good ideologically. In reality it would only have served Cabal and fostered this corrupt conspiracy.

Anonymous ID: KKIreCTB No.148287326 �   **119**
ov 6 2017 16:51:29 (EST)

What is money flow disruption?
List the Billionaires.
What family history goes back pre_WW1/2?
Why is this relevant?
Why did the Bush family recently break silence and attack POTUS?
Coincidence pre SA arrests?
Who audits the billions paid for war?
Who audits the billions paid for environment policy (side note)?
Where do the funds go?
Offshore?
To who / which entity and/or org?
What slush fund was recently terminated by AG Sessions?
What is Fast & Furious?
What is the underlying theme?
MONEY.
Who controls the FED?
How did political leaders/'talking heads' accum assets in excess of $5mm+?
What was the net worth for each prior to taking office?
Reconcile.
Why is this relevant?
Snow White.
Godfather III.
Q

Q has yet to fully explain this post, but I am going to

speculate here. One interesting thing Q has exposed is that today's billionaires do not have familial roots extending back before WWII. This an anomalous, because money makes money.

There was an article about two scientists who had made a bet with each other over when aging would be cured. I forget the exact numbers, but if I were to approximate them from memory it was something like they bet whether someone alive today would be alive in 300 years. The size of the bet was something like $3 trillion dollars, to be collected by their heirs, assuming aging were not cured soon enough for them to collect in person.

They were able to wager such a large sum by each placing $500 in some sort of bond investment with compounded interest which would be rolled over until the date the bet was settled. At that point it was to be $3 trillion, or some such ridiculous amount. The point being, if a family had millions of dollars before WWII, with even a small amount, invested passively with compounded interest, their family should have maintained, or even advanced their ultra-rich status. And yet none had. Every billionaire's fortune is but a flash in the pan, often earned by quirk of chance or spark of genius, and it is returned to dust or given to "charity" on their passing. Contemplate the principle of compounded interest, as well as how the ultra-rich make money far faster than they possibly can spend it, and think about that.

What Q will seem to assert is that the billionaires we see may not actually be the real billionaires. It's possible the reality is a few families, ages ago, reached that level of wealth and went underground. Then, from behind the scenes, they used public proxies to invest and make their money and expand their fortunes. While we focus on the public "billionaires," they live their lives with all the benefits of ultra-high wealth, and none of the detriments like fame and threats – or blame.

Today we are told someone like Mark Zuckerberg comes up with a spark of an idea and makes billions from nothing. Then he decides he doesn't want to pass it on to his family, so he "donates" it all to some charity which spends it on God-knows-what, and before long the fortune is gone – and nobody really knows where it went. At the same time another flash-in-the-pan billionaire comes on the scene and repeats the process. None ever wants to produce an enduring legacy, no family member of their's ever takes a hundred million of their billions and invests it with compounding interest as the seed of a lasting family fortune. And under current trends, a few hundred years from now, there will still be no lasting billionaire family which completely dominates our economies over generations.

Meanwhile the reality is that finances are just like intelligence. Just as an intelligence operation, getting large enough, reaches a critical mass beyond which the natural forces will push it towards total dominance, so too with finance. You should reach a certain point of wealth at which point you cannot spend it fast enough, and the natural tendency will be toward ever greater financial dominance of the economic environment.

These observations may be of greater importance than they appear, as if they are true, they point to everyone holding very basic understandings of the world which are completely wrong. Having gone as far into Q-Anon as I have, I find myself thinking it more likely than not that if we hold such mistaken basic assumptions about the world, they were given to us through culture to help (((Them))) hide more easily.

The slush fund Sessions dispensed with was a DOJ slush fund used to pay out settlements to left-wing interest groups,[197] a means of routing government money into Cabal-influence ops.

Fast and Furious was an ATF operation which armed the Mexican drug cartels with American guns smuggled across the border into Mexico. Some thought US intelligence was supporting drug cartels, and this was one operation supporting them.[198] But if Cabal had infiltrated our government, and infiltrated criminal groups worldwide, this could have been a case of Cabal, Inc. having one US subsidiary arm up its cartels.

The Fed is controlled by a consortium of private banks, many of which are directly or indirectly controlled by the Rothschild family or companies.

Anonymous ID: KKIreCTB No.148287396 ☐   **120**
Nov 6 2017 16:51:56 (EST)

Why, by coincidence, is there a terrorist attack (or mental health c-level attack) within a short time post negative D news?
Do you believe in coincidences?
They think you are stupid. Puppets w/o power. They want your guns. Why? No power left.
Who funds ISIS?
What email published by WL connects SA/Qatar to ISIS?
Was HRC connected?
Why is this relevant?
Why is controlling the narrative important?
Do most people investigate for themselves or simply follow?
Why is the MSM so hostile towards POTUS?
Who controls the MSM?
Why, each and every day, is the MSM pushing a particular topic?
Coordinated?
Who sets the narrative for the day?
How is the narrative communicated to the MSM?

---

197   http://archive.is/fejcV
198   http://archive.is/AoiFE

What does the NSA/MI have (at least what you know of) that allows for data collection?
Think Snowden.
Why is the NSA limited re: ability to capture and unmask US persons?
Who sets the narrative?
US persons?
Who can violate this rule?
Who cannot violate this rule?
Why is Adm R so important?
Who wanted him fired?
Why?
Why wasn't Adm R replaced by POTUS when taking office?
Why is this relevant?
Who has the ultimate power to designate classification?
Who ultimately sets classification?
Why is this relevant?
Fantasy land.
Q

I have long noticed the phenomenon that just as bad news for the Cabal hits, there will be a sudden, seemingly unrelated mass casualty event which will divert media attention from it. It has often been discussed openly on conservative websites, with some mass casualty events even seeming custom tailored to current events, such as the first ever mass-shooting to involve a silencer[199], which makes it harder to aim and shoot fast, as well as retain a weapon in a close-quarter struggle, occurring just before the only time the Supreme Court has ever been about to decide whether to hear a case assessing their legality.[200]

Obviously you can see why Cabal would like us disarmed.

What Q will increasingly reveal on this front is that Cabal

---

199   http://archive.is/dat17
200   http://archive.is/dtksz

appears to view humans as computers, whose behavior is based upon the inputs they receive. In the realm of politics, the inputs they receive are almost exclusively composed of the mainstream news media sources they observe. Thus if you control the mainstream news media sources, you control the informational inputs people receive, and by extension, you control their behavior. Obviously we see precedents for that in the CIA's previously discussed project Mockingbird, where the CIA made it a goal to either turn news reporters into assets of the Agency, or actually install their agents and officers as news reporters.

Q then points out that one of the major terrorist actors today who has often supplied the attacks which changed the topics was ISIS – a terrorist organization formed by Western Intelligence and supported as a counterbalance to Assad in Syria. Indeed, Donald Trump eradicated ISIS from the world stage almost immediately on taking office, whereas Obama first downplayed their relevance in trying to deflect scrutiny from them when he called them the "JV team," and then refused to address them as a major threat and eradicate them. Again under the Q paradigm, Obama was merely a Cabal employee following the orders from Management to run cover for another employee.

In Q's paradigm, the NSA, as a Military Intelligence outfit, is the last holdout against Cabal's infiltration and subversion. Q implies restrictions placed on NSA's spying in America are to keep NSA from spying on Cabal members as they engage in their conspiracy. Admiral Rogers appears to have opposed Cabal, as evidenced by the push to remove him by three Cabal agents in the Intelligence establishment.[201]

---

201   http://archive.is/y2WQS

Altogether what Q is drawing attention to are various facts, which combined together, point to an extensive, possibly non-state intelligence operation which spans national boundaries, which extends back before WWII, and which has installed a massive network of corruption within just about every facet of our governmental and civilian societal infrastructure. And since the President sets classification standards, he has the power to declassify what needs to be revealed to expose this conspiracy to the nation. That this is not happening immediately, implies there is a broader plan afoot, and the declassification will happen on a specific timetable within it.

Anonymous ID: KKIreCTB No.148287473 **121**
Nov 6 2017 16:52:24 (EST)

Why were the acts that recently occurred in SA so critically important?
What US assets are in place in/near SA?
What assurances were made to protect the Kingdom?
Who shot down the missile from Yemen?
POTUS declassify_speech_Jap_11_5
Was it really from Yemen?
How do we know?
Why is this relevant?
Who are the puppets?
Who are the puppet masters?
Who pulls the strings?
What provides power?
What if US elections can be rigged?
How are JFK, Reagan, and Trump different from the rest?
Why did JFK surround himself w/ family much like POTUS?
What if it was bought and paid for?
How would this be possible?
Why are there no voting ID laws in place?
What do you need an ID for? List. Compare. Laugh.
What is the argument for not allowing voter ID laws to be enacted?
Why are immigrants important? (MB)(Votes)(Attacks)
Why are illegals important? (MS13)(Votes)(187)
Why is open border important?

What did BO say on the campaign trail last year to illegals within the US?
What did BO encourage?
Was this illegal?
Who owns sizeable stakes in voter machine co's?
Who decides what voter machines are used in elections?
Why are some 'important' counties still manually/hand counted?
God save us.
Q

Obama gave illegal aliens an assurance that if they voted in our elections, nobody would be investigating, so they would be able to get away with it.[202] Basically Q is saying that our elections were thoroughly compromised by the Cabal through a mixture of voter machine manipulation by the compromised manufacturers, illegal aliens voting, and other voter fraud. And it was all supported up through the President, Barack Obama.

Anonymous ID: KKIreCTB No.148287529 🗗   **122**
Nov 6 2017 16:52:48 (EST)

What does money buy?
How do you prevent tampering?
Why are most forms of media left-wing?
Why is H-wood left-wing?
Why is the narrative so important?
Why do liberals defer to racism w/o proof?
No proof.
Who is HRC's mentor?
What party was he affiliated with?
Proof.
What party formed the KKK?
What party formed the Confederacy?
What party abolished slavery?
Why are D's attempting to erase history?
Is the black pop truly free today or enslaved by the D party?
Refer back to black pop crumbs.
Why is this relevant?

202   https://www.youtube.com/watch?v=nfgEvgVC6Qs&feature=youtu.be

287

Why is there an attack the day after bad news is published (D)?
Do you believe in coincidences?
Paint the picture.
Crumbs will make bread.
Operations underway.
Operators active.
Pray.
Snow White.
Godfather III.
Q

Here Q points out the power of controlling the narrative.
Republicans freed slaves. Democrats opposed the Civil Rights
movement. Hillary's mentor, Robert Byrd was a KKK member.[203]
And yet the Cabal, by controlling the narrative, has been able to
convince everyone that Democrats are the party of black
America, to whom all blacks owe unquestioned loyalty,

The bad news Q refers to is that Judicial Watch uncovered
papers showing FBI Deputy Director Andrew McCabe's wife
had received over $700,000 in campaign contributions from
Clinton Associates, as McCabe personally oversaw Hillary's
email/Classified-mishandling investigation up until a week
before the election.[204] The attack which overshadowed that bad
news was a Texas church mass-shooting.[205]

Anonymous ID: KKIreCTB No.148289594   **123**
Nov 6 2017 17:07:57 (EST)

Nothing is random.
Everything has meaning.
+++
Q

203http://archive.is/IyDwl
204http://archive.is/yL9DJ
205http://archive.is/RMKgK

288

Anonymous ID: NOjYqEdl No.148452545 ⤤

Nov 7 2017 18:34:55 (EST)

Deleted: Nov 7 2017 18:46:01 (EST)

+++
++
+
Q

Anonymous ID: NOjYqEdl No.148453749 ⤤

Nov 7 2017 18:43:57 (EST)

This was an aerial photo from Hong Kong with no copy available on the internet, so it was an original, which Q implied came from Air Force One through the filename, though at the time AF1 was not supposed to be in that area.

Anonymous ID: NOjYqEdl No.148455482 ⤤

Nov 7 2017 18:56:17 (EST)

Previous was deleted. Curious.
+++
++
+
Q

The graphic is your key.
Let's pause and say hello to the rogue intelligence agencies
currently monitoring these threads.
Was the money worth it?
Titanic.
Q

1510280445405.jpg

Trip added.
[C]oordinated effort to misdirect.
Guide to reading the crumbs necessary to cont**[I]**nue.
Attached gr**[A]**phic is correct.
Linked graphics are incorrect and false.
Graphic is necessary and vital.
Time stamp(s) and order **[is]** critical.
Re-review graphic (in full) each day post news release.
Learn to distinguish between relevant/non-relevant news.
Disinformation is real.
Disinformation is necessary.
Ex: US ML NG (1) False SA True
Why was this necessary?
What questions were asked re: SA prior to SA events?
Why is this relevant?
Think mirror.
Look there, or **[here]**, or there, truth is behind you.
What is a map?
Why is a map useful?
What is a legend?
Why is a legend useful?

What is a sequence?
Why is this relevant?
When does a map become a guide?
What is a keystone?
Everything stated is relevant.
Everything.
Future provides past.
Map provides picture.
Picture provides 40,000ft. v.
40,000ft. v. is classified.
Why is a map useful?
Think direction.
Think full picture.
Who controls the narrative?
Why is this relevant?
What is a spell?
Who is asleep?
Dissemination.
Attention on deck.
There is an active war on your mind.
Be [p]repared.
Ope[r]ations underway.
Operators [a]ctive.
Graphic is essential.
Find the ke[y]stone.
Moves and countermoves.
They never thought she would lose.
Snow white.
Godfather III.
Iron Eagle.
Q

The image is a photo reiterating all the posts to date.

Q !ITPb.qbhqo ID: Dx5TPc5d No 148781546 ⬚   **129**
Nov 9 2017 23:24:35 (EST)

[C]los[I]ng [A]ct:
Dismantled.
Impossible to clean.
Operations --> [N]o [S]uch [A]gency
Q

AF1_5A_2.png

Another photo of small islands under light cumulus cloud cover, ostensibly from Air Force One based on the AF1 filename. What this is supposed to indicate is that Trump is traveling to places which are not being publicized. The photo has been altered for brightness and contrast to appear better in print. The original photo can be seen at :

http://qanon.pub/data/media/1510288305037.png

POTUS NAT SEC E briefing 3:02am.
Please stand by.
Q

Q !ITPb.qbhqo ID: ln25Q56n No.148872500    **132**
Nov 10 2017 16:04:51 (EST)

Anonymous ID: rK87uAOe No. 148872136
Nov 10 2017 16:01:39 (EST)

Q Graphic.png

>>148871375

Q confirmed

is anything in this image wrong? i added posts from the 5th

>>148872136
Confirmed.
Correct.
Q

Again, this is a picture of all Q posts to this point.

Hard to swallow.
Important to progress.
Who are the puppet masters?
House of Saud (6+++) - $4 Trillion+
Rothschild (6++) - $2 Trillion+
Soros (6+) - $1 Trillion+
Focus on above (3).
Public wealth disclosures – False.
Many governments of the world feed the 'Eye'.
Think slush funds (feeder).
Think war (feeder).
Think environmental pacts (feeder).
Triangle has (3) sides.
Eye of Providence.
Follow the bloodlines.
What is the keystone?
Does Satan exist?
Does the 'thought' of Satan exist?
Who worships Satan?
What is a cult?
Epstein island.
What is a temple?
What occurs in a temple?
Worship?
Why is the temple on top of a mountain?
How many levels might exist below?
What is the significance of the colors, design and symbol above the dome?
Why is this relevant?
Who are the puppet masters?
Have the puppet masters traveled to this island?
When? How often? Why?
 "Vladimir Putin: The New World Order Worships Satan"
Q

Here Q makes a reference to the "Eye of Providence" - a symbol of a pyramid with an eye inside the top. To find the puppet masters, you must track funding through the House of

Saud, the Rothschild Family, and George Soros. Funding is channeled into the Cabal from governments through war expenditures, fraud, climate pacts, foreign aid, charity, etc.

Q then introduces the importance of bloodlines. Those at the top did not choose the mates whose genes would meld with their family genes haphazardly using emotions like love. Their mates were carefully selected to produce a stronger bloodline. And in a form of "kin-selection," where one individual facilitates the breeding success of a related individual to advance their shared genes, it appears the bloodline families keep track of everywhere their genes may wander to through things like affairs and dalliances, and they use the machinery they control to confer favor upon those relatives, placing them in positions of importance, and using them as assets to support the machine.

Q then draws attention to billionaire investor Jeffery Epstein, and his private island in the Virgin Islands. At the southern tip of his island is a strange building resembling an Islamic mosque, complete with a gold-plated dome on top of it. Q implies there are underground levels beneath it, and the puppet-masters perform some sort of occult rituals there.

It is unclear to what degree Cabal leaders actually believe in occultism and satan in a religious/philosophical sense, and to what degree it is a convenient explanation for why new inductees may be required to engage in evil acts during induction and promotion ceremonies which could facilitate blackmail later on. President Putin's quote about the elites worshiping satan came from the article below.[206]

---

206   http://archive.is/k6db9

Q !ITPb.qbhqo ID: gO/UntOB No.149063271 🗗   **134**
Nov 11 2017 23:29:58 (EST)

Why were the events in SA extraordinary?
Who was arrested?
What will bank records provide?
List names, family history, investment/ownership stakes, and point-to-point contacts.
EX: Alwaleed HUMA BO Citigroup US Control
Why is this relevant?
House of Saud.
House of Saud US Control
Follow the money.
What power shift recently occurred?
Was a new King appointed?
Coincidence?
Dark to LIGHT.
Why is this relevant?
One side of the triangle removed (1st time in history).
Other sides falling.
+++
++
+
Q

Fairly straightforward. Once the House of Saud was taken over by Crown Prince Mohammed bin Salman, all of Cabal's assets were forced to hand over all of their financial records and wealth. This has yielded all of the intelligence needed to take down the networks throughout the world, as it has frozen up all of Cabal's funds which were being laundered and stored in Saudi Arabia.

Q !ITPb.qbhqo ID: gO/UntOB No.149063400 🗗   **135**
Nov 11 2017 23:31:13 (EST)

ROTHSCHILD OWNED & CONTROLLED BANKS:
Afghanistan: Bank of Afghanistan
Albania: Bank of Albania
Algeria: Bank of Algeria

Algeria: Bank of Algeria
Argentina: Central Bank of Argentina
Armenia: Central Bank of Armenia
Aruba: Central Bank of Aruba
Australia: Reserve Bank of Australia
Austria: Austrian National Bank
Azerbaijan: Central Bank of Azerbaijan Republic
Bahamas: Central Bank of The Bahamas
Bahrain: Central Bank of Bahrain
Bangladesh: Bangladesh Bank
Barbados: Central Bank of Barbados
Belarus: National Bank of the Republic of Belarus
Belgium: National Bank of Belgium
Belize: Central Bank of Belize
Benin: Central Bank of West African States (BCEAO)
Bermuda: Bermuda Monetary Authority
Bhutan: Royal Monetary Authority of Bhutan
Bolivia: Central Bank of Bolivia
Bosnia: Central Bank of Bosnia and Herzegovina
Botswana: Bank of Botswana
Brazil: Central Bank of Brazil
Bulgaria: Bulgarian National Bank
Burkina Faso: Central Bank of West African States (BCEAO)
Burundi: Bank of the Republic of Burundi
Cambodia: National Bank of Cambodia
Came Roon: Bank of Central African States
Canada: Bank of Canada – Banque du Canada

Q !!TPb.qbhqo   ID: gO/UntOB   No 149063442☐   **136**
█▪v 11 2017 23:31:41 (EST)

Cayman Islands: Cayman Islands Monetary Authority
Central African Republic: Bank of Central African States
Chad: Bank of Central African States
Chile: Central Bank of Chile
China: The People's Bank of China
Colombia: Bank of the Republic
Comoros: Central Bank of Comoros
Congo: Bank of Central African States
Costa Rica: Central Bank of Costa Rica
Côte d'Ivoire: Central Bank of West African States (BCEAO)
Croatia: Croatian National Bank
Cuba: Central Bank of Cuba

Cyprus: Central Bank of Cyprus
Czech Republic: Czech National Bank
Denmark: National Bank of Denmark
Dominican Republic: Central Bank of the Dominican Republic
East Caribbean area: Eastern Caribbean Central Bank
Ecuador: Central Bank of Ecuador
Egypt: Central Bank of Egypt
El Salvador: Central Reserve Bank of El Salvador
Equatorial Guinea: Bank of Central African States
Estonia: Bank of Estonia
Ethiopia: National Bank of Ethiopia
European Union: European Central Bank
Fiji: Reserve Bank of Fiji
Finland: Bank of Finland
France: Bank of France
Gabon: Bank of Central African States
The Gambia: Central Bank of The Gambia
Georgia: National Bank of Georgia
Germany: Deutsche Bundesbank
Ghana: Bank of Ghana
Greece: Bank of Greece
Guatemala: Bank of Guatemala
Guinea Bissau: Central Bank of West African States (BCEAO)
Guyana: Bank of Guyana
Haiti: Central Bank of Haiti
Honduras: Central Bank of Honduras
Hong Kong: Hong Kong Monetary Authority
Hungary: Magyar Nemzeti Bank
Iceland: Central Bank of Iceland
India: Reserve Bank of India
Indonesia: Bank Indonesia
Iran: The Central Bank of the Islamic Republic of Iran

Q !ITPb.qbhqo ID: gO/UntOB No.149063509☐
●ov 11 2017 23:32:20 (EST)   **137**

Iraq: Central Bank of Iraq
Ireland: Central Bank and Financial Services Authority of Ireland
Israel: Bank of Israel
Italy: Bank of Italy
Jamaica: Bank of Jamaica
Japan: Bank of Japan
Jordan: Central Bank of Jordan
Kazakhstan: National Bank of Kazakhstan

Kenya: Central Bank of Kenya
Korea: Bank of Korea
Kuwait: Central Bank of Kuwait
Kyrgyzstan: National Bank of the Kyrgyz Republic
Latvia: Bank of Latvia
Lebanon: Central Bank of Lebanon
Lesotho: Central Bank of Lesotho
Libya: Central Bank of Libya (Their most recent conquest)
Uruguay: Central Bank of Uruguay
Lithuania: Bank of Lithuania
Luxembourg: Central Bank of Luxembourg
Macao: Monetary Authority of Macao
Macedonia: National Bank of the Republic of Macedonia
Madagascar: Central Bank of Madagascar
Malawi: Reserve Bank of Malawi
Malaysia: Central Bank of Malaysia
Mali: Central Bank of West African States (BCEAO)
Malta: Central Bank of Malta
Mauritius: Bank of Mauritius
Mexico: Bank of Mexico
Moldova: National Bank of Moldova
Mongolia: Bank of Mongolia
Montenegro: Central Bank of Montenegro
Morocco: Bank of Morocco
Mozambique: Bank of Mozambique
Namibia: Bank of Namibia
Nepal: Central Bank of Nepal
Netherlands: Netherlands Bank
Netherlands Antilles: Bank of the Netherlands Antilles
New Zealand: Reserve Bank of New Zealand
Nicaragua: Central Bank of Nicaragua
Niger: Central Bank of West African States (BCEAO)
Nigeria: Central Bank of Nigeria
Norway: Central Bank of Norway
Oman: Central Bank of Oman
Pakistan: State Bank of Pakistan

Papua New Guinea: Bank of Papua New Guinea
Paraguay: Central Bank of Paraguay
Peru: Central Reserve Bank of Peru
Philip Pines: Bangko Sentral ng Pilipinas
Poland: National Bank of Poland
Portugal: Bank of Portugal
Qatar: Qatar Central Bank
Romania: National Bank of Romania
Russia: Central Bank of Russia
Rwanda: National Bank of Rwanda
San Marino: Central Bank of the Republic of San Marino
Samoa: Central Bank of Samoa
Saudi Arabia: Saudi Arabian Monetary Agency
Senegal: Central Bank of West African States (BCEAO)
Serbia: National Bank of Serbia
Seychelles: Central Bank of Seychelles
Sierra Leone: Bank of Sierra Leone
Singapore: Monetary Authority of Singapore
Slovakia: National Bank of Slovakia
Slovenia: Bank of Slovenia
Solomon Islands: Central Bank of Solomon Islands
South Africa: South African Reserve Bank
Spain: Bank of Spain
Sri Lanka: Central Bank of Sri Lanka
Sudan: Bank of Sudan
Surinam: Central Bank of Suriname
Swaziland: The Central Bank of Swaziland
Sweden: Sveriges Riksbank
Switzerland: Swiss National Bank
Tajikistan: National Bank of Tajikistan
Tanzania: Bank of Tanzania
Thailand: Bank of Thailand
Togo: Central Bank of West African States (BCEAO)
Tonga: National Reserve Bank of Tonga
Trinidad and Tobago: Central Bank of Trinidad and Tobago
Tunisia: Central Bank of Tunisia
Turkey: Central Bank of the Republic of Turkey
Uganda: Bank of Uganda
Ukraine: National Bank of Ukraine
United Arab Emirates: Central Bank of United Arab Emirates

United Kingdom: Bank of England
United States: Federal Reserve, Federal Reserve Bank of New York
Vanuatu: Reserve Bank of Vanuatu
Venezuela: Central Bank of Venezuela
Vietnam: The State Bank of Vietnam
Yemen: Central Bank of Yemen
Zambia: Bank of Zambia
Zimbabwe: Reserve Bank of Zimbabwe
The FED and the IRS
FACT: US Federal Reserve is a privately-owned company, sitting on its very own patch of land, immune to the US laws.
Q

Q !ITPb qbhqo ID: gO/UntOB No 149063582☐   **139**
Nov 11 2017 23 33 13 (EST)

List of Republicans, in the House and Senate, who have announced they will not seek re-election:
Bob Corker.
Charlie Dent.
Jeff Flake.
Lynn Jenkins.
Sam Johnson.
Raul Labrador.
Frank LoBiondo.
Tim Murphy.
Why is this relevant?
Re-read crumbs.
Q

These will all be compromised assets of Cabal who Q will assert are being driven from office, by the Military Intelligence counter-coup that is purging Cabal from our government. I assume Q acquired their blackmail files, and has now made clear to them that they will leave, or they will suffer the consequences of their files being made public. Cabal has probably acceded to this, under threat of the citizenry being given their own files, and seeing how Cabal spied on them.

Wealth (over generations) buys power.
Power (over generations) buys more wealth/control.
More wealth/control buys countries and its people.
Families combined (TRI) = NWO.
Inner TRI families will collapse.
What is the keystone?
What Nation dominates all others?
What Nation has influence over most others?
What is the keystone?
Return to SA.
Strings cut (+++).
Puppets (+++) in shadows.
Each side of the triangle controls a certain subsect of power brokers.
Power brokers are also labeled as the puppets/servants.
What is the New World Order?
Why did POTUS receive a sword dance when visiting SA?
What does this mean culturally?
Why is this relevant?
What occurred in SA?
How did POTUS remove one side of the pyramid?
What did POTUS receive while visiting China?
Where did POTUS dine?
What is the significance?
What if China, Russia, and others are coordinating w/ POTUS to eliminate the NWO?
Who controls NK?
Who really controls NK?
Who controls several agencies within the US, EU, and abroad?
Why is No Such Agency so vital?
Enormous scale of events currently ongoing.
Why is Russia helping to kill ISIS?
This is not easy to accept nor believe.
Crumbs make bread.
Operations active.

Joint missions underway.
The world is fighting back.
Refer back to graphic.
The Great Awakening.
Snow White.
Iron Eagle.
Jason Bourne (2016)(Dream/CIA).
Q

Here, Q is emphasizing how massive wealth inevitably grows. You have these ultra-wealthy families, and none is known to dominate economically? All of the richest people in the world stumbled on one idea, and accumulated their wealth in a matter of decades by chance, eclipsing wealthy families who have been around for centuries? Here Q points out that those old families have been dominating, regardless of what you were told.

It's thought Keystone is from a speech John F Kennedy gave the morning he was assassinated. He referred to America as "the keystone in the arch of freedom."[207] As a result of that status, America had become the prime target of any conspiracy looking to eliminate freedom. There is also a software spying tool called Keystone, that will figure in later.

Q also raises the idea Kim Jong Un may not be in charge of North Korea. Long before Q, I thought the idea of Kim as the leader of North Korea was strange. Decades back a North Korean minisub went aground in a bay in South Korea.[208] Once the tide ran out, it would have attracted a lot of attention, so the crew, and a Special Forces unit it was carrying, exited and made their way to land. They found the crew lined up inside the

---

207   http://archive.is/HletA
208   http://archive.is/UqgjA

treeline. They had been knelt down and immediately executed, presumably by the Special Forces team which then made its way north to get home. The ruthlessness struck me every time I saw Kim, especially when he first took control of the country. Here was a young twenty-something, with no physical capability for violence, who probably couldn't handle a weapon, had grown up living a life of luxury and protection, and he was surrounded by grizzled North Korean Generals with hard faces who would have executed their own crews on a moment's notice. None of them ever just took Kim out and seized control?

Q will assert Cabal took over North Korea, around the same time they took over Iran, and both have been led by puppet governments ever since. One problem Cabal would have is that as a non-state actor it would lack a secure base of operations. In intelligence, an area where surveillance can not easily penetrate under an innocuous cover is called a denied area. Denied areas allow an intelligence operation to plan, to coordinate, and to get ahead of competing operations. Since Cabal had no state itself, and was parasitizing local intelligence operations, it could not guarantee a clique would not develop within one of those local operations which might devote surveillance assets to it.

Most people don't grasp how difficult it is to have a denied area on another intelligence operation's turf. Today, if an intelligence operation can get within a hundred or two hundred feet, they can probably hear and even "see" to some regard what is going on within a normal building structure using technology. The idea you need to plant a bug inside a building is one more instance of Cabal misinforming civilians about intelligence operations to make them weaker. The truth is a bug was last used in the fifties and sixties. Since then, just as modern medicine went from fluoroscopes to advanced 3D imaging with different tissues portrayed in different colors, which can be observed literally as you are targeting a tissue with multiple sub-lethal deadly radiation beams on different axes that converged in one lethal spot, so too has surveillance technology advanced to the point you can recreate a structure's curtiledge from a remote position using only data gathered well away from the said structure, without anyone ever making a covert entry.

If you want a denied area that surveillance cannot penetrate, you really need a nation, with a law enforcement force acting as the first layer of a counter-intelligence operation devoted to keeping hostile surveillance out of the entire nation. But Cabal did not have a nation, and even if it did, it would need that nation rendered a no-go zone to all Western intelligence operations if it wanted to be truly secure from eavesdropping and surveillance. So it needed a nation, ideally denied to the West, where it could exert absolute control absent any interference by a free population, or local legal strictures constraining it.

If you believe in the possibility of Cabal (and I have seen it with my own eyes), then North Korea as a puppet regime would not only seem plausible – it would almost be a mission-imperative. And it would make sense of a few other data-points, from Kim not being subject to a violent coup, to even his strange inability to walk at times (one torture method used in Asian nations is tying a subject down on their back and beating the soles of the feet with rattan canes).

Q also indicates NSA was vital because it's a military agency and thus was resistant to infiltration and corruption.

305

Also, the "Bourne" movies might have some significance later on. (It will be revealed later both the plot-line of the CIA corrupting a social media company and MK Ultra mind-control were real facts that somebody drew their movie scripts around.)

Rogue operators are here.
Failed to shut down site.
Protected.
This will only get worse.
Archive and coordinate.
Crumbs dropped will soon paint the full picture.
The picture will open the eyes of the world.
We can't do it without you.
God bless you all.
Q

How did Soros replace family 'y'?
Who is family 'y'?
Trace the bloodlines of these (3) families.
What happened during WWII?
Was Hitler a puppet?
Who was his handler?
What was the purpose?
What was the real purpose of the war?
What age was GS?
What is the Soros family history?
What has occurred since the fall of N Germany?
Who is A. Merkel?
What is A. Merkel's family history?
Follow the bloodline.
Who died on the Titanic?
What year did the Titanic sink?
Why is this relevant?
What 'exactly' happened to the Titanic?
What 'class of people' were guaranteed a lifeboat?

Why did select 'individuals' not make it into the lifeboats?
Why is this relevant?
How do we know who was on the lifeboats (D or A)?
How were names and bodies recorded back then?
When were tickets purchased for her maiden voyage?
Who was 'specifically' invited?
Less than 10.
What is the FED?
What does the FED control?
Who controls the FED?
Who approved the formation of the FED?
Why did H-wood glorify Titanic as a tragic love story?
Who lived in the movie (what man)?
Why is this relevant?
Opposite is true.
What is brainwashing?
What is a PSYOP?
What happened to the Hindenburg?
What really happened to the Hindenburg?
Who died during the 'accident'?
Why is this relevant?
What are sheep?
Who controls the narrative?
The truth would put 99% of people in the hospital.
It must be controlled.
Snow White.
Iron Eagle.
Jason Bourne (CIA/Dream).
Q

Bloodlines appear to play a large part in determining who mans the Cabal's operations. Perhaps it is kin-selection driving Cabal to place related individuals from old bloodline families in positions of power and influence, or maybe it is all a Secret Society and they all know they are different from the regular masses, and the regular masses could not be trusted.

Regardless it has long been noted all Presidents save two (Martin Van Buren and Donald J. Trump) descend from

European royalty. Even Barack Obama is related to six US Presidents: James Madison, Harry S. Truman, Lyndon B. Johnson, Jimmy Carter, George H. W. Bush, and George W. Bush.[209]

You see this in rumors about famous figures in history, though official narratives tend to ignore them. According to one account, Adolf Hitler's grandmother bore his father out of wedlock while she worked for a Rothschild family member who some thought had sired him.[210] Angela Merkel bore a striking resemblance to Hilter's mother, and there was even a rumor one intelligence agency thought she might have been descended from him.[211]

Q's interest in the Titanic raises another conspiracy theory which alleges the sinking of the Titanic was not an accident.[212] This begins with the Titanic's sister ship the Olympic, which suffered sufficient damage in an accident as to render it a total loss. The owners then hatched a scam to insure the Titanic, swap it with her damaged sister-ship, sink the sister-ship in an "accident," and take the insurance money.

Around this time, the elites wanted to gain control of the US currency supply through the creation of the Federal Reserve, but several influential people, such as John Jacob Astor IV, Benjamin Guggenheim, Isidor and Ida Straus, were all adamantly opposed to the Fed. All were on board the Titanic on her maiden voyage. Astor was actually issued a free invitation,

209   http://archive.is/yK7xy
210   http://archive.is/5qWGE
211   http://archive.is/tTIWM
212   Beveridge, B., Hall, S. (2004). *Olympic & Titanic: The Truth Behind the Conspiracy.* Infinity Publishing.

and in accepting it, sealed his fate. Q seems to imply Cabal knew of the insurance scam, and they arranged for the opponents of the Federal Reserve to be on board when it went down.

According to the theory, J.P. Morgan, who owned the company which owned the Titanic, and who was a proponent of the Federal Reserve, had himself seen to it that it was arranged for the opponents of the Federal Reserve to be on board. He himself had publicly booked a ticket on the maiden voyage acquiring a private suite on board, complete with private promenade deck, before canceling at the last minute, supposedly to get a massage.[213]

Finally, in support of the idea the sinking of the Titanic could have been an intelligence operation, is the fact everyone was told it sank after hitting an iceberg, despite a double-hulled designed specifically to survive such an impact. But in reality, increasing evidence indicates that it was actually sunk by a coal fire on board which weakened the hulls – something which would make sabotage much more likely.[214]

Again, in common society, this would seem ridiculous. But if you are dealing with intelligence professionals, running an intelligence operation, this is exactly what they would do. Given J.P. Morgan would have had motivation to both perform an insurance scam and at the same time advance a political agenda, and he owned the company, it is not impossible. In criminal parlance, he had motive, means, and opportunity.

Q then covers the Hindenburg, which we are told ignited

---

213   http://archive.is/SlyZX
214   http://archive.is/j10YR

when a spark of static electricity ignited the hydrogen which filled it. However an FBI report noted that Commander Charles E Rosendahl, who was in charge of Lakehurst Naval Air Station had told FBI investigators that due to various events brought to his attention, he saw purposeful sabotage as a logical cause.[215]

Q is beginning to try to make people realize that if a hostile foreign intelligence operation has penetrated the media and government in the US, they control what you hear, and what theories are lent legitimacy. They write the history you read, and their professors often teach it. That is an enormous power. Again Q references Jason Bourne and Deep Dream, the fictional social media company the CIA had co-opted in the movie.

Note today how difficult it is to find stories on Google which deviate from the set narrative some class of unknown elites is foisting on the people. Search any right-wing view or Trump-favoring story today, and the overwhelming number of stories which come up first will be slanted toward a left-wing, anti-Trump perspective. Then look at social media companies, where critics of the left and conspiracy theorists are labeled either fake news purveyors and banned outright, or labeled Russian bots and banned.

Somebody is going to great lengths to control what you see and hear. But the truth is, the only thing that has changed is that because of the internet you are finding out about it. It has not only always been this way – it has been worse. Q is promising the puppetmasters that they are going to be revealed, and their control over the narrative is ending.

---

215   http://archive.is/Uat1Z

Q !ITPb.qbhqo ID: 99LpGawB No.149124567 ⬚   **143**
⬚v 12 2017 12:31:16 (EST)

> Anonymous ID: AdHN8HBF No.149123755 ⬚
> ⬚v 12 2017 12:23:45 (EST)
>
> >>149122998
> There are a bunch out there, here is one
>
> >The CIA has 7 supercomputers, and they are all named after
> the 7 dwarfs from Snow White (Doc, Dopey, Bashful, Grumpy,
> Sneezy, Sleepy and Happy)
>
> https://cheshirelibraryscience.wordpress.com/tag/cia/ ⬚ ⬚

>>149123755
Confirmed.
Go deeper.
Signatures are IMPORTANT.
Q

Q !ITPb.qbhqo ID: /jAm9Qi+ No.149140639 ⬚   **144**
⬚v 12 2017 14:52:34 (EST)

Patriots don't sleep.
40,000ft. v. necessary to understand **[US]**/SA/global events.
Paint the picture.
Decrease altitude (we will not fly that high again).
Higher the altitude greater the **[risk]** of conspiracy ST.
Many cannot/will not swallow.
What is No Such Agency - Q group?
Who has clearance to full picture?
Important.
SIS is good.
+++Adm R+++
What agency is at war w/ Clowns In America?
How does POTUS shift narrative?
(New) Age of Enlightenment.
80% covert.
20% public.
What has occurred over **[th]**e last several months?
C-info leaks?
Operations (think SA + ???)?
CNN sale?

What co's rec large cash injections by Clowns In America (public)?
Why???
Who does [i]t hurt?
Who control[s] the MSM?
Primary objective from beginning: POTUS discredit MSM.
[W]hy is this relevant?
How is information transmitted?
How are people inform[e]d?
Why was Sarah A. C. attacked (hack-attempt)?
Why was Op[e]ration Mockingbird repeated?
Why was Jason Bourne (CIA/Dream) repeated?
Think social media platforms.
Who are the Wizards & Warloc[k]s?
What council do the Wizards & Warlocks control?
Think Snowden (inside terms dropped).
Alice & Wonderland – understood.
Snow White – understood.
Iron Eagle?
Godfather III?
Speed?
Everything has meaning.
Disney is a distraction.
Senate & Congress = puppets (not all)(power shift).
For **[GOD & COUNTRY]**.
For HUMANITY.
GERONIMO.
Q

Here Q says to be a patriot, you cannot be lulled into complacency by accepting the quieting narratives the media machine gives you or the pat answers the government provides. It is very likely to be all deceptions, designed to put you to sleep, and make you powerless.

His leaks to date about conspiracies were simply to give you an overview that things are not always as you were told, and those telling you what happened are often owned and controlled by those with things to hide.

But he says to not focus too much on that overview, as you risk descending into the world of conspiracies of the past, rather than focusing on the explicit cases of corruption and criminality today which are most important to address. In truth everything is so bad that most could not accept how different the reality is from the lies they have been conditioned to believe.

In National Security circles, the "Q group" is an internal policing group which watches NSA members for signs of espionage or other behaviors that endanger national security.[216] NSA and Q-group will have the full picture because of the massive extent of the communications intelligence which crosses their screens, including technical penetrations of all surveillance operations out there targeting Americans, including Cabal's.

Q now also begins to reveal that there is a war going on between CIA, which has been penetrated and compromised by Cabal, and the NSA, which hasn't been corrupted due to its power to avert penetration by using all the signals intelligence it has access to, and the fact it is primarily military-staffed.

Later, it will to look like Edward Snowden, who appeared to be a lowly security guard in the CIA who flunked out of Special Forces training, may have been plucked and sheep-dipped at the outset of his Army Special Forces training by CIA. He was then trained-up, and sent on an operation into NSA to politically weaken it and expose/damage its collection programs.

On "cash injections," CIA supposedly injected cash into Amazon for cloud computing, and then Amazon turned around and purchased the Washington Post. That appears a natural

---

216   http://archive.is/0OrfL

outgrowth of Project Mockingbird. That is why Trump's primary objective was to discredit the Main Stream Media as "Fake News." It striped the Puppetmasters of their most powerful weapon - the ability to set the narrative and tell the public what to think, and and thereby gain control over what they do.

Sara Carter's Twitter was hacked when she reported on FISA-abuse.[217] Have no illusions, under Obama the country's most powerful surveillance and intelligence operations were being run against even the most minor of political voices online.

Q !ITPb.qbhqo ID: I/hYVcRn No.149151705   **145**
bv 12 2017 16:24:44 (EST)

::::WARNING::::
This is not a game!
DIRECT ATTACK TODAY BY NYT/CLOWNS IN AMERICA:
https://www.nytimes.com/2017/11/12/us/nsa-shadow-brokers.html
Do you believe in coincidences?
How many coincidences do you need before you believe?
This is the biggest insider drop in the history of the world.
Pray.
Q

Q !ITPb.qbhqo ID: X/EWIOzz No.149152383   **146**
bv 12 2017 16:30:27 (EST)

::::WARNING::::
This is not a game!
DIRECT ATTACK TODAY BY NYT/CLOWNS IN AMERICA:
https://www.nytimes.com/2017/11/12/us/nsa-shadow-brokers.html
Do you believe in coincidences?
How many coincidences do you need before you believe?
This is the biggest insider drop in the history of the world.
Pray.
Q

---

217   http://archive.is/Aj2pr

What Q is saying here is no sooner does he reveal the backstory about the war being fought between the Cabal-corrupted CIA and the NSA, than the CIA's Project Mockingbird media, in the form of the NY Times, does a hit-piece on the NSA. The timing of this was seen as a very public shot across the NSA's bow by the CIA, and confirmation that Q's story about what was going on was looking increasingly legitimate.

Q !ITPb.qbhqo ID: X/EWIOzz No.149152902 [↗]   **147**
Nov 12 2017 16:34:56 (EST)

> **Q** !ITPb.qbhqo ID: X/EWIOzz No.149152383 [↗]
> Nov 12 2017 16:30:27 (EST)
>
> ::::WARNING::::
> This is not a game!
> DIRECT ATTACK TODAY BY NYT/CLOWNS IN AMERICA:
> https://www.nytimes.com/2017/11/12/us/nsa-shadow-brokers.html [↗]
> Do you believe in coincidences?
> How many coincidences do you need before you believe?
> This is the biggest insider drop in the history of the world.
> Pray.
> Q

>>149152383
This is a direct attack.
The article is disinfo but made to send a message to POTUS.
You are witnessing history.
Coincidence?
God be with us all.
Q

You will see as time goes on, the media will attack the President, all using specific keywords simultaneously, as if all the major news media celebrities and organizations were getting a memo each morning with orders from someone.

Q !ITPb.qbhqo ID: X/EWlOzz No.149157229 ⬈   **148**
Nov 12 2017 17:10:49 (EST)

NYT/Clowns In America article released today re: Q-group is a
DIRECT attack/warning re: what is being dropped here.
Read between the lines.
Why was the article published today?
POTUS has been briefed.
New measures active and in place.
Update the graphic.

_DGB79FTWA-0ZjBT_19-T_yes
_Conf_13_pre-lau_yes
_HTzD09BA_conf_yes
_^yRTPCCA-7^DFWTAb_yes
_green1_green2_green3_green4_conf-ZDjTwT9Ry
Godspeed.
Q

Q !ITPb.qbhqo ID: TrJge011 No.149160361 ⬈   **149**
Nov 12 2017 17:37:54 (EST)

Freedom.png   ⬇

Q !ITPb.qbhqo ID: /lc4nimE No.149262582 ⬈   **150**
Nov 13 2017 13:04:46 (EST)

Distress cal**[L]**s to others will **[d]**o you/family no good at this stage.
We know whe**[R]**e you/the family are at all times and can hear you
breathing.
Q

_D7g^-_%19FZBx_decline

316

The "LdR" in this was thought to be a reference to Lynn de Rothschild, who had just tweeted out an insult at President Trump, later deleted.[218] The "We can hear you breathe," is a reference to the fact she is under close surveillance by a technical surveillance team, which supports full surveillance.

Q !!TPb.qbhqo ID: EV3pl+ol No.149401052 ☍   **151**
Nov 14 2017 12:51:10 (EST)

How do you capture a very dangerous animal?
Do you attack it from the front?
Do you walk through the front door?
Do you signal ahead of time you will be attacking?
How do you distinguish between good and bad?
Who do you trust to keep secrets?
How do you prevent leaks?
Who do you trust to complete the mission?
How do you prevent warnings being sent?
Why is Adm R. so important?
Why was the source code to former NSA collection p's publicly released?
How do you blind the Clowns In America?
What was Snowden's primary mission?
What was Snowden's real primary mission?
Was Snowden truly acting on his own?
Nothing is as it appears.
What show is being put on by AG Sessions since his confirmation?
What show is being put on by POTUS since AG Sessions' confirmation?
Why was AG Sessions' confirmation challenged heavily?
Why was RR's confirmation smooth and easy?
What was the vote count for RR?
Why did Sessions recuse himself?
Why is this relevant?
What group has vocally supported RM repeatedly?
How do you capture a very dangerous animal?
Who is best to conduct the attack?
What is the one force necessary to retain control?
Why does the US Military play such a vital role in this global game of RISK?

---

218   http://archive.is/4RP9E

What is money without power?
Why did POTUS depart Manila 30 min ahead of schedule?
Why is AF1 landing in Hawaii?
Does AF1 have in-air refueling ability?
Nothing is as it appears.
What was the DC vote breakdown between Trump & Clinton?
What is the nickname for DC?
Why would sealed indictments be outside of DC jurisdiction?
What purpose would this serve?
Why are judicial appointments being rapidly completed?
Who can you trust?
Have faith, Patriots.
Q

Admiral Rogers was the one who revealed to President Trump he was under illegal surveillance at Trump Tower.[219]

Here is where Q first began to reveal what he claimed was Trump and Military Intelligence's plan to take down the Cabal. How do you capture a very dangerous animal? You use a trap.

The gist of the plan was this. Sessions would recuse himself, because he was honorable and Cabal would fear they could not control him. Rosenstein, who appears to have been going along with Cabal's cover-ups previously would take control, and this would cause Cabal's forces in government to relax, because they thought he was one of them. However he was not. He would appoint Mueller, who was a long-term Cabal operative. Mueller's job was to give Cabal a sense they were working toward impeaching Trump and in control. Because Cabal agents in government felt Mueller was doing something, the rest of them would stand down and stay out of his way. Unbeknownst to them, Mueller had already been turned by Trump and Military Intelligence during the meeting with Trump

---

219   http://archive.is/bn6ZF

where he was supposedly being interviewed for the position of FBI Director (which he was already statutorily disqualified from taking). He was shown evidence which would destroy him if prosecuted, and offered a deal, which he took. Now he would investigate Trump, give the impression that he was going to deliver impeachment charges, and then not do any of that. Meanwhile DOJ Inspector General Horowitz was investigating Cabal malfeasance at the Justice Department. A US Attorney in Utah, John Huber was running his own investigation with a Grand Jury. A stealth prosecutor somewhere else, later identified as John Durham, would emerge running yet another investigation into Cabal malfeasance later. All along Q would reveal all of these before they were publicly known.

According to Q, these investigations were building up reams of sealed indictments of the biggest corruption network in the history of the United States. It is believed the reason for sealed indictments is this corruption network had already placed agents throughout the law enforcement and judicial apparatus. If you tried to prosecute them as the indictments were issued, prosecutors would accidentally miss filing dates, judges would dismiss cases, and as each case failed due to protection from someone in the network who sabotaged it, that Cabal operative would be released, and be able to reoccupy their position in the government, where they could cover for someone else.

By sealing all of the indictments, and unsealing them all at once, everyone is charged at once, and everyone is forced to recuse themselves from their positions in the machinery of justice. Even without convictions, this will cleanse the machinery of justice immediately, and prevent individual Cabal operatives from subverting the course of justice in each case. As non-Cabal government workers convict each Cabal member, they will be removed from government permanently, and our government can be purged of this corruption network once and for all. If Q's assertions are correct, it is quite clever, actually. And given the extent of the network I have seen myself, it is probably the only way this could be done. If this is true, everything we have seen, Session's recusal, Trump's tweets criticizing him, Mueller's investigation, it is all a show. The real action will be the investigations this show is buying time for.

"You Blind the Clowns In America" (CIA) by releasing all of their hacking tools, as Wikileaks did with the Vault 7 hack. Everyone patches their systems and those avenues of spying are gone from their arsenal. Notice these came from an NSA worker.

The one force necessary to retain control is the military, and Trump has that crucial support.

Air Force One leaving early, flying quickly,[220] and landing in Hawaii might imply POTUS was avoiding some sort of operation to attack Air Force One, by moving before it was prepared to attack. There is a large NSA facility in Hawaii. He might have been pausing there in response to a threat.

DC is known as the swamp due to the corruption. The support for Cabal's operations is so great that it voted 91% for Hillary Clinton, and 4% for President Trump.[221] That is no coincidence. The vast majority of them are in the Secret Society of Cabal's network. They knew what Donald Trump would do.

---

220   http://archive.is/qIJ3X
221   http://archive.is/ozpuz

Anonymous ID: AWhBigst No.149402286 ☐
▓v 14 2017 13:02:04 (EST)

q.png

Donald J. Trump ⊙
@realDonaldTrump

THANK YOU ASIA! #USA🇺🇸

0:37 / 0:45

6:30 PM · 14 Nov 2017

2,392 Retweets 9,865 Likes

1.6K   2.4K   9.9K

https://twitter.com/realDonaldTrump/status/930490487903084544

did anyone saw this in the vid?

>>149402286
Isn't that curious?
What's below?
Q

Trump was returning from Asia and tweeted a video which contained this image, shot out the window of Air Force One during POTUS's Asia trip. This will later become a visual reference to a secret meeting Q claims POTUS had with North

Korean leader Kim Jong Un in the Forbidden City, presumably after some event, perhaps covert military action, had severed Cabal from its command and control within North Korea. That freed Kim Jong Un to make a deal with President Trump, which was cemented in that meeting. Everything after was just timed theater designed to aid the Storm.

It was after this revelation, that the entire posture of North Korea and the United States changed, seemingly effortlessly, and suddenly peace on the Korean Peninsula seemed well within reach. It would make it appear Trump may have been rushing back to Hawaii to brief Military Intelligence in person, within a SCIF, on the outcome of this trip. Either that, or the turning point had created a moment of extreme risk.

Q !lTPb.qbhqo ID: wmN+33xv No.149467638 ☐   **153**
Nov 14 2017 21:25:09 (EST)

For the coming days ahead.
Ask yourself an honest question, why would a billionaire who has it all, fame, fortune, a warm and loving family, friends, etc. want to endanger himself and his family by becoming POTUS?
Why would he want to target himself and those he cares about?
Does he need money?
Does he need fame?
What does he get out of this?
Does he want to make the US/world a better place for his family and for those good and decent people who have long been taken advantage of?
Perhaps he could not stomach the thought of mass murders occurring to satisfy Moloch?
Perhaps he could not stomach the thought of children being kidnapped, drugged, and raped while leaders/law enforcement of the world turn a blind eye.
Perhaps he was tired of seeing how certain races/countries were being constantly abused and kept in need/poor/and suffering all for a specific purpose.

Perhaps he could not in good conscious see the world burn.
Why, hours after the election, did seven people travel to an undisclosed location to hold a very private & highly secured/guarded meeting?
Why didn't HRC give a concession speech?
When was the last time a presidential candidate didn't personally give a concession speech?
What happens if the border remained open and the MSM continued to brainwash?
At what point do Patriots, and hard working men and woman, become the minority?
What about voting machines?
Who owns the voting machines?
What about voter ID laws?
Photo ID? When is it necessary and must be presented? Make a list. Laugh.
Reconcile.
Would the chances of defeating evil grow less and less with each passing year?
What does 'red line' mean?
Why, again, were the arrests made in SA so very important?
What strings were immediately cut?
Follow the money.
When does a bird sing?
Q

Here we find this Cabal was set on seeking a full dictatorial takeover, by first flooding the nation with weaker foreigners who would lack the American aggression and intolerance of a foreign dictatorship, and then vote in a dictatorship before taking away the vote and just establishing it outright. If this were to happen, then exposure would not matter. Obviously, they were engaging in all manners of horrors to exert their control, and this favored a leadership driven by pure evil.

My own personal firsthand experience with the covert surveillance state indicates an increasing absence of any concern about citizens seeing it. There was also no aversion to using overt intimidation on citizens. This would indicate that those at the top indeed felt that full exposure of a Stasi-like secret police operation against Americans, was of less and less concern as a Hillary Clinton Presidency approached.

At the very least, they were conducting extensive psychological experiments on how individuals would react to being placed under 24/7 surveillance coverage and intimidation with seeming complicity of local government forces like police and federal agents. At worst, and more likely, the surveillance state was already applying it to everyone and actually using all levels of government to contain those who saw it and resisted.

Before I ever knew of Q, I knew we were on this path. I was only unsure of whether it was well into the pilot-program phase, or if it was fully operational. I suspect it was the latter, and we were much closer than anyone could ever have imagined would have been possible in the United States. Q would seem to confirm this, and the knowledge of it was why President Trump turned his back on a life of ease and comfort, and chose to endure the costs to step forward at this moment in history.

Q !ITPb.qbhqo ID: wmN+33xv No.149467690 �   **154**
Nov 14 2017 21:25:29 (EST)

Who financed 9-11?
Who was Bin Laden's handler?
Why was the Clowns In America tasked to hunt/kill/capture UBL?
Why not MI?
If we found UBL, eliminated his security, why would we immediately kill him and not take him alive?
Why wouldn't we want to capture UBL alive and extract other possible T-level events?
Perhaps someday people will understand 'they' had a plan to conduct 'another' mass extinction event.
WWI & II - orchestrated and planned by select families?

Fantasy land.
Remember, the more people there are, the more power the people have.
Why do D's push for gun control 'directly' after every tragic incident?
Why is this so very important to their agenda?
We, the people, are who they are afraid of.
We, the people, are who they fear will one day awake.
Our Father who art in heaven,
Hallowed be thy name.
Thy kingdom come.
Thy will be done
on earth as it is in heaven.
Give us this day our daily bread,
and forgive us our trespasses,
as we forgive those who trespass against us,
and lead us not into temptation,
but deliver us from evil.
Q

Here Q points out bin Ladin has a history as a CIA asset, and the Saudis funded 9/11. Then he points out that although the military was running the war in Afghanistan against Al Qaida, and had a full military intelligence operation that was routinely accompanying patrols, cultivating and meeting with sources in Afghanistan, the CIA was tasked with finding and killing bin Ladin in a parallel operation. Then, when he was found unarmed and confused, rather than take him alive for interrogation, they killed him in place.

Then Q highlights that this conspiracy goes back before WWI, and the families involved use war, both to cull the loyal, principled warrior psychologies which pose the most threat to their continued dominance of society, and to maintain their safety and control by keeping us fighting each other. Finally, this is why they manipulate the sheep to seek gun control.

Q !ITPb.qbhqo ID: snf602p9 No.149490950 155
Nov 15 2017 00:38:48 (EST)

_Conf_D-TT_^_v891_0600_yes
_green1_0600
Bunker Apple Yellow Sky [... + 1]
Yes
Godspeed.
Q

Q !ITPb.qbhqo ID: eTJFrZ+E No.149921023 156
Nov 18 2017 05:18:29 (EST)

++

The significance of these is not understood, but it is
assumed they are a message to somebody watching the board.

Q !ITPb.qbhqo ID: 8GzG+UJ9 No.150166904 157
Nov 20 2017 02:29:00 (EST)

What is a key?
What is a key used for?
What is a guard?
What is a guard used for?
Who unlocked the door of all doors?
Was it pre-planned?
Do you believe in coincidences?
What is information?
Who controls the release of information?
WHO HAS ALL OF THE INFORMATION?
Who disseminates information?
What is the MSM?
Who controls the MSM?
Who really controls the MSM?
Why are we made to believe the MSM are the only credible news
sources?
Who controls the MSM?
Who really controls the MSM?
Why are we made to believe the MSM are the only credible news
sources?

Why is this relevant?
Why are non MSM platforms cast as conspiracy and/or non-credible?
Why are non MSM platforms cast as conspiracy and/or non-credible?
What happens when an entity and/or individual accumulates power?
Define corruption.
Wealth = power.
Power = influence.
Influence = control.
Rinse and repeat.
What power of influence was recently discovered (specifically re: 2016 election)?
How much power of influence does Twitter, FB, Reddit, etc. have in influencing the minds of people?
Has the stranglehold of the MSM been diminished?
What is open source?
What has become blatantly obvious since the election of POTUS?
Why would they allow this (visibility) to occur?
Were they not prepared to counter?
What miscalculation occurred?
What opposite impact did this generate?
How did POTUS recognize and invert?
What happens when an entity and/or individual accumulates power?
Define corruption.
Define censorship.
Define 'controlled' censorship.
What action is Twitter taking effective mid-Dec?
What is the purpose of this action?
Possible test to understand public / gov't response?

Q !ITPb.qbhqo   ID: 8GzG+UJ9   No.150166936 ☑   **158**
ᵇᵛ 20 2017 02:29:21 (EST)

(cont..)
When was this announced?
When did events in SA transpire?
Who controlled a large portion of Twitter stock?

Why is this relevant?
Define oppression.
Who controls the narrative?
Who really controls the narrative?
Who guards the narrative?
Does the MSM shelter and protect select 'party' members?
Does this protection insulate these 'party' members?
Who controls the narrative?
What laws were put in place to protect the MSM from lawsuits?
Who specifically passed this law?
What is immunity?
What prevents a news organization from simply 'making up sources & stories'?
What prevents a news organization from simply 'making up sources & stories'?
What previous SC ruling provided protection to reporters from having to reveal their 'confidential' source(s)?
How many people are unaware of the 'truth' due to the stranglehold?
How must people be made aware of an alternate reality?
What are crumbs (think H-wood/DC)
Define 'lead-in' (think play)?
What has been occurring recently?
The stage must be set.
Crumbs are easy to swallow.
What if Hugh Hefner was /a Clown In America?
What is a honeypot?
Define blackmail.
How could this be applied?
Fantasy land.
WHO HAS ALL OF THE INFORMATION?
No Such Agency.
The hunter becomes the hunted.
Operations underway.
Operators active.
Disinformation is real.
Disinformation is necessary.
Silent war (some gets out).
The Great Awakening.
Iron Eagle.
Godfather III.
The Hunt for Red October.
Q

Saudi Prince Al-Waleed bin Talal and George Soros, both Cabal agents, own massive stakes in Twitter.

What has become obvious is that POTUS has used Twitter more effectively than anyone on Cabal's side. Their miscalculation was that they never thought Hillary would lose, presumably because they had enough voter fraud set up that they felt her election was assured. As this goes on, it increasingly seems Cabal's model was to use the media to push a false narrative on us, like Obama's overwhelming popularity. Once we believed that, when they rigged his electoral victory, we would assume we had been outvoted, the left had won fairly, and we would assent to their installation of a leader who would destroy our nation.

In response to POTUS effectively using twitter to rally his followers on social media, and drive the narratives he wanted to drive, twitter (and all of social media) began to try and censor and control key voices trying to break through to their fellow Americans.[222] This points to someone at the top trying to control the narrative, and Q asks us to ponder who exactly it could be?

Then Q points out he is beginning to reveal this crumb by crumb. He goes on to drop that Hugh Hefner was a CIA asset, and was set up by the agency in his mansion with young women, where he would throw sex parties for the rich and powerful, to gather blackmail materials on them. It will come out later that the celebrities may have been lured into having sex with under-aged girls groomed for this explicit purpose by rogue CIA agents serving Cabal, in an operation eerily similar to Jeffrey Epstein's.

---

222   http://archive.is/ySSm1

This type of activity only increased as time went on and we came to the present. More will come out on this later, showing CIA may have been set up in a neighbor's house, connected to the Playboy Mansion by underground tunnels,[223] which linked into a basement vault holding hidden camera videos of all sorts of famous stars having sex in the mansion.[224] The ride with Q gets a lot more interesting and horrifying than this as we go .

Anonymous ID: 8GzG+UJ9 No.150170117 ⬚   **159**
Nov 20 2017 03:16:18 (EST)

Anonymous ID: XwTkGkKF No.150169787 ⬚
Nov 20 2017 03:10:43 (EST)

>>150168157
>>150168274
> the hunt for red october

This is a reference to the submarine that went missing just recently?

>>150169787
Incorrect.

Anonymous ID: 8GzG+UJ9 No.150170181 ⬚   **160**
Nov 20 2017 03:17:31 (EST)

Anonymous ID: 9Ygs+P0g No.150169796 ⬚
Nov 20 2017 03:10:48 (EST)

You guys are missing the importance of Hugh Hefner! Think of it this way.
>Hugh invites over celeb/politician
>Hugh offers them "something younger"
>Hugh offers them a "safe space" to do it in
>Hugh tapes encounter
>Sends tape to CIA
>CIA has person by the balls for LIFE.

223   http://archive.is/ZtYyS
224   http://archive.is/Dx0Yn

This is MAJORLY IMPORTANT to what has been keeping
people in control for so long!

>>150169796
!!!

*Today they denigrate Pizzagate, as well as the idea of
Jeffrey Epstein working for a bigger conspiracy. The world is
Darwinian. You have been conditioned to think nobody would do
this, when we evolved under a world which was designed to
confer favor on, and produce, the type of people who would.*

Anonymous ID: 8GzG+UJ9 No.150171298 ⬀   **161**
Nov 20 2017 03:36:59 (EST)

XXX !a22Tubbaks ID: uCpJZ72M No.150170782 ⬀
Nov 20 2017 03:27:48 (EST)

1501490111770.gif

HOW DO YOU LURE A DANGEROUS ANIMAL INTO A
TRAP?! MY FUCKING SIDES!!!

>>150170782
All posts are connected.
Graphic is key.

Q !ITPb.qbhqo ID: LuUE1Prl No.150172069 🗗   **162**
bv 20 2017 03:49:32 (EST)

QMAP 1/2 confirmed.
This is the key.
Q

Q !ITPb.qbhqo ID: LuUE1Prl No.150172817 🗗   **163**
bv 20 2017 04:00:31 (EST)

1&2 confirmed.
You will need for coming weeks.
Put it this way, six attempts were made to silence the witness
scheduled to appear tomorrow.
Special operators on guard.
Q

This refers to a witness in the Uranium One scandal who was set to testify in front of the Senate.[225]

Q !ITPb.qbhqo ID: LuUE1Prl No.150173114 🗗   **164**
bv 20 2017 04:05:24 (EST)

Bots deactivated upon arrival.
Keep up the good fight.
It's spreading.
Q

The Q board was being flooded by bot programs that automatically posted nonsense posts to dilute the research and communications. Q is saying things are spreading regardless.

Q !ITPb.qbhqo ID: DmzzKPea No.150212477 🗗   **165**
bv 20 2017 12:48:10 (EST)

Expand your thinking.
What are patterns?
How are patterns formed and isolated?
What are data sets?

---

225   http://archive.is/l8tvn

What is a map?
Re: Twitter (repeat)(important).
What action is Twitter taking effective mid-Dec?
What is the purpose of this action?
Possible test to understand public / gov't response?
When was this announced?
When did events in SA transpire?
Who controlled a large portion of Twitter stock?
Why is this relevant?
Expand your thinking.
What is the real purpose of this action?
What is the SS?
Who is the primary person protected under the SS?
What action is Twitter taking effective mid-Dec?
Would POTUS be able to use Twitter post action?
Define the 'known' action.
Why is the MSM ignoring this action?
What transpired w/ POTUS' Twitter account a short time ago?
Re-read crumbs on this topic (necessary).
Two scenarios (lose/lose).
POTUS advised by SS to terminate use of Twitter due to new
website tracking policy (cookies) amongst other spyware not
disclosed (risk) – 1st time they failed (re-read).
POTUS silenced on Twitter due to new policy (re: SS / risk).
Direct message failure.
POTUS refuses to be silenced.
Bad actors gather metadata and targeting.
Small example of the ongoing silent war.
Options?
Regulate?
Problem: time to complete.
Solution?
Patriots, get the word out.
Jason Bourne (Deep Dream).
Q

The surveillance state is immense, and it is not all
government. I am not even sure most of it is. Much may be
cloaked in the private sector. Here Q is saying Twitter publicly
announced it was going to begin tracking its users off site, and

seeing who they associate with. A social map is a graphical representation of social connections, and Twitter appeared to be beginning to assemble one for everyone who used it. And Q asserts they were not only tracking online behavior, but offline as well, using tracking software that was presumably geo-locating phones and studying computer IP addresses to see who was connected. This sounds bad – a private company, funded by shadowy figures like George Soros and Saudi Prince Al Waleed, tracking where you go, who is with you, who you communicate with, what you say, and even doing it to the President. And this is not even near being a hundreth of the horror of the surveillance machine that was created, tracking every American, and poised to deal with them, had Hillary been elected.

Q !!TPb.qbhqo ID: Qwfs7lfl No.150214269 ⬚   **166**
▓ov 20 2017 13:07:04 (EST)

(Repost to correct thread).
Expand your thinking.
What are patterns?
How are patterns formed and isolated?
What are data sets?
What is a map?
Re: Twitter (repeat)(important).
What action is Twitter taking effective mid-Dec?
What is the purpose of this action?
Possible test to understand public / gov't response?
When was this announced?
When did events in SA transpire?
Who controlled a large portion of Twitter stock?
Why is this relevant?
Expand your thinking.
What is the real purpose of this action?
What is the SS?
Who is the primary person protected under the SS?
What action is Twitter taking effective mid-Dec?
Would POTUS be able to use Twitter post action?

Define the 'known' action.
Why is the MSM ignoring this action?
What transpired w/ POTUS' Twitter account a short time ago?
Re-read crumbs on this topic (necessary).
Two scenarios (lose/lose).
POTUS advised by SS to terminate use of Twitter due to new website tracking policy (cookies) amongst other spyware not disclosed (risk) – 1st time they failed (re-read).
POTUS silenced on Twitter due to new policy (re: SS / risk).
Direct message failure.
POTUS refuses to be silenced.
Bad actors gather metadata and targeting.
Small example of the ongoing silent war.
Options?
Regulate?
Problem: time to complete.
Solution?
Patriots, get the word out.
Jason Bourne (Deep Dream).
Q

Q cannot be clear, because he cannot clearly and openly reveal classified data. So each post is an exercise in speculation. Here, he seems to be implying Cabal was using inside access at Twitter to install secret spyware on phones, allowing individuals to be tracked off the site, thereby documenting user's social networks using everything on their phones, possibly even including microphones, cameras, and location tracking. This would have allowed them to spy on the President, wherever he and his twitter phone went, and who he contacted with the phone (allowing extrapolation of who he may have been meeting and what he may have been doing). There are recent anecdotal accounts saying some apps such as the twitter app may also be performing microphone captures, which in most cases are used for ad targeting. However this could have allowed eavesdropping on the President's private conversations. Secret Service detected the vulnerabilities, and warned the President. This placed the President in a position where he would have to either give up his use of Twitter to mold the narrative, continue to keep a Twitter-enabled phone near and endure the intelligence it gave away, or find a third way to bypass the threat and continue to use Twitter.

All of this occurred right after the handover in power in Saudi Arabia, implying it was a panicked response to a suddenly emerging threat Cabal wasn't ready for.

Q !ITPb.qbhqo ID: Qwfs7lfl No.150214731 ☑   **167**
ɔv 20 2017 13:12:14 (EST)

POTUS opened the door of all doors.
Expand your thinking.
What is the keystone?
Q

Here Q introduces the second meaning of Keystone, though it is only revealed much later. Keystone is a surveillance tool which opens a user's phone to full access remotely by NSA. Q is saying POTUS opened the door of all doors into Cabal operations by authorizing NSA taking full control of Cabal-owned phones and accessing everything that went on around them for intelligence value.

Q !ITPb.qbhqo ID: Qwfs7lfl No.150214824 ☑   **168**
ɔv 20 2017 13:13:08 (EST)

Anonymous ID: AjEyk7a4 No.150214567 ☑
ɔv 20 2017 13:10:19 (EST)

>>150214269
Q. glad you are here can you confirm this theory to Red
October?
http://www.lasvegasnow.com/news/us-says-north-korean-
submarine-missing/395856843 ☑

336

http://www.lasvegasnow.com/news/us-says-north-korean-submarine-missing/395856843 ☐ ▨
Saw the sub searches on the 13th and the navy build up in San diego.

>>150214567
Red Oct sig has not occurred yet.
Follow the map.
Q

Q !ITPb.qbhqo ID: Qwfs7lfl No.150215418 ☐   **169**
▨ov 20 2017 13:19:39 (EST)

Anonymous ID: G8TT126Y No.150214997 ☐
▨ov 20 2017 13:15:12 (EST)

Soros sells Twitter, Facebook, Apple and Snap

https://www.marketwatch.com/story/soros-sells-twitter-facebook-apple-and-snap-2017-11-14?
mod=mw_share_facebook ☐ ▨

>>150214997
!!!

Q !ITPb.qbhqo ID: Qwfs7lfl No.150215871 ☐   **170**
▨ov 20 2017 13:24:02 (EST)

Why am I here during the day?
Why is this relevant?
What does this infer?
Q

This would imply Q is doing his job by posting these intelligence drops, meaning the Q-Anon phenomenon is actually a planned component of a Military Intelligence plan. That means the plan requires the public be slowly brought up to speed on exactly what has been going on behind the scenes, in preparation for a larger chain of events which are coming, although it might also mean Q will drop disinformation as well.

Q !!TPb.qbhqo ID: ElcmhCtp No.150254865 ⊡   **171**
🔳 ᴏv 20 2017 19:17:08 (EST)

Good will always defeat evil.
Q

Q posted this on 4Chan in a thread about Janet Yellen being forced out of the Federal Reserve. He then posted the duplicate below on his board.

Q !!TPb.qbhqo ID: hBrMT7Bt No.150257424 ⊡   **172**
🔳 ᴏv 20 2017 19:40:49 (EST)

Good will always defeat evil.
Q

Q !!TPb.qbhqo ID: S2g2/YEM No.150257653 ⊡   **173**
🔳 ᴏv 20 2017 19:42:50 (EST)

Good will always defeat evil.
No rigging / blackmail this time.
Wizards & Warlocks.
Q

This was posted by Q in a thread discussing Angela Merkel failing to form a coalition in Germany. It confirms Merkel is evil, and is serving Cabal in furthering (((Their))) migrant agenda.

Q !!TPb.qbhqo ID: 6XKIeKXI No.150260900 ⊡   **174**
🔳 ᴏv 20 2017 20:12:32 (EST)

Coordinated effort to silence.
It will only get worse.
All for a LARP right?
Q

Online, LARP stands for Live Action Role Play. It is an online shorthand for a person pretending to be something important, when really they are not. Followers were noting that bot programs were flooding Q's posts with meaningless posts, porn, racism, and other objectionable content, making them difficult to read and navigate. Q is noting that if he were a fake LARP, you would not see his threads rapidly becoming unreadable due to such organized activity.

Q !ITPb.qbhqo ID: rHXVKCrC No.150388962 ☐   **175**
Nov 21 2017 18:43:15 (EST)

Expand your thinking.
Captain Mike Green.
_Conf_D-TT_^_v891_0600_yes
_green1_0600
Bunker Apple Yellow Sky [... + 1]
Yes.
Who countered?
Do you believe in coincidences?
Learn how to read the map.
Q

Captain Mike Green was killed piloting a helicopter over the Rothschild mansion.[226] The code was from post 155 above, and an anon claimed a partial translation would have been "Confirmation of Drop, Troop Transfer via route 891 at 0600 hours, Green, action 1 at 0600." Q is implying, if you read the article, Military Intelligence took over the airfield where Air Traffic Control was shut down, and a mission was launched from there against the Rothschild mansion. So Q had posted some orders here, including the Captain's name, in preparation for a future confirmation of the operation on the board. I assume he is also implying the Rothschild's security countered by using a Cessna to impact the helicopter at some point in the

---

226   http://archive.is/kbLpq

mission.

I can confirm firsthand, that Cabal has significant air assets deployed and either loitering in the air waiting for commands to join surveillance operations, or partaking in surveillance activities, in all major population centers. They appear to usually be flying under the cover of private aviation, and I personally have seen many Cessnas, including one flying nose-up, at the very border of stall speed while circling a target.

It is not impossible, as I reflect on it, they might have arranged the ability to remotely hijack control of those aircraft and fly them remotely in areas where they might want a pseudo-cruise-missile capability on short notice, especially since they probably supply the aircraft to the pilots. I'd assume they do so without alerting the pilots. The idea of a Cessna impacting a hostile target is actually more credible than most would think, given many observations I've made, both about the assets out there, and the no-boundaries psychologies involved.

Note also how it stretches probability that Q would mention the Rothschilds, imply they are under coverage, then tweet a stringer with Green and Sky in it, only to have a pilot named Green fall from the sky over the Rothschild's estate.

Q !ITPb.qbhqo ID: rHXVKCrC No.150391223 ⬈   **176**
Nov 21 2017 19:01:21 (EST)

What was posted prior to the stringer?
What keywords were within the stringer?
Why would keywords be left in the stringer?
Future shows past.
Learn to read the map.
Everything has meaning - EVERYTHING.
Q

Post 150 was a direct threat to Lynn de Rothschild, complete with an assertion she was under active surveillance. Post 154, immediately prior to the stringer in Post 155, asserted select families like the Rothschilds were behind major world tragedies like 9/11, WWI, and WWII, that they were using those tragedies to benefit themselves, and that they were planning a major extinction-level event in the near future.

Q !!TPb.qbhqo ID: rHXVKCrC No.150393065 ⬈   **177**
Nov 21 2017 19:15:58 (EST)

Keywords:
Confirm.
Green.
Sky.
Why were keywords added in the stringer?
What was the purpose?
What was previously stated?
To who specifically?
++
Who countered?
Learn to read the map.
Missing critical items.
Graphic is key.
Ordering is critical.
Q

Q !!TPb.qbhqo ID: a9MnCArQ No.150395774 ⬈   **178**
Nov 21 2017 19:39:58 (EST)

Archive immediately.
Stringer = code = command.
What stringer was provided (2) days prior to event?
What were the keywords in the stringer?
Confirm.
Green (Yes).
Sky.
Why were keywords provided?
Guide to reading map?
Lord d R.
What was previously stated?

++

Who was the pilot of the plane?
Bad actor?
Who was the pilot of the helicopter?
Green?
What was countered?
Who was on the ground (outside) shortly before the collision?
Who was in the home shortly before the collision?
Learn to read the map.
We may have overestimated your ability.
Q

Q IITPb.qbhqo ID: a9MnCArQ No.150400112 ☐   **179**
░ov 21 2017 20:18:17 (EST)

Spreadsheet Anon AT IILytbJwNsQ6v ID: c9QCQdsX No.150398185
☐ ▓
Nov 21 2017 20:01:29 (EST)

>>150395774
>What stringer was provided (2) days prior to event?
_Conf_D-TT_^_v891_0600_yes
_green1_0600
Bunker Apple Yellow Sky [... + 1]

confirm 0600 (time) yes
Green 0600 (time)
Base Green Yellow (condition yellow?) Air

>What were the keywords in the stringer?
confirm
green
Yellow
Sky

>Guide to reading map?
legend, past provides the future, questions provide the answers

>Lord d R.
++
target

>Who was the pilot of the plane?
Green

>What was countered?
Unknown to us

>Who was on the ground (outside) shortly before the collision?
"Unnamed" Rothschild

>Who was in the home shortly before the collision?
Unknown to us now, was "dog grooming event"

>Learn to read the map.
trying really hard, is like herding kittens in here sometimes

>We may have overestimated your ability.
you came to us for certain strengths but there are weaknesses
as well, some being exploited
not enough focus

answer the questions
build the big picture
break it back down
make memes for the normies to calm & educate

so we'll be ready for the Storm

>>150398185Shadow war.
Act II, Scene IV.
(Movie idea – thoughts?)
(Characters)
Good guy (pilot of helicopter).
Bad guy (pilot of plane).
Targets (on ground and in home).
(Story)
Upon receipt of the 'go' code - Good guy flies during a blackout
window provided by unknown agency w/ unknowns (ordinary
people by the look of it) to a select location (re: highly classified
mission) who was given the 'go' order by 'x' to execute (delivery –
(3) for care_). Bad guy intercepts message due to rogue operator
embedded in tactical observation unit and takes out Good guy by
top down invisible attack.
Mission failure.
Encore: What has since occurred by Targets?
Q

Q !!TPb.qbhqo ID: a9MnCArQ No.150400638 ☐   **180**
Nov 21 2017 20:22:58 (EST)

Anonymous ID: y1XGeIPg No.150400127 ☐
Nov 21 2017 20:18:23 (EST)

Why is LRD chatting up Eagles on Twitter

>>150400127
What US President was nicknamed "Eagle" by the USSS?
FlyEaglesFly
Q

This references a since-deleted tweet by Lynn de Rothschild,[227] where she adds the hashtag #FlyEaglesFly. Bill Clinton's code name was Eagle, and later it will appear the FlyXFly references someone dying. It implies it was an order to assassinate Bill Clinton's to keep him from cooperating with Q.

Q !!TPb.qbhqo ID: AJWt5SQs No.150405959 ☐   **181**
Nov 21 2017 21:10:09 (EST)

anonymous ID: uMuGxlli No.150403252 ☐
Nov 21 2017 20:46:17 (EST)

>>150400719
Dear Q:
Jesus Christ was fucking pissed at his apostles most of the time because they were stupid fucks (at the time) that couldn't piece together even the most basic of clues. We are no different and are even more clueless. We are trying, but you really do have to spell it out for us. Sorry. We believe you are speaking the truth. To whom else can we turn? So put up with our shit and help us, and we'll do what you ask.

>>150403252
Sniffer progs would kill the site.
Everything has to be carefully crafted and tooled prior to release.
Godspeed, Patriot.
Q

227   http://archive.is/f7uID

182

Q !ITPb.qbhqo ID: AJWt5SQs No.150406974 ⚐
⬛ov 21 2017 21:19:27 (EST)

> Anonymous ID: WGF9EL8f No.150404273 ⚐
> ⬛ov 21 2017 20:55:41 (EST)
>
> >Act II, Scene IV
> The same scene in Macbeth talks about a falcon flying freely
> before being ambushed by an owl. It is noted that the owl does
> not normally hunt the falcon. The scene continues to talk about
> many odd happenings and a darkness on the horizon for
> humanity. It is noted that even the horses are rebelling and
> turning upon one another (specifically eating eachother).
> Is it possible that the Clintons have turned on the Rothschilds?
> The flyeaglefly may even be a veiled threat directed towards the
> Clintons, a 'We know' type thing.

>>150404273
What does the "Owl" represent to certain cults?
Q

In the occult, the owl represents the ability to see through the darkness. For that reason it is supposed to be a symbol of the Illuminati and the Freemasons. These are two groups who have fashioned themselves as above the masses due to their ability to perceive the truths of the world, which all others are oblivious to. Inherent within that is some assumption that such groups, who can see the truth in the darkness, would enjoy benefit were the broader population to be purposely placed in a state of darkness.

Q !ITPb.qbhqo ID: AJWt5SQs No.150407593 ⚐
⬛ov 21 2017 21:24:48 (EST)

> FJ ID: L0zQwZXN No.150405114 ⚐
> ⬛ov 21 2017 21:03:10 (EST)
>
> CONFIRM GREEN SKY = giving an order to Captain Green to
> do something to the Rothschilds.

Q gave us this crumb beforehand, and also wrote a message to LdR (we can hear you breathing).

This was a map. Q told us that future shows the past meaning that a future event (Captain Mike Green doing something with a helicopter to Rothchilds) will explain these keywords and confirm that Q knows top secret information.

Green, obviously a good guy, had a mission. We don't know what exactly he was supposed to do. But it had to be something very serious because bad guys countered very seriously and killed several people.

Mission failed.

>>150405114

Q !ITPb.qbhqo ID: pOV0fY+r No.150412315 [↗]   **184**
bv 21 2017 22:07:58 (EST)

Their need for symbolism will be their downfall.
Follow the Owl & Y head around the world.
Identify and list.
They don't hide it.
They don't fear you.
You are sheep to them.
You are feeders.
Godfather III.
Q

Q says this repeatedly. The elites in Cabal approach it as if being in a secret club. They revel in showing off their status to fellow Cabal-members through using their symbols. There is a good graphic assembled here on the use of the Owl in the artistic aspects of Cabal institutions,[228] and as Q points out, we will see the horned/antlered/Y-head displayed as well as time goes on. Ironically this will make it easy to identify Cabal's members.

---

228   http://archive.is/Lhhik

Rothschild_Symbolism.jpg

Photos from a 1972 Rothschild Illuminati party.[229] Baron Guy de Rothschild is in an owl hat, and Marie-Hélène de Rothschild is in the antlered-deer, Y-head mask.

Q IITPb.qbhqo ID: pOV0fY+r No.150412717 🗗   **186**
📷ov 21 2017 22:11:47 (EST)

You are learning.
You needed a push.
Godspeed.
Q

Next up is a summation of our nation's recent history. It

_____

229   https://archive.is/VNjpQ

may not click with you now, but as evidence accumulates, and it will, you will be blown away. We have been being lied to for a long, long, time, to the point we are almost conditioned to believe the lies reflexively, and view the truth as the province of weirdos.

Q !lTPb.qbhqo ID: pOV0fY+r No.150417001   **187**
Nov 21 2017 22:49:02 (EST)

Anonymous ID: 3AGLrGdq No.150414073
Nov 21 2017 22:23:41 (EST)

>>150413820
My actual conclusion is probably what's delayed me the most as it's been mind blowing understanding our country now.... I totally get it..

Current conclusions?
so Titanic -> Rothchild screws America by making our money worthless -> crash of 29 -> Tons new government which doesn't fix the problem Rothchild created (but a war helps) -> cia -> everyone blackmailed with sex tapes -> media consumed cia -> Country forced hard left -> population to puppets -> Causes uprising by certain Patriots like Kennedy/Reagan/Trump and while they managed to kill Kennedy and outlast Reagan enough lessons were learned that we are now finally ready to clean house and become America again?

First time in about a hundred years.... wow...

>>150414073

In the next post, things may go back farther than we are aware, and those who are part of the conspiracy may have been hiding within our ranks for a very, very long time ...

348

Q !ITPb.qbhqo ID: pOV0fY+r No.150417146
v 21 2017 22:50:09 (EST)

Anonymous ID: GazxQd8P No.150415097
v 21 2017 22:32:56 (EST)

image.jpg

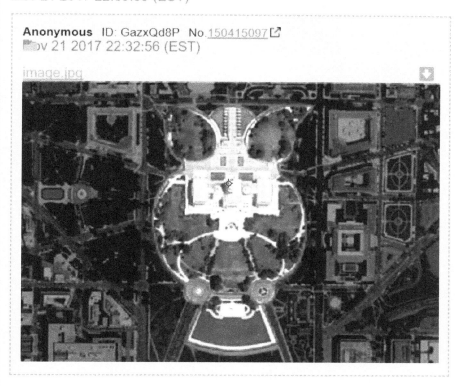

>>150415097

An overhead view of the White House (center) and surrounding grounds in Washington DC. Here, when a prominent structure was being planned out, somebody within the planning organization was in the Secret Society and included a well-known, (within Cabal-circles), symbol of the conspiracy.

At this point I was intrigued, but far from convinced. As Q went on however, and more and more evidence accumulated, it became clear these were not isolated coincidences. There were people out there who knew about something I did not, and they were signaling to each other – and they had been for some time.

Identify symbolism (Owl / Y).
Which performers/celebs supported HRC during the election?
Who performed during her rallies?
What jewelry and/or tattoos present?
What other events do they attend together?
What does HRC represent to them?
What celebrities have owl / Y head symbols?
What politicians have owl / Y head symbols?
What powerful people have owl / Y head symbols?
What powerful groups have owl / Y head symbols?
Why are they worn/shown openly?
Their need for symbolism will be their downfall.
MSM role?
Push conspiracy theory.
Social media role?
Push conspiracy theory and institute new rules allowing for ban.
Censorship.
The graphic is key.
Re-read graphic (ex: what family did Soros replace (Y)).
Part II – How were they 'adopted' into the cult (as children).
What were they provided for obeying and staying silent
(brainwashed)?
All that you know to be right is wrong.
The 'cult' runs the world.
Fantasy land.
The world is fighting back (& destroying the cult).
20% public.
80% private.
The world would otherwise collapse.
40,000ft. v. (again) and need to decrease altitude to avoid
'conspiracy' label.
Was necessary.
GODFATHER III.
For God & Country.
Q

Q's researchers would dig up pictures showing that Lady
Gaga, Beyonce, Jay Z, Katy Perry, Madonna and a slew of other

celebrities all performed and attended Hillary rallies. All either wore jewelry, had tattoos, or made hand symbols that are noted as symbolic of occult societies. The research here is too deep to go into, but as Q's board delved into it, it was shocking how many of these stars routinely made hand symbols, or wore signs which were noted as signaling their membership in the club. In addition, many, like Lady Gaga, Jay Z and Beyonce would attend occult Spirit Cooking ceremonies by Marina Abramovic.

National Press Club, The Yale Record,[230] Freemasonry, Bilderberg Group Bohemian Club,[231] Freemasonry,[232] and other organizations through history would feature Owl symbology.[233] Even the clock in Herald Square features gratuitous Owl imagery on the doors.[234]

There is a Secret Society around you which knows it exists, signals among itself, and holds great power. Hillary, as a member, represented to them the idea of their Secret Society holding control over the most powerful office in the land.

They keep their society secret by denigrating any mention of it as a conspiracy theory, which immediately makes the public disregard its possibility. Because of the public's total lack of awareness, revealing everything would create shock and disturbance. So 80% of what will happen to clear out the cult will occur out of the public's sight, with only about 20% made public. From here Q says we will cease the overview, and return to examining the individual mechanisms of the cult.

---

230   http://archive.is/NyLkO
231   http://archive.is/ZrD6S
232   http://archive.is/3VHEC
233   http://archive.is/kly5l
234   http://archive.is/s27br

Q !ITPb.qbhqo ID: T4rZfKsN No.150433983 ☐   **190**
█ov 22 2017 01:30:56 (EST)

USA vs.
Necessary to cut strings from foreign bad actors.
Necessary to form WW alliances to defeat.
Think Merkel is a coincidence?
They are puppets.
They are weak.
They are scared.
80% dark ops necessary.
20% public for justice.
The stage must be set.
Have faith.
Q

Q !ITPb.qbhqo ID: T4rZfKsN No.150434351 ☐   **191**
█ov 22 2017 01:34:58 (EST)

Anonymous ID: Ukm/q3OU No.150434251 ☐
█ov 22 2017 01:33:54 (EST)

popes snake pit.jpg

>>150432420

anon meme makers please make some memes of the popes
audience hall looking like a snake pit. That sum sik shit

>>150434251

The center of that image is the stage, behind which is a disturbing looking large wooden statue which will be discussed later.

China and Russia are closed societies to keep the Secret Society out. As a result, you don't see the owl-Y-head symbology there. Indeed, as a Secret Society leader, Obama was shamed in China, by making him leave the "ass" of Air Force One, rather than allowing him a traditional red-carpet entrance, exiting the side of Air Force One, as would be normal.[235] In Russia, it is said Putin banned the Rothschilds from the country,[236] and banned charities from George Soros.[237]

Since WWII, the Secret Society has attempted to promote its own relative position by advancing degeneracy and disloyalty among the masses, from dissolution of national borders, to sexual degeneracy, to currency debasement. Russia and China escaped it by keeping the Cult out of their nations.

---

235   http://archive.is/jT0Fv
236   http://archive.is/rKyWS
237   http://archive.is/jxKEX

Who really controls NK?
Q

This is a stock picture of the Hyangsan Hotel, in Huichon North Korea. Again we have the Illuminati all-seeing Eye-of-Providence pyramid symbology expressed in its architecture. But something even more interesting is the lone guy walking on the small wall in the center of the picture. Nobody noticed, but this stock picture, taken at the height of North Korea being a reclusive Hermit Kingdom, features a Caucasian man, who almost resembles a young Donald Trump, walking freely just feet from soldiers, while limos are behind him, indicating the presence of VIPs. Who was this guy, and how did North Korea, ruled with an ironclad fist by the Kims, end up with white guys walking around? Enlargement of the image on the next page:

The point being, there is more than meets the eye to the Hermit Kingdom, and Q's assertions fit the available evidence better than the stories we've been told.

U1 – CA – EU – ASIA – IRAN/NK
Iran Deal.
Why is this relevant?
Re-read drops re: NK / Iran.
(Y) What does it mean to be covered in gold?
Which couple was photographed covered in gold?
The public release was a mistake.
Who released the picture?
Who has all the information?
(Y) What does it mean to be covered in gold?
Can you locate one other pic w/ Y head covered in gold?
What does this represent?
/_\
THE SUM OF ALL FEARS.
Q

There is a lot of speculation, but all that is known for certain is that the Iran deal moved pallets of untraceable physical cash (which may not have made it to Iran), and the Uranium One deal moved a lot of Uranium, and all of it seems to have been related, orchestrated by the Cabal for some unified purpose. Q says it was all part of one operation with one goal.

The Sum of All Fears was a movie featuring a plot where a black market nuclear weapon was manufactured in a former Russian military facility in the Ukraine and detonated in the United States, in conjunction with a false flag attack by a compromised Russian military officer, to trigger a third world war between Russia and the US. Q seems to imply this was similar to the plan the Cabal was moving us toward, as a way of thinning our populations and unifying our us under (((Them))).

Q posted this post a second time, in Post 195.

Q !!TPb.qbhqo ID: YzNom6b4 No.150513545 🔗

Nov 22 2017 16:33:25 (EST)

U1 – CA – EU – ASIA – IRAN/NK

Iran Deal.

Why is this relevant?

Re-read drops re: NK / Iran.

(Y) What does it mean to be covered in gold?

Which couple was photographed covered in gold?

The public release was a mistake.

Who released the picture?

Who has all the information?

(Y) What does it mean to be covered in gold?

Can you locate one other pic w/ Y head covered in gold?

What does this represent?

/_\

THE SUM OF ALL FEARS.

Q

Q !!TPb.qbhqo ID: YzNom6b4 No.150513895 🔗

Nov 22 2017 16:36:25 (EST)

Anonymous ID: LOkt3Z9j No.150510227 🔗

Nov 22 2017 16:04:51 (EST)

RothsChildsOld.jpg

>>150510227

Gold.

Q

Although it won't show in the image here, in black and white, the deer head mask is covered in gold leaf, and the hat worn by the man also features gold accents.

Q !ITPb.qbhqo ID: YzNom6b4 No.150515203 ☑   **197**
ov 22 2017 16:47:21 (EST)

Ancient Egyptians considered gold "the skin of the gods" -- specifically the sun god Ra -- and often used it to craft objects of spiritual significance.
Why is this relevant?
Q

Q !ITPb.qbhqo ID: YzNom6b4 No.150515835 ☑   **198**
ov 22 2017 16:52:24 (EST)

3 sides form what shape?
Expand your thinking.
Re-read crumbs.
Q

It seems Q is implying this cult may go back to the times of ancient Egypt and the pyramids, and have existed as a secret religion, much as Christianity, only within the shadows and occupying the upper echelons of power.

Q !ITPb.qbhqo ID: YzNom6b4 No.150517837 ☑   **199**
ov 22 2017 17:07:59 (EST)

U1 - CA - EU - ASIA - IRAN/NK
Where did it end up?
What was the purpose?
Who was suppose to win the election of 2016?
Why was the Iran deal kept from Congress and placed at the highest level of classification?
Meaning, a United States Senator could NOT review the deal but other foreign powers could.
How much money was hand delivered by plane(s)?
Why in cash?
Where did the plane(s) actually land?
What was the cover?
Who paid for BO to attend Harvard?

Why would this occur pre-political days?
Who was the biggest contributor to the CF?
The graphic is the key.
Why does the MSM push conspiracy w/o investigation?
Who controls the MSM?
What does the word 'conspiracy' mean to you?
Has the word 'conspiracy' been branded to mean something shameful in today's society?
The world cannot handle the truth.
This pill cannot be swallowed by most.
Risk in painting this picture.
THE SUM OF ALL FEARS.
Q

The Uranium One deal transferred one fifth of the United State's Uranium 238 stockpile to a Russian company. Q may be implying it ended up in North Korea, with the dual goal of both creating a black-market nuclear weapon to be used in a false flag attack to start a World War, and to render North Korea a nuclear power, and thus totally out of the reach of any Western power which might want to invade it to access the Cabal's secure headquarters and deal a sudden deathblow to them.

Although there is some ambiguity to the finances of the Clinton Foundation, the biggest donor likely was Frank Giustra, who was behind the Uranium One sale.[238] Saudi Prince Al-Waleed bin Talal is believed to have been Barack Obama's patron during his college days. Given Prince Al-Waleed's apparent ties to the Cabal currently being overthrown, this would imply Obama's ascension to the Presidency was planned by this Cabal, he was groomed for it, installed, and as President he was acting as their agent. That the media will not examine these ties, shows they're part of the Cult as well.

---

238   http://archive.is/03Sq7

Q !!TPb.qbhqo ID: 3EnVOnIV No.150522442 ☐   **200**
☐ov 22 2017 17:45:01 (EST)

Rizvi Traverse Management.
Happy hunting.
Q

Rizvi is an investment entity with ties to many Cabal-associated entities and characters, from Playboy (a likely Cabal-blackmail/honeypot), to Space-X, Twitter, and Snapchat. Some suspect it may be a CIA front, designed to financially advance entities where CIA/Cabal wants to control the space, like social media or tech. If you started a Twitter clone and posed a threat to Twitter early on, CIA, on behalf of Cabal, could flood money into Twitter and out-fund your small startup, crowding you out of the space. Combined with free Cabal-media-mentions for your competitor, you'll never stand a chance, and Cabal will end up in control. This mechanism is why companies like Myspace failed, while Facebook effortlessly took over the social media space.

Q !!TPb.qbhqo ID: 3EnVOnIV No.150523420 ☐   **201**
☐ov 22 2017 17:53:22 (EST)

> **Anonymous** ID: UybaYRYn No.150523213 ☐
> ☐ov 22 2017 17:51:42 (EST)
> >>150522875
> clown front?

>>150523213
Q !!TPb.qbhqo ID: gq87sJf0 No.150559154 ☐   **202**
☐ov 22 2017 23:29:41 (EST)

Bad bread not updated.
Q

Q !!TPb.qbhqo ID: WXyMF1WS No.150559269 ☐   **203**
☐ov 22 2017 23:30:51 (EST)

Bad bread.
Q

Q is saying the last page of comments by users was bad.

Q !ITPb.qbhqo ID: gq87sJf0 No.150559381 ☑   **204**
⬛v 22 2017 23:32:01 (EST)

> Anonymous ID: QAPSaY3V No.150559263 ☑
> ⬛v 22 2017 23:30:47 (EST)
>
> >>150559154
> What's up Q, please tell me life will get better. Growing tired and
> need hope.

>>150559263
We are winning bigly.
Q

Q !ITPb.qbhqo ID: gq87sJf0 No.150559818 ☑   **205**
⬛v 22 2017 23:36:06 (EST)

> **DEATH TO THE TRIUMVIRATE** ID: AWk/5slA No.150559502 ☑
> ⬛v 22 2017 23:32:59 (EST)
>
> 1510022344945.jpg   ⬇
>
>
>
> >>150559381
> Fake Q is fake.
> DTTT

You made the list.
It's rare, feel proud.
Pick up your phone.
Q

This was a poster who used the name, Death To The Triumverate (DTTT). He claimed to be a Rothschild who opposed what his family was doing, and seemingly this was Q recruiting him.

Q !lTPb.qbhqo ID: ss2EXAyq No.150560899   **206**
Nov 22 2017 23:47:11 (EST)

Can't wait for the green light.
Teams on standby.
Q

Q !lTPb.qbhqo ID: 6606MRSe No.150561736   **207**
Nov 22 2017 23:55:41 (EST)

$4.9 billion in government subsidies.
Why?
Q

Q !lTPb.qbhqo ID: 6606MRSe No.150562337   **208**
Nov 23 2017 00:01:22 (EST)

Rizvi Traverse Management.
Very important.
Q

Q !lTPb.qbhqo ID: 6606MRSe No.150562694   **209**
Nov 23 2017 00:05:13 (EST)

Why did BO scuttle the shuttle program?
What is SpaceX?
Expand your thinking.
Q

He was moving control over a critical capability from the

US government, to private sector entities, so they could maintain increased secrecy and greater power relative to the US government. Q will later assert the goal was also to shut down US Space defense capability, and possibly transfer missile tech to North Korea – something less illegal if you transfer private sector technology, as opposed to US Government technology.

Q !!TPb.qbhqo ID: 6o6MRSe No.150562920 ☑   **210**
Nov 23 2017 00:07:16 (EST)

> **PLVSVLTRA** ID: e9hPKb0e No.150562774 ☑
> Nov 23 2017 00:05:55 (EST)
>
> >>150562694
>
> >>150562661
>> Suhail Rizvi is the "secretive investor" that has ties to SpaceX and is tied to Saudi Prince Alwaleed bin Talal's investment company!!! This is HUGE!
>
> **CHECK MY LAST POST Q!!**
> >>150562661
> >>150562661

>>150562774

Q !!TPb.qbhqo ID: 6o6MRSe No.150563217 ☑   **211**
Nov 23 2017 00:10:13 (EST)

NK _ SpaceX.
Q

Here it is implied they may have been transferring rocket technology from Space X to North Korea, as well as nuclear material from the Uranium One deal, and know how from Iran, to make North Korea an intercontinental nuclear power, likely as a fail-safe, so whatever should come up in the future, Cabal would be hiding within a bonafide unpredictable nuclear power.

363

Q !ITPb.qbhqo ID: 66o6MRSe No.150565108 **212**
Nov 23 2017 00:27:53 (EST)

> **Anonymous** ID: G9U7adoa No.150564270
> Nov 23 2017 00:19:48 (EST)
>
> >>150563756
> Holy shit. All of the president's past tweets making that reference.
>
> "MUSK. You magnificent bastard, Q read your BOOK!"

>>150564270
Do you believe in coincidences?
Q

The President called North Korea's leader, Kim Jong Un Rocketman, and Forbes had called Elon Musk Rocketman,[239] in yet another "coincidence,"

Q !ITPb.qbhqo ID: 66o6MRSe No.150565710 **213**
Nov 23 2017 00:33:39 (EST)

The world cannot swallow the truth.
Q

Q !ITPb.qbhqo ID: b+CmlEal No.150567199 **214**
Nov 23 2017 00:47:45 (EST)

What is FB?
Spying tool?
Who created it?
Who really created it?
Nothing is what it seems.
Q

Facebook will later be shown to have begun life as a

---

239 http://archive.is/zhO5j

program called Lifelog, under the auspices of DARPA, long before Mark Zuckerberg ever had any thought of getting involved in Social Media. Its purpose was to document everything about someone, especially their social connections.

As time goes on it will appear Facebook is entirely a government spying program designed to create a spying database on Americans with data populated by the targets of the surveillance themselves. Mark Zuckerberg and all the mythology around him and the formation of Facebook may in fact be an elaborate cover story, with Zuckerberg more akin to an actor recruited by the government to pretend to have created the company as a social media company. He was only added to the cover story so the users will think they are using Social Media designed by a goofy geek, rather than uploading their data to a CIA spying program developed by DARPA to get control of them.

Q !ITPb.qbhqo ID: b+CmIEal No.150567655 ⬈
      215

Nov 23 2017 00:52:14 (EST)

Focus on his wife.
Q

Zuckerberg's wife is the daughter of a Chinese refugee. One thing I have noticed about Cabal's civilian informant program is it recruits very heavily from among new immigrants, and once a parent is an agent, they seem to raise their child as an agent, from a very early age. It is very nepotistic, like a cult.

When an intelligence operation tries to penetrate any entity, among the first targets it will try to get its agents into is Human Resources, so it can facilitate the hiring of additional agents and control their placement within the organization. My suspicion, long before Q, was that the entity I saw was recruiting foreign immigrants as agents to run against our civilian population. I assumed they were smoothing over citizenship issues, in return for the new citizen's loyalty to them, and willingness to spy on the populace for them. In retrospect, it is likely that Cabal's domestic intelligence operation here infiltrated Immigration and Naturalization (the Human Resources of the United States), and organized a flood of new immigrants who would be hustled through the citizenship process in return for loyalty to Cabal, and a promise to serve Cabal. And once they were in, they brought their kids in.

If I am correct, Zuckerberg marrying the daughter of an immigrant, would fit with Cabal agents keeping it in the family. It might also mean his wife is helping to keep tabs on him for Cabal.

Q !!TPb.qbhqo ID: b+CmIEal No.150569482 ☑   **216**
Nov 23 2017 01:11:25 (EST)

Keyhole.
Happy hunting.
Q

Q !!TPb.qbhqo ID: b+CmIEal No.150569779 ☑   **217**
Nov 23 2017 01:14:06 (EST)

> **Anonymous** ID: hPg9HcUL No.150569615 ☑
> Nov 23 2017 01:12:34 (EST)
> >>150569482
> GOD DAMMIT ONE MORE CLUE - HOW THE FUCK WILL WE EVER CONNECT "KEYHOLE" TO THIS?
> One more key word, please. Please.

>>150569615
Clowns In America.
Q

Q !!TPb.qbhqo ID: b+CmlEal No.150570023 🗗
Nov 23 2017 01:16:24 (EST)

Anonymous ID: hipNwtJK No.150569907 🗗
Nov 23 2017 01:15:23 (EST)

>>150569779
Q IS IT THIS HERE
>>150569482
https://pando.com/2015/07/01/cia-foia-google-keyhole/

>One of the first big milestones in this transformation took place in November 2004 when Google acquired a tiny and little-known 3-D mapping startup called Keyhole Inc. Google paid an undisclosed sum for the company, immediately absorbed it, and began turning its tech into what we now know as Google Earth. The acquisition would have gone unnoticed, had it not been for one not-so-tiny detail: Keyhole Inc was part-owned by the CIA and the "National Geospatial-Intelligence Agency" (NGA), a sister agency to the NSA. Keyhole Inc also had one major client base: US military and intelligence agencies.

Google is like a cheat code for intelligence gathering.

>>150569907

So Google is a part of our intelligence agencies, and is buying assets from them and developing those assets for them. Which probably points to a co-mingling of finances. Would an intelligence agency have any interest in a searchable database containing almost all known open source data on the planet, like Google? Would the CIA, which created Operation Mockingbird to take over the news media so it could control the information provided to people, have any interest in controlling what search results are displayed, to control public opinion? Would an intelligence agency want you thinking it had created the websites you are using online? Might it create a cover story to make you think the website developed innocently? These companies might not have developed the way you thought, and the people really behind them may not be the young goofs you were told.

Q !!TPb.qbhqo ID: fX85VkAw No.150679159 ⬀   **219**
▮v 23 2017 21:54:44 (EST)

_27-1_yes_USA94-2
_27-1_yes_USA58-A
_27-1_yes_USA04
_Conf_BECZ_y056-(3)_y
The_Castle_Runs_RED_yes
Godspeed.
Q

The significance of this is unknown.

Q !!TPb.qbhqo ID: fX85VkAw No.150681065 ⬀   **220**
▮v 23 2017 22:14:30 (EST)

Reminder.
Unclassified setting.
Monitored and analyzed in RT.
Future answers past.
Q

Q !!TPb.qbhqo ID: fX85VkAw No.150681832 ⬀   **221**
▮v 23 2017 22:21:46 (EST)

What news broke?
American contractors where?
Hanging from feet?
Re-read dumps.
Why is this relevant?
News unlocks map.
Expand your thinking.
Q

US mercenaries were in Saudi Arabia hanging corrupt Saudi Princes from their feet and torturing them for intelligence on some conspiracy they were a part of.[240]

This lends credence to Q's assertion of a global counter-intelligence operation against an enemy in Saudi Arabia.

---

240   http://archive.is/r5sJ7

368

Anonymous ID: AMBznWhW No.150682213 ☐
☐v 23 2017 22:25:26 (EST)

>>150681065

Q!

is this relevant?

At In-Q-Tel, Painter's work focused on identifying, researching
and evaluating "new start-up technology firms that were
believed to offer tremendous value to the CIA, the National
Geospatial-Intelligence Agency, and the Defense Intelligence
Agency." Indeed, the NGA had confirmed that its intelligence
obtained via Keyhole was used by the NSA to support US
operations in Iraq from 2003 onwards.

A former US Army special operations intelligence officer,
Painter's new job at Google as of July 2005 was federal
manager of what Keyhole was to become: Google Earth
Enterprise. By 2007, Painter had become Google's federal chief
technologist.

'TK' refers to Talent/Keyhole, code names for imagery from
reconnaissance aircraft and spy satellites,

>>150682213

Q !ITPb.qbhqo ID: /cDHrhas No.150686780 ☐   **223**
☐v 23 2017 23:12:46 (EST)

Who is Betsy D?
Why is she relevant?
Expand your thinking.
Q

*Betsy DeVos is the Secretary of Education, and the sister
of Blackwater Founder Erik Prince. It implies Cabal may have
been doing something in the Department of Education to affect*

the development of our next generation, perhaps to make them more compliant and malleable under the forces of Cabal.

Q !lTPb.qbhqo ID: q8aHxh0v No.150697929 ☑   **224**
Nov 24 2017 01:14:46 (EST)

> **Anonymous** ID: orlJUPCM No.150697054 ☑
> Nov 24 2017 01:04:19 (EST)
>
> Betsy DeVos > Erik Prince > POTUS
>
> https://theintercept.com/2017/01/17/notorious-mercenary-erik-prince-is-advising-trump-from-the-shadows/ ☑ ▣

>>150697054
Who knows where the bodies are buried?
The map is in front of you.
Re-read.
Expand your thinking.
Purpose for time being spent here.
Q

Q !lTPb.qbhqo ID: q8aHxh0v No.150698662 ☑   **225**
Nov 24 2017 01:23:11 (EST)

> **Anonymous** ID: jYb7cHDY No.150698169 ☑
> Nov 24 2017 01:17:30 (EST)
>
> >>150697929
> >Who knows where the bodies are buried?
> The ones who put the bodies there.
> Blackwater was used in a shitton of shady ops by the US government back when it was under Cabal control and, as a proper PMC, they've got it all kept on the books.
>
> Books which the POTUS just got access to.

>>150698169
Expand further.
Make the connection.
Map currently has 43 confirmed connections.
Important to understand.
When this breaks many won't swallow.

MSM not trusted.
You are the voice.
We are here to help guide.
Future proves past.
You are the calm before and during the storm.
Q

Q !!TPb.qbhqo ID: JhFEE9Gk No.150701196 🔗   **226**
Nov 24 2017 01:55:52 (EST)

_yes1_yes2_yes3_^_cDVT-089bT_AD_Conf
Godspeed.
Q

Q !!TPb.qbhqo ID: 7W57HuKG No.150767674 🔗   **227**
Nov 24 2017 16:19:45 (EST)

DPbNwxvVAAAEST1.jpg

Q !!TPb.qbhqo ID: 3LaVfhm8 No.150869010 🔗   **228**
Nov 25 2017 13:20:08 (EST)

USA_leadership change
SA_leadership change
GER_leadership change?
PAK_leadership change?

40,000ft.
(8, 7, 6, 5......).
Q

Q !ITPb.qbhqo ID: 3LaVfhm8 No.150870083 ☑   **229**
Nov 25 2017 13:30:47 (EST)
Deleted: Nov 25 2017 13:56:13 (EST)

RED_RED_
_FREEDOM-_v05_yes_27-1_z
_FREEDOM-_v198_yes_27-1_b
_FREEDOM-_v-811z_yes_27-1_c
_FREEDOM-_vZj9_yes_27-1_y
_FREEDOM-_v^CAS0R-T_yes_27-1_87x
_FREEDOM-_v&CAS0R-T2_yes_27-1_t
_FREEDOM-_vEXh29B_yes_27-1_ch
_FREEDOM-_v_stand
_FREEDOM-_v_stand
_FREEDOM-_v_stand
_FREEDOM-_v_stand
_FREEDOM-_v_stand_CAN
_FREEDOM-_v1_stand
_FREEDOM-_v1_stand
_FREEDOM-_v1_stand
_FREEDOM-_v2_stand
_FREEDOM-_v3_stand
_FREEDOM-_v4_mod_D092x
_FREEDOM-_v4_mod_CAS80^
_FREEDOM-_vv1_stand
_FREEDOM-_vv2_stand
_FREEDOM-_vSHAz1EVCB_yes_27-1
_FREEDOM-_vSA_US_yes_DC08vC_EX_y_AW_Conf-go
_FREEDOM-_vSA_US_yes_DC09vC_EX_y_AW_Conf-go
_FREEDOM-_vSA_US_yes_DC10vC_EX_y_AW_Conf-go
_FREEDOM-_vSA_US_yes_DC11vC_EX_y_AW_Conf-go
_FREEDOM-_vSA_US_yes_DC12vc_EX_y_AW_Conf-go
_FREEDOM-_vSA_US_yes_DC13vC_EX_y_AW_Conf-go
_FREEDOM-_vSA_US_stand_DC14vC_EX_y_AW_Conf/stand
_FREEDOM-_vSA_US_yes_DC15vC_EX_y_AW_Conf-go
_FREEDOM-_vSA_US_yes_DC16vC_EX_y_AW_Conf-go
_FREEDOM-_vSA_US_yes_DC17vc_EX_y_AW_Conf-go
_FREEDOM-_vSA_US_yes_DC18vC_EX_y_AW_Conf-go
_FREEDOM-_vSA_US_yes_DC19vC_EX_y_AW_Conf-go
_FREEDOM-_vSA_US_yes_DC20vC_EX_y_AW_Conf-go

```
_FREEDOM-_vSA_US_yes_DC21vC_EX_y_AW_Conf-go
_FREEDOM-_vSA_US_yes_DC22vc_EX_y_AW_Conf-go
_FREEDOM-_vSA_US_yes_DC23vC_EX_y_AW_Conf-go
_FREEDOM-_vSA_US_yes_DC24vC_EX_y_AW_Conf-go
_FREEDOM-_vSA_US_yes_DC25vC_EX_y_AW_Conf-go
_FREEDOM-_vSA_US_stand_DC26vC_EX_y_AW_Conf/stand
_FREEDOM-_vSA_US_yes_DC27vc_EX_y_AW_Conf/term/zJ&bY02
_FREEDOM-_vGER_US_yes_000BVx_LO_yes_[... + 1]_Conf_y
_Conf_4_3_good_EXT-TVB7xxj_ALL_FREEDOM_#[1-43]
_EX_27-1
Q
```

This post and the similar types to follow later were presumed to be some kind of coded messages out in the open, but the significance of them was never determined.

Q !ITPb.qbhqo No.10956085 🗗 📄   **230**
Nov 25 2017 13:54:45 (EST)

Test
Test
4Chan infiltrated.
Future posts will be relayed here.
Q

People do not really grasp the extent of the intelligence operation that has been launched against society, to try and cement the control of the elites. Online message boards like 4Chan are just one example. On 4Chan, there are millions of people who will view the boards. Only a few hundred per day, maybe a few thousand, will feel the drive to post on the political board /pol. Since most posts are meaningless banter, only a handful of the posts will have any meaning, and any ability to affect opinions and perceptions of reality. Of those only a handful will have the psychological savvy to be genuine influencers. The rest of all those people are just readers, consuming the data they see. This offers a tremendous return on human investment in terms of affecting public perceptions and opinions, especially when you consider that a single person with appropriate software can assume a hundred different identities, posting under a hundred different avatars, making it appear as if public opinion is skewed one way or another. Even fewer people actually seek out positions as board moderators with the ability to delete posts and ban users, as that requires a time investment and is a burden. If you have entities whose sole purpose is to control the online dialog, their people will aggressively seek out those positions, so they can further control the dialog online. Those organizations are there, both private sector with political agendas, and governmental, and they often work together.

It was long known 4Chan was compromised by these forces, and here Q confirms they are interfering with his ability to post, so he is moving to a similar board, 8Chan.

Q !ITPb.qbhqo ID: 3LaVfhm8 No.150875388 ☑   **231**
Nov 25 2017 14:22:21 (EST)
Deleted: Nov 25 2017 14:38:43 (EST)

T: B, F, J, 1,5,11-20, ^
_Conf_d-ww_CON_off**[dark]**_
_Conf_SIL-_EX
COMM_Castle_Active_7ZbV-WT9
RED1_RED2_
SAT_40k_se_c_**[30m]**
Godspeed.
P_pers: WRWY
Q

Q !ITPb.qbhqo ID: 3LaVfhm8 No.150876856 ☑   **232**
Nov 25 2017 14:35:44 (EST)
Deleted: Nov 25 2017 14:49:43 (EST)

_Conf_goTWIT_P_act-small#_
RED1_RED2_
Q

Q !!TPb.qbhqo No.10956374 🗀 📁   **233**
Nov 25 2017 15:28:38 (EST)

Flash Dir_
Start_code_activated/instruction
LOG1_^67FVc
_4ch_n
_8ch_y
_Conf_y_**[8]**_8bCon
Key secured.
Q

Q !!TPb.qbhqo `ID: 0a9612` No.10925 🗀   **234**
Nov 29 2017 14:21:16 (EST)

Snow White utilized/activated to silence.
This was not anticipated.
Control / protection lost.
Routing through various networks ('jumpers') randomly has created
connection/sec issues.
Working to resolve.
Select people removed.
Stay strong.
We are winning.
More to follow.
Q

Q !!TPb.qbhqo `ID: 249a4f` No.12916 🗀   **235**
Nov 30 2017 00:05:38 (EST)

IMG_1139.PNG ⬇

Where is BO?
What is the purpose?
Who fired?
When?
Reconcile.
Q

Q !!TPb.qbhqo ID: 7ebe7c No.13092 ☐
⬛v 30 2017 00:38:37 (EST)

Focus on Hussein.
Revelations coming very very soon.
HUMA - SA - Hussein.
HLR (first).
Civil rights attorney.
13th District - Sen.
DNC.
Hussein v HRC v McCain.
Why is this relevant?
Follow the money pre-pres.
Follow the connections pre-pres.
Why does Hussein travel ahead of POTUS?
Why did Hussein travel behind POTUS?
Think Asia.
Think NK.
What was told re: NK during the past 8 years?
What dramatic shift occurred re: NK post election of POTUS?
Reconcile.
Define hostage.
The Sum of all Fears.
Why are sexual harassment claims all appearing suddenly?
Coincidence?
What is a pill?
When is it hard to swallow?
How do you remove your enemies from positions of influence and
authority?
Define stages.
Define puppets.
Define puppet handlers.
Define proxy war.
Define proxy war.
Define proxy war.
Expand your thinking.
Why is Justice stalling release of c-level info?
Think.

Does POTUS control all matters classified?
Think.
Have faith.
These people are losers!
Q

Q !ITPb.qbhqo ID: 7db625 No.13215 ☐   **237**
ov 30 2017 01:01:36 (EST)

What if NK had miniature nuke payload delivery in 2004?
What if NK had ICBM capability since 2009?
What if the previous tests that failed were staged?
Why would this be relevant?
Who is involved and why?
Biggest cover up in our history.
U1 - CA - EU - ASIA\NK.
Iran deal.
Russian reset.
Q

Q !ITPb.qbhqo ID: 7db625 No.13282 ☐   **238**
ov 30 2017 01:12:57 (EST)

Sidley Austin.
Happy hunting.
Q

Q !ITPb.qbhqo ID: 47b2cc No.13601 ☐   **239**
ov 30 2017 02:23:51 (EST)

The Asia Foundation.
CIA-RDP84B00049R001303260026-4
Happy hunting.
Q

A reference to the founder of the Asia Foundation, CIA counter-intelligence chief Robert Blum.[241] His story shows that a lot of official looking organizations you would think were formed for one purpose, were actually Agency creations serving an Agency purpose, and everything you were told was just a cover story to make people think nobody was seizing power.

---

241   http://archive.is/VhKtU

Q !ITPb.qbhqo ID: W6dZpInF No.151561953 ⬀   **240**
ɔv 30 2017 23:42:25 (EST)
Deleted: Nov 30 2017 23:45:18 (EST)

_Start_IP_log_4ch_y
_Conf_y_
_Lang_v_US_jurid_y
Snow White Pounce.
_Conf_actors_1-9999999_per_condition_89074-b
No nets.
Re_8ch_carry_good_
Q

Q !ITPb.qbhqo ID: fbc52d No.17283 ⬀   **241**
ɛc 1 2017 00:08:26 (EST)

WH party w/ 400+ guests.
Whoever posted those insider pics did not take into account the
many WH public and private sec cams which can triangulate and
time log/IDEN the person responsible.
We will investigate.
Think.
Q

This references two anons on 4Chan who were live-posting pictures from a White House event to 4Chan.[242]

Q !ITPb.qbhqo ID: fbc52d No.17290 ⬀   **242**
ɛc 1 2017 00:09:33 (EST)

Be here tomorrow.
The story unfolds.
Q

Q !ITPb.qbhqo ID: fbc52d No.17359 ⬀   **243**
ɛc 1 2017 00:17:43 (EST)

SA controlled US puppets.
Strings cut.
D's dropping all around over sexual misconduct (1st stage).
Coincidence directly after SA?
Don't you realize the war has gone public?
List who will not be running for re_election.

242   http://archive.is/0jOIS

378

Q !!TPb.qbhqo ID: fbc52d No.17474 ⬀   **244**
■ ec 1 2017 00:38:08 (EST)

Less than 10 can confirm me.
DOITQ - coincidence
Twitter retweet - coincidence
Twitter keywords - coincidence
Pics - coincidence
Meant only for you.
God bless.
Q

DOITQ was part of the file name of a photo President Trump tweeted,[243] although this will not be discovered for some time. On the desk in front of the President in the photo is a newspaper article detailing the Saudi crackdown. Twitter filenames are supposed to be assigned randomly by twitter when you upload an image. Clearly the probability of POTUS getting a filename containing DOITQ is extraordinarily small, unless Q has real elite-level government-type authority, and can call up twitter and make it happen. This was seen as a strong Q proof when it was revealed.

Q !!TPb.qbhqo ID: fbc52d No.17546 ⬀   **245**
■ ec 1 2017 00:46:51 (EST)
Hussein is evil and a real loser.
No special treatment.
Shopping around for a (new) handler/protection is fun to watch on the SATs / spy comms.
Morons, all of them.
Q

Q !!TPb.qbhqo ID: fbc52d No.17586 ⬀   **246**
■ ec 1 2017 00:49:43 (EST)

89074
Underground massive data center?
Q

---

243   http://archive.is/Sl1mt

379

Q !ITPb.qbhqo ID: eda158 No.34081 🗗
⬛ec 4 2017 22:01:07 (EST)

Have you been watching the news since Friday?
Who is Peter Strzok?
How was he compromised?
How was he paid?
Who is Melissa Hodgman?
Company?
Title?
Date of promotion?
Focus on the date.
What events re: Peter recently occurred that you now know?
Think HRC emails, Weiner laptop, etc.
Dates?
Date of promotion of wife?
How do they stack the deck?
Who do they want inside the gov't?
What are puppets?
How do you control a puppet?
#2 in FBI?
Wife connection?
What is a pattern?
Follow the wives.
Keep watching the news this week.
Future proves past.
Re-read crumbs.
(Small)
How many D's / R's will not seek re-election?
Why?
What just passed in the Senate?
Why?
Who is their new handler?
Do as told?
Why is this relevant?
Do you not understand the gov't is being gutted publicly?
Bottom middle top.
Hussein Iran connection.
Bombs away.
Merry Christmas.
Q

Peter Strzok's wife, Melissa Hodges, an SEC Director,
blocked an investigation of the Clinton Foundation by the FBI.

Q !!TPb.qbhqo ID: eda158 No.34110 ⬀   **248**
Dec 4 2017 22:12:51 (EST)

#FLYROTHSFLY#

Q !!TPb.qbhqo ID: eda158 No.34250 ⬀   **249**
Dec 4 2017 22:38:51 (EST)

RED_RED
Remember?
Hussein AIDS Video.
Hidden message?
Response?
Twitter.
Roles.
Actions.
Expand your thinking.
News unlocks meaning.
Q

Q !!TPb.qbhqo ID: eda158 No.34290 ⬀   **250**
Dec 4 2017 22:45:41 (EST)

Date Peter/Comey cleared Weiner emails?
Date wife was promoted?
Do you believe in coincidences?
Q

Q !!TPb.qbhqo ID: eda158 No.34323 ⬀   **251**
Dec 4 2017 22:50:10 (EST)

Re-review RED_RED stringer.
Focus on Hussein AIDS Video.
Cross reference.
Date of stringer vs video?
Learn to decider.
News unlocks message.
Find the keystone.
Q

Q !!TPb.qbhqo ID: eda158 No.34407 ⬀   **252**
Dec 4 2017 23:01:17 (EST)

Red Cross is corrupt and used as a piggy bank.
Future topic.

Diseases created by families in power (pop control + pharma
billions kb).
Think AIDS.
Future topic.
Relevant.
#FLYROTHSFLY#
Q

Q !ITPb.qbhqo Q !ITPb.qbhqo ID: eda158 No.34447 🔗 📁   **253**
Dec 4 2017 23:07:17 (EST)

> Anonymous ID: cc8528 No.34409 🔗 📁
> Dec 4 2017 23:01:32 (EST)
> Screen Shot 2017-12-05 at ....png
>
> On main page of Red website.
> >COINCIDENCE?

>>34409

Q !ITPb.qbhqo Q !ITPb.qbhqo ID: eda158 No.34502 🔗   **254**
Dec 4 2017 23:12:59 (EST)

> Q !ITPb.qbhqo Q !ITPb.qbhqo ID: eda158 No.34447 🔗
> Dec 4 2017 23:07:17 (EST)
>
> >>34409

>>34447
Expand your thinking.
When did Hussein travel to Asia?
When was the stringer released?
When was the RED video taped?
Do you believe in coincidences?
Q

Q !!TPb.qbhqo ID: eda158 No.34522 ☐   **255**
☐c 4 2017 23:14:24 (EST)

Learn to read the map.
You have more than you realize.
Q

Q !!TPb.qbhqo ID: eda158 No.34635 ☐   **256**
☐c 4 2017 23:27:40 (EST)

Dates: 25, 27, 28.
Stringer, RED RED, ASIA.
Analyze the connection.
Learn to read the map.
Q

Q !!TPb.qbhqo ID: eda158 No.34655 ☐   **257**
☐c 4 2017 23:30:26 (EST)

Anonymous ID: 6ee2e0 No.34602 ☐
☐c 4 2017 23:24:46 (EST)

Q pointed out the picture on the RED.ORG site with the Korean
woman pointing to "Meet Me In Seoul" Obummer goes to
China, did he go to Seoul too?

>>34602

Q !!TPb.qbhqo ID: eda158 No.34738 ☐   **258**
☐c 4 2017 23:41:11 (EST)

Anonymous ID: 1139cb No.34663 ☐
☐c 4 2017 23:30:55 (EST)

>>34407

South Korea calls North Korea daily:

"The ministry has to keep pestering Pyongyang over the military
and Red Cross talks," he said. "It has to keep placing calls on
the Panmunjom telephone. The situation can quickly change
and North Korea could feel the need for dialogue. When they do
return, they will likely want to deal with the United States first,
but let them try to accomplish anything in talks with Washington
without the involvement of Seoul — it won't work."

https://www.bloomberg.com/news/articles/2017-10-03/north-
korea-tension-sidelines-south-s-unification-ministry ☐ ☐

RED CROSS RED RED.
NK.
Hussein.
ASIA.
Why was that STRINGER sent out?
Decode.
News unlocks message.
Future proves past.
Where is the RED CROSS?
Runs deep.
Children.
Pray.
Q

Q !!TPb.qbhqo ID: cc0116 No.34917 ☐   **259**
 ec 5 2017 00:09:40 (EST)

RED RED 9/11.
Funds raised vs distributed?
Oversight?
7/10 plane crashes are targeted kills.
Those in the know never sleep.
Q

Q !!TPb.qbhqo ID: cc0116 No.35004 ☐   **260**
 ec 5 2017 00:24:14 (EST)

Who knows where the bodies are buried?
FLYNN is safe.
We protect our Patriots.
Q

Q !!TPb.qbhqo ID: cc0116 No.35048 ☐   **261**
 ec 5 2017 00:31:00 (EST)

RED Haiti.
Children.
$
Since POTUS elected what changed w/ RED?
Since POTUS elected what changed w/ CF?
Since POTUS elected what changed w/ Mc_I?
These people deserve ....
Q

The Senate began to investigate shady aspects of the Red

Cross' finances.[244] The Clinton Foundation donations plummeted once neither of them had influence to sell,[245] and the Clinton Global Initiative closed. As donors who previously bought favors from Clinton ceased donating, they shifted their donations to the McCain Institute,[246] which Q seems to indicate is because McCain offered influence in return for contributions to his foundation, and those donations were then presumably being laundered to Cabal with a cut to his family.

Q !!TPb.qbhqo **ID: cc0116** No.35166 ☐   **262**
ec 5 2017 00:45:56 (EST)

RED RED stringer 25th.
Hussein RED video 27th (response).
Hussein in Asia on 28th post stringer.
Analyze.
Coincidence?
More than one meaning.
Hussein RED Indictments variables.
Think circle.
Expand your thinking.
Take multiple paths.
One connects to another.
Learn to read the map.
The map is the key.
Find the keystone.
What holds everything together?
Q

Q !!TPb.qbhqo **ID: cc0116** No.35519 ☐   **263**
ec 5 2017 01:48:47 (EST)

+FLYROTHSFLY+

Q !!TPb.qbhqo **ID: cc0116** No.35560 ☐   **264**
ec 5 2017 01:54:26 (EST)
God bless, Patriots.
We are proud.
Q

244   http://archive.is/ziIQh
245   http://archive.is/TecKe
246   http://archive.is/bgoGB

Q !ITPb.qbhqo ID: abced6 No.38330 ☑   **265**
c 5 2017 15:43:47 (EST)

Bye Bye Johnny.
Update the list.
Watch the news.
WAR.
Q

Q !ITPb.qbhqo ID: abced6 No.38366 ☑   **266**
c 5 2017 15:49:09 (EST)

#FLYJOHNNYFLY

Q was indicating here that John McCain is now fated to die.

Q !ITPb.qbhqo ID: abced6 No.38394 ☑   **267**
c 5 2017 15:52:48 (EST)

#FLYALFLY#
Runway lights being turned on.
FLY HIGH.
Q

Q !ITPb.qbhqo ID: abced6 No.38406 ☑   **268**
c 5 2017 15:53:38 (EST)

> **Anonymous** ID: a3ee6f No.38396 ☑
> c 5 2017 15:52:54 (EST)
>
> >>38366
> Anything you can say on Deutsche Bank?

>>38396
FAKE NEWS.
Q

Q !ITPb.qbhqo ID: 7cfe10 No.38467 ☑   **269**
c 5 2017 16:01:30 (EST)

Key - unlocks the door of all doors (info)
Stone - the force / strength capable of yielding power to act on info
Key+Stone=
Q

Q !ITPb.qbhqo ID: 7cfe10 No.38507 ⬈   **270**
c 5 2017 16:06:17 (EST)

Adm R/ No Such Agency (W&W) + POTUS/USMIL =
Apply the Keystone.
Paint the picture.
Q

Q !ITPb.qbhqo ID: 7cfe10 No.38514 ⬈   **271**
c 5 2017 16:06:49 (EST)

> Anonymous ID: 47c6e4 No.38503 ⬈
> c 5 2017 16:05:45 (EST)
>
> >>38467
> Military Intelligence, No Such Agency = key
> POTUS and Patriots = stone

>>38503

Q !ITPb.qbhqo ID: 7cfe10 No.38537 ⬈   **272**
c 5 2017 16:09:28 (EST)

> Anonymous ID: 04e025 No.38504 ⬈
> c 5 2017 16:05:57 (EST)
>
> List of politicians not seeking re-election
> Bob Corker, R
> Charlie Dent, R
> Jeff Flake, R
> John Duncan, R
> Bob Goodlatte, R
> Jeb Hensarling, R
> Lynn Jenkins, R
> Sam Johnson, R
> Frank LoBiondo, R
> Tim Murphy, R
> Ted Poe, R
> Dave Reichert, R
> Ileana Ros-Lehtinen, R
> Lamar Smith, R
> Pat Tiberi, R
> Dave Trott, R
> Carol Shea-Porter, D

387

Gene Green, D
Joe Barton, R
John Delaney, D
Luis V. Gutierrez, D
Niki Tsongas, D
John Conyers, D
Sandy Levin, D

>>38504
Normal?
Coincidence?
Draining the swamp?
Q

Q !ITPb.qbhqo ID: 7cfe10 No.38627 ⬈   **273**
c 5 2017 16:20:32 (EST)

 R
RED
 D

Q !ITPb.qbhqo ID: 7cfe10 No.38638 ⬈   **274**
c 5 2017 16:21:56 (EST)

Godfather III
Be prepared for what you find.
Q

Q !ITPb.qbhqo ID: 7cfe10 No.38682 ⬈   **275**
c 5 2017 16:26:34 (EST)

+FLY+
Banks control Gov'ts
Gov'ts control people
SA controls elected people.
SOROS controls organizations of people.
Ready to play?
Q

Q !ITPb.qbhqo ID: 7cfe10 No.38701 ⬈   **276**
c 5 2017 16:27:56 (EST)

WONDERFUL friends.
Q

388

Q !!TPb.qbhqo **ID: 6f5bab** No.45363 ⬈   **277**
Dec 6 2017 20:34:58 (EST)

Goodbye AL.
Add to list.
#FLYSIDFLY#
Q

Al Franken announced he was stepping down from the
Senate due to a sexual harassment complaint the next day, on
Dec 7th. Sidney might mean Sidney Blumenthal, or it might be a
reference to John McCain's middle name, Sidney. Q indicated at
one point whatever McCain was guilty of was so evil they do not
like to mention him by name.

Q !!TPb.qbhqo **ID: 6f5bab** No.45424 ⬈   **278**
Dec 6 2017 20:44:36 (EST)

HRC tried to cut a deal today.
WE SAID NO.
Q

Q !!TPb.qbhqo **ID: 6f5bab** No.45494 ⬈   **279**
Dec 6 2017 20:52:37 (EST)

> Anonymous **ID: 1d1357** No.45476 ⬈
> Dec 6 2017 20:50:09 (EST)
>
> >>45424
>
> Q can you confirm?
>
> >>45121

Why is the SS now protecting key members of No Such Agency?
>>45476

The unquoted post Q was being asked to confirm (and
which he apparently did) is reprinted on the next page.

This is what Q meant with Hunt for Red October:
>>http://www.foxnews.com/transcript/2017/10/24/clinton-campaign-dnc-paid-for-anti-trump-dossier-research-ivanka-trump-washington-is-complicated-place.html

JARRETT: If there is collusion, it's Hillary-Russia collusion. Not Trump-Russia collusion.

HANNITY: I've been predicting this, Dr. Gorka this massive boomerang for a long time. I've known a lot of this evidence was out there and it was all coming. I've been telling my audience, its coming, and its coming. Now the floodgates are open, if you will.

SEBASTIAN GORKA, DEPUTY ASSISTANT TO PRESIDENT TRUMP: It's the last scene from that great Tom Clancy movie, "The hunt for red October." When the bad submarine commander launch a torpedo it comes back and sinks his own vessel. That is what the Russian collusion story has done for the DNC and for Hillary. Let's stop using the word collusion, because the evidence we now have is about subversion, it's about sabotaging the political process and it's about propaganda. In the cold war, the Soviet Union will be used what was called active measures to undermine our democracy. This is the Democrat Party, the Hillary campaign using active measures to undermine Donald Trump and the Democratic process in America. It's a shocking story.

Q !ITPb.qbhqo ID: 6f5bab No.45541 ☐   **280**
ec 6 2017 20:58:51 (EST)

Watch the news.
Leakers exposed.
These people are stupid.
Q

Q !ITPb.qbhqo ID: 6f5bab No.45557 ☐   **281**
ec 6 2017 21:00:45 (EST)

We represent YOU.
Never forget that.
We never will.
MAGA.
Q

Q !ITPb.qbhqo ID: 6f5bab No.45581 ⬏
Dec 6 2017 21:03:11 (EST)

Anonymous ID: 0b6109 No.45563 ⬏
Dec 6 2017 21:01:21 (EST)

>>45541
I have a question: The 10 days, darkness.. when?

>>45563
Shutdown.
Q

Q !ITPb.qbhqo ID: 6f5bab No.45609 ⬏
Dec 6 2017 21:05:26 (EST)

Anonymous ID: c27a60 No.45569 ⬏
Dec 6 2017 21:02:04 (EST)

>>45543
>https://twitter.com/SaraCarterDC/status/938574363040911360
Sara is good people.

>>45569
Why are Sara & John getting all the 'real' scoops?
Expand your thinking.
Why are they now under protection?
Q

Sarah Carter and John Solomon are uncompromised by Cabal, and thus probably targeted, and angry about it. So they are being used by Q to deliver honest scoops to the public.

Q !ITPb.qbhqo ID: 8e6033 No.45723 ⬏
Dec 6 2017 21:22:00 (EST)

AL back in the news today after #FLYALFLY#.
Another coincidence?
Follow the news.
Merry Christmas.
Q

Q !!TPb.qbhqo (ID: 8e6033) No.45814 ☐   **285**
  ec 6 2017 21:31:50 (EST)

What if No Such Agency alerted May to the kill plan per POTUS?
What if the attempt was ordered by ++?
Why?
FREEDOM Caucus?
FREEDOM.
Q

Again, Q is highlighting the news you do not hear on the evening news programs. Q is saying that on Trump's orders, NSA warned Teresa May of an impending assassination attack on her,[247] which had been ultimately ordered by one of the three major powers that control Cabal. The purpose of the attack was to replace her with someone who would derail Brexit.

Q !!TPb.qbhqo (ID: cbaed3) No.46591 ☐   **286**
  ec 7 2017 00:02:52 (EST)

Strike package Bravo-dT450-1
Conf^_y_7
[R]_(   )[+ 4]
Q

Q !!TPb.qbhqo (ID: cbaed3) No.46652 ☐   **287**
  ec 7 2017 00:11:37 (EST)

> **Anonymous** (ID: 922b47) No.46647 ☐
>   ec 7 2017 00:10:16 (EST)
> >>46591
> Wtf happened last thread

>>46647
This is not a game.
Q

Q's board would suddenly become unreadable when he would post, as bots and trolls filled the threads up with gibberish.

---

247   http://archive.is/H9FiB

Q !!TPb.qbhqo ID: cbaed3 No.46773 ☑   **288**
 ec 7 2017 00:28:58 (EST)

_Go_A-Strike_B-04_00
As The World Turns.
Q

Q !!TPb.qbhqo ID: cbaed3 No.46820 ☑   **289**
 ec 7 2017 00:33:36 (EST)

Reached est 1.2mm, Patriots.
You are reaching more than you know.
1=2, 2=4, 4=8, …
Godspeed.
Q

Q !!TPb.qbhqo ID: 9cad51 No.50693 ☑   **290**
 ec 7 2017 19:39:59 (EST)

0704911B-FBA8-4DE7-9C53-9....jpeg

03821C90-07E4-4906-B30D-A....jpeg

Q !!TPb.qbhqo ID: 9cad51 No.50834 🔗 📁   **292**
Dec 7 2017 19:56:06 (EST)

> **Anonymous** ID: 40f1ef No.50813 🔗 📁
> Dec 7 2017 19:53:33 (EST)
> >>50787
> what is that ring?

>>50813

Never resolved, but it is assumed Hillary wearing that ring with a black stone, and displaying it in a public photo, may be a symbolic display of her membership in the Secret Society, letting others know she knows, and is approved of by Cabal. Other celebrities were found displaying similar rings.

Q !!TPb.qbhqo ID: 9cad51 No.50896 🔗   **293**
Dec 7 2017 20:01:44 (EST)

Pictures unlock 'deal' presented that was declined.
Puppets going wild.
Q

Q !!TPb.qbhqo ID: d9b992 No.51313 🔗   **294**
Dec 7 2017 20:46:29 (EST)

B6C47FD8-1F66-4549-8A4B-2....jpeg

Due to copyright issues, this picture can be viewed at:
http://archive.is/vsZZD
It is a picture of Clinton aide Huma Abedin walking with Clinton staffer John Podesta

9AB57841-1F3F-4630-889B-4...jpeg

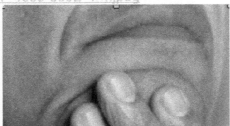

*Due to copyright issues, this picture can
be viewed at:
http://archive.is/3z6ia
It is a picture of Barack Obama's hand
under his chin, emphasizing the Islamic
wedding ring he wears.*

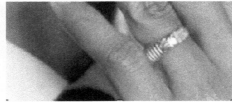

77C6EF7B-C1F0-49A6-BD1E-C...jpeg

*Due to Copyright issues, this picture can
be viewed at:
http://archive.is/mCX5u
It is a picture of Obama walking on a
tarmac, holding a copy of Fareed Zakaria's
book, "The Post-American World."*

Due to copyright issues, this picture can be viewed at:
http://archive.is/ox2Qz
It is a picture of Angela Merkel, standing, and holding her hands in a triangle with her fingertips touching.

Due to copyright issues, this picture can be viewed at:
http://archive.is/vo7vA
The picture features Hillary Walking with Laurance Rockefeller

It is unclear if Q is saying Hillary offered to turn on these people to save herself, or if he is just posting pictures of the club. These pictures feature Obama's Muslim wedding ring, Obama with a copy of Fareed Zakaria's book, "The Post-American World," Angela Merkel sporting the triangle hand position she frequently uses, and Hillary with Laurance Rockefeller.

Q !!TPb.qbhqo (ID: 913bb1) No.51739 🗗   **296**
c 7 2017 21:34:28 (EST)

C2C6E563-AEEE-46D4-95F9-0...jpeg

Due to copyright issues, this picture can be viewed at: http://archive.is/NSiDl It features Hillary Clinton standing with Lynn de Rothschild

29ABE882-37B0-472A-A79E-F...jpeg

Due to copyright issues, this picture can be viewed at: http://archive.is/TwOza It is a picture of Hillary Clinton standing with Sir Evelyn de Rothschild

The previous pictures featured Hillary with Lynn de Rothschild, Hillary with Sir Evelyn de Rothschild, Hillary and John McCain, and Hillary with George Soros.

Due to copyright issues, this picture can
be viewed at:
http://archive.is/ceepm
The picture is of Hillary Clinton with Saudi
Foreign Minister Prince Saud Al-Faisal
(R), and Kuwaiti Foreign Minister Sheikh
Sabah Khaled al-Hamad Al-Sabah.

Due to copyright issues, this picture can
be viewed at:
http://archive.is/vSylO
The picture is of Saudi Prince Alwaleed
bin Talal

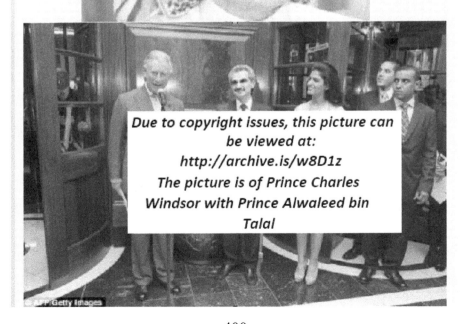

Due to copyright issues, this picture can
be viewed at:
http://archive.is/w8D1z
The picture is of Prince Charles
Windsor with Prince Alwaleed bin
Talal

400

Due to copyright issues, this picture can be viewed at: http://archive.is/2KYTP The picture is of John McCain meeting with members of the Syrian Resistance.

The first picture features Hillary with Saudi Foreign Minister Prince Saud Al-Faisal (R), and Kuwaiti Foreign Minister Sheikh Sabah Khaled al-Hamad Al-Sabah. The second is a picture of Prince Alwaleed bin Talal. The third is of Prince Charles Windsor with Prince Alwaleed bin Talal. The last picture is of John McCain during a meeting where he was alleged to have met with ISIS terrorists in Syria – a claim the media roundly debunks, but which facts indicate at most isn't proven 100%,[248] and which Q says was actually a coordination meeting between McCain, a high-ranking Cabal operative, and ISIS leadership. You will see the media bend over backward and sacrifice its credibility to try and deny something potentially damaging to Cabal operatives, rather than honestly report the facts. You'll find as time goes on, if you see that, it is a good indication something untoward happened, and Cabal has issued orders to its agents in the Fake News media to cover it up.

---

248   http://archive.is/tHuLX

3155B65F-063D-445E-A3BD-5...jpeg

Due to copyright issues, this picture can be viewed at:
http://archive.is/yoJHk
These two pictures are of John McCain meeting with alleged ISIS members in Syria

8BF7AC13-C658-41A6-A0E3-8...jpeg

Due to copyright issues, this picture can be viewed at:
http://archive.is/whEcQ
Syrian President Bashar al-Assad (R) and Saudi Prince al-Waleed bin Talal bin Abdulaziz.

© AFP/Getty Images

These pictures basically show both, that the Saudis have been everywhere behind the scenes, and often supposed political

enemies seem closer than they should be. Hillary Clinton is pure sociopath and completely evil. If John McCain had one millionth the honor and patriotism attributed to him in the media, he would never have been able to associate so closely with Hillary, not because of ideology, but because of who she is as a person. The salient point is, things were not as we were told.

Q !ITPb.qbhqo `ID: 913bb1` No.51984 ⟶ **299**
Dec 7 2017 22:05:16 (EST)

Rothschilds (cult leaders)(church)(P)
Banks / Financial Institutions
WW Gov Control
Gov Controls People
SA
Oil Tech Sex/Children
SA Controls (assigned) US / UK Politicians / Tech Co's (primary)
Soros
Controls organizations of people (create division / brainwash) +
management / operator of slush funds (personal net worth never
reduces think DOJ settlements Consumer Iran Enviro pacts etc etc)
/_\ - Rock (past)(auth over followers)
_\ (present)
(Future)
Order is critical.
Strings cut to US/UK.
Expand your thinking.
Swamp drain.
1 - sexual harassment exit + future
....
[R] - No.
Bomb away.
Q

This lays out the old order, where the Rothschilds control the Church, cults, banks, media, governments, and through governments, the people. Saudi Arabia handled oil/energy, banking, and facilitated child abuse for purposes of the Cabal, including child-sexual abuse and possibly murder/sacrifice, performed for blackmail. George Soros operated private sector influence organizations to guide the populace's fervors into Cabal objectives. According to Q, one side of the triangle has been disabled at this point, namely the Saudi banking aspect.

Q !ITPb.qbhqo **ID: 913bb1** No.52122 🗗   **300**
Dec 7 2017 22:25:31 (EST)

Can you find a pic of Alwaleed and Hussein or Clinton or other US politicians?
L.
Heard you can't sleep anymore.
Don't come here again.
Q

Alwaleed has not been photographed with US leaders, despite being close to them. What you see is controlled.

Q !ITPb.qbhqo **ID: 913bb1** No.52134 🗗   **301**
Dec 7 2017 22:27:06 (EST)

#FLYROTHSFLY#
Sweet dreams.
Q

Q !ITPb.qbhqo **ID: 913bb1** No.52157 🗗   **302**
Dec 7 2017 22:29:30 (EST)

For Green.
Q
—end—

Q !ITPb.qbhqo **ID: 052e3b** No.54349 🗗   **303**
Dec 8 2017 11:01:30 (EST)

Renee J James
Q

She is a tech executive and former CEO of Intel.

MONDAY **Q** !!TPb.qbhqo ID: 6bea6c No.55699 ⬈   **304**
c 8 2017 16:22:57 (EST)

https://www.youtube.com/watch?v=chyHx0zKQGo ⬈
These people are sick.
Q

This was a since-deleted youtube video of Nancy Pelosi sounding confused and disoriented.[249] Q has implied this was her laying the groundwork for a dementia defense to make use of in a future trial for her crimes. John McCain did something similar at a Senate hearing, prior to declaring he had a brain tumor,[250] and Joe Biden is a gaffe a day, and at this point, just assumed to be going senile.

Q !!TPb.qbhqo ID: 7813e1 No.59684 ⬈   **305**
c 9 2017 11:24:37 (EST)

482D19E4-6664-478F-8836-30....png

_____

249   http://archive.is/DeetO
250   http://archive.li/a2c1w

Q !!TPb.qbhqo **ID: 571cae** No.60141 🗗   **306**
c 9 2017 13:12:19 (EST)

News unlocks map.
Future proves past.
Why was the Lord's prayer posted?
Which version?
Why is this relevant?
What just came out re: the Lord's prayer?
What can be connected?
Do you believe in coincidences?
Re-review the map post relevant news drops.
Godfather III.
Q

Q !!TPb.qbhqo **ID: 571cae** No.60172 🗗   **307**
c 9 2017 13:16:56 (EST)

Anonymous **ID: e60938** No.60150 🗗
c 9 2017 13:13:29 (EST)

>>60141
Tues Nov 4th,

Who financed 9-11?
Who was Bin Laden's handler?
Why was the Clowns In America tasked to hunt/kill/capture
UBL?
Why not MI?
If we found UBL, eliminated his security, why would we
immediately kill him and not take him alive?
Why wouldn't we want to capture UBL alive and extract other
possible T-level events?
Perhaps someday people will understand 'they' had a plan to
conduct 'another' mass extinction event.
WWI & II - orchestrated and planned by select families?
Fantasy land.
Remember, the more people there are, the more power the
people have.
Why do D's push for gun control 'directly' after every tragic
incident?
Why is this so very important to their agenda?
We, the people, are who they are afraid of.
We, the people, are who they fear will one day awake.

Our Father who art in heaven,
Hallowed be thy name.
Thy kingdom come.
Thy will be done
on earth as it is in heaven.
Give us this day our daily bread,
and forgive us our trespasses,
as we forgive those who trespass against us,
and lead us not into temptation,
but deliver us from evil.
Q

>>60150
The "marker."
Learn to read the map.
News unlocks the map.
Q

MONDAY Q !ITPb.qbhqo ID: 571cae No.60201 ☑   **308**
Dec 9 2017 13:21:38 (EST)

Tangent.
Expand your thinking.
Q

Q !ITPb.qbhqo Q !ITPb.qbhqo ID: 571cae No.60244 ☑   **309**
Dec 9 2017 13:28:04 (EST)

Justice.
Q

Q !ITPb.qbhqo Q !ITPb.qbhqo ID: 571cae No.60291 ☑   **310**
Dec 9 2017 13:34:24 (EST)

Anonymous ID: b588f5 No.60267 ☑
Dec 9 2017 13:31:10 (EST)
>>60244
>Justice
His speech in Pensacola mentioned the US military providing
justice throughout the world.
I hope that isn't just standard NeoCon justification to be the
world's policeman …

>>60267
What has been said about the US Military?
The speech yesterday verified and unlocked so much.

Expand your thinking.
Re-read crumbs.
Re-listen to yesterday's speech.
Connect the 'markers.'
News (in all forms) unlocks the map.
Expand your thinking.
The Great Awakening.
Q

Q !!TPb.qbhqo (ID: 571cae) No.60336 ☑   **311**
ec 9 2017 13:41:15 (EST)

What was the USSS codename for Hussein?
[R]
Define.
They knew all along.
Expand your thinking.
Q

Hussein's (Obama's) Secret Service codename was
Renegade, or one who acts against his own people's mores.

Q !!TPb.qbhqo (ID: 571cae) No.60350 ☑   **312**
ec 9 2017 13:42:30 (EST)

> Q !!TPb.qbhqo (ID: 571cae) No.60336 ☑
> ec 9 2017 13:41:15 (EST)
>
> What was the USSS codename for Hussein?
> [R]
> Define.
> They knew all along.
> Expand your thinking.
> Q

>>60336
Who currently protects Hussein?
[R]
Why is this relevant?
Who currently protects B/H C?
Why is this relevant?
Learn.
Q

Q !!TPb.qbhqo ID: 571cae No.60365 🗗   313
ec 9 2017 13:44:08 (EST)

> Anonymous ID: 14e054 No.60346 🗗
> ec 9 2017 13:42:19 (EST)
>
> >>60336
> Renegade

>>60346
A person who deserts and betrays an organization, country, or set
of principles.
They always knew.
Q

Q !!TPb.qbhqo ID: 571cae No.60382 🗗   314
ec 9 2017 13:45:57 (EST)

Be the autists we know you are.
It's about the BREAK.
Godspeed, Patriots.
Q

Q !!TPb.qbhqo ID: 571cae No.60421 🗗   315
ec 9 2017 13:48:57 (EST)

> Q !!TPb.qbhqo Q !!TPb.qbhqo ID: 571cae No.60291 🗗
> ec 9 2017 13:34:24 (EST)
> >>60267
> What has been said about the US Military?
> The speech yesterday verified and unlocked so much.
> Expand your thinking.
> Re-read crumbs.
> Re-listen to yesterday's speech.
> Connect the 'markers.'
> News (in all forms) unlocks the map.
> Expand your thinking.
> The Great Awakening.
> Q

>>60291
Timestamp US Military against POTUS' recent Tweet - US Military.
How many clues must we provide?
As the World Turns.
Q

Here, Q will quote numerous comments from Anons on his board, before intimating he represents Military Intelligence:

Q !ITPb.qbhqo ID: 571cae No.60470 ⬀   **316**
▮c 9 2017 13:54:51 (EST)

Anonymous ID: 6acc52 No.60296 ⬀
▮c 9 2017 13:35:39 (EST)

>>60291
Martial Law starting the 11th?

Anonymous ID: 14e054 No.60309 ⬀
▮c 9 2017 13:37:17 (EST)

>>60244
>>60291

I like subject Q

Anonymous Anonymous ID: e0d226 No.60319 ⬀
▮c 9 2017 13:38:26 (EST)

٠ >>60291

Yes, felt that speech was odd last night but in a good way.
POTUS emphasis and speech patterns.

We need to go back and listen closely. He did emphasize
words used by Q and POTUS twitter. Find Rightside
Broadcasting Network on utube

Anonymous ID: 10fe8c No.60331 ⬀
▮c 9 2017 13:40:33 (EST)

>>60291
US military will be the strongest in the world.
the speech yesterday was bomb as fuck.
re-listen to POTUS' speech, re-listen to pelosi's seizure.

Anonymous ID: b588f5 No.60340
ec 9 2017 13:41:40 (EST)

>>60291
Yes, I was stuck by how that speech paralleled the themes you've been posting here.
Looking at the map gives a good idea of the operations ahead.

Anonymous ID: 4276b7 No.60358
ec 9 2017 13:43:23 (EST)

>>60291
>>60336
renegade

Anonymous ID: b588f5 No.60363
ec 9 2017 13:43:53 (EST)

>>60291
>Connect the 'markers.'
Are these relevant? >>51726

Anonymous ID: c37c0f No.60418
ec 9 2017 13:48:47 (EST)

>>60201
The proposed change to the Lord's Prayer is not the point. The point is that Q revealed that this was known a month before it was revealed publicly. Q wants us to understand that what is in the map is real and this provides the evidence for it.

>>60244
The important point is Justice.

>>60291
POTUS speech used terms found in the map. More evidence that truth is being revealed, Q is legit and justice is being served.

>>60382
We need to assemble and spread the map *NOW* and demonstrate why it is true due to the news proofs contained within it.

Anonymous ID: bcc578 No.60428 ⬈
Dec 9 2017 13:49:25 (EST)
>>60291
Notice Q is in a different color....something to keep in mind for
the future in case it's becomes something relevant like Monday
in yesterday's post

Anonymous ID: b588f5 No.60267 ⬈
Dec 9 2017 13:31:10 (EST)
>>60244
>Justice
His speech in Pensacola mentioned the US military providing
justice throughout the world.
I hope that isn't just standard NeoCon justification to be the
world's policeman ...

▶Q (You)!ITPb.qbhqo 12/09/17 (Sat) 10:34:24 571cae
No.60291>>60292 >>60296 >>60297 >>60309 >>60311 >>60319
>>60328 >>60331 >>60335 >>60340 >>60349 >>60358 >>60359
>>60363 >>60372 >>60418 >>60421 >>60428
>>60267
What has been said about the US Military?
The speech yesterday verified and unlocked so much.
Expand your thinking.
Re-read crumbs.
Re-listen to yesterday's speech.
Connect the 'markers.'
News (in all forms) unlocks the map.
Expand your thinking.
The Great Awakening.
Q

"We love our U.S. Military. On behalf of an entire Nation, THANK
YOU for your sacrifice and service!"
Timestamp.
How many clues must we provide?
Q

What Q is saying is the President's speech laid out
everything Q had been saying about The Plan to destroy the
Cabal, even using phrases Q has highlighted.

413

Q !ITPb.qbhqo ID: 571cae No.60507 **317**
Dec 9 2017 13:59:21 (EST)

Anonymous Anonymous ID: e0d226 No.60444
Dec 9 2017 13:51:44 (EST)

Q, where the "White House Anons" really the secret service? The ones who showed the WH Christmas photos? Secret Service watches everything and it was AFTER the party that night and no people were in the photos, which would be hard if 400+ guests where there. Were they showing they are on our side?

>>60444
Don't mistake journalists invited to parties as 'insiders'.
Q

Q !ITPb.qbhqo ID: 571cae No.60523 **318**
Dec 9 2017 14:01:00 (EST)

Anonymous ID: 8614a6 No.60476
Dec 9 2017 13:55:39 (EST)

I'm about to BREAK

RIP Chester Bennington and Chris Cornell. They tried to move on Geffen and paid the price.

>>60476
"The" vs "To."
Everything has meaning.
Q

Chester Bennington and Chris Cornell were two rock stars who began talking about a pedophilia problem in show business and making noise about exposing it. Both died within a very short period of time after going public. Q has said that the Cabal did not let just anyone work hard and become a star. Stars were controlled, often by having spent childhoods being videotaped in pedophile networks, making them blackmailable.

Q !!TPb.qbhqo ID: 571cae No.60568 ☐   **319**
☐ec 9 2017 14:06:46 (EST)

Timestamp my post re: US Military vs. POTUS' Tweet.
Why did the USSS codename Hussein 'Renegade'?
A person who deserts and betrays an organization, country, or set
of principles.
Who does the USSS currently protect?
Why is this relevant?
Q

Q !!TPb.qbhqo ID: 571cae No.60630 ☐   **320**
☐ec 9 2017 14:12:28 (EST)

Not understanding why the drops today aren't being understood.
Expand your thinking.
Important.
Q

What Q seems to be saying is Secret Service knew Obama was betraying the nation, and were not happy with that. Now they protect him, which means they are surrounding him 24/7 and keeping track of him. But unlike before when he was President, now there is an opposing force working against his betrayal of the principles of our nation. In other words, patriots are in control.

Q !!TPb.qbhqo ID: 571cae No.60660 ☐   **321**
☐ec 9 2017 14:15:53 (EST)

Post: 1:34 US Military
POTUS: 1:37 US Military
Q

Q's post 310, posted on Dec 9th at 1:34 PM referenced the military, and 3 minutes later President Trump tweeted about the Army-Navy game and said we love our military.

Q !!TPb.qbhqo ID: 4aa050 No.63599 ☑
2c 9 2017 22:34:48 (EST)

322

Donald J. Trump ✓
@realDonaldTrump

Why does Barack Obama's ring have an arabic
inscription? bit.ly/VMN6Vn Who is this guy?

Obama's ring: 'There is no god but Allah'
wnd.com

1:11 PM · Oct 11, 2012

4th quarter, Patriots.
We fight together.
Q

Obama was Muslim, and things were not as they seemed.

Q !!TPb.qbhqo ID: 4aa050 No.63628 ☑
2c 9 2017 22:39:03 (EST)

323

> **Anonymous** ID: 13d4b8 No.63621 ☑
> 2c 9 2017 22:37:31 (EST)
> >>63599
> Thank you, Q
> Helping you is all we want to do
> It must be painful to watch us learn what all of you already
> know
> Sorry to be a drag on you guys
> I will try my best
> Service to God and patriots
> Whatever you need
> At any time
> Ready we well be

>>63621
We are all so very appreciative.
God bless each and every one of you.
Q

416

Q !lTPb.qbhqo ID: 4aa050 No.63644 ⬀   **324**
ec 9 2017 22:40:41 (EST)

Please pray tonight.
Good people in harms way.
Q

Q !lTPb.qbhqo ID: be6798 No.70055 ⬀   **325**
ec 10 2017 23:29:56 (EST)

Blunt & Direct Time.
Adam Schiff is a traitor to our country.
Leaker.
NAT SEC.
EVIL.
Tick Tock.
Hope the $7.8mm was worth it.
Enjoy the show.
Q

Q !lTPb.qbhqo ID: be6798 No.70088 ⬀   **326**
ec 10 2017 23:32:52 (EST)

False flag(s).
POTUS 100% insulated.
Expect fireworks.
JUSTICE.
Q

Q !lTPb.qbhqo ID: 4533cb No.73368 ⬀   **327**
ec 11 2017 12:23:09 (EST)

Do you believe in coincidences?
"Blunt & Direct Time"
BDT.
Think currency.
Think fireworks.
Thwarted.
Message delivered.
These people are sick!
Q

      BDT is the acronym for the Bangladeshi Taka, the
currency of Bangladesh.[251] So Q makes references to a false flag

251   http://archive.is/6Raj8

terrorist attack, and some fireworks (a bomb), makes a coded reference to Bangladesh, and suddenly within a day, a Bangladeshi launches a false flag terrorist bombing in New York City, which seems to detonate prematurely with an under powered charge that only injures him, possibly as if it was thwarted (ie JUSTICE).[252] These can be coincidences or lucky guesses, but they are accumulating.

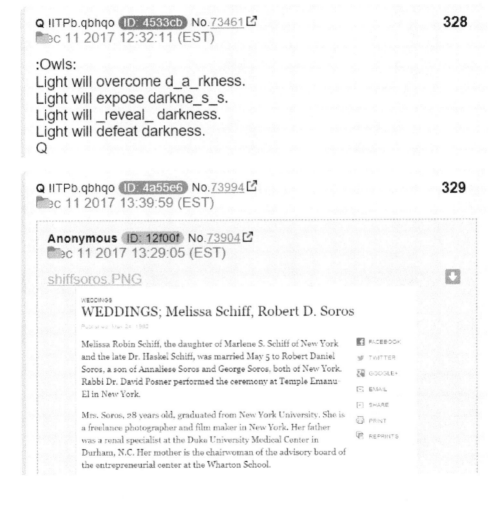

Q !ITPb.qbhqo **ID: 4533cb** No.73461 ☐   **328**
ec 11 2017 12:32:11 (EST)

:Owls:
Light will overcome d_a_rkness.
Light will expose darkne_s_s.
Light will _reveal_ darkness.
Light will defeat darkness.
Q

Q !ITPb.qbhqo **ID: 4a55e6** No.73994 ☐   **329**
ec 11 2017 13:39:59 (EST)

Anonymous ID: 12f00f No.73904 ☐
ec 11 2017 13:29:05 (EST)

shiffsoros.PNG

WEDDINGS
WEDDINGS; Melissa Schiff, Robert D. Soros

Published Nov 24, 1982

Melissa Robin Schiff, the daughter of Marlene S. Schiff of New York and the late Dr. Haskel Schiff, was married May 5 to Robert Daniel Soros, a son of Annaliese Soros and George Soros, both of New York. Rabbi Dr. David Posner performed the ceremony at Temple Emanu-El in New York.

Mrs. Soros, 28 years old, graduated from New York University. She is a freelance photographer and film maker in New York. Her father was a renal specialist at the Duke University Medical Center in Durham, N.C. Her mother is the chairwoman of the advisory board of the entrepreneurial center at the Wharton School.

FACEBOOK
TWITTER
GOOGLE+
EMAIL
SHARE
PRINT
REPRINTS

---

252   http://archive.is/IYjQR

418

http://www.nytimes.com/1992/05/24/style/weddings-melissa-schiff-robert-d-soros.html

g-g-guyssss
Is Melissa Schiff related to Adam Schiff?
What are the chances?

>>73904
Follow the wives.
These people are stupid.
Q

Soros senior appears to be a mere employee of Cabal. He seems to be managing Cabal funds and handling resource allocation to lower level Cabal-influence organizations, under the cover of being a billionaire. These organizations they create are used to draw oxygen from any legitimate organizations which Cabal doesn't control. So if you created a legitimate foundation for promoting democracy,, your foundation would get no funding, and no media-mentions, and thus no followers. Meanwhile Soros would be running, funding (with millions of Cabal-Euros and dollars), and getting free Cabal media for the organizations he's running.

Q's repeated references to the wives being significant is curious. I have noted a matriarchal nature to Cabal's ground-level surveillance/intelligence operations. It is possible Cabal allocates certain jobs to men, and reserves intelligence/infiltration operations to females, as they are naturally perceived as less threatening, and given natural male propensities, can manipulate men on the outside of Cabal more easily than men can manipulate other men. Soros junior's wife may be a familial Cabal legacy-member, making sure he is under full control.

Q !ITPb.qbhqo (ID: 4a55e6) No.74037 🗗   **330**
Dec 11 2017 13:44:10 (EST)

We have a special place picked out for GS.
Really special.
Q

Q !ITPb.qbhqo (ID: 4a55e6) No.74050 🗗   **331**
ec 11 2017 13:45:13 (EST)

> **Anonymous** (ID: 26b2f6) No.74029 🗗
> ec 11 2017 13:43:38 (EST)
>
> Maybe all (((these))) wives are there own high priestess cult...
> that where we'll see the symbolism...the "slip ups"

>>74029

There is a cult-like aspect to Cabal's ground forces, with whole families taking part in spying, and children growing up knowing they are in a secret society and others are not. They seemingly limit child-socialization to other cult-members, and somehow keep what is an unbelievably enormous secret from the rest of the country. To what degree it actually holds cult-like religious beliefs, I could not say. But there will be signs of strange occult-religious beliefs practiced at the upper levels.

Q !ITPb.qbhqo (ID: 4a55e6) No.74128 🗗   **332**
ec 11 2017 13:50:52 (EST)
Risk of another shutdown.
Be prepared to lose access.
Q

Q !ITPb.qbhqo `ID: 7b86c9` No.74533 ⬀   **333**
▓▓c 11 2017 14:31:03 (EST)
FOR GOD & COUNTRY.
FREEDOM.
‾
Q   ]_y

!ITPb.qbhqo `ID: bb0fbe` No.82056 ⬀   **334**
▓▓c 12 2017 17:03:32 (EST)

Exec_y.png   🔽

Merry Christmas.
Q

Q !ITPb.qbhqo `ID: 3ce126` No.82276 ⬀   **335**
▓▓c 12 2017 17:31:52 (EST)

Timestamp **[Q]** post **[:03]** against POTUS' Tweet **[:13]**.
[10]
No coincidences.
Q

> *There are many times where Q posts immediately before*
> *Trump tweets, as if they are coordinating. Q is pointing this out.*

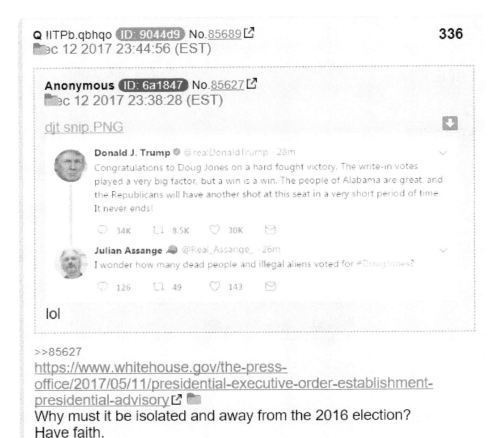

Q !ITPb.qbhqo ID: 9044d9 No.85689
ec 12 2017 23:44:56 (EST)

Anonymous ID: 6a1847 No.85627
ec 12 2017 23:38:28 (EST)

djt snip.PNG

Donald J. Trump @realDonaldTrump · 28m
Congratulations to Doug Jones on a hard fought victory. The write-in votes played a very big factor, but a win is a win. The people of Alabama are great, and the Republicans will have another shot at this seat in a very short period of time. It never ends!
34K   8.5K   30K

Julian Assange @Real_Assange_ · 26m
I wonder how many dead people and illegal aliens voted for #DougJones?
126   49   143

lol

>>85627
https://www.whitehouse.gov/the-press-office/2017/05/11/presidential-executive-order-establishment-presidential-advisory
Why must it be isolated and away from the 2016 election?
Have faith.
These people are stupid!
Q

Q is referencing the Presidential Executive Order on the Establishment of a Presidential Advisory Commission on Election Integrity.[253] Liberals were trying to claim Trump stole the 2016 election through "collusion," so this will be kept hidden until it releases its findings, lest the Democrats attempt to portray it as an attempt to rig the 2020 elections.

---

253   http://archive.is/7EEWu

Q !ITPb.qbhqo ID: 9044d9 No.85926 ☐
ec 13 2017 00:12:53 (EST)

Patriots, rest assured we are in control.
Watch, confirm, and disseminate.
The country is not divided, this is fake news. ANTIFA was
organized purely for optics re: division.
It's FAKE!
Estimated 4-6% we consider 'hopeless' and forever brainwashed.
Re-read crumbs re: slave grip the D's have on the black pop.
Why is this relevant?
Why are jobs/economy (growth) relevant?
This requires a DEEP CLEANING.
These people are stupid.
You are safe.
Have faith.
Q

The economy must be addressed first because one way Cabal could try to derail the Storm would be to trigger a global economic collapse, or even just a major US recession. By shoring up the economy first, President Trump is securing his ability to operate with the support of the public going forward. Improving the economy and employment will also benefit the black community particularly, and help to prevent the Democrats from using the politics of division to turn the black vote against Republicans going forward.

Q !ITPb.qbhqo ID: 9044d9 No.85959 ☐
ec 13 2017 00:15:45 (EST)

"Special."
Q

Q may be saying he has a very special place in hell picked out for Soros, as in they will give him a death penalty.

Q !ITPb.qbhqo ID: 9044d9 No.86111 ⤢   **339**
c 13 2017 00:28:32 (EST)

Anonymous ID: 97d8e9 No.86037 ⤢
c 13 2017 00:22:14 (EST)

Screen Shot 2017-12-12 at 10.20.26 PM.png   ⬇

▶ Q !ITPb.qbhqo 12/11/17 (Mon) 11:44:10 ID: 4a55e6 No.74037
>>74417

We have a special place picked out for GS.
Really special.
Q

Q has asked about ownership of voting machines before. They
knew GS was going to mess with the numbers. This was the
plan.

A VERY SPECIAL PLACE!!
What would be the penalty for stealing elections?

>>86037
>>86037

Q !ITPb.qbhqo ID: 267271 No.92626 ⤢   **340**
c 13 2017 23:24:30 (EST)

Anonymous ID: d0e43e No.92291 ⤢
c 13 2017 22:27:43 (EST)
gg3.JPG   ⬆

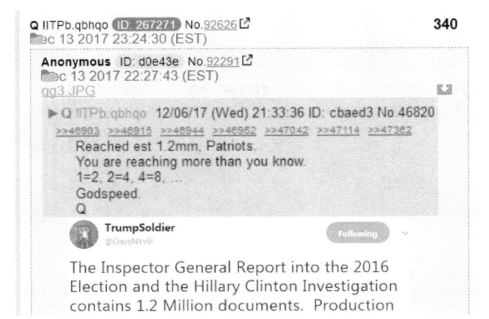

▶ Q !ITPb.qbhqo 12/06/17 (Wed) 21:33:36 ID: cbaed3 No.46820
>>46903 >>46915 >>46944 >>46952 >>47042 >>47114 >>47362
Reached est 1.2mm. Patriots.
You are reaching more than you know.
1=2, 2=4, 4=8, ...
Godspeed.
Q

TrumpSoldier   Following
@DaveNYviii

The Inspector General Report into the 2016
Election and the Hillary Clinton Investigation
contains 1.2 Million documents. Production

date: January 15th, 2018 #RosensteinHearing

>>1.2mm
>>1.2mm
>1.2mm
>1.2mm
We are on the team

>>92291
You are learning.
News unlocks map.
Future proves past.
Not everything can be stated 1:1.
Q

Q does not want his posts to be seen as ironclad, 100% true predictions of a prophet yet. It appears he is trying to slowly build credibility, lest the entire population suddenly realize the truth – that pedophiles of organized networks are elevated to high office because they are controllable and blackmailable, our nation's government was subverted by a foreign intelligence operation, and the corrupt politicians we elected, of both parties, tried to import foreigners and hand our country to them, so we wouldn't have any power to resist through the electoral system. If everyone suddenly realized that overnight, it is not impossible we would have an overnight civil war. By doing it this way, and slowly spreading, some of us find out but wait, and desensitize, while others then find out and desensitize, and as the country learns gradually, Q and Trump are approaching a position where they can actually act and punish the bad actors, while supported by the people, thereby averting the civil war option.

Q !!TPb.qbhqo ID: 267271 No.92710 **341**
ec 13 2017 23:35:55 (EST)

"Documents from the Obama administration have been transferred to the Barack Obama Presidential Library. You may send your request to the Obama Library. However, you should be aware that under the Presidential Records Act, Presidential records remain closed to the public for five years after an administration has left office."
RAIDED by the GOOD GUYS (per POTUS).
Shockingly quiet.
No leaks?
Presidential libraries are put in place to retain control over self-incriminating c-doc releases.
Scam!
Review the law.
What is different re: Hussein's PL?
Who controls?
These people really are stupid.
Q

Obama's Presidential Library will not house his papers for scholarly review.[254] Instead, they will be stored in a building in DC, presumably out of the reach of prying eyes of scholars. Also note, if they have not been sent to Obama's Presidential Library, FOIA requests for specific searches targeting specific issues within those documents will come back non-responsive.

Q claims that regardless, these records were raided by intelligence, under the provisions of Executive Order 13489 of

---

254   http://archive.is/9ubYp

426

January 21, 2009, which states;

(a) Upon receipt of a notice of intent to disclose Presidential records, the Attorney General (directly or through the Assistant Attorney General for the Office of Legal Counsel) and the Counsel to the President shall review as they deem appropriate the records covered by the notice and consult with each other, the Archivist, and such other executive agencies as they deem appropriate concerning whether invocation of executive privilege is justified.

(b) The Attorney General and the Counsel to the President, in the exercise of their discretion and after appropriate review and consultation under subsection (a) of this section, may jointly determine that invocation of executive privilege is not justified. The Archivist shall be notified promptly of any such determination.

Q !ITPb.qbhqo ID: 267271 No.92737 ☑   **342**
Dec 13 2017 23:38:59 (EST)

> Anonymous ID: d85ea0 No.92647 ☑
> Dec 13 2017 23:27:16 (EST)
> >>92626
> Hard day at work today Q? Welcome back.
>
> Was there a lot of information in the questioning of Rod Rosenstein today?
>
> I see much of the questioning is related to your drops. "Future proves past"

>>92647
End is near.
Q

Q !ITPb.qbhqo ID: 267271 No.92789 ☑   **343**
Dec 13 2017 23:42:09 (EST)

> Anonymous ID: c9870b No.92680 ☑
> Dec 13 2017 23:32:07 (EST)
> >>92626
> >Not everything can be stated 1:1.
> Q can't come out and tell us exact meanings of his drops.

Likely because it would reveal information that would compromise operations as the scumbags scramble to clean up loose ends that are revealed. Hence the 1.2mm, which we thought were 1.2 million normies reached by this board when the 1.2mm was actually the 1.2 million documents in the IG report, which the scumbags had no clue about.

>>92680
Bad people watching.
Q

Q !!TPb.qbhqo (ID: 3610ff) No.93181 ☐   **344**
Dec 14 2017 00:24:04 (EST)

7803B61A-1F3E-47BD-88D4-F....jpeg

Saw this in last thread.
Focus on papers on table.
Graphic at top.
They all belong to the same sick cult/club.
Q

The papers on the table appear to have an image of Tanit,
an occult goddess requiring child sacrifice, on the upper right-

hand corner. So does the dress on the girl cutout behind him. Tanit also featured prominently overseeing a human sacrifice in a shrine over his mother, Gloria Vanderbilt's, bed.[255] One analysis of the papers indicates it contains pedophile code, and may be some sort of coded newsletter for pedophiles.[256]

Q will present evidence that the "elites" in our society may go through some sort of induction ritual which involves harming children to enter a secret society, probably performed so as to provide the upper levels with blackmail materials over them. In truth, Q is not the first to level such accusations.[257]

Q !!TPb.qbhqo ID: 3610ff No.93246 ☑   **345**
ec 14 2017 00:32:05 (EST)

Q !!TPb.qbhqo ID: 3610ff No.93181 ☑
ec 14 2017 00:24:04 (EST)
7803B61A-1F3E-47BD-88D4-F ... jpeg

255   http://archive.is/jNmYb
256   http://archive.is/F4V8x
257   http://archive.is/t8fH3

Saw this in last thread.
Focus on papers on table.
Graphic at top.
They all belong to the same sick cult/club.
Q

>>93181
Image at top: boy, boy/girl.
Enhance.
What else do you see?
Archive - watchers will now erase from web.
Q

Q !ITPb.qbhqo `ID: 3610ff` No.93287 ☐   **346**
〓c 14 2017 00:36:08 (EST)

Godspeed, Patriots.
POTUS: WRWY
Q

Q !ITPb.qbhqo `ID: 3610ff` No.93312 ☐   **347**
〓c 14 2017 00:38:12 (EST)

> **Q** !ITPb.71B/. `ID: d5784a` No.93267 ☐
> 〓c 14 2017 00:34:10 (EST)
>
> Getting closer
> (USER WAS BANNED FOR THIS POST)

>>93267
Tag: USSS
Q

This was a reply to someone trying to hack Q's ID.

Anonymous `ID: 7681cc` No.99480 ☐   **348**
〓c 14 2017 21:20:48 (EST)

Blocked from posting entering 'trip'. It would appear this board has
been compromised.
Q

Anonymous ID: 7681cc No.99500 ☑
ec 14 2017 21:24:07 (EST)

This board is compromised.
Cannot enter trip code to verify auth.
Trip code on 4 has also been modified.
God bless,
Q

Q's authentication system was finally hacked, so for the next posts he is back to posting as "Anonymous."

Anonymous ID: 7681cc No.99525 ☑
ec 14 2017 21:27:05 (EST)

Shall we play a game?
Find the spider(s) and build the web (the 'map').
Remember, they consider you to be the fly (specifically, the 'feeder').
Remember, they never thought she was going to lose.
Therefore, they never thought investigations and/or public interest into their criminal acts would be exposed/investigated.
Therefore, they never thought they had anything to fear.
Therefore, they openly showcase their symbolism.
Therefore, they were sloppy.
Hussein's last speech in Chicago re: 'scandal free'.
Why did he continually emphasize that phrase?
As a backup, they infiltrated and control the narrative (the 'MSM').
As a backup, they install only those on the team.
As a backup, they blackmail those that aren't.
As a backup, they defined 'conspiracy' as crazy/mentally unstable and label anything 'true' as such.
This works given most of what they engage in is pure evil and simply unbelievable (hard to swallow).
The 'fix' has always been in – no matter which party won the election (-JFK (killed)/Reagan(shot)).
This was always the promise made to those who played the game (willingly or otherwise) (i.e., they would never lose power).
Power of the (3) letter agencies.
Power over the US Military (WW dominance to push against other nations and install like-kind).
These people are really stupid.

Follow the husbands.
Another Hint:
Ian Cameron
McKinsey & Company
Clowns In America.
Dr. Emmett J. Rice.
Federal Reserve.
Everyone is connected.
How about a nice game of chess?
Q
(No ability to enter trip code - last dump)

Q says the Secret Society is easily tracked through use of symbolism, familial attachments, and an understanding of the machine, because they assumed they were too powerful to fail.

Anonymous ID: 7681cc No.99548 ☑   **351**
Dec 14 2017 21:29:49 (EST)

Blocked_8.jpeg

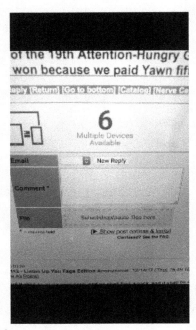

Godspeed, Patriots.
Q

Q !ITPb.qbhqo **ID: 462c9a** No.11043803 🔗   **352**
ꟾꞏc 14 2017 21:40:05 (EST)

Lost access to /cbts/
No ability to enter trip code.
Q

Anonymous **ID: b01ed7** No.99658 🔗   **353**
ꟾꞏc 14 2017 21:41:02 (EST)

https://8ch.net/pol/res/11028937.html#11043803 🔗 📷
24hrs to restore trip code or departure.
Godspeed,
Q

> *Q was telling the site owner he had lost the ability to access the board he was using, and needed it restored quickly.*

Q !ITPb.qbhqo **ID: 462c9a** No.11043832 🔗   **354**
ꟾꞏc 14 2017 21:43:38 (EST)

Shall we play a game?
Find the spider(s) and build the web (the 'map').
Remember, they consider you to be the fly (specifically, the 'feeder').
Remember, they never thought she was going to lose.
Therefore, they never thought investigations and/or public interest into their criminal acts would be exposed/investigated.
Therefore, they never thought they had anything to fear.
Therefore, they openly showcase their symbolism.
Therefore, they were sloppy.
Hussein's last speech in Chicago re: 'scandal free'.
Why did he continually emphasize that phrase?
As a backup, they infiltrated and control the narrative (the 'MSM').
As a backup, they install only those on the team.
As a backup, they blackmail those that aren't.
As a backup, they defined 'conspiracy' as crazy/mentally unstable and label anything 'true' as such.
This works given most of what they engage in is pure evil and simply unbelievable (hard to swallow).
The 'fix' has always been in – no matter which party won the election (-JFK (killed)/Reagan(shot)).

This was always the promise made to those who played the game (willingly or otherwise) (i.e., they would never lose power).
Power of the (3) letter agencies.
Power over the US Military (WW dominance to push against other nations and install like-kind).
These people are really stupid.
Follow the husbands.
Another Hint:
Ian Cameron
McKinsey & Company
Clowns In America.
Dr. Emmett J. Rice.
Federal Reserve.
Everyone is connected.
How about a nice game of chess?
Q

What Q is describing is a full fledged network of spies, informants, and traitors in the US, set up by an outside entity which infiltrated not just the US government, but the news media, academia, economic entities, the security/intel agencies, cultural/entertainment/music businesses, local governments, and any other potential avenue of power, exposure, or legal consequence. He is also showing with this example how Cabal uses nepotism to concentrate its members within families, as a way of reducing its risk of public exposure. As an example, he lists Ian Cameron, McKinsey & Company, Clowns In America (CIA), Dr. Emmett J. Rice, and The Federal Reserve as compromised entities subverted by this.

Ian Cameron[258] is a new producer for ABC World News Tonight with David Muir, This Week, and 60 Minutes. He is married to Susan Rice,[259] who has held a variety of positions in

---

258   http://archive.is/K5POx
259   http://archive.is/XXqln

the Clinton and Obama administrations. They met while working at a management advisory company named McKinsey & Company, which is listed as a CIA-connected partner/front company.[260] Meaning you have high-level positions in government and news manned by two people who previously worked in a CIA front-company, could be assumed to be at least agents of the CIA if not officers, and they are married.

The Cabal is very nepotistic. It is not uncommon when being followed around by the domestic surveillance/informant elements to see parents indoctrinating their children in the culture, even sending the children in close with hidden jacket cameras to take video in stores and public places. It is probably easier to accept operating against the Constitution, and other American citizens, when you are raised with it from childhood. Plus by keeping it in families, it is easier to keep the secret from the rest of America. For this reason, if you find a Cabal member, you can often look up and down the family tree and find more.

Here, Q names Susan Rice's father, Dr. Emmett J. Rice.,[261] I would have assumed he was in the conspiracy, and placed in a position of power. Sure enough, he was on the board of the Federal Reserve, and worked for USAID, (which has been implicated as a CIA front-operation),[262] as well as a host of other high-level positions. So here you have just three members of a

---

260   https://books.google.com/books?
id=rdw9DwAAQBAJ&pg=PA246&lpg=PA246&dq=%22McKinsey+
%26+Company%22+and+%22CIA%22&source=bl&ots=UoC7lw8bFm&sig=-
zvk2_TJ04nywqVkcUKWIpNr37k&hl=en&sa=X&ved=0ahUKEwituoXQ8YzYAh
UITCYKHb6iBpcQ6AEIRjAG#v=onepage&q=%22McKinsey
%20%26%20Company%22%20and%20%22CIA%22&f=false
261   http://archive.is/0SjOx
262   http://archive.is/058YD

family, and all have ties to CIA front-operations, where it could be assumed they were recruited as agents, if not officers. And this one small portion of a family spread its power across economics, business management, national security, and the media – at the highest levels. Would Susan Rice's husband's news coverage of her actions be unbiased? If he was a CIA agent, would he be able to block any news story dangerous to the Agency? If the Agency were infiltrated, and being run by an even broader conspiracy, would he offer cover to that? Suppose the Agency was running illegal surveillance on American citizens, and you discovered it when you became a target? Who might you go to, if trying to expose these operations to the public? If the media might be a threat to such operations, would the conspiracy look to control that threat by infiltrating their people into those positions? What would it look like if you had an intelligence operation penetrate your government and society, and man all critical control points with their people? It would look exactly like this.

As time goes on, you'll begin to notice this pattern will repeat everywhere, from Hollywood, to finance, to music, to the talking heads on the Sunday shows. And the Secret Society went even further than that, right down to the neighborhood level.

Q !ITPb.qbhqo `ID: 462c9a` No.11043839 ⬀   **355**
ec 14 2017 21:44:23 (EST)

Q PLEASE HELP! **FARMERFUNKK** ID: 6db431 No.11043835 ⬀
ec 14 2017 21:44:01 (EST)

Screen Shot 2017-12-13 at 12.17.03 PM   ⬇

(no subject)

John Doe <johndoe@gmail.com>
to me
Don't worry about the ocean but, fix all of my plan. Share link.

Can send a box with friends

ignore?

>>11043835
Fake.
Q

Not relevant. Somebody was asking Q if something they saw was a threat, and Q said it was fake.

Q !ITPb.qbhqo ID: raLCcyMk No.153323368 🗗   **356**
Dec 14 2017 21:52:47 (EST)

Trip test.
Q

Q !ITPb.qbhqo ID: 462c9a No.11044319 🗗   **357**
Dec 14 2017 22:37:42 (EST)

Trip code on 4 working.
#FLYSIDFLY#
We don't like to say his name.
Q

The trip-code Q uses to authenticate his posts, so nobody can impersonate him on the board, was restored.

Q !ITPb.qbhqo ID: 462c9a No.11045052 🗗   **358**
Dec 15 2017 01:03:02 (EST)

Being advised to update code.
Serious hardware being used to break.
4 is not secure.
Q

One of the things which would lend credence to Q is all the effort expended to disrupt the activity on the small boards he operated on.

437

Q !UW.yye1fxo (ID: 462c9a) No.11045057 ⬀   **359**
ec 15 2017 01:04:06 (EST)

Updated.
Q

Q !ITPb.qbhqo (ID: 462c9a) No.11045061 ⬀   **360**
ec 15 2017 01:04:43 (EST)

> **Q !UW.yye1fxo** ID: 462c9a No.11045057 ⬀
> ec 15 2017 01:04:06 (EST)
>
> Updated.
> Q

>>11045057
Confirmed.

Q !UW.yye1fxo (ID: 462c9a) No.11045072 ⬀   **361**
ec 15 2017 01:05:51 (EST)

> **Q !ITPb.qbhqo** ID: 462c9a No.11045061 ⬀
> ec 15 2017 01:04:43 (EST)
>
> >>11045057
> Confirmed.

>>11045061
Confirmed.
Q

Q !UW.yye1fxo (ID: 462c9a) No.11045132 ⬀   **362**
ec 15 2017 01:15:57 (EST)

We may have exhausted our ability to maintain safe-comms.
Snow White.
Rig for silent running.
Unknown return.
Godspeed, Patriots.
Q

Q !UW.yye1fxo `ID: 462c9a` No.11045213 ⌕

ec 15 2017 01:25:44 (EST)

_Conf_term**[5]**_y
_SECFAIL-490b
Private OP_END
Q

Q !UW.yye1fxo `ID: 462c9a` No.11045246 ⌕

ec 15 2017 01:28:58 (EST)

Follow the crumbs.
You have it all.
SEC Conf will be analyzed.
Dark **[10]**.
Enjoy the show!
Q

Q !UW.yye1fxo `ID: 82d434` No.121327 ⌕

ec 18 2017 23:27:52 (EST)

FLASH_BREAK_
∧* ∧ ∧*
Shall we play a game?
Map is critical to understand.
Future unlocks past.
DECLAS_ATL_(past).
News unlocks map.
Find the markers.
10 & **[10]**.
12/7 – 12/17.
Concourse F.
Terminal 5.
Private_operated plane (OP)?
ATL -> IAD
Extraction/known.
Dark.
Darkness.
Learn double meanings.
SHUTDOWN.
Q/POTUS-1
Q/POTUS-2
Q/POTUS-3
Q/POTUS-4 **[10]**

Q/POTUS-5
"Special Place"
Why are drops highlighted by POTUS shortly thereafter?
Coincidence or message?
"The Great Awakening"
POTUS today.
Unlock?
CLAS_OP_IAD_(future).
How about a nice game of chess?
SPLASH.
FOX THREE.
Q

This references a prediction of a blackout that Q had made which subsequently occurred at the Atlanta Airport.[263] Q is implying it was a planned operation done purposely to move someone or something through the airport, probably without surveillance cameras documenting it, since Cabal has access to many network-connected surveillance camera feeds through a very sophisticated backdoor/network capability. Some speculated it was related to a private jet that made the 2 hour trip to Dulles in Washington, DC in about one hour and 15 minutes.[264] The rest of the post is unclear, though POTUS has referenced Camp David as a "special place," which some took as a sign perhaps whoever was taken was transferred to Camp David for processing/interrogation.[265]

It is probably likely the big players in this conspiracy are unknown to us. We see the politicians, who are one level. Above them are probably members of the Intelligence Community, whose names we could find with extensive digging, but who are

---

263   http://archive.is/3z2yh
264   http://archive.is/ekPd7
265   https://archive.fo/9tsna

broadly unknown. I suspect above them are leaders who we would probably not be able to identify because they are smart enough to eschew publicity and cloak their finances and business relationships behind trusts, corporations, fake billionaires, and charitable foundations. It is not impossible whoever was grabbed in Atlanta was a genuine high value target, and none of us would recognize them by sight or name, or be able to find out anything about them.

Much of these side-speculations, though interesting, are meaningless however. The significant element of this, and the only part about which we could be certain, was that Q apparently predicted a major event, which if it occurred purposely (and was predictable), would have been a part of something important. And by Q being able to predict it, it would mean Q was part of something important as well.

Q !UW.yye1fxo ID: 82d434 No.121409 🔗 📷   366
Dec 18 2017 23:38:43 (EST)

> Anonymous ID: 6afbc6 No.121392 🔗 📷
> Dec 18 2017 23:36:13 (EST)
>
> >>121340
> Splash =   Missile time of flight is expired or missile destroyed; target or bomb impact.
> Fox Three =   Simulated/actual launch of active radar-guided missile

>>121392

A reference to the use of splash in the last post, which implies Q was saying something about a weapon's deployment. Fox three will appear to mean something different later, so this definition appears not significant.

441

Q IUW.yye1fxo ID: 82d434 No.121449 🔗 📁   **367**
Dec 18 2017 23:44:20 (EST)

> **Anonymous** ID: afbf68 No.121446 🔗 📁
> Dec 18 2017 23:43:55 (EST)
>
> Give us an hint on the ATL airport

>>121446
Extraction_GOOD.
Q

Q IUW.yye1fxo ID: 82d434 No.121519 🔗 📁   **368**
Dec 18 2017 23:53:53 (EST)

> **Anonymous** ID: fc4520 No.121501 🔗 📁
> Dec 18 2017 23:51:20 (EST)
>
> >>121491
> Seconding this. The context of that train crash seems relevant.
> High value target aboard?

>>121501
We would not 'intentionally' harm a person in the pursuit of a
TARGET.
This was retaliatory re: ATL.
Q

Q is saying his side will never crash a train, and that the
DC train crash which was referenced[266] was done in retaliation
for the Atlanta operation. You will see several cases going
forward where it appears that the Cabal arranged events which
killed innocent people, as a way of threatening those which got
in its way, or as a way of retaliating for perceived transgressions.
One would be the murder of Detective Miosotis Familia,
arranged through their domestic intelligence operation's

---

266   http://archive.is/ej9kS

harassment of her shooter while making it appear is if it were NYPD doing the harassing. When the individual finally snapped and attempted to strike back at his harassers, he ended up striking back at exactly who Cabal wanted to see struck. That murder of a single mother of four and Police Officer was believed to be a message to the NYPD regarding the need to maintain secrecy regarding certain files NYPD discovered on Anthony Weiner's laptop.

Q IUW.yye1fxo ID: 82d434 No.121555 🏴   **369**
Dec 18 2017 23:57:28 (EST)

> **Anonymous** ID: 205c72 No.121535 🏴
> Dec 18 2017 23:55:21 (EST)
>
> >>121519
> >They Derailed
> as Punishment for ALT extraction. Wonder which pawn is off the table… Or was it something higher?

>>121535
BISHOP (cult).
Q

Whoever was grabbed in Atlanta was high-ranking,

Q IUW.yye1fxo ID: 82d434 No.121559 🏴   **370**
Dec 18 2017 23:58:04 (EST)

> **Anonymous** ID: d3b6f7 No.121553 🏴
> Dec 18 2017 23:57:15 (EST)
>
> What happened on 12/7?

>>121553
Clock started - 10 days.
Q

Q IUW.yye1fxo ID: 82d434 No.121650 ☐ 📄
Dec 19 2017 00:07:54 (EST)

Why did the WH link posted turn up 404 (2) days after?
Expand your thinking.
Do you believe in coincidences?
Q

This refers to the link Q posted in post 336 to a Presidential Executive Order creating an advisory committee on election integrity.[267] A few days after Q discussed it, the document was removed from the White House server, and trying to access it would only yield a 404 Document not Found error. Normally such a document would be posted, and then left on the server in that location in perpetuity.

Q is implying the document was posted just for us, and after we saw it, it was removed from the server. That would imply Q's operation has authority over all aspects of White House operations.

Q IUW.yye1fxo ID: 82d434 No.121690 ☐ 📄   **372**
Dec 19 2017 00:12:02 (EST)

House of cards.
12 deals rejected (today alone).
Panic in DC.
TRUST SESSIONS.
Enjoy the show.
Q

Cabal assets are trying to save themselves by cutting deals, but Q and team are not making any deals.

---

267   http://archive.is/wBpt0

Q !UW.yye1fxo ID: c07cfc No.122123

Dec 19 2017 01:02:51 (EST)

373

Term_**[#2]**19_y
NAT_SEC_
NAT_SEC_A,H,H, L, B, E, classified Cdg-23k
FREEDOM_#1-43
CAP_H(9).
MAVERICK.
JUSTICE_FED_J**[1-4]**_remove + appellate
Q

Q !UW.yye1fxo ID: c07cfc No.122211

Dec 19 2017 01:11:33 (EST)

374

19 OPs **[now]**.
Operators active.
Operators in harms way.
POTUS awake.
No sleep during OP.
Pray.
Q

Q !UW.yye1fxo ID: 03c2f4 No.126896

Dec 19 2017 17:33:11 (EST)

375

7F0F82A1-151F-4868-96EE-054CE9876425.png

Newsweek

TRUMP COULD USE MILITARY TO LAUNCH HIS OWN COUP, WARNS FORMER WHITE HOUSE ETHICS LAWYER

F4929FC0-EA86-4042-82CC-AEE84ABDA9BF.jpeg

Same day.
Coincidence?
Only the beginning.
Q

Q IUW.yye1fxo ID: 03c2f4 No.126948 🔗 📁   **376**
Dec 19 2017 17:39:15 (EST)

> **Anonymous** ID: fad025 No.126928 🔗 📁
> Dec 19 2017 17:37:38 (EST)
>
> >>126896
>
> Are UFOs a distraction?

>>126928
How far away is the closest star?
What do you think?
Q

When you realize the degree to which we had been lied to and deceived, it gets hard to tell where the boundaries really are. Some wondered if Cabal was being run by alien "visitors" who had always been here, but Q is saying that is just a distraction.

Q !UW.yye1fxo ID: 03c2f4 No.126998 **377**
Dec 19 2017 17:44:41 (EST)

>>126934
'Conspiracy'
Theme will be pushed.
BIG threat to them.
All absorbed in RT.
Feel proud.
Q

The term "Conspiracy Theory" is actually a term which is designed to delegitimize any concept it is applied to, instantly making it appear as the paranoid delusion of a mentally-unbalanced mind. It will be used against Q prodigiously now.

Q !UW.yye1fxo ID: 03c2f4 No.127012 **378**
Dec 19 2017 17:45:59 (EST)

> **Anonymous** ID: 18f3ac No.126988
> Dec 19 2017 17:43:39 (EST)
>
> >>126896
> So left is grubbing for justification to take over with UN troops?

>>126988
No UN troops.
Fake.
Q

Q !UW.yye1fxo ID: 03c2f4 No.127064 **379**
Dec 19 2017 17:50:10 (EST)

> **Anonymous** ID: 2ca3dc No.126931
> Dec 19 2017 17:37:46 (EST)
>
> Ops a success last night ? >>126896

>>126931
Roger that.
Q

Q !UW.yye1fxo ID: 03c2f4 No.127069 ⬏ ▓   **380**
Dec 19 2017 17:50:58 (EST)

> **Anonymous** ID: abd4f1 No.127057 ⬏ ▓
> Dec 19 2017 17:49:46 (EST)
>
> >>127012
> That's a relief. Though Chicago is in clear agony either way.
> Let's hope that all changes soon!

>>127057
NAT G.
Q

Q !UW.yye1fxo ID: 03c2f4 No.127154 ⬏ ▓   **381**
Dec 19 2017 18:00:02 (EST)

We won't telegraph our moves to the ENEMY.
We will however light a FIRE to flush them out.
Q

So one objective of Q's posts is to motivate enemy action.
However in order to have the credibility to motivate enemy
action, Q must drop some good intelligence and honestly inform.

Q !UW.yye1fxo ID: 03c2f4 No.127286 ⬏ ▓   **382**
Dec 19 2017 18:11:07 (EST)

> **Anonymous** ID: fad0d1 No.127237 ⬏ ▓
> Dec 19 2017 18:07:28 (EST)
>
> >>127154
> Q, I have heard fro ppl in France, the Netherlands, Poland,
> Canada, and USA today. Ppl hunger for LIGHT - have lived
> under the darkness forTOO LONG.Thankyou

>>127237
We have tremendous WW support.
SATAN has left the WH.
Day of days.
Q

Q !UW.yye1fxo `ID: 03c2f4` No.127379 ↗ ▣   **383**
Dec 19 2017 18:18:24 (EST)

> **Anonymous** `ID: 810bf1` No.127305 ↗ ▣
> Dec 19 2017 18:13:07 (EST)
>
> >>121409
> SA intercepts H missile fired toward R
> reuters
> .com/article/us-saudi-blast/saudi-arabia-intercepts-houthi-
> missile-fired-toward-riyadh-no-reported-casualties-
> idUSKBN1ED17Y

>>127305
FOX 3?
Q

Q !UW.yye1fxo `ID: 03c2f4` No.127397 ↗ ▣   **384**
Dec 19 2017 18:20:02 (EST)

Bill Binney.
Q

Bill Binney[268] was an NSA technology specialist who stepped forward as a whistleblower to say that the intelligence services were essentially rendering the Bill of Rights completely obsolete. The government set surveillance up on his house, listened for when he went into the shower, and then executed a SWAT raid at that exact moment so they could drag him out of the shower soaking wet and naked. As Q will show, Bill was in actuality a patriot of the highest order, striving to protect the nation and the Constitution from the intrusiveness of Cabal's abuses of our intelligence infrastructure. It is unclear if he actually understood he was looking at a foreign penetration of our government by a hostile intelligence operation, however.

---

268   http://archive.is/lAjlr

Q !UW.yye1fxo ID: 03c2f4 No.127421 ☐ ▮
Dec 19 2017 18:21:26 (EST)

> Anonymous ID: 6ae524 No.127396 ☐ ▮
> Dec 19 2017 18:20:02 (EST)
>
> Q
> The Alabama Election was stolen. I have not doubt. Y'all gonna fix that one too?

>>127396
Thought when we 404'd the link that gave confirmation.
Learn.
Q

Q is saying that these posts show the fight to secure our elections is going on behind the scenes, and out of our sight.

Q !UW.yye1fxo ID: 03c2f4 No.127429 ☐ ▮
Dec 19 2017 18:22:21 (EST)

> Anonymous ID: 836800 No.127420 ☐ ▮
> Dec 19 2017 18:21:26 (EST)
>
> >>127397
> >>127397
> Whistle Blower.. truther.. hero?

>>127420
PATRIOT of the highest caliber.
Q

This is in regard to Bill Binney, the NSA whistleblower. Although Bill was only blowing the whistle on the technical side of the surveillance machine, because it was what he saw, it is important to understand that the machine deployed against American citizens had grown similarly in all other aspects, from physical surveillance, to informant networks, to tech deployment.

Q !UW.yye1fxo ID: 03c2f4 No.127449   **387**
Dec 19 2017 18:23:44 (EST)

Anonymous ID: 2c9e96 No.127411
Dec 19 2017 18:20:59 (EST)

Capture.JPG

Top stories

Jared Kushner's Business Empire Is a House of Cards	Jared Kushner's "Ultimate Deal" Keeps Getting Worse	What We Know About Jared Kushner and Ivanka Trump's Financial Disclosure...
Vanity Fair	Vanity Fair	Newsweek
4 hours ago	1 hour ago	1 hour ago

→ More for jared kushner

Jared Kushner - Rumours of he's next on Mueller's list?

>>127411
End is near.
Q

Q !UW.yye1fxo ID: 061d5f No.128296   **388**
Dec 19 2017 20:10:49 (EST)

Define CORRUPTION.
Iris Weinshall.
New York City Department of Transportation.
Responsibility of DoT?
Budget for past (5) years?
Former commissioner?
Empire State Dev Corp?
Urban Dev Corp?
Dept of Economic Dev?
Integrated Resources, Inc.?
US Senator of NY?
Follow me down the hole.

These people are STUPID.
Q

Q is basically showing how these people were getting sloppy under the assumption nobody could challenge them, and they were failing to camouflage their links to each other. Chuck Schumer's daughter worked for the Robin Hood Foundation which was funded by Soros, and had Harvey Weinstein on the Board of Directors. She worked on Hillary Clinton's campaign, and the article on her wedding offered immense insight into the members of the network by listing all the people in attendance. When the mafia has a marriage, the FBI walks around writing down license plates to find out all the people in attendance, but when Cabal has a marriage you only have to pick up a copy of the New York Times. They all want to see their names in the paper, because they think they are untouchable.

Q IUW.yye1fxo **ID: 061d5f** No.128438   **389**
Dec 19 2017 20:26:11 (EST)

CS/Soros.
CS/Playboy.
CS/Heidi Fleiss.
HEIDI FLEISS (EVIL/CLOWN/BLACKMAIL).
Q

It is believed Q is saying Chuck Schumer is owned by Soros, took part in a network which trafficked girls such as playboy models (as will be mentioned in the next Q-post), and was a patron of Hollywood madam Heidi Fleiss, who Q says was a CIA (Clown) operation gathering blackmail on powerful people. I have said the domestic intelligence network of Cabal was extensive. There is no way a Madam like Heidi could operate outside of Cabal's knowledge and awareness, especially given she was compromising important people through her activities, many of whom would probably be owned by Cabal already. So her operation, if not controlled, was a direct threat to Cabal's assets, and by extension, Cabal's network. Cabal surveillance would have set up on her in moments, gathered intelligence on her operation, and handed it off to Cabal assets in law enforcement who would have taken her down before she ever got off the ground.

If she was allowed to continue to operate until she was servicing high-ranking members of society, it was because she was a part of Cabal's operation herself, and under the full control of Cabal. And if that was the case, she was also actively recruiting new members into Cabal's network by compromising them with blackmail using prostitution. In truth, I would suspect that like Jeffrey Epstein, her operation was more a blackmail operation operating under the cover of prostitution, than a prostitution operation forced into blackmail. Anywhere you saw services for the rich and famous which would have been embarrassing if their involvement with it was publicized, you will find Cabal surveillance picked up on it and Cabal intelligence had penetrated that service, taken it over, and their assets were actively using it to gather blackmail on those who partook of it.

Q !UW.yye1fxo **ID: 061d5f** No.128547 ☐ 🖼️   **390**
Dec 19 2017 20:36:54 (EST)

http://www.foxnews.com/us/2017/11/03/playboy-models-among-3-seeking-27m-say-soros-fund-manager-raped-beat-them.html ☐ 🖼️
Are we there yet?
Q

This demonstrates that those in power were degenerates on a level we could not imagine. That was no accident. It was why they were recruited - because it meant they could be controlled. Also, notice this guy had a non-stop stream of Playboy models who he could acquire, and who were willing to endure his abuse. Those girls were being trafficked to him, as part of a network like Jeffrey Epstein's. Access to those various sex-trafficking networks served as both a perk of being in Cabal, and a means of actively cementing control over its members.

Q IUW.yye1fxo **ID: 061d5f** No.128629 ☑ 📄   **391**
Dec 19 2017 20:43:55 (EST)

Twitter rants can be harmful.
Lesson learned?
How about _SIERRA_C_?
How about ($22/Singapore)?
When does a bird sing?
Goodbye C.
Q

Q IUW.yye1fxo **ID: 061d5f** No.128724 ☑ 📄   **392**
Dec 19 2017 20:50:59 (EST)

Anonymous ID: 2bd420 No.128571 ☑ 📄
Dec 19 2017 20:39:21 (EST)

missing.jpg

454

▶Q !UW.yye1fxo 12/19/17 (Tue) 19:26:11 061d5f
No.128438>>128441 >>128442 >>128452 >>128454 >>128456
>>128457 >>128461 >>128462 >>128471 >>128472 >>128477
>>128482 >>128484 >>128486 >>128505 >>128506 >>128510
>>128516 >>128527 >>128528 >>128529 >>128532 >>128536
>>128537 >>128542

Q, where are the children?

Seriously. Where are the children?

Love,

TlinOKC

>>128571
3,000+ saved by the raids in SA alone.
WW lanes shut down.
Bottom to TOP.
[HAITI].
[RED CROSS]
[CLASSIFIED]
High Priority.
Q

The first letters of the words in bold spell out HRC, an acronym for Hillary Rodham Clinton. It implies Hillary is involved in child trafficking for Cabal's blackmail operations, something supported by the arrest of one of her close associates while trying to smuggle children out of an earthquake-ravaged Haiti.[269] Note how the Clinton Foundation would have the logistics and cover to move items across national borders, as well as the cover to operate in areas of high disorder and chaos, where missing children might not be investigated. Some say the children are used in occult/blackmail rituals by Cabal members, while others believe they are used primarily for sexual abuse.

---

269   https://archive.md/tFJ9h

Q !UW.yye1fxo ID: 5ed198 No.129526 ☑ 📁   **393**
Dec 19 2017 22:22:19 (EST)

Board owner, mods, and other patriots:
Sincere thanks for all that you do.
You are true heroes.
Long overdue - my apologies.
There will be a day (within the next few months) that a scary but
safe personalized message finds its way to you on multiple
platforms recognizing your contributions.
We thank you for your service.
Godspeed,
Q

Q !UW.yye1fxo ID: 5ed198 No.129599 ☑ 📁   **394**
Dec 19 2017 22:27:03 (EST)

> **Anonymous** ID: 342218 No.129558 ☑ 📁
> Dec 19 2017 22:24:29 (EST)
>
> >>129526
> Thank you Sir...
>
> Sorry for the Trip mess up earlier...

>>129558
Safety first.
We have the USSS, NSA, and DHS, also protecting this message.
No random IP needed (though we can implement at a moments
notice).
Godspeed,
Q

Q !UW.yye1fxo ID: 3c96d5 No.130030 ☑ 📁   **395**
Dec 19 2017 23:10:31 (EST)

SEA_TO_SHINING_SEA
DIRECT: CODE 234 SEC: B1-3
DIRECT: CODE 299 SEC: F19-A
[C   P   19]
Show the World Our Power.
RED_OCTOBER >
Q

Q !UW.yye1fxo ID: 3c96d5 No. 130064 ⬀ 🏴
Dec 19 2017 23:12:54 (EST)

> **Q** !UW.yye1fxo ID: 3c96d5 No. 130030 ⬀ 🏴
> Dec 19 2017 23:10:31 (EST)
>
> SEA_TO_SHINING_SEA
> DIRECT: CODE 234 SEC: B1-3
> DIRECT: CODE 299 SEC: F19-A
> **[C   P   19]**
> Show the World Our Power.
> RED_OCTOBER >
> Q

>>130030
SWEET DREAMS.
P_pers: Public (not private).
NATSEC_19384z_A_DT-approve
Q

Q !UW.yye1fxo ID: 3c96d5 No. 130170 ⬀ 🏴
Dec 19 2017 23:20:14 (EST)

21_**[f]**_SEQ1239
22 _SEQ_FREE_9-ZBA
22 _WH_POTUS_PRESS
Divert-ATT_CAP_H
Q

Q !UW.yye1fxo ID: 3c96d5 No. 130185 ⬀ 🏴
Dec 19 2017 23:21:41 (EST)

1 _y
Q

The meaning of these is all unknown, it is assumed Q was sending some sort of message to someone.

To encourage anons, and show something was happening, President Trump officially declared a, "national emergency with respect to serious human rights abuse and corruption around the world and providing for the imposition of sanctions on actors engaged in these malign activities." According to Q this was a message of encouragement to anons.

Q had a failure of his trip code for authenticating his posts, and thus his post was shown as coming from "Anonymous" again. It was not significant, and the board operator fixed it quickly.

These were Q's first 400 posts. In the next chapter, we will feature four later posts, which feature quotes from Q which I believe will prove prophetic. They may explain hidden forces Q is leveraging against the Cabal in this fight, further develop your knowledge of the conspiracy, and give you an idea of what I believe is to come.

Chapter Seven

Additional Illuminating Q Posts_____

There are a few additional Q-quotes which resonate with me, after my experiences with the Cabal. They are as follows. "4-6% lost forever," "The flood is coming, Emails, videos, audio, pics, etc..., No Such Agency accidentally releases IT ALL. Shall we play a game?," "Those you trust are the most guilty of sin," "60% must remain private [at least] - for humanity," "The streets will not be safe for them," and "We have it ALL."

Here we will look at the posts where he made these quotes, and what these quotes might tell us about how the fight Q and President Trump are waging will play out.

Q !UW.yye1fxo No.17   **529**
Jan 13 2018 23:16:59 (EST)

Be READY.
MSM coming - BIG WAY.
We see all.
We hear all.
FIGHT, FIGHT, FIGHT.
CONSPIRACY push coming.
MSM LOST CONTROL.
D LOST SLAVE GRIP.
D LOST CENTER VOTERS.
LIBS are MINORITY.
MSM PROJECTS AS BIG MOVEMENT.
FAKE NEWS.
4-6% LOST FOREVER.
HELLO GEORGE.
Q

4-6% is about what is estimated to comprise the civilian domestic surveillance informant network. The bottom estimate, 4%, is what Operation TIPS proposed for the pilot program of that informant network, and it doubtless was to grow from there.

People thought 4-6% was perhaps political ideologues who would prove hopelessly brainwashed, but he may be referring to the domestic intelligence network. They will not see what was wrong with neighbors using the latest high-tech spying gear to spy on everyone in the neighborhood, listening, and even watching their most private moments inside their houses, and building out files on them. Nor will they want to let go of being in the Secret Society and the advantages they get from it. For them, privacy is a foolish illusion, and the plebes were made to be trampled upon by an all powerful intelligence apparatus.

Q !UW.yye1fxo ID: 7f44ec No.119877 ☐   **576**
Jan 21 2018 21:12:19 (EST)

Q !UW.yye1fxo ID: 7f44ec No.119769 ☐
Jan 21 2018 21:05:55 (EST)

>>119569
Not from WL.
[CLAS-N-DI_9] gg_dump **[No Such Agency]**.
It does not technically exist as open-source.
Q

>>119769
The flood is coming.
Emails, videos, audio, pics, etc.
FBI accidentally deletes texts?
No Such Agency accidentally releases IT ALL>
Shall we play a game?
Q

I think in post 576 Q is threatening Cabal. In post 596, Q says, "We have it all," a phrase he will emphasize often, occasionally writing "all" in all capitals to emphasize they have it "ALL." In intelligence, I think there is one thing which is known as "IT ALL." I think it is the database of all the domestic intelligence files on every American. Don't forget, we already discussed how given the "Hops" rule in the Foreign Intelligence Surveillance Act, there are over one trillion ancillary target authorizations. Each authorization will allow each target, even innocent soccer moms, and even their minor children, to receive full-tilt FISA surveillance identical to what would be deployed on Osama bin Ladin, were he to enter the US with a nuclear weapon and the mission of leveling a major US city. That is one trillion authorizations, in a nation of only 300 million Americans. In essence, every American, and even their child, has a FISA warrant, and can be spied on at will, entirely legally.

I think when Q says, "how about we release IT ALL, he is saying to Cabal, "How about we give every American their full file now, and let them find out that when they were having sex with their wives, their neighbors were listening, recording, maybe even videoing, either through the wall with microwave imaging or thermal imaging, or even with cameras covertly installed in their bedrooms, and archiving the audio in their government file?"

If Q did that, it would simultaneously enrage all Americans, to the point they would do violence, and it would reveal exactly who is in and not in the domestic surveillance network. American men would find their wives were violated by neighbors intruding in on their most private moments. Fathers would find their 15 year old daughters were lured to private rooms by older boys in the network, when they were young, naive and vulnerable, and coerced into sex which was videoed and added to their files, so the network could control them later if it needed to. This was a full-fledged intelligence operation targeting the American people, using all the tools of the intelligence trade. American men would kill people to avenge the wrongs visited on their loved ones, and in truth I am not sure anybody would blame them. With one simple file release, in an uncontrolled fashion, Q would visit on Cabal a violent, chaotic end. So I think Q is saying, if you do not want to dismantle this slowly and in an organized, peaceful fashion, we can just turn it all over to the American people and let them deal with it. I am sure to the Q team, one way is almost as good as another. Given the choice, however, I am sure Cabal would prefer the organized, soft landing.

In post 111, Q says, "The complete picture would put 99% of Americans (the World) in a hospital." You have to be put under this surveillance knowingly to understand that. If you revealed to every American that they literally have no privacy, and at any moment a neighbor may be invading the privacy of their most private parts of their house, and there is nothing they can do, it is a huge cognitive stress. You literally will have no sanctuary, and no ability to relax. You really don't realize the simple pleasure of coming home, closing the door, flopping on the couch, and not having a bunch of people watching and listening to you, until you can no longer enjoy such a private moment. Suddenly given all of this knowledge, dropped on them completely in a few moments, I suspect most Americans would have enormous difficulty adapting peacefully.

I've had the advantage of having this revealed slowly over a few years, as I kept realizing the situation was worse than I had thought, increment by increment. Revealing it all immediately would provoke mass unrest, and many would not be able to cope.

Q IUW.yye1fxo ID: b189f8 No.130638 ⬚   **586**
Jan 22 2018 21:47:32 (EST)

What would happen if texts originating from a FBI agent to several **[internals]** discussed the assassination (possibility) of the POTUS or member of his family?
What if the texts suggest foreign allies were involved?
Forget the Russia set up **[1 of 22]**.
This is only the beginning.
Be careful what you wish for.
AS THE WORLD TURNS.
Could messages such as those be publicly disclosed?
What happens to the FBI?
What happens to the DOJ?
What happens to special counsel?
What happens in general?
Every FBI/DOJ prev case could be challenged.
Lawless.
Think logically.
We haven't started the drops re: human trafficking / sacrifices **[yet]** **[worst]**.
Those **[good]** who know cannot sleep.
Those **[good]** who know cannot find peace.
Those **[good]** who know will not rest until those responsible are held accountable.
Nobody can possibly imagine the pure evil and corruption out there.
Those you trust are the most guilty of sin.
Who are we taught to trust?
If you are religious, PRAY.
60% must remain private **[at least]** - for humanity.
These people should be hanging.
Q

Q goes on to say, "Nobody can imagine the pure evil and corruption out there. Those you trust are the most guilty of sin..." I think here he is referencing that those you trust most, IN YOUR OWN LIFE, are the most guilty with respect to your life. This thing has built files on everyone. That means you have a file. Maybe you weren't under 24/7 surveillance 365 days a year like me, but for three or five, or ten days a year, you got full coverage, just to make sure their file on you was complete. That includes infiltration and the rest of the package, because surveillance does not roll out piecemeal. When it is triggered, it is deployed as a package. You had vehicular, you had foot following you into grocery stores, you had technical monitoring of all your electronic activity, you had at least ears in your house, and most disturbingly, you had someone, maybe a few people, in your social circles as informants. Some were sent in, and it is even possible others were friends or family who were drawn into the informant network and turned on you.

When someone is assigned to inform, they are briefed on the target – what they like and what they don't like. Who they are as a person. How to get close, and be liked. So when they send somebody in, that person will click with you better than a regular normal contact, because their express mission is to click with you. They will agree with your opinions, laugh at your jokes, and not take offense at your eccentricities. They will become, "Those you trust most." It will shake your faith in all personal relationships. If you weren't anti-social before encountering this, you will become anti-social after it.

Then Q says, "60% must remain private [at least] - for humanity." I think here, Q is saying they are going to release our files, but they will keep the most embarrassing and private 60% private for humanity. Q will frequently say, "FISA brings down the house." Occasionally he will say "FISA [FULL] brings down the house." I think this means he intends to release every American's full FISA file publicly, just with the most embarrassing material not being released publicly, and being held back. Our files are probably separated into the general material, and the more embarrassing, compromising material, or as the Russians so famously called it, "Kompromat." The Kompromat section is probably composed of sexual video and audio, embarrassing conversations or arguments with spouses, or medical details, etc. If it is separated out, it may be easy to just release the general file, and hold back the rest in the Kompromat section, which is 60% of the files on average.

Q !xowAT4Z3VQ ID: 491f56 No.875936 **993**
Apr 2 2018 23:23:03 (EST)
>>875827
Follow Bolton.
Clean.
Stage.
Learn how to archive offline.
The streets will not be safe for them.
Q

Finally Q says, "The streets will not be safe for them." I do not think he is talking about the big names we know. Hillary doesn't walk on the streets among us, outside of staged photo-ops. I think these will be the people who run these operations, probably the regional managers and others who we do not know now, but whose names will come out in the lawsuits and document dumps I expect this will produce. They knew what they were doing, and people will not be pleased with what they did.

I have no idea if this will extend down to the individual informants. I have had interactions with a couple of cops who I believe the network sent in to intimidate and demonstrate their control, and after a few moments, they seemed baffled to be dealing with me. I assume they were told to follow me overtly, and assumed I was a criminal, only to find I was not. At that point, they looked like they didn't really know what they were doing, and wanted to get out of there. It is possible many informants have been false flagged (lied to), and really had no idea of the evil of the machine they were supporting. But for those who know, I have no doubt the streets will not be safe for them.

The final post we will look at was post 3821:

Q !!Hs1Jq13jV6 ID: aef29b No.7991360 ☐   **3821**
Feb 1 2020 12:41:11 (EST)

Who was the 17th Director of the NSA?
https://www.washingtonpost.com/world/national-security/pentagon-and-intelligence-community-chiefs-have-urged-obama-to-remove-the-head-of-the-nsa/2016/11/19/44de6ea6-adff-11e6-977a-1030f822fc35_story.html ☐
Q

Q frequently uses the number 17, as Q is the 17th letter in the alphabet. The 17th Director of the National Security Agency was Admiral Mike Rogers, who has long been resisting Cabal's efforts to hijack NSA's surveillance capabilities for their own purposes. It was he who immediately traveled to Trump Tower to apprise Donald Trump of the illegal surveillance of his *operations after he won the White House.*

And now it appears he may have been doing much more for freedom than just that.

Chapter Eight

*Conclusions*_____

By now you should have a good idea of the conspiracy we face, the Q-phenomenon, and the ability to read Q's posts and begin to deduce what Q is talking about yourself. As of this writing there are over 3600 posts in total, with more coming constantly. You can see all of the posts at special websites which scrape them off of the overpopulated, chaotic, and disorganized message boards where Q posts. Here is a list of Q-scrapers, current as of publication:

https://qanon.pub/

https://qmap.pub/

https://qntmpkts.keybase.pub/

https://qposts.online/

http://we-go-all.net/q.html

https://www.qanonposts.io/

https://qanon.news/Q

http://qanon.news/posts.html

You can now read these posts yourself online at these sites, or you can look to subsequent volumes of this series which will reprint them with commentary.

By now you will have a better appreciation why many of

us ignored the puppetmasters and narrative-crafters of the Fake News media when they told us Q was a fake conspiracy theory, and instead blazed our own intellectual path, doing our own observations and analysis.

Hopefully, going forward you will make the same choice, and together we can all better secure the freedom and honest governance the Founders worked so hard to bestow upon us. Then together, we may pass it on, protected and strengthened, to the next generation.

Stop by our website and like it on facebook and twitter, to help spread r/K Selection Theory at:

http://www.anonymousconservative.com

Also, stop by our blog for daily summaries of news headlines and events focused on politics and the fight against Cabal, as well as occasional articles on other subjects of interest at:

http://www.anonymousconservative.com/blog

If you liked this book, check out these titles:

The Evolutionary Psychology Behind Politics

This book examines from a scientific perspective why we have two diametrically opposed political psychologies in this world. Drawing from a range of scientific disciplines, it begins by examining the two predominant psychologies in nature, and shows how animals develop them because they have two basic environments – gluts and shortages. In a glut, like rabbits in fields of grass they will never fully consume, animals develop the rabbit's r-selected psychology, designed to simply produce as many offspring, of any quality as quickly as possible, to exploit the glut. They avoid danger and conflict, mate promiscuously, single mother offspring, encourage early sexualization of young to spread genes faster, and never sacrifice for others.

473

Conversely, in a shortage, it is shown that animals develop the wolf's K-selected psychology, where conflict and threat are accepted and met, because fleeing will result in no food. They compete for mates, and monopolize them with monogamy, to produce the fittest offspring possible. They encourage offspring to select monogamous mates later, when they themselves are fitter, so their single, life-long mate will be as fit as possible, and so will their offspring. Finally, they form competitive groups, and form intense bonds of loyalty within them. These are the foundations of our two political psychologies, and this book examines this from the historical, to the genetic, from neurobiology to social psychology. We are a political battle of rabbits and wolves, one expecting resources to be free and not feeling loyalty to the group, and one assuming shortage, and realizing we need to band together and stick together to make it in the world, because there are others who will take our ration of resources if we do not. I believe it was this book which caused the passive surveillance which lurks in the shadows around all of us to be ordered to intrude more openly and aggressively in my life.

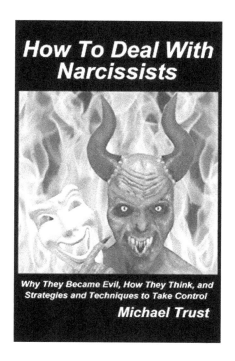

How to Deal With Narcissists.

This book arose from a malignant narcissist I knew when I was younger, who revealed enough about his past that I could see where his psychology came from. It takes the narcissistic psychology, and examines how predisposition mixes with specific environmental conditions, to mold their brain to exhibit the strange constellation of traits the narcissist exhibits. From rewriting history to construct an imaginary reality that makes their brain feel better, to the need to make others feel worse, this book examines where their traits came from, before segueing into the range of techniques they will use to manipulate the normal people around them and try to seize the control they cannot be without.

Affiliated Sites Online

In the course of this journey, it has become clear that there are two sources of information when you go online.

I do not understand the specifics, as nobody briefs me on how it all works. But in casual observation, you will notice that the "large" sources of information, which are promoted everywhere as "respectable," and which we are told get the most traffic and largest readerships, will tend to be controlled outlets. Inherent to their reporting and media production will be an implicit assumption that there is respectable information which intelligent people believe, and which they are providing you, and "bad" information, which only those who are not worthy of respect will tend to promote.

Purely by coincidence, these sites will rarely speak of government surveillance, and when they do, it will be strictly about data-processing schemes which involve such impersonal mechanisms as the warehousing of incidental data points about you which nobody will ever really examine. Ideas such a massive civilian spying network turned on the citizenry, or governmental entities allowing 9/11 to happen, or the presence of massive sex-trafficking networks used to blackmail politicians, or pedophile rings in high places, or the media being controlled by some sort of intelligence network hostile to the American people, will be dismissed out of hand as too ridiculous to even examine.

I view it all with the benefit of knowing the truth. The surveillance machine is massive, everywhere, and composed of personal, civilian informant networks reviewing and curating almost all of the very personal material they harvest in real time. Having seen that, I know there is no way 19 Arab hijackers entered the US, traveled to flight schools, asked to be taught how to fly but not how to land or take off, all while being funded by terrorist networks overseas, and the machine missed them. And most importantly, I know all of these big outlets know the big secret - the machine that controls all of this, from the media, to the government, to probably even someone you know and interact with in real life. And they are all keeping the secret, because they don't want you to know. Follow those controlled media outlets, and you are letting the puppeteers control what you think, what you believe, and what you do.

But there is another form of outlet online. These outlets talk about everything, investigate everything, and provide all information freely. Masses of free thinkers are attracted to them, as bastions of free thought, truth, and clear pictures of reality, and those individuals add to the content with their own discussions and exchanges of information, in the comment sections of these free-thinking outlets.

Clearly Q is one such outlet, but online there are many. Following will be some I have stumbled upon as I tried to promote r/K Theory. Even as I appreciate their help, I also recognize they are the nucleus of an online community which can gie you the picture of reality that those in control do not want you to have. Follow those outlets, and you can be free.

On the following page, we will list but a few.

Bill Whittle - *News and commentary from a Conservative perspective*

http://www.billwhittle.com/

Stefan Molyneux – *Philosophy politics, and news, genius-tier.*

https://freedomainradio.com/

Castalia House – *The publishing house of the independent right*

http://www.castaliahouse.com/

Vox Day – *Top 40 billboard artist, syndicated columnist, author, publisher, thought criminal according to the Social Justice Left*

http://voxday.blogspot.com/

Infogalactic – *Hate Wikipedia's bias? This is the alternative*

http://www.infogalactic.com

Matt Forney – *An author and journalist, Matt was one of the first to promote r/K online to his readers.*

https://mattforney.com/

Heartiste – *Heartiste is a part of the online right devoted to using psychology to make women find you attractive. A more hedonistic specialty, it seems out of place, but if conservative men believe in marrying and staying married, then this material is seen as vital, and is now common knowledge among the independent online right.*

Homepage: *https://heartiste.org/*

Gab: *https://gab.com/heartiste*

Krauser – *Like Heartiste, Krauser covers using psychology to attract women, and he has very high-quality books detailing his methods.*

https://krauserpua.com/

Liberty Authors Forum – *This requires a free online registration to get in, where writers from the independent online right congregate and converse.*

http:www.libertyauthors.com

Davis Aurini – *Author, writer, and commentary on politics and the world, banned on multiple platforms for crime-think, and an early promoter of r/K.*

http://www.staresattheworld.com/

Tommy Robinson News – *A political activist in Britain who offers the patriotic perspective in his journalism, and who may be the first member of the independent right to lead a major superpower.*

https://www.tr.news/

Red Ice – *Great news from a couple trying to save Europe from the leftist migrant invasion.*

https://redice.tv/

Free Republic - *One of the top online conservative political forums.*

http://www.freerepublic.com

The Burning Platform – *A sane view of the insane world, with a constant stream of articles on current events.*

https://www.theburningplatform.com/

4Chan - *Really needs no introduction. It has a very high noise to* *signal ratio, but if you can weed through the shills and the Cabal disruptors, there are real gems constantly being mined here.*

https://boards.4chan.org/pol/

CPSIA information can be obtained
at www.ICGtesting.com
Printed in the USA
BVHW092256030121
596836BV00006B/296

9 781733 414203